Family Maps
of
Gibson County, Indiana
Deluxe Edition

With Homesteads, Roads, Waterways, Towns, Cemeteries, Railroads, and More

Family Maps
of
Gibson County, Indiana
Deluxe Edition

With Homesteads, Roads, Waterways, Towns, Cemeteries, Railroads, and More

by Gregory A. Boyd, J.D.

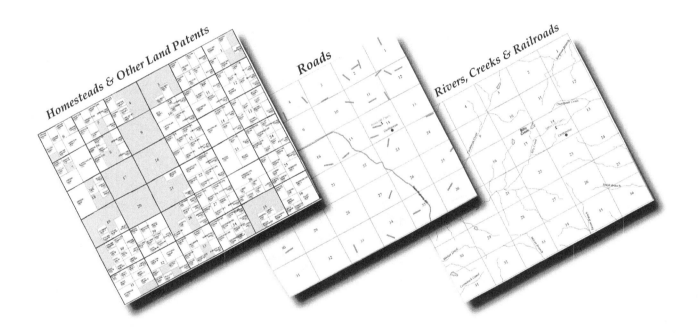

Featuring 3 *Maps Per Township...*

Arphax Publishing Co.
www.arphax.com

Family Maps of Gibson County, Indiana, Deluxe Edition: With Homesteads, Roads, Waterways, Towns, Cemeteries, Railroads, and More.
by Gregory A. Boyd, J.D.

ISBN 1-4203-1303-7

Published by Arphax Publishing Co., 2210 Research Park Blvd., Norman, Oklahoma, USA 73069
www.arphax.com

First Edition

ATTENTION HISTORICAL & GENEALOGICAL SOCIETIES, UNIVERSITIES, COLLEGES, CORPORATIONS, FAMILY REUNION COORDINATORS, AND PROFESSIONAL ORGANIZATIONS: Quantity discounts are available on bulk purchases of this book. For information, please contact Arphax Publishing Co., at the address listed above, or at (405) 366-6181, or visit our web-site at www.arphax.com and contact us through the "Bulk Sales" link.

—LEGAL—

This book is dedicated to my wonderful family:

Vicki, Jordan, & Amy Boyd

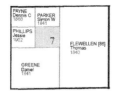

Contents

- Part I -

The Big Picture

- Part II -

Township Map Groups

(Map Groups contain a Patent Index, Patent Map, Road Map, & Historical Map)

Appendices

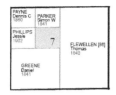

Preface

The quest for the discovery of my ancestors' origins, migrations, beliefs, and life-ways has brought me rewards that I could never have imagined. The *Family Maps* series of books is my first effort to share with historical and genealogical researchers, some of the tools that I have developed to achieve my research goals. I firmly believe that this effort will allow many people to reap the same sorts of treasures that I have.

Our Federal government's General Land Office of the Bureau of Land Management (the "GLO") has given genealogists and historians an incredible gift by virtue of its enormous database housed on its web-site at glorecords.blm.gov. Here, you can search for and find millions of parcels of land purchased by our ancestors in about thirty states.

This GLO web-site is one of the best FREE on-line tools available to family researchers. But, it is not for the faint of heart, nor is it for those unwilling or unable to to sift through and analyze the thousands of records that exist for most counties.

My immediate goal with this series is to spare you the hundreds of hours of work that it would take you to map the Land Patents for this county. Every Gibson County homestead or land patent that I have gleaned from public GLO databases is mapped here. Consequently, I can usually show you in an instant, where your ancestor's land is located, as well as the names of nearby land-owners.

Originally, that was my primary goal. But after speaking to other genealogists, it became clear that there was much more that they wanted. Taking their advice set me back almost a full year, but I think you will agree it was worth the wait. Because now, you can learn so much more.

Now, this book answers these sorts of questions:

- Are there any variant spellings for surnames that I have missed in searching GLO records?
- Where is my family's traditional home-place?
- What cemeteries are near Grandma's house?
- My Granddad used to swim in such-and-such-Creek—where is that?
- How close is this little community to that one?
- Are there any other people with the same surname who bought land in the county?
- How about cousins and in-laws—did they buy land in the area?

And these are just for starters!

The rules for using the *Family Maps* books are simple, but the strategies for success are many. Some techniques are apparent on first use, but many are gained with time and experience. Please take the time to notice the roads, cemeteries, creek-names, family names, and unique first-names throughout the whole county. You cannot imagine what YOU might be the first to discover.

I hope to learn that many of you have answered age-old research questions within these pages or that you have discovered relationships previously not even considered. When these sorts of things happen to you, will you please let me hear about it? I would like nothing better. My contact information can always be found at www.arphax.com.

One more thing: please read the "How To Use This Book" chapter; it starts on the next page. This will give you the very best chance to find the treasures that lie within these pages.

My family and I wish you the very best of luck, both in life, and in your research.   Greg Boyd

How to Use This Book - A Graphical Summary

Part I
"The Big Picture"

Map A ▸ *Counties in the State*
Map B ▸ *Surrounding Counties*
Map C ▸ *Congressional Townships (Map Groups) in the County*
Map D ▸ *Cities & Towns in the County*
Map E ▸ *Cemeteries in the County*
Surnames in the County ▸ *Number of Land-Parcels for Each Surname*
Surname/Township Index ▸ *Directs you to Township Map Groups in Part II*

The <u>Surname/Township Index</u> can direct you to any number of **Township Map Groups**

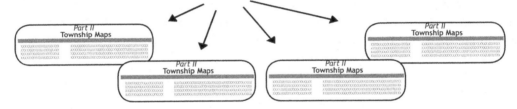

Part II
Township Map Groups
(1 for each Township in the County)

Each Township Map Group contains all four of of the following tools . . .

Land Patent Index ▸ *Every-name Index of Patents Mapped in this Township*
Land Patent Map ▸ *Map of Patents as listed in above Index*
Road Map ▸ *Map of Roads, City-centers, and Cemeteries in the Township*
Historical Map ▸ *Map of Railroads, Lakes, Rivers, Creeks, City-Centers, and Cemeteries*

Appendices

Appendix A ▸ *Congressional Authority enabling Patents within our Maps*
Appendix B ▸ *Section-Parts / Aliquot Parts (a comprehensive list)*
Appendix C ▸ *Multi-patentee Groups (Individuals within Buying Groups)*

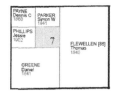

How to Use This Book

The two "Parts" of this *Family Maps* volume seek to answer two different types of questions. Part I deals with broad questions like: what counties surround Gibson County, are there any ASHCRAFTs in Gibson County, and if so, in which Townships or Maps can I find them? Ultimately, though, Part I should point you to a particular Township Map Group in Part II.

Part II concerns itself with details like: where exactly is this family's land, who else bought land in the area, and what roads and streams run through the land, or are located nearby. The Chart on the opposite page, and the remainder of this chapter attempt to convey to you the particulars of these two "parts", as well as how best to use them to achieve your research goals.

Part I
"The Big Picture"

Within Part I, you will find five "Big Picture" maps and two county-wide surname tools.

These include:

- Map A - Where Gibson County lies within the state
- Map B - Counties that surround Gibson County
- Map C - Congressional Townships of Gibson County (+ Map Group Numbers)
- Map D - Cities & Towns of Gibson County (with Index)
- Map E - Cemeteries of Gibson County (with Index)
- Surnames in Gibson County Patents (with Parcel-counts for each surname)
- Surname/Township Index (with Parcel-counts for each surname by Township)

The five "Big-Picture" Maps are fairly self-explanatory, yet should not be overlooked. This is particularly true of Maps "C", "D", and "E", all of which show Gibson County and its Congressional Townships (and their assigned Map Group Numbers).

Let me briefly explain this concept of Map Group Numbers. These are a device completely of our own invention. They were created to help you quickly locate maps without having to remember the full legal name of the various Congressional Townships. It is simply easier to remember "Map Group 1" than a legal name like: "Township 9-North Range 6-West, 5th Principal Meridian." But the fact is that the TRUE legal name for these Townships IS terribly important. These are the designations that others will be familiar with and you will need to accurately record them in your notes. This is why both Map Group numbers AND legal descriptions of Townships are almost always displayed together.

Map "C" will be your first intoduction to "Map Group Numbers", and that is all it contains: legal Township descriptions and their assigned Map Group Numbers. Once you get further into your research, and more immersed in the details, you will likely want to refer back to Map "C" from time to time, in order to regain your bearings on just where in the county you are researching.

Remember, township boundaries are a completely artificial device, created to standardize land descriptions. But do not let them become a boundary in your mind when choosing which townships to research. Your relative's in-laws, children, cousins, siblings, and mamas and papas, might just as easily have lived in the township next to the one your grandfather lived in—rather than in the one where he actually lived. So Map "C" can be your guide to which other Townships/ Map Groups you likewise ought to analyze.

Of course, the same holds true for County lines; this is the purpose behind Map "B". It shows you surrounding counties that you may want to consider for further reserarch.

Map "D", the Cities and Towns map, is the first map with an index. Map "E" is the second (Cemeteries). Both, Maps "D" and "E" give you broad views of City (or Cemetery) locations in the County. But they go much further by pointing you toward pertinent Township Map Groups so you can locate the patents, roads, and waterways located near a particular city or cemetery.

Once you are familiar with these *Family Maps* volumes and the county you are researching, the "Surnames In Gibson County" chapter (or its sister chapter in other volumes) is where you'll likely start your future research sessions. Here, you can quickly scan its few pages and see if anyone in the county possesses the surnames you are researching. The "Surnames in Gibson County" list shows only two things: surnames and the number of parcels of land we have located for that surname in Gibson County. But whether or not you immediately locate the surnames you are researching, please do not go any further without taking a few moments to scan ALL the surnames in these very few pages.

You cannot imagine how many lost ancestors are waiting to be found by someone willing to take just a little longer to scan the "Surnames In Gibson County" list. Misspellings and typographical errors abound in most any index of this sort. Don't miss out on finding your Kinard that was written Rynard or Cox that was written Lox. If it looks funny or wrong, it very often is. And one of those little errors may well be your relative.

Now, armed with a surname and the knowledge that it has one or more entries in this book, you are ready for the "Surname/Township Index." Unlike the "Surnames In Gibson County", which has only one line per Surname, the "Surname/Township Index" contains one line-item for each Township Map Group in which each surname is found. In other words, each line represents a different Township Map Group that you will need to review.

Specifically, each line of the Surname/Township Index contains the following four columns of information:

1. Surname
2. Township Map Group Number (these Map Groups are found in Part II)
3. Parcels of Land (number of them with the given Surname within the Township)
4. Meridian/Township/Range (the legal description for this Township Map Group)

The key column here is that of the Township Map Group Number. While you should definitely record the Meridian, Township, and Range, you can do that later. Right now, you need to dig a little deeper. That Map Group Number tells you where in Part II that you need to start digging.

But before you leave the "Surname/Township Index", do the same thing that you did with the "Surnames in Gibson County" list: take a moment to scan the pages of the Index and see if there are similarly spelled or misspelled surnames that deserve your attention. Here again, is an easy opportunity to discover grossly misspelled family names with very little effort. Now you are ready to turn to . . .

Part II
"Township Map Groups"

You will normally arrive here in Part II after being directed to do so by one or more "Map Group Numbers" in the Surname/Township Index of Part I.

Each Map Group represents a set of four tools dedicated to a single Congressional Township that is either wholly or partially within the county. If you are trying to learn all that you can about a particular family or their land, then these tools should usually be viewed in the order they are presented.

These four tools include:

1. a Land Patent Index
2. a Land Patent Map
3. a Road Map, and
4. an Historical Map

As I mentioned earlier, each grouping of this sort is assigned a Map Group Number. So, let's now move on to a discussion of the four tools that make up one of these Township Map Groups.

Land Patent Index

Each Township Map Group's Index begins with a title, something along these lines:

MAP GROUP 1: Index to Land Patents
Township 16-North Range 5-West (2nd PM)

The Index contains seven (7) columns. They are:

1. ID (a unique ID number for this Individual and a corresponding Parcel of land in this Township)
2. Individual in Patent (name)
3. Sec. (Section), and
4. Sec. Part (Section Part, or Aliquot Part)
5. Date Issued (Patent)
6. Other Counties (often means multiple counties were mentioned in GLO records, or the section lies within multiple counties).
7. For More Info . . . (points to other places within this index or elsewhere in the book where you can find more information)

While most of the seven columns are self-explanatory, I will take a few moments to explain the "Sec. Part." and "For More Info" columns.

The "Sec. Part" column refers to what surveryors and other land professionals refer to as an Aliquot Part. The origins and use of such a term mean little to a non-surveyor, and I have chosen to simply call these sub-sections of land what they are: a "Section Part". No matter what we call them, what we are referring to are things like a quarter-section or half-section or quarter-quarter-section. See Appendix "B" for most of the "Section Parts" you will come across (and many you will not) and what size land-parcel they represent.

The "For More Info" column of the Index may seem like a small appendage to each line, but please

recognize quickly that this is not so. And to understand the various items you might find here, you need to become familiar with the Legend that appears at the top of each Land Patent Index.

Here is a sample of the Legend . . .

LEGEND

"For More Info . . . " column

A = Authority (Legislative Act, See Appendix "A")
B = Block or Lot (location in Section unknown)
C = Cancelled Patent
F = Fractional Section
G = Group (Multi-Patentee Patent, see Appendix "C")
V = Overlaps another Parcel
R = Re-Issued (Parcel patented more than once)

Most parcels of land will have only one or two of these items in their "For More Info" columns, but when that is not the case, there is often some valuable information to be gained from further investigation. Below, I will explain what each of these items means to you you as a researcher.

A = Authority
(Legislative Act, See Appendix "A")

All Federal Land Patents were issued because some branch of our government (usually the U.S. Congress) passed a law making such a transfer of title possible. And therefore every patent within these pages will have an "A" item next to it in the index. The number after the "A" indicates which item in Appendix "A" holds the citation to the particular law which authorized the transfer of land to the public. As it stands, most of the Public Land data compiled and released by our government, and which serves as the basis for the patents mapped here, concerns itself with "Cash Sale" homesteads. So in some Counties, the law which authorized cash sales will be the primary, if not the only, entry in the Appendix.

B = Block or Lot (location in Section unknown)
A "B" designation in the Index is a tip-off that the EXACT location of the patent within the map is not apparent from the legal description. This Patent will nonetheless be noted within the proper

Section along with any other Lots purchased in the Section. Given the scope of this project (many states and many Counties are being mapped), trying to locate all relevant plats for Lots (if they even exist) and accurately mapping them would have taken one person several lifetimes. But since our primary goal from the onset has been to establish relationships between neighbors and families, very little is lost to this goal since we can still observe who all lived in which Section.

C = Cancelled Patent

A Cancelled Patent is just that: cancelled. Whether the original Patentee forfeited his or her patent due to fraud, a technicality, non-payment, or whatever, the fact remains that it is significant to know who received patents for what parcels and when. A cancellation may be evidence that the Patentee never physically re-located to the land, but does not in itself prove that point. Further evidence would be required to prove that. *See also*, Re-issued Patents, *below*.

F = Fractional Section

A Fractional Section is one that contains less than 640 acres, almost always because of a body of water. The exact size and shape of land-parcels contained in such sections may not be ascertainable, but we map them nonetheless. Just keep in mind that we are not mapping an actual parcel to scale in such instances. Another point to consider is that we have located some fractional sections that are not so designated by the Bureau of Land Management in their data. This means that not all fractional sections have been so identified in our indexes.

G = Group
(Multi-Patentee Patent, see Appendix "C")

A "G" designation means that the Patent was issued to a GROUP of people (Multi-patentees). The "G" will always be followed by a number. Some such groups were quite large and it was impractical if not impossible to display each individual in our maps without unduly affecting readability. EACH person in the group is named in the Index, but they won't all be found on the Map. You will find the name of the first person in such a Group

on the map with the Group number next to it, enclosed in [square brackets].

To find all the members of the Group you can either scan the Index for all people with the same Group Number or you can simply refer to Appendix "C" where all members of the Group are listed next to their number.

O = Overlaps another Parcel

An Overlap is one where PART of a parcel of land gets issued on more than one patent. For genealogical purposes, both transfers of title are important and both Patentees are mapped. If the ENTIRE parcel of land is re-issued, that is what we call it, a Re-Issued Patent (*see below*). The number after the "O" indicates the ID for the overlapping Patent(s) contained within the same Index. Like Re-Issued and Cancelled Patents, Overlaps may cause a map-reader to be confused at first, but for genealogical purposes, all of these parties' relationships to the underlying land is important, and therefore, we map them.

R = Re-Issued (Parcel patented more than once)

The label, "Re-issued Patent" describes Patents which were issued more than once for land with the EXACT SAME LEGAL DESCRIPTION. Whether the original patent was cancelled or not, there were a good many parcels which were patented more than once. The number after the "R" indicates the ID for the other Patent contained within the same Index that was for the same land. A quick glance at the map itself within the relevant Section will be the quickest way to find the other Patentee to whom the Parcel was transferred. They should both be mapped in the same general area.

I have gone to some length describing all sorts of anomalies either in the underlying data or in their representation on the maps and indexes in this book. Most of this will bore the most ardent reseracher, but I do this with all due respect to those researchers who will inevitably (and rightfully) ask: *"Why isn't so-and-so's name on the exact spot that the index says it should be?"*

In most cases it will be due to the existence of a Multi-Patentee Patent, a Re-issued Patent, a Cancelled Patent, or Overlapping Parcels named in separate Patents. I don't pretend that this discussion will answer every question along these lines, but I hope it will at least convince you of the complexity of the subject.

Not to despair, this book's companion web-site will offer a way to further explain "odd-ball" or errant data. Each book (County) will have its own web-page or pages to discuss such situations. You can go to www.arphax.com to find the relevant web-page for Gibson County.

Land Patent Map

On the first two-page spread following each Township's Index to Land Patents, you'll find the corresponding Land Patent Map. And here lies the real heart of our work. For the first time anywhere, researchers will be able to observe and analyze, on a grand scale, most of the original land-owners for an area AND see them mapped in proximity to each one another.

We encourage you to make vigorous use of the accompanying Index described above, but then later, to abandon it, and just stare at these maps for a while. This is a great way to catch misspellings or to find collateral kin you'd not known were in the area.

 Each Land Patent Map represents one Congressional Township containing approximately 36-square miles. Each of these square miles is labeled by an accompanying Section Number (1 through 36, in most cases). Keep in mind, that this book concerns itself solely with Gibson County's patents. Townships which creep into one or more other counties will not be shown in their entirety in any one book. You will need to consult other books, as they become available, in order to view other countys' patents, cities, cemeteries, etc.

But getting back to Gibson County: each Land Patent Map contains a Statistical Chart that looks like the following:

Township Statistics

Parcels Mapped	:	173
Number of Patents	:	163
Number of Individuals	:	152
Patentees Identified	:	151
Number of Surnames	:	137
Multi-Patentee Parcels	:	4
Oldest Patent Date	:	11/27/1820
Most Recent Patent	:	9/28/1917
Block/Lot Parcels	:	0
Parcels Re-Issued	:	3
Parcels that Overlap	:	8
Cities and Towns	:	6
Cemeteries	:	6

This information may be of more use to a social statistician or historian than a genealogist, but I think all three will find it interesting.

Most of the statistics are self-explanatory, and what is not, was described in the above discussion of the Index's Legend, but I do want to mention a few of them that may affect your understanding of the Land Patent Maps.

First of all, Patents often contain more than one Parcel of land, so it is common for there to be more Parcels than Patents. Also, the Number of Individuals will more often than not, not match the number of Patentees. A Patentee is literally the person or PERSONS named in a patent. So, a Patent may have a multi-person Patentee or a single-person patentee. Nonetheless, we account for all these individuals in our indexes.

On the lower-righthand side of the Patent Map is a Legend which describes various features in the map, including Section Boundaries, Patent (land) Boundaries, Lots (numbered), and Multi-Patentee Group Numbers. You'll also find a "Helpful Hints" Box that will assist you.

One important note: though the vast majority of Patents mapped in this series will prove to be reasonably accurate representations of their actual locations, we cannot claim this for patents lying along state and county lines, or waterways, or that have been platted (lots).

Shifting boundaries and sparse legal descriptions in the GLO data make this a reality that we have nonetheless tried to overcome by estimating these patents' locations the best that we can.

Road Map

On the two-page spread following each Patent Map you will find a Road Map covering the exact same area (the same Congressional Township).

For me, fully exploring the past means that every once in a while I must leave the library and travel to the actual locations where my ancestors once walked and worked the land. Our Township Road Maps are a great place to begin such a quest.

Keep in mind that the scaling and proportion of these maps was chosen in order to squeeze hundreds of people-names, road-names, and place-names into tinier spaces than you would traditionally see. These are not professional road-maps, and like any secondary genealogical source, should be looked upon as an entry-way to original sources— in this case, original patents and applications, professionally produced maps and surveys, etc.

Both our Road Maps and Historical Maps contain cemeteries and city-centers, along with a listing of these on the left-hand side of the map. I should note that I am showing you city center-points, rather than city-limit boundaries, because in many instances, this will represent a place where settlement began. This may be a good time to mention that many cemeteries are located on private property, Always check with a local historical or genealogical society to see if a particular cemetery is publicly accessible (if it is not obviously so). As a final point, look for your surnames among the road-names. You will often be surprised by what you find.

Historical Map

The third and final map in each Map Group is our attempt to display what each Township might have looked like before the advent of modern roads. In frontier times, people were usually more determined to settle near rivers and creeks than they were near roads, which were often few and

far between. As was the case with the Road Map, we've included the same cemeteries and city-centers. We've also included railroads, many of which came along before most roads.

While some may claim "Historical Map" to be a bit of a misnomer for this tool, we settled for this label simply because it was almost as accurate as saying "Railroads, Lakes, Rivers, Cities, and Cemeteries," and it is much easier to remember.

In Closing . . .

By way of example, here is *A Really Good Way to Use a Township Map Group.* First, find the person you are researching in the Township's Index to Land Patents, which will direct you to the proper Section and parcel on the Patent Map. But before leaving the Index, scan all the patents within it, looking for other names of interest. Now, turn to the Patent Map and locate your parcels of land. Pay special attention to the names of patent-holders who own land surrounding your person of interest. Next, turn the page and look at the same Section(s) on the Road Map. Note which roads are closest to your parcels and also the names of nearby towns and cemeteries. Using other resources, you may be able to learn of kin who have been buried here, plus, you may choose to visit these cemeteries the next time you are in the area.

Finally, turn to the Historical Map. Look once more at the same Sections where you found your research subject's land. Note the nearby streams, creeks, and other geographical features. You may be surprised to find family names were used to name them, or you may see a name you haven't heard mentioned in years and years—and a new research possibility is born.

Many more techniques for using these *Family Maps* volumes will no doubt be discovered. If from time to time, you will navigate to Gibson County's web-page at www.arphax.com (use the "Research" link), you can learn new tricks as they become known (or you can share ones you have employed). But for now, you are ready to get started. So, go, and good luck.

– Part I –

The Big Picture

Map A - Where Gibson County, Indiana Lies Within the State

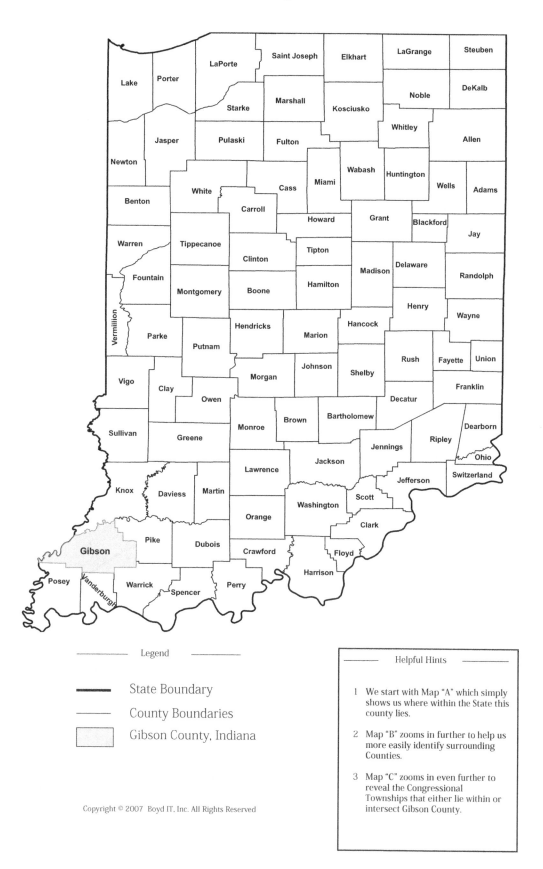

Legend

State Boundary

County Boundaries

Gibson County, Indiana

Helpful Hints

1 We start with Map "A" which simply shows us where within the State this county lies.

2 Map "B" zooms in further to help us more easily identify surrounding Counties.

3 Map "C" zooms in even further to reveal the Congressional Townships that either lie within or intersect Gibson County.

Map B - Gibson County, Indiana and Surrounding Counties

Jasper

Sullivan

Greene

Crawford

Lawrence

Richland

Knox

Daviess

Illinois

Wabash

Wayne

Gibson

Edwards

Indiana

Pike

Dubois

White

Warrick

Posey

Vanderburgh

Spencer

Gallatin

Henderson

Kentucky

Union

Daviess

——— Legend ———

━━━ State Boundaries (when applicable)

——— County Boundary

———— Helpful Hints ————

1 Many Patent-holders and their families settled across county lines. It is always a good idea to check nearby counties for your families.

2 Refer to Map "A" to see a broader view of where this County lies within the State, and Map "C" to see which Congressional Townships lie within Gibson County.

Map C - Congressional Townships of Gibson County, Indiana

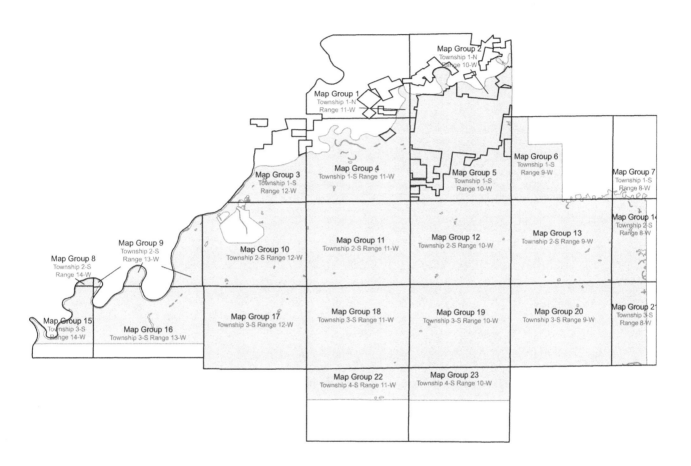

─── Legend ───

Gibson County, Indiana

Congressional Townships

─── Helpful Hints ───

1   Many Patent-holders and their families settled across county lines. It is always a good idea to check nearby counties for your families (See Map "B").

2   Refer to Map "A" to see a broader view of where this county lies within the State, and Map "B" for a view of the counties surrounding Gibson County.

Map D Index: Cities & Towns of Gibson County, Indiana

The following represents the Cities and Towns of Gibson County, along with the corresponding Map Group in which each is found. Cities and Towns are displayed in both the Road and Historical maps in the Group.

City/Town	Map Group No.
Baldwin Heights	12
Buckskin	20
Crawleyville	16
Dongola	14
Douglas	12
Durham	18
East Mount Carmel	3
Egg Harbor	17
Fort Branch	18
Fort Gibson (historical)	19
Francisco	13
Giro	2
Gray Junction	14
Gudgel	13
Haubstadt	19
Hazleton	2
Hickory Ridge	16
Jimtown	16
Johnson	17
King	11
Lyles	11
Mackey	20
McGary	18
Mount Olympus	5
Mounts	17
Oak Hill	13
Oakland City	14
Oatsville	6
Owensville	17
Patoka	4
Princeton	12
Saint James	23
Skelton	10
Somerville	20
Warrenton	23
Wheeling	6
White River	3

Map D - Cities & Towns of Gibson County, Indiana

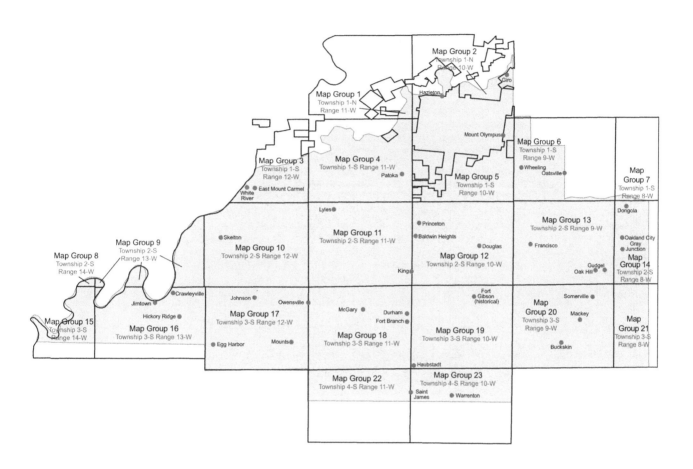

─── Legend ───

Gibson County, Indiana

Congressional Townships

─── Helpful Hints ───

1   Cities and towns are marked only at their center-points as published by the USGS and/or NationalAtlas.gov. This often enables us to more closely approximate where these might have existed when first settled.

2   To see more specifically where these Cities & Towns are located within the county, refer to both the Road and Historical maps in the Map-Group referred to above. See also, the Map "D" Index on the opposite page.

Map E Index: Cemeteries of Gibson County, Indiana

The following represents many of the Cemeteries of Gibson County, along with the corresponding Township Map Group in which each is found. Cemeteries are displayed in both the Road and Historical maps in the Map Groups referred to below.

Cemetery	Map Group No.
Albright Cem.	20
Archer Cem.	11
Armstrong Cem.	5
Barnett Cem.	2
Benson Cem.	17
Clark Cem.	18
Decker Chapel Cem.	5
Durham Cem.	18
Eden Cem.	21
Field Cem.	5
Hitch Cem.	4
Humphrey Cem.	4
Kilpatrick Cem.	21
Kirk Cem.	6
Kirk-McRoberts Cem.	5
Knowles Cem.	17
Maple Hill Cem.	12
Mauck Cem.	17
Meade Cem.	13
Milburn Cem.	5
Montgomery Cem.	14
Morrison Cem.	5
Mount Mariah Cem.	18
Nobles Cem.	23
Oak Grove Cem.	17
Odd Fellows Cem.	12
Old Union Cem.	17
Phillips Cem.	2
Powell Cem.	22
Richardson Cem.	6
Robb Cem.	5
Saint Josephs Cem.	12
Sand Hill Cem.	11
Skelton Cem.	17
Stunkel Cem.	19
Townsley Cem.	20
Trippet Cem.	5
Walnut Hill Cem.	19
Warnock Cem.	12
Williams Cem.	22
Wilson Cem.	17

Map E - Cemeteries of Gibson County, Indiana

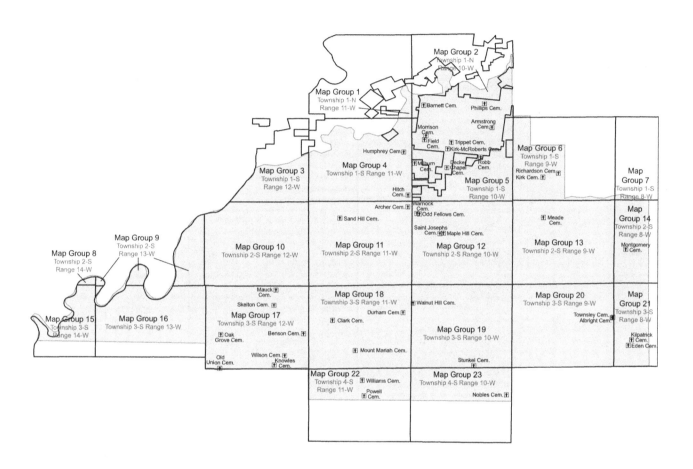

———— Legend ————

Gibson County, Indiana

Congressional Townships

———— Helpful Hints ————

1   Cemeteries are marked at locations as published by the USGS and/or NationalAtlas.gov.

2   To see more specifically where these Cemeteries are located, refer to the Road & Historical maps in the Map Group referred to above. See also, the Map "E" Index on the opposite page to make sure you don't miss any of the Cemeteries located within this Congressional township.

Surnames in Gibson County, Indiana Patents

The following list represents the surnames that we have located in Gibson County, Indiana Patents and the number of parcels that we have mapped for each one. Here is a quick way to determine the existence (or not) of Patents to be found in the subsequent indexes and maps of this volume.

Surname	# of Land Parcels	Surname	# of Land Parcels	Surname	# of Land Parcels	Surname	# of Land Parcels
ADAMS	11	BRILES	1	CREEK	9	FARMER	14
ALSOP	2	BRILS	1	CRISWELL	1	FARR	1
ALVIS	1	BRITTENHAM	1	CROCK	1	FARRIS	2
AMES	1	BRITTONHAM	1	CROCKETT	1	FERRIS	3
AMORY	12	BROKAW	3	CROSS	1	FIELD	8
AMOS	1	BROSE	1	CROW	6	FIELDS	5
ANDERSON	3	BROTHERS	8	CROWLEY	7	FIELER	1
ARBURN	2	BROWN	20	CRUSE	7	FIFER	3
ASH	2	BROWNLEE	7	CULBERTSON	2	FILED	1
ASHLEY	5	BRUMFIELD	1	CUNINGHAM	1	FINCH	1
ASHMEAD	1	BRUNER	2	CUNNINGHAM	3	FINNEY	2
ATKINS	1	BUCKNER	1	CURRY	4	FISHER	5
ATKINSON	1	BUMP	2	CURTIS	1	FLOWER	3
AULDREDGE	1	BURCHFIELD	3	DANIEL	5	FORBIS	2
AULDRIDGE	3	BURGET	1	DASH	1	FORREST	2
AYERS	3	BURRUCKER	1	DAUGHERTY	1	FOSTER	3
AYRES	1	BURTCH	2	DAVIDSON	5	FRAZER	3
BAECHEL	4	BURTON	8	DAVIS	20	FREEMAN	5
BAIRD	1	BUSING	3	DAVISSON	1	FRENCH	3
BAKER	10	BYERS	1	DAWSON	2	FULLERTON	2
BALDRIDGE	1	BYRN	1	DAY	7	FURGUSON	1
BALDWIN	4	CALVERT	1	DECKER	9	GALLOWAY	3
BALENTINE	2	CALVIN	1	DENBO	2	GARDNER	3
BALLARD	3	CANNON	1	DENBY	3	GARRET	8
BALLENGER	1	CARBAUGH	6	DEPRIEST	6	GARRETT	4
BALLINTINE	4	CARITHERS	1	DEVIN	7	GARTEN	2
BARBER	3	CARPENTER	3	DICK	4	GARTON	2
BARKER	11	CARTER	4	DICKMEIR	1	GEDNEY	1
BARLOW	1	CARTWRIGHT	2	DICKMIRE	1	GEISE	1
BARNES	1	CASBOLT	2	DIKMAR	1	GEISLER	1
BARNETT	7	CASEY	1	DILL	7	GENTER	2
BARRETT	8	CASH	2	DILLBECK	1	GERAULD	1
BASS	2	CASSELBERRY	1	DILLON	1	GOOCH	2
BAULDWIN	2	CATLIN	1	DIVEN	2	GOODWIN	1
BEASLEY	6	CATT	2	DOCKER	1	GOORLEY	2
BEAVIS	2	CHAFFIN	6	DORRELL	3	GORDON	1
BEDELL	2	CHALMERS	2	DOSON	2	GRAHAM	1
BELL	10	CHAMBERS	2	DOUGLASS	10	GRANT	1
BELLASS	1	CHAPMAN	2	DOWNEY	1	GRAPER	1
BELOAT	3	CHRISTY	3	DOWNING	1	GRAY	4
BENNETT	2	CHURCH	1	DRAKE	6	GRAYSON	2
BENSON	1	CIDELS	2	DUFF	6	GREATER	1
BERLIN	1	CLARK	8	DUNCAN	11	GREATHOUSE	4
BESING	2	COCKRUM	16	EATON	1	GREEK	1
BETTEOLFF	1	COFFMAN	3	EDRINGTON	1	GREP	1
BIGHAM	4	COLEMAN	4	EDWARDS	1	GRIER	2
BISHOP	1	COLLINS	2	EGGLESTON	2	GRIFFEN	1
BITTROLFF	1	COLVIN	3	ELDER	1	GRIFFITH	2
BIXLER	2	COMPTON	1	ELWYNE	1	GRIGGS	3
BLACK	5	CONGER	2	EMBEE	1	GRIGSBY	2
BLYTHE	3	CONNER	6	EMBNER	3	GRIGSLY	1
BOICOURT	1	CONNOR	4	EMBREE	22	GRUNDER	1
BOOKER	1	COOPER	1	EMISON	3	GUDGEL	4
BOREN	16	CORNWELL	1	EMMERSON	1	GUIREY	1
BORLAND	8	CORY	2	ENLOW	1	GULLICK	4
BOSWELL	6	COULTER	1	ENNIS	1	GUTHRIE	2
BOYCE	2	COVEY	3	ERVIN	3	GWIN	3
BRADLEY	1	COX	2	ESTES	2	HALBROOK	1
BRADSHAW	1	CRAVENS	2	EVANS	2	HALBROOKS	5
BRATCHER	1	CRAVINS	1	EVINS	1	HALCOMBE	1
BRAZELTON	1	CRAW	1	EWING	4	HALL	12
BREEDLOVE	2	CRAWFORD	5	FALLS	1	HAMER	1

Surname	# of Land Parcels	Surname	# of Land Parcels	Surname	# of Land Parcels	Surname	# of Land Parcels
HAMILTON	3	JOHNSON	26	MANCK	1	MINIS	2
HAMPTON	3	JOHNSTON	1	MANGRUM	1	MINNIS	5
HANFT	2	JONES	10	MANIFOLD	2	MINTON	1
HANNAH	3	JORDAN	19	MANNING	6	MITCHELL	7
HARBISON	8	JORDEN	1	MARINER	1	MOCK	5
HARDMAN	2	JORDON	3	MARKLE	1	MOFFATT	3
HARDY	1	KAVANAUGH	1	MARSHALL	1	MONTGOMERY	16
HARGROVE	10	KEERTZ	1	MARTIN	28	MOONEY	1
HARGROW	1	KELL	8	MARVEL	6	MOORE	8
HARMAN	1	KENEIPP	1	MARVELL	1	MOOTRY	1
HARMON	10	KENNERLY	3	MASON	8	MORRIS	6
HARNESS	2	KENT	1	MAUCH	1	MOUNCE	1
HARPER	10	KESTER	2	MAUCK	3	MOUNTS	4
HARRINGTON	1	KEY	4	MAXAM	1	MOUTRAY	1
HARRIS	6	KEYS	1	MAXWELL	2	MOWRER	1
HARRISON	4	KILLPATRICK	16	MAYER	2	MOWREY	1
HARRISS	2	KIME	1	MAYHALL	5	MUNFORD	1
HART	1	KIMMONS	1	MCADAMS	1	MURFITT	1
HARTEN	1	KINCADE	1	MCCARTNEY	2	MURPHEY	4
HARTIN	2	KINCHELOE	1	MCCARTY	1	MURPHY	6
HARVEY	1	KING	6	MCCCULLOUGH	1	MUSE	2
HASKIN	1	KINGSBURY	1	MCCLEARY	5	MUSIC	1
HASSELBRINK	2	KIRK	15	MCCLELLAN	5	MYER	1
HATTON	1	KIRKMAN	1	MCCLELLAND	3	MYERS	2
HAVIN	1	KIRKPATRICK	1	MCCONELL	1	NEABARGER	1
HAWKINS	6	KITCHEN	5	MCCONNEL	3	NEELY	1
HAYES	1	KLUSMANN	1	MCCONNELL	4	NEIPERT	1
HAYHURST	4	KNEREMER	1	MCCRARY	4	NEWMAN	2
HAYS	2	KNIGHT	1	MCCRAY	2	NEWSOM	1
HEAD	1	KNOLES	11	MCCRORY	1	NEWSUM	2
HEDGES	1	KNOX	1	MCCULLOCH	5	NICHOL	1
HEDRICK	1	KUHL	1	MCCULLOH	2	NICKELS	1
HENDERSON	1	KURTZ	5	MCCULLOM	1	NIXON	6
HENING	1	LAGOW	3	MCCULLOUGH	7	NOFOET	1
HEPNER	2	LANCE	2	MCCURDY	2	NULL	6
HERSHEY	1	LAND	2	MCDANIEL	1	OBERT	2
HILL	2	LANDSDOWN	1	MCDILL	4	OGLESBY	1
HINDE	1	LANE	2	MCDONALD	3	OLIPHANT	1
HOBBS	1	LANSDOWN	2	MCDOWELL	3	OLMSTED	1
HOESELE	1	LATHAN	1	MCFADEN	1	ONEAL	2
HOGE	2	LATHOM	1	MCFADIN	1	ONEIL	1
HOGUE	1	LATHORN	1	MCGAREY	1	ONEILL	1
HOLCOM	2	LAW	1	MCGARRAH	13	ORIN	8
HOLCOMB	9	LAWRENCE	6	MCGARY	3	ORR	8
HOLCOMBE	15	LEACH	1	MCGEHEE	2	OVERTON	2
HOLLIS	1	LEATHERS	1	MCGOWEN	1	OWENS	1
HOPKINS	3	LEECH	1	MCGREGER	10	PADEN	3
HOSACK	4	LEGRANGE	1	MCGREGOR	3	PANLEY	1
HOSICK	2	LEMAR	1	MCGREW	2	PARKER	2
HOWE	7	LEMASTERS	3	MCHISSICK	2	PARKINSON	1
HUDELSON	1	LEPRIEST	1	MCINTIRE	2	PARRETT	1
HUDSON	2	LETHERS	1	MCKEE	2	PATTERSON	1
HUDSPETH	3	LEWIS	2	MCKEMSON	1	PAUL	3
HUGHES	5	LININGER	1	MCKIDDY	1	PAYNE	3
HUGO	1	LOCKWOOD	3	MCMILLAN	5	PEARCE	1
HULL	1	LOLLMAN	1	MCMILLEN	1	PERKINS	1
HUMMER	1	LONG	1	MCMULLEN	1	PHILIPS	6
HUMPHREYS	21	LOOMIS	1	MCMULLIN	15	PHILLIPS	16
HUNT	2	LOSE	1	MCREYNOLDS	1	PIERCE	5
HUNTER	2	LOVEBAUGH	1	MCWILLIAMS	6	PINNEY	1
HURD	2	LOVELLETT	1	MEEK	2	POE	1
HUSE	1	LOW	1	MEISENHELTER	2	POTTER	3
HUSSEY	4	LOYD	4	MEKEMSON	1	POWELL	3
HUTHER	2	LUCAS	5	MELTON	1	PRATT	12
INGRAM	4	LUKRING	1	MERKEL	1	PRICE	7
INGRUM	1	LUTZ	1	MIKESELL	2	PRINCE	1
IRELAND	6	LYNN	7	MILBURN	13	PRITCHETT	3
JACKSON	1	MADISON	3	MILLER	19	PRIVETT	1
JACOBUS	5	MAIL	1	MILLS	6	PURCELL	6
JARREL	1	MANAHAN	2	MILN	1	PUTNAM	4

Surname	# of Land Parcels	Surname	# of Land Parcels	Surname	# of Land Parcels
RACHELS	2	SLAVEN	2	WARD	2
RAINEY	3	SLOAN	1	WARTH	4
RALSTON	1	SMIDT	1	WASSON	1
RAMSEY	1	SMITH	23	WATERS	2
RATZE	2	SPAIN	5	WATKINS	2
REAVIS	25	SPEAR	10	WATT	7
REDBURN	3	SPEER	2	WATTERS	2
REDMAN	6	SPENCER	3	WATTS	2
REED	2	SPROUL	1	WEBB	4
REEDER	1	SPROWL	3	WEED	1
REEL	3	STALLINGS	3	WEHNER	1
REEVES	1	STASER	4	WELBORN	1
REITZEL	2	STASIR	1	WELLER	2
RENNIS	1	STEEL	11	WEST	2
REVES	2	STEEN	2	WESTFALL	3
REYNOLDS	7	STEPHENS	7	WHEATON	2
RICE	1	STERETT	4	WHEELER	13
RICHARDS	1	STERNS	1	WHITE	9
RICHARDSON	2	STEWART	14	WHITING	2
RICK	1	STILLWELL	1	WHITNEY	1
RICKEY	2	STILWELL	1	WHITSETT	4
RILEY	1	STOCKLAND	1	WHITSITT	2
ROBB	7	STONE	2	WIDENER	1
ROBBISON	1	STORMENT	1	WIGGINS	1
ROBERTS	3	STORMON	2	WILHOW	1
ROBERTSON	1	STORMONT	5	WILKINS	3
ROBINSON	14	STRICKLAND	14	WILKINSON	5
ROCKWELL	3	STRICTMOERDER	1	WILKISON	1
RODBURN	1	STUNKEL	2	WILKS	3
RODERICK	5	STUNKLE	1	WILLIAMS	28
ROLFSMEYER	2	SULLIVAN	18	WILLY	1
ROSBOROUGH	3	SUMNER	1	WILSON	34
ROSE	1	SUMNERS	2	WINKELMANN	1
ROUTT	1	SUMPTER	1	WIRE	3
ROWE	2	SUTPHEN	1	WISE	4
RUSSELL	1	SUTTON	2	WITHERSPOON	5
RUTLEDGE	8	SWANEY	1	WITHRAW	1
RUTTER	1	TALES	1	WITHROW	14
SAIBART	1	TARRET	2	WITTMAN	1
SANDALL	3	TAYLOR	12	WONZER	2
SAULMAN	1	TERRELL	3	WOOD	8
SAULMON	2	TERRY	3	WOODHOUSE	1
SAWYER	2	THACHER	12	WOODS	21
SAXTON	1	THOMAS	9	WRIGHT	5
SCANTLIN	1	THOMPSON	6	YAGER	12
SCHMOLL	2	TOMPSON	2	YEAGER	4
SCHONK	1	TOWNSEND	10	YIERLING	1
SCOTT	4	TRENCH	1	YOUNG	3
SECHMAN	1	TRIBBLE	1	YOUNGMAN	1
SELSOR	1	TRIBLE	5	ZIMMERMAN	6
SHADLE	2	TRIPPET	5		
SHAFER	2	TRIPPETT	2		
SHANNER	1	TRUITT	2		
SHANNON	6	TUCKER	1		
SHARNST	1	TURNER	3		
SHARP	13	TURPIN	3		
SHAW	2	TWEEDLE	8		
SHELTON	1	ULM	1		
SHERRY	1	VANDERHOOF	4		
SHERWOOD	1	VANDERHOOP	1		
SHIELDS	2	VAUGHN	1		
SIDES	4	VICKERS	5		
SIDLE	2	VON PRICE	1		
SIDLES	1	WALDEN	6		
SILLAVEN	4	WALK	1		
SIMPSON	19	WALKER	2		
SINZICK	1	WALLACE	5		
SKELSON	1	WALLER	1		
SKELTEN	1	WALLIS	3		
SKELTON	21	WALTERS	9		

Surname/Township Index

This Index allows you to determine which *Township Map Group(s)* contain individuals with the following surnames. Each *Map Group* has a corresponding full-name index of all individuals who obtained patents for land within its Congressional township's borders. After each index you will find the Patent Map to which it refers, and just thereafter, you can view the township's Road Map and Historical Map, with the latter map displaying streams, railroads, and more.

So, once you find your Surname here, proceed to the Index at the beginning of the **Map Group** indicated below.

Surname	Map Group	Parcels of Land	Meridian/Township/Range		
ADAMS	**4**	7	2nd PM	1-S	11-W
" "	**19**	3	2nd PM	3-S	10-W
" "	**18**	1	2nd PM	3-S	11-W
ALSOP	**18**	2	2nd PM	3-S	11-W
ALVIS	**4**	1	2nd PM	1-S	11-W
AMES	**18**	1	2nd PM	3-S	11-W
AMORY	**19**	8	2nd PM	3-S	10-W
" "	**20**	4	2nd PM	3-S	9-W
AMOS	**5**	1	2nd PM	1-S	10-W
ANDERSON	**23**	3	2nd PM	4-S	10-W
ARBURN	**19**	1	2nd PM	3-S	10-W
" "	**23**	1	2nd PM	4-S	10-W
ASH	**17**	2	2nd PM	3-S	12-W
ASHLEY	**16**	4	2nd PM	3-S	13-W
" "	**9**	1	2nd PM	2-S	13-W
ASHMEAD	**12**	1	2nd PM	2-S	10-W
ATKINS	**2**	1	2nd PM	1-N	10-W
ATKINSON	**7**	1	2nd PM	1-S	8-W
AULDREDGE	**17**	1	2nd PM	3-S	12-W
AULDRIDGE	**17**	2	2nd PM	3-S	12-W
" "	**9**	1	2nd PM	2-S	13-W
AYERS	**19**	2	2nd PM	3-S	10-W
" "	**18**	1	2nd PM	3-S	11-W
AYRES	**19**	1	2nd PM	3-S	10-W
BAECHEL	**23**	4	2nd PM	4-S	10-W
BAIRD	**17**	1	2nd PM	3-S	12-W
BAKER	**9**	9	2nd PM	2-S	13-W
" "	**2**	1	2nd PM	1-N	10-W
BALDRIDGE	**6**	1	2nd PM	1-S	9-W
BALDWIN	**17**	3	2nd PM	3-S	12-W
" "	**21**	1	2nd PM	3-S	8-W
BALENTINE	**3**	2	2nd PM	1-S	12-W
BALLARD	**23**	2	2nd PM	4-S	10-W
" "	**6**	1	2nd PM	1-S	9-W
BALLENGER	**5**	1	2nd PM	1-S	10-W
BALLINTINE	**3**	4	2nd PM	1-S	12-W
BARBER	**13**	2	2nd PM	2-S	9-W
" "	**12**	1	2nd PM	2-S	10-W
BARKER	**18**	5	2nd PM	3-S	11-W
" "	**16**	3	2nd PM	3-S	13-W
" "	**9**	2	2nd PM	2-S	13-W
" "	**21**	1	2nd PM	3-S	8-W
BARLOW	**18**	1	2nd PM	3-S	11-W
BARNES	**14**	1	2nd PM	2-S	8-W

Surname	Map Group	Parcels of Land	Meridian/Township/Range		
BARNETT	**1**	4	2nd PM	1-N	11-W
" "	**15**	2	2nd PM	3-S	14-W
" "	**16**	1	2nd PM	3-S	13-W
BARRETT	**13**	7	2nd PM	2-S	9-W
" "	**14**	1	2nd PM	2-S	8-W
BASS	**20**	2	2nd PM	3-S	9-W
BAULDWIN	**10**	2	2nd PM	2-S	12-W
BEASLEY	**13**	4	2nd PM	2-S	9-W
" "	**20**	2	2nd PM	3-S	9-W
BEAVIS	**12**	1	2nd PM	2-S	10-W
" "	**13**	1	2nd PM	2-S	9-W
BEDELL	**10**	2	2nd PM	2-S	12-W
BELL	**21**	8	2nd PM	3-S	8-W
" "	**3**	1	2nd PM	1-S	12-W
" "	**14**	1	2nd PM	2-S	8-W
BELLASS	**10**	1	2nd PM	2-S	12-W
BELOAT	**18**	3	2nd PM	3-S	11-W
BENNETT	**16**	2	2nd PM	3-S	13-W
BENSON	**9**	1	2nd PM	2-S	13-W
BERLIN	**5**	1	2nd PM	1-S	10-W
BESING	**23**	2	2nd PM	4-S	10-W
BETTEOLFF	**12**	1	2nd PM	2-S	10-W
BIGHAM	**12**	3	2nd PM	2-S	10-W
" "	**13**	1	2nd PM	2-S	9-W
BISHOP	**16**	1	2nd PM	3-S	13-W
BITTROLFF	**12**	1	2nd PM	2-S	10-W
BIXLER	**22**	2	2nd PM	4-S	11-W
BLACK	**9**	2	2nd PM	2-S	13-W
" "	**3**	1	2nd PM	1-S	12-W
" "	**10**	1	2nd PM	2-S	12-W
" "	**21**	1	2nd PM	3-S	8-W
BLYTHE	**22**	2	2nd PM	4-S	11-W
" "	**18**	1	2nd PM	3-S	11-W
BOICOURT	**12**	1	2nd PM	2-S	10-W
BOOKER	**20**	1	2nd PM	3-S	9-W
BOREN	**22**	13	2nd PM	4-S	11-W
" "	**18**	2	2nd PM	3-S	11-W
" "	**15**	1	2nd PM	3-S	14-W
BORLAND	**13**	8	2nd PM	2-S	9-W
BOSWELL	**5**	5	2nd PM	1-S	10-W
" "	**13**	1	2nd PM	2-S	9-W
BOYCE	**20**	2	2nd PM	3-S	9-W
BRADLEY	**10**	1	2nd PM	2-S	12-W
BRADSHAW	**20**	1	2nd PM	3-S	9-W
BRATCHER	**4**	1	2nd PM	1-S	11-W
BRAZELTON	**12**	1	2nd PM	2-S	10-W
BREEDLOVE	**9**	1	2nd PM	2-S	13-W
" "	**13**	1	2nd PM	2-S	9-W
BRILES	**22**	1	2nd PM	4-S	11-W
BRILS	**22**	1	2nd PM	4-S	11-W
BRITTENHAM	**4**	1	2nd PM	1-S	11-W
BRITTONHAM	**4**	1	2nd PM	1-S	11-W
BROKAW	**19**	3	2nd PM	3-S	10-W
BROSE	**23**	1	2nd PM	4-S	10-W
BROTHERS	**18**	7	2nd PM	3-S	11-W
" "	**22**	1	2nd PM	4-S	11-W
BROWN	**2**	5	2nd PM	1-N	10-W
" "	**12**	4	2nd PM	2-S	10-W
" "	**1**	3	2nd PM	1-N	11-W
" "	**14**	3	2nd PM	2-S	8-W

Surname	Map Group	Parcels of Land	Meridian/Township/Range		
BROWN (Cont'd)	**13**	2	2nd PM	2-S	9-W
" "	**5**	1	2nd PM	1-S	10-W
" "	**4**	1	2nd PM	1-S	11-W
" "	**10**	1	2nd PM	2-S	12-W
BROWNLEE	**5**	7	2nd PM	1-S	10-W
BRUMFIELD	**18**	1	2nd PM	3-S	11-W
BRUNER	**4**	2	2nd PM	1-S	11-W
BUCKNER	**4**	1	2nd PM	1-S	11-W
BUMP	**9**	2	2nd PM	2-S	13-W
BURCHFIELD	**13**	3	2nd PM	2-S	9-W
BURGET	**3**	1	2nd PM	1-S	12-W
BURRUCKER	**19**	1	2nd PM	3-S	10-W
BURTCH	**4**	2	2nd PM	1-S	11-W
BURTON	**20**	7	2nd PM	3-S	9-W
" "	**15**	1	2nd PM	3-S	14-W
BUSING	**23**	3	2nd PM	4-S	10-W
BYERS	**23**	1	2nd PM	4-S	10-W
BYRN	**18**	1	2nd PM	3-S	11-W
CALVERT	**22**	1	2nd PM	4-S	11-W
CALVIN	**16**	1	2nd PM	3-S	13-W
CANNON	**2**	1	2nd PM	1-N	10-W
CARBAUGH	**15**	6	2nd PM	3-S	14-W
CARITHERS	**5**	1	2nd PM	1-S	10-W
CARPENTER	**15**	2	2nd PM	3-S	14-W
" "	**14**	1	2nd PM	2-S	8-W
CARTER	**22**	2	2nd PM	4-S	11-W
" "	**5**	1	2nd PM	1-S	10-W
" "	**23**	1	2nd PM	4-S	10-W
CARTWRIGHT	**16**	2	2nd PM	3-S	13-W
CASBOLT	**12**	2	2nd PM	2-S	10-W
CASEY	**10**	1	2nd PM	2-S	12-W
CASH	**9**	1	2nd PM	2-S	13-W
" "	**17**	1	2nd PM	3-S	12-W
CASSELBERRY	**16**	1	2nd PM	3-S	13-W
CATLIN	**4**	1	2nd PM	1-S	11-W
CATT	**2**	2	2nd PM	1-N	10-W
CHAFFIN	**18**	3	2nd PM	3-S	11-W
" "	**22**	3	2nd PM	4-S	11-W
CHALMERS	**2**	1	2nd PM	1-N	10-W
" "	**17**	1	2nd PM	3-S	12-W
CHAMBERS	**12**	2	2nd PM	2-S	10-W
CHAPMAN	**4**	2	2nd PM	1-S	11-W
CHRISTY	**5**	2	2nd PM	1-S	10-W
" "	**12**	1	2nd PM	2-S	10-W
CHURCH	**17**	1	2nd PM	3-S	12-W
CIDELS	**19**	2	2nd PM	3-S	10-W
CLARK	**16**	3	2nd PM	3-S	13-W
" "	**12**	2	2nd PM	2-S	10-W
" "	**7**	1	2nd PM	1-S	8-W
" "	**18**	1	2nd PM	3-S	11-W
" "	**15**	1	2nd PM	3-S	14-W
COCKRUM	**14**	13	2nd PM	2-S	8-W
" "	**13**	3	2nd PM	2-S	9-W
COFFMAN	**20**	3	2nd PM	3-S	9-W
COLEMAN	**13**	2	2nd PM	2-S	9-W
" "	**6**	1	2nd PM	1-S	9-W
" "	**14**	1	2nd PM	2-S	8-W
COLLINS	**14**	2	2nd PM	2-S	8-W
COLVIN	**6**	3	2nd PM	1-S	9-W
COMPTON	**19**	1	2nd PM	3-S	10-W

Surname	Map Group	Parcels of Land	Meridian/Township/Range		
CONGER	**2**	2	2nd PM	1-N	10-W
CONNER	**19**	3	2nd PM	3-S	10-W
" "	**18**	2	2nd PM	3-S	11-W
" "	**16**	1	2nd PM	3-S	13-W
CONNOR	**19**	4	2nd PM	3-S	10-W
COOPER	**15**	1	2nd PM	3-S	14-W
CORNWELL	**4**	1	2nd PM	1-S	11-W
CORY	**19**	2	2nd PM	3-S	10-W
COULTER	**13**	1	2nd PM	2-S	9-W
COVEY	**23**	3	2nd PM	4-S	10-W
COX	**13**	2	2nd PM	2-S	9-W
CRAVENS	**14**	2	2nd PM	2-S	8-W
CRAVINS	**14**	1	2nd PM	2-S	8-W
CRAW	**6**	1	2nd PM	1-S	9-W
CRAWFORD	**5**	3	2nd PM	1-S	10-W
" "	**14**	2	2nd PM	2-S	8-W
CREEK	**17**	5	2nd PM	3-S	12-W
" "	**16**	3	2nd PM	3-S	13-W
" "	**10**	1	2nd PM	2-S	12-W
CRISWELL	**20**	1	2nd PM	3-S	9-W
CROCK	**2**	1	2nd PM	1-N	10-W
CROCKETT	**17**	1	2nd PM	3-S	12-W
CROSS	**17**	1	2nd PM	3-S	12-W
CROW	**6**	4	2nd PM	1-S	9-W
" "	**2**	1	2nd PM	1-N	10-W
" "	**12**	1	2nd PM	2-S	10-W
CROWLEY	**9**	4	2nd PM	2-S	13-W
" "	**16**	2	2nd PM	3-S	13-W
" "	**15**	1	2nd PM	3-S	14-W
CRUSE	**23**	7	2nd PM	4-S	10-W
CULBERTSON	**4**	2	2nd PM	1-S	11-W
CUNINGHAM	**6**	1	2nd PM	1-S	9-W
CUNNINGHAM	**2**	2	2nd PM	1-N	10-W
" "	**5**	1	2nd PM	1-S	10-W
CURRY	**13**	4	2nd PM	2-S	9-W
CURTIS	**4**	1	2nd PM	1-S	11-W
DANIEL	**4**	4	2nd PM	1-S	11-W
" "	**5**	1	2nd PM	1-S	10-W
DASH	**23**	1	2nd PM	4-S	10-W
DAUGHERTY	**16**	1	2nd PM	3-S	13-W
DAVIDSON	**12**	4	2nd PM	2-S	10-W
" "	**19**	1	2nd PM	3-S	10-W
DAVIS	**17**	9	2nd PM	3-S	12-W
" "	**16**	5	2nd PM	3-S	13-W
" "	**22**	2	2nd PM	4-S	11-W
" "	**12**	1	2nd PM	2-S	10-W
" "	**9**	1	2nd PM	2-S	13-W
" "	**13**	1	2nd PM	2-S	9-W
" "	**19**	1	2nd PM	3-S	10-W
DAVISSON	**12**	1	2nd PM	2-S	10-W
DAWSON	**5**	2	2nd PM	1-S	10-W
DAY	**2**	2	2nd PM	1-N	10-W
" "	**4**	2	2nd PM	1-S	11-W
" "	**19**	2	2nd PM	3-S	10-W
" "	**18**	1	2nd PM	3-S	11-W
DECKER	**2**	6	2nd PM	1-N	10-W
" "	**4**	3	2nd PM	1-S	11-W
DENBO	**10**	2	2nd PM	2-S	12-W
DENBY	**16**	3	2nd PM	3-S	13-W
DEPRIEST	**19**	4	2nd PM	3-S	10-W

Surname	Map Group	Parcels of Land	Meridian/Township/Range
DEPRIEST (Cont'd)	18	1	2nd PM 3-S 11-W
" "	20	1	2nd PM 3-S 9-W
DEVIN	20	3	2nd PM 3-S 9-W
" "	4	2	2nd PM 1-S 11-W
" "	13	2	2nd PM 2-S 9-W
DICK	2	4	2nd PM 1-N 10-W
DICKMEIR	23	1	2nd PM 4-S 10-W
DICKMIRE	23	1	2nd PM 4-S 10-W
DIKMAR	23	1	2nd PM 4-S 10-W
DILL	13	6	2nd PM 2-S 9-W
" "	14	1	2nd PM 2-S 8-W
DILLBECK	23	1	2nd PM 4-S 10-W
DILLON	6	1	2nd PM 1-S 9-W
DIVEN	3	2	2nd PM 1-S 12-W
DOCKER	4	1	2nd PM 1-S 11-W
DORRELL	13	3	2nd PM 2-S 9-W
DOSON	5	2	2nd PM 1-S 10-W
DOUGLASS	18	9	2nd PM 3-S 11-W
" "	23	1	2nd PM 4-S 10-W
DOWNEY	13	1	2nd PM 2-S 9-W
DOWNING	18	1	2nd PM 3-S 11-W
DRAKE	12	4	2nd PM 2-S 10-W
" "	19	2	2nd PM 3-S 10-W
DUFF	23	5	2nd PM 4-S 10-W
" "	13	1	2nd PM 2-S 9-W
DUNCAN	13	4	2nd PM 2-S 9-W
" "	5	3	2nd PM 1-S 10-W
" "	10	2	2nd PM 2-S 12-W
" "	18	2	2nd PM 3-S 11-W
EATON	17	1	2nd PM 3-S 12-W
EDRINGTON	21	1	2nd PM 3-S 8-W
EDWARDS	2	1	2nd PM 1-N 10-W
EGGLESTON	13	2	2nd PM 2-S 9-W
ELDER	9	1	2nd PM 2-S 13-W
ELWYNE	13	1	2nd PM 2-S 9-W
EMBEE	12	1	2nd PM 2-S 10-W
EMBNER	14	3	2nd PM 2-S 8-W
EMBREE	19	12	2nd PM 3-S 10-W
" "	13	6	2nd PM 2-S 9-W
" "	14	2	2nd PM 2-S 8-W
" "	18	1	2nd PM 3-S 11-W
" "	23	1	2nd PM 4-S 10-W
EMISON	10	2	2nd PM 2-S 12-W
" "	2	1	2nd PM 1-N 10-W
EMMERSON	22	1	2nd PM 4-S 11-W
ENLOW	19	1	2nd PM 3-S 10-W
ENNIS	5	1	2nd PM 1-S 10-W
ERVIN	19	3	2nd PM 3-S 10-W
ESTES	19	2	2nd PM 3-S 10-W
EVANS	4	2	2nd PM 1-S 11-W
EVINS	4	1	2nd PM 1-S 11-W
EWING	12	3	2nd PM 2-S 10-W
" "	21	1	2nd PM 3-S 8-W
FALLS	19	1	2nd PM 3-S 10-W
FARMER	13	12	2nd PM 2-S 9-W
" "	14	1	2nd PM 2-S 8-W
" "	21	1	2nd PM 3-S 8-W
FARR	5	1	2nd PM 1-S 10-W
FARRIS	14	1	2nd PM 2-S 8-W
" "	21	1	2nd PM 3-S 8-W

Surname	Map Group	Parcels of Land	Meridian/Township/Range		
FERRIS	**12**	3	2nd PM	2-S	10-W
FIELD	**4**	7	2nd PM	1-S	11-W
" "	**18**	1	2nd PM	3-S	11-W
FIELDS	**4**	2	2nd PM	1-S	11-W
" "	**18**	2	2nd PM	3-S	11-W
" "	**5**	1	2nd PM	1-S	10-W
FIELER	**4**	1	2nd PM	1-S	11-W
FIFER	**16**	3	2nd PM	3-S	13-W
FILED	**4**	1	2nd PM	1-S	11-W
FINCH	**22**	1	2nd PM	4-S	11-W
FINNEY	**5**	1	2nd PM	1-S	10-W
" "	**13**	1	2nd PM	2-S	9-W
FISHER	**12**	2	2nd PM	2-S	10-W
" "	**23**	2	2nd PM	4-S	10-W
" "	**22**	1	2nd PM	4-S	11-W
FLOWER	**15**	3	2nd PM	3-S	14-W
FORBIS	**10**	2	2nd PM	2-S	12-W
FORREST	**17**	1	2nd PM	3-S	12-W
" "	**22**	1	2nd PM	4-S	11-W
FOSTER	**13**	2	2nd PM	2-S	9-W
" "	**19**	1	2nd PM	3-S	10-W
FRAZER	**17**	2	2nd PM	3-S	12-W
" "	**10**	1	2nd PM	2-S	12-W
FREEMAN	**2**	2	2nd PM	1-N	10-W
" "	**19**	2	2nd PM	3-S	10-W
" "	**1**	1	2nd PM	1-N	11-W
FRENCH	**4**	1	2nd PM	1-S	11-W
" "	**12**	1	2nd PM	2-S	10-W
" "	**20**	1	2nd PM	3-S	9-W
FULLERTON	**4**	2	2nd PM	1-S	11-W
FURGUSON	**18**	1	2nd PM	3-S	11-W
GALLOWAY	**20**	3	2nd PM	3-S	9-W
GARDNER	**6**	3	2nd PM	1-S	9-W
GARRET	**17**	8	2nd PM	3-S	12-W
GARRETT	**17**	3	2nd PM	3-S	12-W
" "	**16**	1	2nd PM	3-S	13-W
GARTEN	**17**	2	2nd PM	3-S	12-W
GARTON	**17**	1	2nd PM	3-S	12-W
" "	**16**	1	2nd PM	3-S	13-W
GEDNEY	**19**	1	2nd PM	3-S	10-W
GEISE	**12**	1	2nd PM	2-S	10-W
GEISLER	**22**	1	2nd PM	4-S	11-W
GENTER	**23**	2	2nd PM	4-S	10-W
GERAULD	**4**	1	2nd PM	1-S	11-W
GOOCH	**18**	2	2nd PM	3-S	11-W
GOODWIN	**17**	1	2nd PM	3-S	12-W
GOORLEY	**19**	1	2nd PM	3-S	10-W
" "	**21**	1	2nd PM	3-S	8-W
GORDON	**4**	1	2nd PM	1-S	11-W
GRAHAM	**19**	1	2nd PM	3-S	10-W
GRANT	**19**	1	2nd PM	3-S	10-W
GRAPER	**19**	1	2nd PM	3-S	10-W
GRAY	**15**	4	2nd PM	3-S	14-W
GRAYSON	**15**	2	2nd PM	3-S	14-W
GREATER	**23**	1	2nd PM	4-S	10-W
GREATHOUSE	**4**	2	2nd PM	1-S	11-W
" "	**3**	2	2nd PM	1-S	12-W
GREEK	**17**	1	2nd PM	3-S	12-W
GREP	**22**	1	2nd PM	4-S	11-W
GRIER	**17**	2	2nd PM	3-S	12-W

Surname	Map Group	Parcels of Land	Meridian/Township/Range		
GRIFFEN	**15**	1	2nd PM	3-S	14-W
GRIFFITH	**13**	2	2nd PM	2-S	9-W
GRIGGS	**4**	2	2nd PM	1-S	11-W
" "	**5**	1	2nd PM	1-S	10-W
GRIGSBY	**5**	1	2nd PM	1-S	10-W
" "	**6**	1	2nd PM	1-S	9-W
GRIGSLY	**5**	1	2nd PM	1-S	10-W
GRUNDER	**19**	1	2nd PM	3-S	10-W
GUDGEL	**13**	2	2nd PM	2-S	9-W
" "	**18**	2	2nd PM	3-S	11-W
GUIREY	**12**	1	2nd PM	2-S	10-W
GULLICK	**5**	4	2nd PM	1-S	10-W
GUTHRIE	**16**	2	2nd PM	3-S	13-W
GWIN	**3**	1	2nd PM	1-S	12-W
" "	**10**	1	2nd PM	2-S	12-W
" "	**17**	1	2nd PM	3-S	12-W
HALBROOK	**18**	1	2nd PM	3-S	11-W
HALBROOKS	**18**	3	2nd PM	3-S	11-W
" "	**19**	2	2nd PM	3-S	10-W
HALCOMBE	**19**	1	2nd PM	3-S	10-W
HALL	**12**	5	2nd PM	2-S	10-W
" "	**19**	3	2nd PM	3-S	10-W
" "	**4**	1	2nd PM	1-S	11-W
" "	**13**	1	2nd PM	2-S	9-W
" "	**17**	1	2nd PM	3-S	12-W
" "	**20**	1	2nd PM	3-S	9-W
HAMER	**17**	1	2nd PM	3-S	12-W
HAMILTON	**13**	2	2nd PM	2-S	9-W
" "	**3**	1	2nd PM	1-S	12-W
HAMPTON	**23**	3	2nd PM	4-S	10-W
HANFT	**22**	2	2nd PM	4-S	11-W
HANNAH	**19**	3	2nd PM	3-S	10-W
HARBISON	**21**	4	2nd PM	3-S	8-W
" "	**20**	3	2nd PM	3-S	9-W
" "	**5**	1	2nd PM	1-S	10-W
HARDMAN	**22**	2	2nd PM	4-S	11-W
HARDY	**18**	1	2nd PM	3-S	11-W
HARGROVE	**14**	5	2nd PM	2-S	8-W
" "	**5**	3	2nd PM	1-S	10-W
" "	**12**	2	2nd PM	2-S	10-W
HARGROW	**14**	1	2nd PM	2-S	8-W
HARMAN	**15**	1	2nd PM	3-S	14-W
HARMON	**17**	5	2nd PM	3-S	12-W
" "	**10**	3	2nd PM	2-S	12-W
" "	**15**	2	2nd PM	3-S	14-W
HARNESS	**4**	2	2nd PM	1-S	11-W
HARPER	**13**	10	2nd PM	2-S	9-W
HARRINGTON	**4**	1	2nd PM	1-S	11-W
HARRIS	**22**	4	2nd PM	4-S	11-W
" "	**6**	1	2nd PM	1-S	9-W
" "	**10**	1	2nd PM	2-S	12-W
HARRISON	**4**	3	2nd PM	1-S	11-W
" "	**5**	1	2nd PM	1-S	10-W
HARRISS	**17**	2	2nd PM	3-S	12-W
HART	**6**	1	2nd PM	1-S	9-W
HARTEN	**12**	1	2nd PM	2-S	10-W
HARTIN	**12**	2	2nd PM	2-S	10-W
HARVEY	**6**	1	2nd PM	1-S	9-W
HASKIN	**10**	1	2nd PM	2-S	12-W
HASSELBRINK	**12**	2	2nd PM	2-S	10-W

Surname	Map Group	Parcels of Land	Meridian/Township/Range
HATTON	**3**	1	2nd PM 1-S 12-W
HAVIN	**5**	1	2nd PM 1-S 10-W
HAWKINS	**18**	6	2nd PM 3-S 11-W
HAYES	**2**	1	2nd PM 1-N 10-W
HAYHURST	**19**	4	2nd PM 3-S 10-W
HAYS	**2**	2	2nd PM 1-N 10-W
HEAD	**18**	1	2nd PM 3-S 11-W
HEDGES	**5**	1	2nd PM 1-S 10-W
HEDRICK	**13**	1	2nd PM 2-S 9-W
HENDERSON	**20**	1	2nd PM 3-S 9-W
HENING	**16**	1	2nd PM 3-S 13-W
HEPNER	**16**	2	2nd PM 3-S 13-W
HERSHEY	**4**	1	2nd PM 1-S 11-W
HILL	**18**	1	2nd PM 3-S 11-W
" "	**23**	1	2nd PM 4-S 10-W
HINDE	**3**	1	2nd PM 1-S 12-W
HOBBS	**17**	1	2nd PM 3-S 12-W
HOESELE	**20**	1	2nd PM 3-S 9-W
HOGE	**12**	1	2nd PM 2-S 10-W
" "	**13**	1	2nd PM 2-S 9-W
HOGUE	**12**	1	2nd PM 2-S 10-W
HOLCOM	**19**	1	2nd PM 3-S 10-W
" "	**18**	1	2nd PM 3-S 11-W
HOLCOMB	**19**	4	2nd PM 3-S 10-W
" "	**20**	3	2nd PM 3-S 9-W
" "	**21**	2	2nd PM 3-S 8-W
HOLCOMBE	**19**	12	2nd PM 3-S 10-W
" "	**23**	3	2nd PM 4-S 10-W
HOLLIS	**19**	1	2nd PM 3-S 10-W
HOPKINS	**12**	1	2nd PM 2-S 10-W
" "	**19**	1	2nd PM 3-S 10-W
" "	**18**	1	2nd PM 3-S 11-W
HOSACK	**5**	3	2nd PM 1-S 10-W
" "	**19**	1	2nd PM 3-S 10-W
HOSICK	**19**	2	2nd PM 3-S 10-W
HOWE	**19**	3	2nd PM 3-S 10-W
" "	**4**	1	2nd PM 1-S 11-W
" "	**12**	1	2nd PM 2-S 10-W
" "	**14**	1	2nd PM 2-S 8-W
" "	**21**	1	2nd PM 3-S 8-W
HUDELSON	**5**	1	2nd PM 1-S 10-W
HUDSON	**15**	2	2nd PM 3-S 14-W
HUDSPETH	**12**	2	2nd PM 2-S 10-W
" "	**19**	1	2nd PM 3-S 10-W
HUGHES	**10**	2	2nd PM 2-S 12-W
" "	**18**	2	2nd PM 3-S 11-W
" "	**9**	1	2nd PM 2-S 13-W
HUGO	**19**	1	2nd PM 3-S 10-W
HULL	**18**	1	2nd PM 3-S 11-W
HUMMER	**21**	1	2nd PM 3-S 8-W
HUMPHREYS	**4**	13	2nd PM 1-S 11-W
" "	**5**	6	2nd PM 1-S 10-W
" "	**12**	1	2nd PM 2-S 10-W
" "	**13**	1	2nd PM 2-S 9-W
HUNT	**16**	2	2nd PM 3-S 13-W
HUNTER	**17**	2	2nd PM 3-S 12-W
HURD	**4**	2	2nd PM 1-S 11-W
HUSE	**10**	1	2nd PM 2-S 12-W
HUSSEY	**12**	3	2nd PM 2-S 10-W
" "	**6**	1	2nd PM 1-S 9-W

Surname	Map Group	Parcels of Land	Meridian/Township/Range		
HUTHER	**12**	2	2nd PM	2-S	10-W
INGRAM	**19**	3	2nd PM	3-S	10-W
" "	**20**	1	2nd PM	3-S	9-W
INGRUM	**20**	1	2nd PM	3-S	9-W
IRELAND	**23**	6	2nd PM	4-S	10-W
JACKSON	**10**	1	2nd PM	2-S	12-W
JACOBUS	**1**	3	2nd PM	1-N	11-W
" "	**4**	2	2nd PM	1-S	11-W
JARREL	**13**	1	2nd PM	2-S	9-W
JOHNSON	**17**	6	2nd PM	3-S	12-W
" "	**13**	5	2nd PM	2-S	9-W
" "	**10**	4	2nd PM	2-S	12-W
" "	**2**	3	2nd PM	1-N	10-W
" "	**3**	3	2nd PM	1-S	12-W
" "	**4**	2	2nd PM	1-S	11-W
" "	**14**	1	2nd PM	2-S	8-W
" "	**18**	1	2nd PM	3-S	11-W
" "	**22**	1	2nd PM	4-S	11-W
JOHNSTON	**12**	1	2nd PM	2-S	10-W
JONES	**6**	7	2nd PM	1-S	9-W
" "	**2**	1	2nd PM	1-N	10-W
" "	**4**	1	2nd PM	1-S	11-W
" "	**23**	1	2nd PM	4-S	10-W
JORDAN	**16**	9	2nd PM	3-S	13-W
" "	**9**	5	2nd PM	2-S	13-W
" "	**17**	3	2nd PM	3-S	12-W
" "	**22**	2	2nd PM	4-S	11-W
JORDEN	**16**	1	2nd PM	3-S	13-W
JORDON	**16**	3	2nd PM	3-S	13-W
KAVANAUGH	**3**	1	2nd PM	1-S	12-W
KEERTZ	**13**	1	2nd PM	2-S	9-W
KELL	**14**	4	2nd PM	2-S	8-W
" "	**21**	2	2nd PM	3-S	8-W
" "	**20**	2	2nd PM	3-S	9-W
KENEIPP	**3**	1	2nd PM	1-S	12-W
KENNERLY	**18**	2	2nd PM	3-S	11-W
" "	**19**	1	2nd PM	3-S	10-W
KENT	**19**	1	2nd PM	3-S	10-W
KESTER	**19**	2	2nd PM	3-S	10-W
KEY	**3**	2	2nd PM	1-S	12-W
" "	**2**	1	2nd PM	1-N	10-W
" "	**5**	1	2nd PM	1-S	10-W
KEYS	**19**	1	2nd PM	3-S	10-W
KILLPATRICK	**20**	10	2nd PM	3-S	9-W
" "	**21**	5	2nd PM	3-S	8-W
" "	**13**	1	2nd PM	2-S	9-W
KIME	**6**	1	2nd PM	1-S	9-W
KIMMONS	**2**	1	2nd PM	1-N	10-W
KINCADE	**20**	1	2nd PM	3-S	9-W
KINCHELOE	**16**	1	2nd PM	3-S	13-W
KING	**4**	3	2nd PM	1-S	11-W
" "	**19**	3	2nd PM	3-S	10-W
KINGSBURY	**12**	1	2nd PM	2-S	10-W
KIRK	**6**	12	2nd PM	1-S	9-W
" "	**5**	2	2nd PM	1-S	10-W
" "	**21**	1	2nd PM	3-S	8-W
KIRKMAN	**12**	1	2nd PM	2-S	10-W
KIRKPATRICK	**21**	1	2nd PM	3-S	8-W
KITCHEN	**18**	5	2nd PM	3-S	11-W
KLUSMANN	**12**	1	2nd PM	2-S	10-W

Surname	Map Group	Parcels of Land	Meridian/Township/Range		
KNEREMER	**19**	1	2nd PM	3-S	10-W
KNIGHT	**7**	1	2nd PM	1-S	8-W
KNOLES	**17**	6	2nd PM	3-S	12-W
" "	**18**	5	2nd PM	3-S	11-W
KNOX	**19**	1	2nd PM	3-S	10-W
KUHL	**23**	1	2nd PM	4-S	10-W
KURTZ	**23**	2	2nd PM	4-S	10-W
" "	**6**	1	2nd PM	1-S	9-W
" "	**14**	1	2nd PM	2-S	8-W
" "	**19**	1	2nd PM	3-S	10-W
LAGOW	**12**	2	2nd PM	2-S	10-W
" "	**4**	1	2nd PM	1-S	11-W
LANCE	**5**	2	2nd PM	1-S	10-W
LAND	**22**	2	2nd PM	4-S	11-W
LANDSDOWN	**10**	1	2nd PM	2-S	12-W
LANE	**2**	2	2nd PM	1-N	10-W
LANSDOWN	**4**	1	2nd PM	1-S	11-W
" "	**10**	1	2nd PM	2-S	12-W
LATHAN	**13**	1	2nd PM	2-S	9-W
LATHOM	**5**	1	2nd PM	1-S	10-W
LATHORN	**14**	1	2nd PM	2-S	8-W
LAW	**18**	1	2nd PM	3-S	11-W
LAWRENCE	**12**	5	2nd PM	2-S	10-W
" "	**13**	1	2nd PM	2-S	9-W
LEACH	**4**	1	2nd PM	1-S	11-W
LEATHERS	**5**	1	2nd PM	1-S	10-W
LEECH	**4**	1	2nd PM	1-S	11-W
LEGRANGE	**18**	1	2nd PM	3-S	11-W
LEMAR	**16**	1	2nd PM	3-S	13-W
LEMASTERS	**13**	2	2nd PM	2-S	9-W
" "	**5**	1	2nd PM	1-S	10-W
LEPRIEST	**19**	1	2nd PM	3-S	10-W
LETHERS	**5**	1	2nd PM	1-S	10-W
LEWIS	**6**	1	2nd PM	1-S	9-W
" "	**18**	1	2nd PM	3-S	11-W
LININGER	**19**	1	2nd PM	3-S	10-W
LOCKWOOD	**19**	2	2nd PM	3-S	10-W
" "	**18**	1	2nd PM	3-S	11-W
LOLLMAN	**23**	1	2nd PM	4-S	10-W
LONG	**22**	1	2nd PM	4-S	11-W
LOOMIS	**14**	1	2nd PM	2-S	8-W
LOSE	**12**	1	2nd PM	2-S	10-W
LOVEBAUGH	**13**	1	2nd PM	2-S	9-W
LOVELLETT	**9**	1	2nd PM	2-S	13-W
LOW	**22**	1	2nd PM	4-S	11-W
LOYD	**23**	3	2nd PM	4-S	10-W
" "	**13**	1	2nd PM	2-S	9-W
LUCAS	**4**	2	2nd PM	1-S	11-W
" "	**17**	2	2nd PM	3-S	12-W
" "	**10**	1	2nd PM	2-S	12-W
LUKRING	**23**	1	2nd PM	4-S	10-W
LUTZ	**22**	1	2nd PM	4-S	11-W
LYNN	**4**	3	2nd PM	1-S	11-W
" "	**21**	2	2nd PM	3-S	8-W
" "	**5**	1	2nd PM	1-S	10-W
" "	**10**	1	2nd PM	2-S	12-W
MADISON	**4**	3	2nd PM	1-S	11-W
MAIL	**23**	1	2nd PM	4-S	10-W
MANAHAN	**20**	2	2nd PM	3-S	9-W
MANCK	**10**	1	2nd PM	2-S	12-W

Surname	Map Group	Parcels of Land	Meridian/Township/Range
MANGRUM	**22**	1	2nd PM 4-S 11-W
MANIFOLD	**2**	1	2nd PM 1-N 10-W
" "	**6**	1	2nd PM 1-S 9-W
MANNING	**19**	3	2nd PM 3-S 10-W
" "	**13**	2	2nd PM 2-S 9-W
" "	**4**	1	2nd PM 1-S 11-W
MARINER	**20**	1	2nd PM 3-S 9-W
MARKLE	**5**	1	2nd PM 1-S 10-W
MARSHALL	**5**	1	2nd PM 1-S 10-W
MARTIN	**20**	13	2nd PM 3-S 9-W
" "	**4**	5	2nd PM 1-S 11-W
" "	**22**	5	2nd PM 4-S 11-W
" "	**21**	3	2nd PM 3-S 8-W
" "	**12**	2	2nd PM 2-S 10-W
MARVEL	**18**	5	2nd PM 3-S 11-W
" "	**22**	1	2nd PM 4-S 11-W
MARVELL	**17**	1	2nd PM 3-S 12-W
MASON	**20**	5	2nd PM 3-S 9-W
" "	**14**	3	2nd PM 2-S 8-W
MAUCH	**10**	1	2nd PM 2-S 12-W
MAUCK	**10**	3	2nd PM 2-S 12-W
MAXAM	**12**	1	2nd PM 2-S 10-W
MAXWELL	**2**	2	2nd PM 1-N 10-W
MAYER	**19**	2	2nd PM 3-S 10-W
MAYHALL	**20**	3	2nd PM 3-S 9-W
" "	**19**	2	2nd PM 3-S 10-W
MCADAMS	**7**	1	2nd PM 1-S 8-W
MCCARTNEY	**5**	2	2nd PM 1-S 10-W
MCCARTY	**12**	1	2nd PM 2-S 10-W
MCCCULLOUGH	**19**	1	2nd PM 3-S 10-W
MCCLEARY	**20**	5	2nd PM 3-S 9-W
MCCLELLAN	**13**	5	2nd PM 2-S 9-W
MCCLELLAND	**21**	2	2nd PM 3-S 8-W
" "	**20**	1	2nd PM 3-S 9-W
MCCONELL	**13**	1	2nd PM 2-S 9-W
MCCONNEL	**13**	2	2nd PM 2-S 9-W
" "	**21**	1	2nd PM 3-S 8-W
MCCONNELL	**13**	2	2nd PM 2-S 9-W
" "	**22**	2	2nd PM 4-S 11-W
MCCRARY	**18**	3	2nd PM 3-S 11-W
" "	**17**	1	2nd PM 3-S 12-W
MCCRAY	**12**	2	2nd PM 2-S 10-W
MCCRORY	**20**	1	2nd PM 3-S 9-W
MCCULLOCH	**13**	3	2nd PM 2-S 9-W
" "	**20**	2	2nd PM 3-S 9-W
MCCULLOH	**20**	2	2nd PM 3-S 9-W
MCCULLOM	**4**	1	2nd PM 1-S 11-W
MCCULLOUGH	**20**	6	2nd PM 3-S 9-W
" "	**19**	1	2nd PM 3-S 10-W
MCCURDY	**9**	2	2nd PM 2-S 13-W
MCDANIEL	**4**	1	2nd PM 1-S 11-W
MCDILL	**20**	2	2nd PM 3-S 9-W
" "	**13**	1	2nd PM 2-S 9-W
" "	**21**	1	2nd PM 3-S 8-W
MCDONALD	**19**	2	2nd PM 3-S 10-W
" "	**22**	1	2nd PM 4-S 11-W
MCDOWELL	**22**	2	2nd PM 4-S 11-W
" "	**18**	1	2nd PM 3-S 11-W
MCFADEN	**17**	1	2nd PM 3-S 12-W
MCFADIN	**10**	1	2nd PM 2-S 12-W

Surname	Map Group	Parcels of Land	Meridian/Township/Range
MCGAREY	**18**	1	2nd PM 3-S 11-W
MCGARRAH	**19**	8	2nd PM 3-S 10-W
" "	**23**	3	2nd PM 4-S 10-W
" "	**20**	2	2nd PM 3-S 9-W
MCGARY	**18**	2	2nd PM 3-S 11-W
" "	**17**	1	2nd PM 3-S 12-W
MCGEHEE	**23**	2	2nd PM 4-S 10-W
MCGOWEN	**2**	1	2nd PM 1-N 10-W
MCGREGER	**21**	7	2nd PM 3-S 8-W
" "	**20**	3	2nd PM 3-S 9-W
MCGREGOR	**18**	1	2nd PM 3-S 11-W
" "	**21**	1	2nd PM 3-S 8-W
" "	**20**	1	2nd PM 3-S 9-W
MCGREW	**20**	2	2nd PM 3-S 9-W
MCHISSICK	**12**	2	2nd PM 2-S 10-W
MCINTIRE	**18**	2	2nd PM 3-S 11-W
MCKEE	**19**	2	2nd PM 3-S 10-W
MCKEMSON	**5**	1	2nd PM 1-S 10-W
MCKIDDY	**18**	1	2nd PM 3-S 11-W
MCMILLAN	**20**	5	2nd PM 3-S 9-W
MCMILLEN	**20**	1	2nd PM 3-S 9-W
MCMULLEN	**4**	1	2nd PM 1-S 11-W
MCMULLIN	**18**	6	2nd PM 3-S 11-W
" "	**4**	4	2nd PM 1-S 11-W
" "	**20**	4	2nd PM 3-S 9-W
" "	**5**	1	2nd PM 1-S 10-W
MCREYNOLDS	**17**	1	2nd PM 3-S 12-W
MCWILLIAMS	**12**	6	2nd PM 2-S 10-W
MEEK	**20**	2	2nd PM 3-S 9-W
MEISENHELTER	**4**	2	2nd PM 1-S 11-W
MEKEMSON	**5**	1	2nd PM 1-S 10-W
MELTON	**3**	1	2nd PM 1-S 12-W
MERKEL	**6**	1	2nd PM 1-S 9-W
MIKESELL	**2**	2	2nd PM 1-N 10-W
MILBURN	**4**	5	2nd PM 1-S 11-W
" "	**5**	4	2nd PM 1-S 10-W
" "	**12**	4	2nd PM 2-S 10-W
MILLER	**18**	9	2nd PM 3-S 11-W
" "	**2**	4	2nd PM 1-N 10-W
" "	**1**	2	2nd PM 1-N 11-W
" "	**4**	2	2nd PM 1-S 11-W
" "	**5**	1	2nd PM 1-S 10-W
" "	**22**	1	2nd PM 4-S 11-W
MILLS	**5**	3	2nd PM 1-S 10-W
" "	**19**	2	2nd PM 3-S 10-W
" "	**13**	1	2nd PM 2-S 9-W
MILN	**4**	1	2nd PM 1-S 11-W
MINIS	**13**	2	2nd PM 2-S 9-W
MINNIS	**13**	3	2nd PM 2-S 9-W
" "	**14**	1	2nd PM 2-S 8-W
" "	**21**	1	2nd PM 3-S 8-W
MINTON	**18**	1	2nd PM 3-S 11-W
MITCHELL	**12**	4	2nd PM 2-S 10-W
" "	**22**	2	2nd PM 4-S 11-W
" "	**5**	1	2nd PM 1-S 10-W
MOCK	**10**	4	2nd PM 2-S 12-W
" "	**3**	1	2nd PM 1-S 12-W
MOFFATT	**19**	2	2nd PM 3-S 10-W
" "	**6**	1	2nd PM 1-S 9-W
MONTGOMERY	**18**	7	2nd PM 3-S 11-W

Surname	Map Group	Parcels of Land	Meridian/Township/Range		
MONTGOMERY (Cont'd)	10	4	2nd PM	2-S	12-W
" "	22	3	2nd PM	4-S	11-W
" "	14	2	2nd PM	2-S	8-W
MOONEY	4	1	2nd PM	1-S	11-W
MOORE	5	4	2nd PM	1-S	10-W
" "	22	2	2nd PM	4-S	11-W
" "	3	1	2nd PM	1-S	12-W
" "	13	1	2nd PM	2-S	9-W
MOOTRY	17	1	2nd PM	3-S	12-W
MORRIS	20	3	2nd PM	3-S	9-W
" "	4	1	2nd PM	1-S	11-W
" "	18	1	2nd PM	3-S	11-W
" "	23	1	2nd PM	4-S	10-W
MOUNCE	17	1	2nd PM	3-S	12-W
MOUNTS	18	4	2nd PM	3-S	11-W
MOUTRAY	16	1	2nd PM	3-S	13-W
MOWRER	9	1	2nd PM	2-S	13-W
MOWREY	10	1	2nd PM	2-S	12-W
MUNFORD	5	1	2nd PM	1-S	10-W
MURFITT	19	1	2nd PM	3-S	10-W
MURPHEY	17	2	2nd PM	3-S	12-W
" "	12	1	2nd PM	2-S	10-W
" "	22	1	2nd PM	4-S	11-W
MURPHY	20	3	2nd PM	3-S	9-W
" "	22	2	2nd PM	4-S	11-W
" "	12	1	2nd PM	2-S	10-W
MUSE	10	2	2nd PM	2-S	12-W
MUSIC	10	1	2nd PM	2-S	12-W
MYER	23	1	2nd PM	4-S	10-W
MYERS	19	2	2nd PM	3-S	10-W
NEABARGER	23	1	2nd PM	4-S	10-W
NEELY	19	1	2nd PM	3-S	10-W
NEIPERT	19	1	2nd PM	3-S	10-W
NEWMAN	20	2	2nd PM	3-S	9-W
NEWSOM	18	1	2nd PM	3-S	11-W
NEWSUM	18	1	2nd PM	3-S	11-W
" "	16	1	2nd PM	3-S	13-W
NICHOL	14	1	2nd PM	2-S	8-W
NICKELS	19	1	2nd PM	3-S	10-W
NIXON	5	5	2nd PM	1-S	10-W
" "	4	1	2nd PM	1-S	11-W
NOFOET	14	1	2nd PM	2-S	8-W
NULL	20	6	2nd PM	3-S	9-W
OBERT	23	2	2nd PM	4-S	10-W
OGLESBY	16	1	2nd PM	3-S	13-W
OLIPHANT	2	1	2nd PM	1-N	10-W
OLMSTED	4	1	2nd PM	1-S	11-W
ONEAL	6	1	2nd PM	1-S	9-W
" "	12	1	2nd PM	2-S	10-W
ONEIL	2	1	2nd PM	1-N	10-W
ONEILL	2	1	2nd PM	1-N	10-W
ORIN	20	8	2nd PM	3-S	9-W
ORR	12	6	2nd PM	2-S	10-W
" "	4	1	2nd PM	1-S	11-W
" "	18	1	2nd PM	3-S	11-W
OVERTON	10	1	2nd PM	2-S	12-W
" "	16	1	2nd PM	3-S	13-W
OWENS	23	1	2nd PM	4-S	10-W
PADEN	16	2	2nd PM	3-S	13-W
" "	17	1	2nd PM	3-S	12-W

Surname	Map Group	Parcels of Land	Meridian/Township/Range
PANLEY	9	1	2nd PM 2-S 13-W
PARKER	13	2	2nd PM 2-S 9-W
PARKINSON	12	1	2nd PM 2-S 10-W
PARRETT	4	1	2nd PM 1-S 11-W
PATTERSON	21	1	2nd PM 3-S 8-W
PAUL	6	3	2nd PM 1-S 9-W
PAYNE	4	3	2nd PM 1-S 11-W
PEARCE	18	1	2nd PM 3-S 11-W
PERKINS	13	1	2nd PM 2-S 9-W
PHILIPS	5	3	2nd PM 1-S 10-W
" "	6	3	2nd PM 1-S 9-W
PHILLIPS	2	8	2nd PM 1-N 10-W
" "	5	5	2nd PM 1-S 10-W
" "	6	3	2nd PM 1-S 9-W
PIERCE	18	2	2nd PM 3-S 11-W
" "	5	1	2nd PM 1-S 10-W
" "	19	1	2nd PM 3-S 10-W
" "	16	1	2nd PM 3-S 13-W
PINNEY	12	1	2nd PM 2-S 10-W
POE	18	1	2nd PM 3-S 11-W
POTTER	13	3	2nd PM 2-S 9-W
POWELL	22	3	2nd PM 4-S 11-W
PRATT	7	7	2nd PM 1-S 8-W
" "	14	3	2nd PM 2-S 8-W
" "	12	2	2nd PM 2-S 10-W
PRICE	5	3	2nd PM 1-S 10-W
" "	17	3	2nd PM 3-S 12-W
" "	4	1	2nd PM 1-S 11-W
PRINCE	4	1	2nd PM 1-S 11-W
PRITCHETT	18	2	2nd PM 3-S 11-W
" "	4	1	2nd PM 1-S 11-W
PRIVETT	18	1	2nd PM 3-S 11-W
PURCELL	2	4	2nd PM 1-N 10-W
" "	4	1	2nd PM 1-S 11-W
" "	9	1	2nd PM 2-S 13-W
PUTNAM	4	4	2nd PM 1-S 11-W
RACHELS	15	2	2nd PM 3-S 14-W
RAINEY	21	3	2nd PM 3-S 8-W
RALSTON	19	1	2nd PM 3-S 10-W
RAMSEY	3	1	2nd PM 1-S 12-W
RATZE	12	2	2nd PM 2-S 10-W
REAVIS	12	9	2nd PM 2-S 10-W
" "	13	6	2nd PM 2-S 9-W
" "	20	6	2nd PM 3-S 9-W
" "	19	4	2nd PM 3-S 10-W
REDBURN	5	3	2nd PM 1-S 10-W
REDMAN	18	2	2nd PM 3-S 11-W
" "	17	2	2nd PM 3-S 12-W
" "	22	2	2nd PM 4-S 11-W
REED	19	2	2nd PM 3-S 10-W
REEDER	16	1	2nd PM 3-S 13-W
REEL	18	3	2nd PM 3-S 11-W
REEVES	10	1	2nd PM 2-S 12-W
REITZEL	23	2	2nd PM 4-S 10-W
RENNIS	12	1	2nd PM 2-S 10-W
REVES	12	2	2nd PM 2-S 10-W
REYNOLDS	12	5	2nd PM 2-S 10-W
" "	14	1	2nd PM 2-S 8-W
" "	19	1	2nd PM 3-S 10-W
RICE	20	1	2nd PM 3-S 9-W

Surname	Map Group	Parcels of Land	Meridian/Township/Range
RICHARDS	10	1	2nd PM 2-S 12-W
RICHARDSON	6	2	2nd PM 1-S 9-W
RICK	5	1	2nd PM 1-S 10-W
RICKEY	19	2	2nd PM 3-S 10-W
RILEY	4	1	2nd PM 1-S 11-W
ROBB	18	5	2nd PM 3-S 11-W
" "	2	1	2nd PM 1-N 10-W
" "	12	1	2nd PM 2-S 10-W
ROBBISON	17	1	2nd PM 3-S 12-W
ROBERTS	4	2	2nd PM 1-S 11-W
" "	10	1	2nd PM 2-S 12-W
ROBERTSON	18	1	2nd PM 3-S 11-W
ROBINSON	22	7	2nd PM 4-S 11-W
" "	18	4	2nd PM 3-S 11-W
" "	17	2	2nd PM 3-S 12-W
" "	5	1	2nd PM 1-S 10-W
ROCKWELL	23	3	2nd PM 4-S 10-W
RODBURN	5	1	2nd PM 1-S 10-W
RODERICK	2	5	2nd PM 1-N 10-W
ROLFSMEYER	23	2	2nd PM 4-S 10-W
ROSBOROUGH	18	2	2nd PM 3-S 11-W
" "	22	1	2nd PM 4-S 11-W
ROSE	23	1	2nd PM 4-S 10-W
ROUTT	6	1	2nd PM 1-S 9-W
ROWE	12	1	2nd PM 2-S 10-W
" "	13	1	2nd PM 2-S 9-W
RUSSELL	3	1	2nd PM 1-S 12-W
RUTLEDGE	18	6	2nd PM 3-S 11-W
" "	12	1	2nd PM 2-S 10-W
" "	22	1	2nd PM 4-S 11-W
RUTTER	10	1	2nd PM 2-S 12-W
SAIBART	19	1	2nd PM 3-S 10-W
SANDALL	23	3	2nd PM 4-S 10-W
SAULMAN	17	1	2nd PM 3-S 12-W
SAULMON	17	2	2nd PM 3-S 12-W
SAWYER	9	2	2nd PM 2-S 13-W
SAXTON	20	1	2nd PM 3-S 9-W
SCANTLIN	19	1	2nd PM 3-S 10-W
SCHMOLL	12	2	2nd PM 2-S 10-W
SCHONK	19	1	2nd PM 3-S 10-W
SCOTT	18	3	2nd PM 3-S 11-W
" "	15	1	2nd PM 3-S 14-W
SECHMAN	2	1	2nd PM 1-N 10-W
SELSOR	10	1	2nd PM 2-S 12-W
SHADLE	4	2	2nd PM 1-S 11-W
SHAFER	22	2	2nd PM 4-S 11-W
SHANNER	20	1	2nd PM 3-S 9-W
SHANNON	12	4	2nd PM 2-S 10-W
" "	5	1	2nd PM 1-S 10-W
" "	19	1	2nd PM 3-S 10-W
SHARNST	23	1	2nd PM 4-S 10-W
SHARP	3	8	2nd PM 1-S 12-W
" "	10	4	2nd PM 2-S 12-W
" "	17	1	2nd PM 3-S 12-W
SHAW	19	2	2nd PM 3-S 10-W
SHELTON	20	1	2nd PM 3-S 9-W
SHERRY	19	1	2nd PM 3-S 10-W
SHERWOOD	18	1	2nd PM 3-S 11-W
SHIELDS	4	1	2nd PM 1-S 11-W
" "	20	1	2nd PM 3-S 9-W

Surname	Map Group	Parcels of Land	Meridian/Township/Range		
SIDES	**18**	4	2nd PM	3-S	11-W
SIDLE	**19**	2	2nd PM	3-S	10-W
SIDLES	**19**	1	2nd PM	3-S	10-W
SILLAVEN	**18**	4	2nd PM	3-S	11-W
SIMPSON	**17**	8	2nd PM	3-S	12-W
" "	**21**	6	2nd PM	3-S	8-W
" "	**18**	2	2nd PM	3-S	11-W
" "	**20**	2	2nd PM	3-S	9-W
" "	**16**	1	2nd PM	3-S	13-W
SINZICK	**20**	1	2nd PM	3-S	9-W
SKELSON	**13**	1	2nd PM	2-S	9-W
SKELTEN	**13**	1	2nd PM	2-S	9-W
SKELTON	**20**	11	2nd PM	3-S	9-W
" "	**19**	4	2nd PM	3-S	10-W
" "	**13**	3	2nd PM	2-S	9-W
" "	**17**	2	2nd PM	3-S	12-W
" "	**12**	1	2nd PM	2-S	10-W
SLAVEN	**5**	2	2nd PM	1-S	10-W
SLOAN	**4**	1	2nd PM	1-S	11-W
SMIDT	**23**	1	2nd PM	4-S	10-W
SMITH	**18**	7	2nd PM	3-S	11-W
" "	**16**	5	2nd PM	3-S	13-W
" "	**12**	4	2nd PM	2-S	10-W
" "	**3**	2	2nd PM	1-S	12-W
" "	**19**	2	2nd PM	3-S	10-W
" "	**6**	1	2nd PM	1-S	9-W
" "	**10**	1	2nd PM	2-S	12-W
" "	**17**	1	2nd PM	3-S	12-W
SPAIN	**19**	3	2nd PM	3-S	10-W
" "	**5**	1	2nd PM	1-S	10-W
" "	**4**	1	2nd PM	1-S	11-W
SPEAR	**21**	5	2nd PM	3-S	8-W
" "	**20**	4	2nd PM	3-S	9-W
" "	**19**	1	2nd PM	3-S	10-W
SPEER	**19**	2	2nd PM	3-S	10-W
SPENCER	**12**	3	2nd PM	2-S	10-W
SPROUL	**3**	1	2nd PM	1-S	12-W
SPROWL	**12**	3	2nd PM	2-S	10-W
STALLINGS	**19**	2	2nd PM	3-S	10-W
" "	**23**	1	2nd PM	4-S	10-W
STASER	**23**	2	2nd PM	4-S	10-W
" "	**22**	2	2nd PM	4-S	11-W
STASIR	**23**	1	2nd PM	4-S	10-W
STEEL	**20**	8	2nd PM	3-S	9-W
" "	**13**	2	2nd PM	2-S	9-W
" "	**17**	1	2nd PM	3-S	12-W
STEEN	**4**	2	2nd PM	1-S	11-W
STEPHENS	**20**	4	2nd PM	3-S	9-W
" "	**19**	2	2nd PM	3-S	10-W
" "	**15**	1	2nd PM	3-S	14-W
STERETT	**20**	3	2nd PM	3-S	9-W
" "	**13**	1	2nd PM	2-S	9-W
STERNS	**12**	1	2nd PM	2-S	10-W
STEWART	**3**	3	2nd PM	1-S	12-W
" "	**10**	3	2nd PM	2-S	12-W
" "	**5**	2	2nd PM	1-S	10-W
" "	**4**	2	2nd PM	1-S	11-W
" "	**18**	2	2nd PM	3-S	11-W
" "	**22**	2	2nd PM	4-S	11-W
STILLWELL	**3**	1	2nd PM	1-S	12-W

Surname	Map Group	Parcels of Land	Meridian/Township/Range
STILWELL	**3**	1	2nd PM 1-S 12-W
STOCKLAND	**19**	1	2nd PM 3-S 10-W
STONE	**18**	2	2nd PM 3-S 11-W
STORMENT	**5**	1	2nd PM 1-S 10-W
STORMON	**12**	2	2nd PM 2-S 10-W
STORMONT	**12**	3	2nd PM 2-S 10-W
" "	**4**	1	2nd PM 1-S 11-W
" "	**10**	1	2nd PM 2-S 12-W
STRICKLAND	**19**	9	2nd PM 3-S 10-W
" "	**10**	3	2nd PM 2-S 12-W
" "	**12**	2	2nd PM 2-S 10-W
STRICTMOERDER	**23**	1	2nd PM 4-S 10-W
STUNKEL	**23**	2	2nd PM 4-S 10-W
STUNKLE	**19**	1	2nd PM 3-S 10-W
SULLIVAN	**7**	7	2nd PM 1-S 8-W
" "	**2**	6	2nd PM 1-N 10-W
" "	**14**	3	2nd PM 2-S 8-W
" "	**12**	2	2nd PM 2-S 10-W
SUMNER	**19**	1	2nd PM 3-S 10-W
SUMNERS	**16**	1	2nd PM 3-S 13-W
" "	**22**	1	2nd PM 4-S 11-W
SUMPTER	**16**	1	2nd PM 3-S 13-W
SUTPHEN	**2**	1	2nd PM 1-N 10-W
SUTTON	**2**	1	2nd PM 1-N 10-W
" "	**22**	1	2nd PM 4-S 11-W
SWANEY	**20**	1	2nd PM 3-S 9-W
TALES	**5**	1	2nd PM 1-S 10-W
TARRET	**17**	2	2nd PM 3-S 12-W
TAYLOR	**19**	4	2nd PM 3-S 10-W
" "	**13**	3	2nd PM 2-S 9-W
" "	**20**	3	2nd PM 3-S 9-W
" "	**3**	2	2nd PM 1-S 12-W
TERRELL	**3**	3	2nd PM 1-S 12-W
TERRY	**13**	2	2nd PM 2-S 9-W
" "	**5**	1	2nd PM 1-S 10-W
THACHER	**7**	7	2nd PM 1-S 8-W
" "	**14**	3	2nd PM 2-S 8-W
" "	**12**	2	2nd PM 2-S 10-W
THOMAS	**18**	7	2nd PM 3-S 11-W
" "	**16**	1	2nd PM 3-S 13-W
" "	**15**	1	2nd PM 3-S 14-W
THOMPSON	**18**	3	2nd PM 3-S 11-W
" "	**9**	2	2nd PM 2-S 13-W
" "	**5**	1	2nd PM 1-S 10-W
TOMPSON	**5**	2	2nd PM 1-S 10-W
TOWNSEND	**5**	9	2nd PM 1-S 10-W
" "	**3**	1	2nd PM 1-S 12-W
TRENCH	**20**	1	2nd PM 3-S 9-W
TRIBBLE	**18**	1	2nd PM 3-S 11-W
TRIBLE	**18**	3	2nd PM 3-S 11-W
" "	**19**	1	2nd PM 3-S 10-W
" "	**22**	1	2nd PM 4-S 11-W
TRIPPET	**5**	5	2nd PM 1-S 10-W
TRIPPETT	**5**	2	2nd PM 1-S 10-W
TRUITT	**13**	2	2nd PM 2-S 9-W
TUCKER	**19**	1	2nd PM 3-S 10-W
TURNER	**4**	1	2nd PM 1-S 11-W
" "	**6**	1	2nd PM 1-S 9-W
" "	**22**	1	2nd PM 4-S 11-W
TURPIN	**5**	2	2nd PM 1-S 10-W

Surname	Map Group	Parcels of Land	Meridian/Township/Range		
TURPIN (Cont'd)	**6**	1	2nd PM	1-S	9-W
TWEEDLE	**15**	5	2nd PM	3-S	14-W
" "	**16**	3	2nd PM	3-S	13-W
ULM	**4**	1	2nd PM	1-S	11-W
VANDERHOOF	**1**	2	2nd PM	1-N	11-W
" "	**4**	2	2nd PM	1-S	11-W
VANDERHOOP	**4**	1	2nd PM	1-S	11-W
VAUGHN	**15**	1	2nd PM	3-S	14-W
VICKERS	**20**	3	2nd PM	3-S	9-W
" "	**19**	2	2nd PM	3-S	10-W
VON PRICE	**20**	1	2nd PM	3-S	9-W
WALDEN	**15**	5	2nd PM	3-S	14-W
" "	**16**	1	2nd PM	3-S	13-W
WALK	**5**	1	2nd PM	1-S	10-W
WALKER	**12**	2	2nd PM	2-S	10-W
WALLACE	**13**	3	2nd PM	2-S	9-W
" "	**19**	1	2nd PM	3-S	10-W
" "	**18**	1	2nd PM	3-S	11-W
WALLER	**15**	1	2nd PM	3-S	14-W
WALLIS	**19**	3	2nd PM	3-S	10-W
WALTERS	**19**	5	2nd PM	3-S	10-W
" "	**18**	4	2nd PM	3-S	11-W
WARD	**10**	1	2nd PM	2-S	12-W
" "	**15**	1	2nd PM	3-S	14-W
WARTH	**1**	4	2nd PM	1-N	11-W
WASSON	**17**	1	2nd PM	3-S	12-W
WATERS	**10**	1	2nd PM	2-S	12-W
" "	**16**	1	2nd PM	3-S	13-W
WATKINS	**22**	2	2nd PM	4-S	11-W
WATT	**14**	5	2nd PM	2-S	8-W
" "	**21**	2	2nd PM	3-S	8-W
WATTERS	**19**	1	2nd PM	3-S	10-W
" "	**18**	1	2nd PM	3-S	11-W
WATTS	**16**	2	2nd PM	3-S	13-W
WEBB	**15**	4	2nd PM	3-S	14-W
WEED	**18**	1	2nd PM	3-S	11-W
WEHNER	**23**	1	2nd PM	4-S	10-W
WELBORN	**17**	1	2nd PM	3-S	12-W
WELLER	**12**	2	2nd PM	2-S	10-W
WEST	**18**	1	2nd PM	3-S	11-W
" "	**20**	1	2nd PM	3-S	9-W
WESTFALL	**17**	2	2nd PM	3-S	12-W
" "	**2**	1	2nd PM	1-N	10-W
WHEATON	**20**	2	2nd PM	3-S	9-W
WHEELER	**12**	6	2nd PM	2-S	10-W
" "	**17**	3	2nd PM	3-S	12-W
" "	**14**	2	2nd PM	2-S	8-W
" "	**19**	2	2nd PM	3-S	10-W
WHITE	**10**	2	2nd PM	2-S	12-W
" "	**19**	2	2nd PM	3-S	10-W
" "	**15**	2	2nd PM	3-S	14-W
" "	**5**	1	2nd PM	1-S	10-W
" "	**9**	1	2nd PM	2-S	13-W
" "	**13**	1	2nd PM	2-S	9-W
WHITING	**18**	2	2nd PM	3-S	11-W
WHITNEY	**20**	1	2nd PM	3-S	9-W
WHITSETT	**5**	2	2nd PM	1-S	10-W
" "	**12**	2	2nd PM	2-S	10-W
WHITSITT	**12**	2	2nd PM	2-S	10-W
WIDENER	**23**	1	2nd PM	4-S	10-W

Surname	Map Group	Parcels of Land	Meridian/Township/Range		
WIGGINS	**17**	1	2nd PM	3-S	12-W
WILHOW	**23**	1	2nd PM	4-S	10-W
WILKINS	**15**	2	2nd PM	3-S	14-W
" "	**16**	1	2nd PM	3-S	13-W
WILKINSON	**22**	3	2nd PM	4-S	11-W
" "	**18**	2	2nd PM	3-S	11-W
WILKISON	**23**	1	2nd PM	4-S	10-W
WILKS	**1**	2	2nd PM	1-N	11-W
" "	**5**	1	2nd PM	1-S	10-W
WILLIAMS	**19**	6	2nd PM	3-S	10-W
" "	**17**	6	2nd PM	3-S	12-W
" "	**22**	6	2nd PM	4-S	11-W
" "	**16**	5	2nd PM	3-S	13-W
" "	**12**	2	2nd PM	2-S	10-W
" "	**5**	1	2nd PM	1-S	10-W
" "	**10**	1	2nd PM	2-S	12-W
" "	**15**	1	2nd PM	3-S	14-W
WILLY	**17**	1	2nd PM	3-S	12-W
WILSON	**20**	9	2nd PM	3-S	9-W
" "	**13**	7	2nd PM	2-S	9-W
" "	**21**	6	2nd PM	3-S	8-W
" "	**12**	5	2nd PM	2-S	10-W
" "	**22**	4	2nd PM	4-S	11-W
" "	**18**	3	2nd PM	3-S	11-W
WINKELMANN	**23**	1	2nd PM	4-S	10-W
WIRE	**20**	2	2nd PM	3-S	9-W
" "	**19**	1	2nd PM	3-S	10-W
WISE	**4**	2	2nd PM	1-S	11-W
" "	**20**	2	2nd PM	3-S	9-W
WITHERSPOON	**18**	4	2nd PM	3-S	11-W
" "	**4**	1	2nd PM	1-S	11-W
WITHRAW	**23**	1	2nd PM	4-S	10-W
WITHROW	**23**	14	2nd PM	4-S	10-W
WITTMAN	**23**	1	2nd PM	4-S	10-W
WONZER	**3**	1	2nd PM	1-S	12-W
" "	**9**	1	2nd PM	2-S	13-W
WOOD	**12**	4	2nd PM	2-S	10-W
" "	**13**	2	2nd PM	2-S	9-W
" "	**19**	1	2nd PM	3-S	10-W
" "	**20**	1	2nd PM	3-S	9-W
WOODHOUSE	**4**	1	2nd PM	1-S	11-W
WOODS	**19**	10	2nd PM	3-S	10-W
" "	**18**	6	2nd PM	3-S	11-W
" "	**20**	5	2nd PM	3-S	9-W
WRIGHT	**18**	3	2nd PM	3-S	11-W
" "	**5**	1	2nd PM	1-S	10-W
" "	**22**	1	2nd PM	4-S	11-W
YAGER	**22**	6	2nd PM	4-S	11-W
" "	**10**	3	2nd PM	2-S	12-W
" "	**18**	2	2nd PM	3-S	11-W
" "	**6**	1	2nd PM	1-S	9-W
YEAGER	**22**	3	2nd PM	4-S	11-W
" "	**18**	1	2nd PM	3-S	11-W
YIERLING	**19**	1	2nd PM	3-S	10-W
YOUNG	**2**	1	2nd PM	1-N	10-W
" "	**1**	1	2nd PM	1-N	11-W
" "	**19**	1	2nd PM	3-S	10-W
YOUNGMAN	**2**	1	2nd PM	1-N	10-W
ZIMMERMAN	**5**	6	2nd PM	1-S	10-W

– Part II –

Township Map Groups

Map Group 1: Index to Land Patents

Township 1-North Range 11-West (2nd PM)

After you locate an individual in this Index, take note of the Section and Section Part then proceed to the Land Patent map on the pages immediately following. You should have no difficulty locating the corresponding parcel of land.

The "For More Info" Column will lead you to more information about the underlying Patents. See the *Legend* at right, and the "How to Use this Book" chapter, for more information.

```
┌─────────────────────────────────────────────────────┐
│                    LEGEND                            │
│         "For More Info . . . " column                │
│ A = Authority (Legislative Act, See Appendix "A")    │
│ B = Block or Lot (location in Section unknown)       │
│ C = Cancelled Patent                                 │
│ F = Fractional Section                               │
│ G = Group  (Multi-Patentee Patent, see Appendix "C") │
│ V = Overlaps another Parcel                          │
│ R = Re-Issued (Parcel patented more than once)       │
│                                                      │
│ (A & G items require you to look in the Appendixes   │
│ referred to above. All other Letter-designations     │
│ followed by a number require you to locate line-items│
│ in this index that possess the ID number found after │
│ the letter).                                         │
└─────────────────────────────────────────────────────┘
```

ID	Individual in Patent	Sec.	Sec. Part	Date Issued	Other Counties	For More Info . . .
18	BARNETT, Vincent	25	8N½	1850-12-10	Knox	A1 F
19	"	25	9N½	1850-12-10	Knox	A1 F
16	"	25	10	1852-10-01	Knox	A1 F
17	"	25	7	1858-08-30	Knox	A1
9	BROWN, John	36	N½N½	1826-05-20	Knox	A1 F
10	"	36	NWSE	1835-10-07	Knox	A1 F
20	BROWN, William	25	11	1837-03-20	Knox	A1 F
15	FREEMAN, Stephen	36	SWSE	1839-08-01	Knox	A1 F
6	JACOBUS, Jacob	25	N½N½	1839-08-01	Knox	A1 F
12	JACOBUS, Peter	25	1	1837-11-07	Knox	A1 F
13	"	25	2	1839-02-01	Knox	A1 F
7	MILLER, Jacob	25	6	1837-08-05	Knox	A1 F
8	"	36	1	1839-02-01	Knox	A1 F
5	VANDERHOOF, Harvey	36	S½	1835-10-01	Knox	A1 F
4	"	36	2N½	1835-10-23	Knox	A1 F
3	WARTH, Harrison	24	SE	1838-09-01	Knox	A1 F
1	"	24	4	1839-08-01	Knox	A1 F
2	"	24	N½NE	1857-07-01	Knox	A1 F
11	WARTH, John	25	4	1840-10-01	Knox	A1 F
21	WILKS, Willis	25	3	1837-03-30	Knox	A1 F
22	"	25	5	1837-11-07	Knox	A1 F
14	YOUNG, Sparling	36	E½SE	1825-06-11	Knox	A1 F

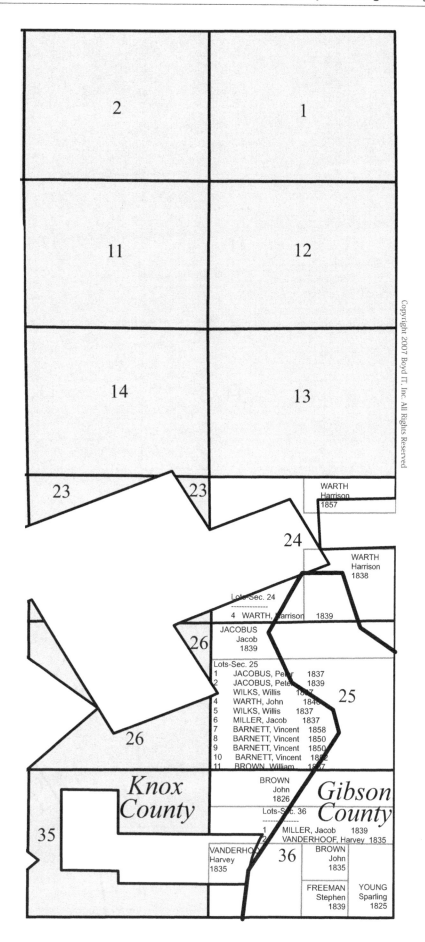

Patent Map

T1-N R11-W
2nd PM Meridian

M a p   G r o u p   1

Township Statistics

Parcels Mapped	:	22
Number of Patents	:	21
Number of Individuals	:	12
Patentees Identified	:	12
Number of Surnames	:	9
Multi-Patentee Parcels	:	0
Oldest Patent Date	:	6/11/1825
Most Recent Patent	:	8/30/1858
Block/Lot Parcels	:	238
Parcels Re - Issued	:	0
Parcels that Overlap	:	0
Cities and Towns	:	0
Cemeteries	:	0

Note: the area contained in this map amounts to far less than a full Township. Therefore, its contents are completely on this single page (instead of a "normal" 2-page spread).

Legend

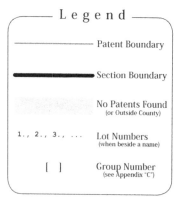

————— Patent Boundary

━━━━━ Section Boundary

No Patents Found
(or Outside County)

1., 2., 3., ... Lot Numbers
(when beside a name)

[ ] Group Number
(see Appendix "C")

Scale: Section = 1 mile X 1 mile
(generally, with some exceptions)

43

Road Map

T1-N R11-W
2nd PM Meridian

Map Group 1

Note: the area contained in this map amounts to far less than a full Township. Therefore, its contents are completely on this single page (instead of a "normal" 2-page spread).

Cities & Towns
None

Cemeteries
None

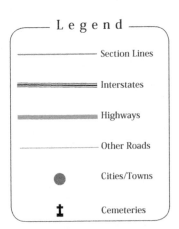

Legend

————	Section Lines
═══════	Interstates
————	Highways
————	Other Roads
●	Cities/Towns
✝	Cemeteries

Scale: Section = 1 mile X 1 mile
(generally, with some exceptions)

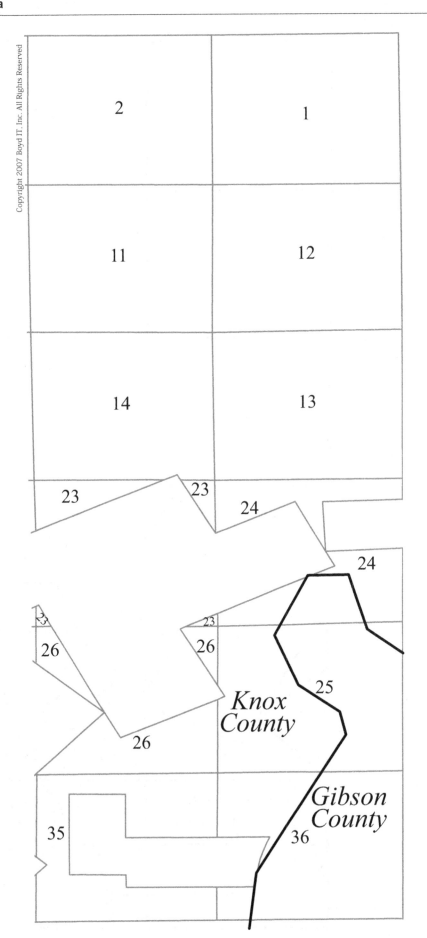

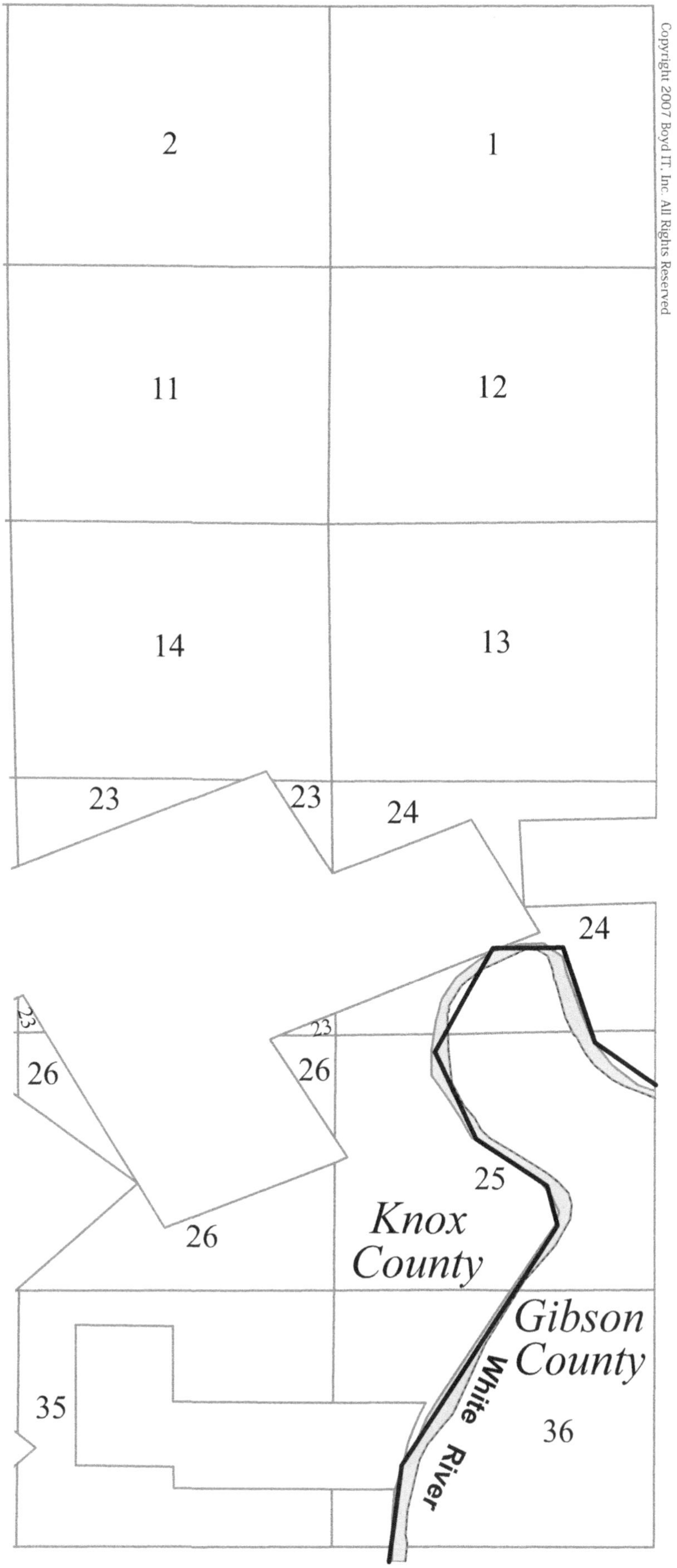
2
1
11
12
14
13
23
23
24
24
23
23
26
26
26
25
Knox County
Gibson County
White River
35
36

Historical Map

T1-N R11-W
2nd PM Meridian

Map Group 1

Note: the area contained in this map amounts to far less than a full Township. Therefore, its contents are completely on this single page (instead of a "normal" 2-page spread).

Cities & Towns

None

Cemeteries

None

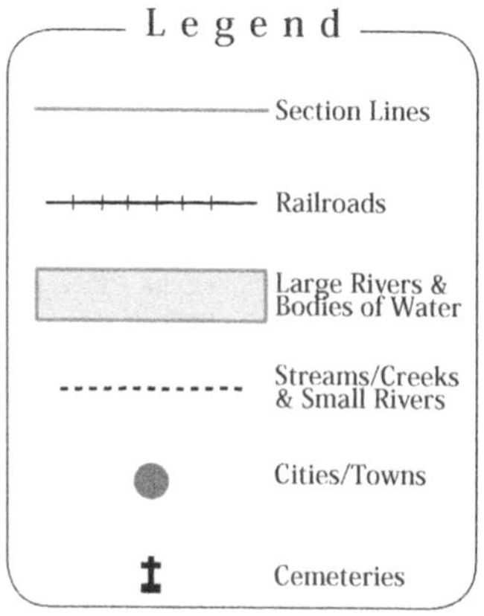
Legend
Section Lines
Railroads
Large Rivers & Bodies of Water
Streams/Creeks & Small Rivers
Cities/Towns
Cemeteries

Scale: Section = 1 mile X 1 mile
(there are some exceptions)

Map Group 2: Index to Land Patents

Township 1-North Range 10-West (2nd PM)

After you locate an individual in this Index, take note of the Section and Section Part then proceed to the Land Patent map on the pages immediately following. You should have no difficulty locating the corresponding parcel of land.

The "For More Info" Column will lead you to more information about the underlying Patents. See the *Legend* at right, and the "How to Use this Book" chapter, for more information.

ID	Individual in Patent	Sec.	Sec. Part	Date Issued	Other Counties	For More Info . . .
55	ATKINS, Jarret	22	6	1839-08-01	Knox	A1
56	BAKER, John	12	E½E½	1829-05-01	Knox	A1 F
60	BROWN, John	31	1	1835-10-01		A1 F
59	" "	30	N½S½	1837-03-18	Knox	A1 F R77
57	" "	30	3	1839-08-01	Knox	A1 F
58	" "	30	4	1839-08-01	Knox	A1 F
105	BROWN, William	31	2	1837-03-20		A1 F
61	CANNON, John	14	E½SW	1849-05-30	Knox	A1 F
62	CATT, John	17	2	1839-08-01	Knox	A1 F
80	CATT, Lewis	21	2	1837-03-30	Knox	A1 F
86	CHALMERS, Peter	21	N½	1839-08-01	Knox	A1 F
63	CONGER, John D	13	6	1840-10-01	Knox	A1 F
94	CONGER, Sebastian	13	5	1839-08-01	Knox	A1 F
36	CROCK, David	20	E½S½S½	1837-08-05	Knox	A1 F
78	CROW, Joseph G	17	1	1839-08-01	Knox	A1 F
28	CUNNINGHAM, Andrew	22	E½S½	1840-10-01	Knox	A1 F
43	CUNNINGHAM, Green	27	5	1839-08-01		A1 F
87	DAY, Peter	22	2	1840-10-01	Knox	A1 F
88	" "	22	W½E½	1840-10-01	Knox	A1 F
41	DECKER, Elizabeth	24	1	1837-03-15	Knox	A1 F
64	DECKER, John	17		1835-09-10	Knox	A1 F
89	DECKER, Ransom	23	NE	1839-08-01	Knox	A1 F
100	DECKER, Thomas J	27	1	1853-04-15		A1 F
101	" "	27	2W½E½	1853-04-15		A1 F
102	" "	27	6	1853-04-15		A1 F
49	DICK, James	20	SWSW	1853-10-10	Knox	A1
50	" "	28	W½	1855-01-03		A1 F
98	DICK, Thomas	19	NE	1838-09-05	Knox	A1 G11 F
99	" "	20	N½	1838-09-05	Knox	A1 G11 F
53	EDWARDS, James S	23	3	1844-08-01	Knox	A1 F
93	EMISON, Samuel	29	N½	1835-10-01	Knox	A1 G14 F
97	FREEMAN, Stephen	31	4	1837-03-15		A1 F
96	"	31	3	1838-09-01		A1 F
32	HAYES, Benjamin	26	NENW	1852-10-01		A1
51	HAYS, James L	26	2SE	1855-01-03		A1 F
54	HAYS, James S	26	SWNW	1853-10-10		A1
82	JOHNSON, Nicholas	17	W½	1830-12-02	Knox	A1 F
104	JOHNSON, Thomas	12	7	1837-03-15	Knox	A1 F
103	" "	12	6	1837-03-18	Knox	A1 F
81	JONES, Morgan	20	SESW	1837-11-07	Knox	A1 F
65	KEY, John L	12	E½	1853-04-15	Knox	A1 G25 F
65	KEY, Stewart C	12	E½	1853-04-15	Knox	A1 G25 F
65	KEY, William	12	E½	1853-04-15	Knox	A1 G25 F
44	KIMMONS, Henry	13	S½N½	1839-08-01	Knox	A1 F
34	LANE, Danfred	12	2	1837-03-20	Knox	A1 F
35	" "	12	3	1837-03-20	Knox	A1 F

ID	Individual in Patent	Sec.	Sec. Part	Date Issued	Other Counties	For More Info . . .
79	MANIFOLD, Joseph	36	S½	1841-05-25		A1 F
27	MAXWELL, Alexander	13	1	1838-09-01	Knox	A1 F
66	MAXWELL, John	12	4	1837-08-05	Knox	A1 F
67	MCGOWEN, John	30	N½	1837-11-07	Knox	A1 F
42	MIKESELL, Garret W	20	6	1837-03-18	Knox	A1 F
68	MIKESELL, John	19	SW	1837-03-18	Knox	A1 F
23	MILLER, Adam	21	SE	1837-03-30	Knox	A1 F
24	" "	22	5	1839-08-01	Knox	A1 F
26	" "	28	1	1840-10-01		A1 F
25	" "	22	7	1841-05-25	Knox	A1 F
52	OLIPHANT, James	23	SESE	1850-12-10	Knox	A1 F
45	ONEIL, Henry	21	S½N½	1837-03-30	Knox	A1 F
46	ONEILL, Henry	28	2	1839-08-01		A1 F
29	PHILLIPS, Andrew	26	SENE	1839-02-01		A1
39	PHILLIPS, Edwin	26	NENE	1859-04-01		A1
83	PHILLIPS, Payton	23	W½SE	1839-08-01	Knox	A1 F
84	" "	24	2	1839-08-01	Knox	A1 F
85	" "	25	1	1839-08-01		A1 F
90	PHILLIPS, Roda	26	SENW	1857-07-01		A1
91	" "	26	SW	1857-07-01		A1 F
92	" "	26	SWNE	1859-04-01		A1
98	PURCELL, Andrew	19	NE	1838-09-05	Knox	A1 G11 F
99	" "	20	N½	1838-09-05	Knox	A1 G11 F
30	" "	20	3	1839-08-01	Knox	A1 F
31	" "	20	4	1839-08-01	Knox	A1 F
37	ROBB, David	21	S½	1826-05-20	Knox	A1 F
72	RODERICK, John	14	NE	1829-04-10	Knox	A1 F
71	" "	14	4	1840-10-01	Knox	A1 F
73	" "	22	1	1840-10-01	Knox	A1 F
70	" "	14	2	1841-05-25	Knox	A1 F
69	" "	14	1W½SE	1851-02-01	Knox	A1 F
33	SECHMAN, Charles	22	W½N½	1839-08-01	Knox	A1 F
47	SULLIVAN, Henry	20	2	1840-10-01	Knox	A1 F
74	SULLIVAN, John	21	1	1835-10-28	Knox	A1 F
75	" "	27	3	1839-02-01		A1 F
76	" "	27	4	1839-02-01		A1 F
77	" "	30	N½S½	1839-02-01	Knox	A1 F R59
106	SULLIVAN, William	23	NESE	1857-07-01	Knox	A1 F
40	SUTPHEN, Elias	26	NWNW	1857-07-01		A1
38	SUTTON, Ebenezer	14	E½SE	1837-08-01	Knox	A1 F
93	WESTFALL, Thomas	29	N½	1835-10-01	Knox	A1 G14 F
95	YOUNG, Sparling	19	W½	1838-09-07	Knox	A1 F
48	YOUNGMAN, Jacob S	20	5	1837-03-18	Knox	A1 F

Patent Map

T1-N R10-W
2nd PM Meridian

Map Group 2

Township Statistics

Parcels Mapped	:	84
Number of Patents	:	77
Number of Individuals	:	61
Patentees Identified	:	58
Number of Surnames	:	42
Multi-Patentee Parcels	:	4
Oldest Patent Date	:	5/20/1826
Most Recent Patent	:	4/1/1859
Block/Lot Parcels	:	1180
Parcels Re - Issued	:	1
Parcels that Overlap	:	0
Cities and Towns	:	2
Cemeteries	:	2

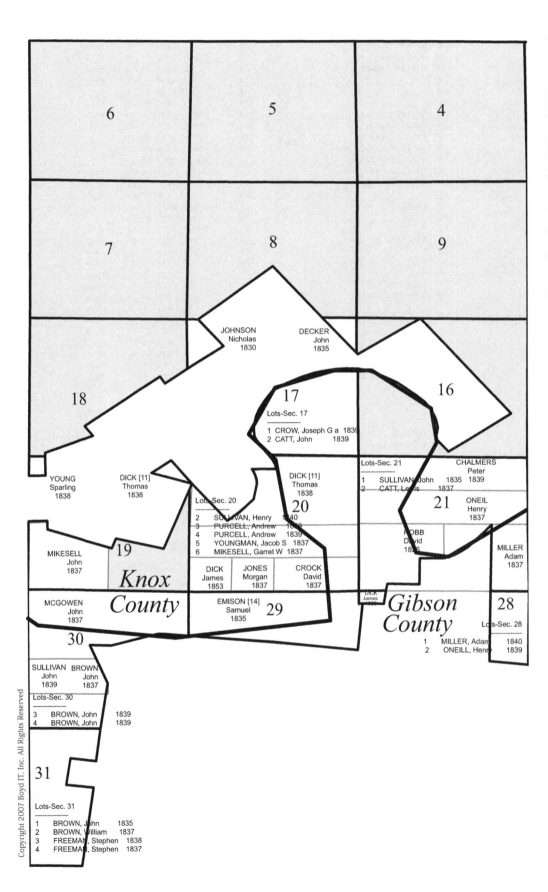

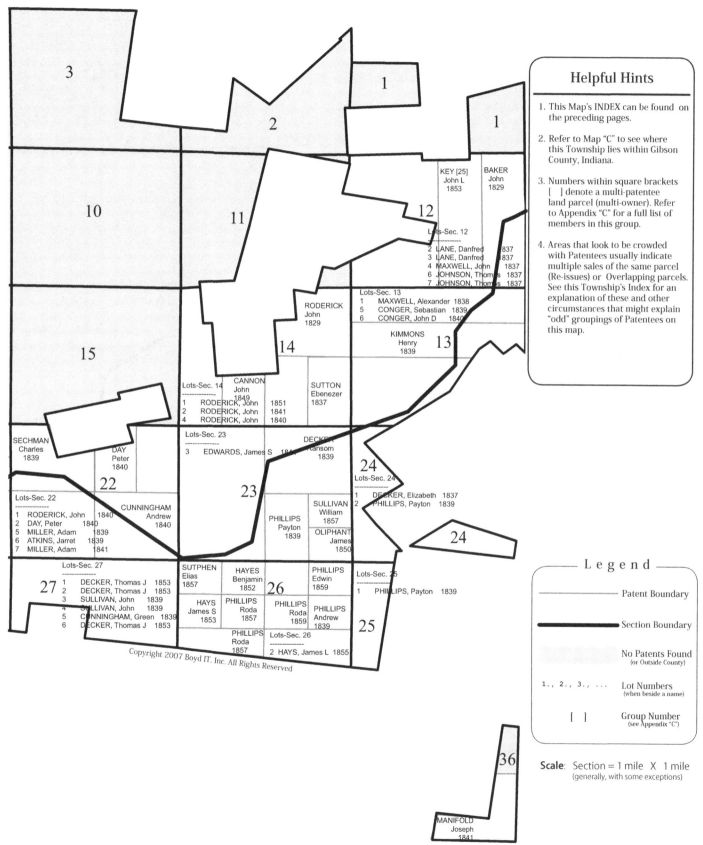

Helpful Hints

1. This Map's INDEX can be found on the preceding pages.

2. Refer to Map "C" to see where this Township lies within Gibson County, Indiana.

3. Numbers within square brackets [ ] denote a multi-patentee land parcel (multi-owner). Refer to Appendix "C" for a full list of members in this group.

4. Areas that look to be crowded with Patentees usually indicate multiple sales of the same parcel (Re-issues) or Overlapping parcels. See this Township's Index for an explanation of these and other circumstances that might explain "odd" groupings of Patentees on this map.

Legend

——————— Patent Boundary

━━━━━━ Section Boundary

No Patents Found
(or Outside County)

1., 2., 3., ...   Lot Numbers
(when beside a name)

[ ]   Group Number
(see Appendix "C")

Scale: Section = 1 mile X 1 mile
(generally, with some exceptions)

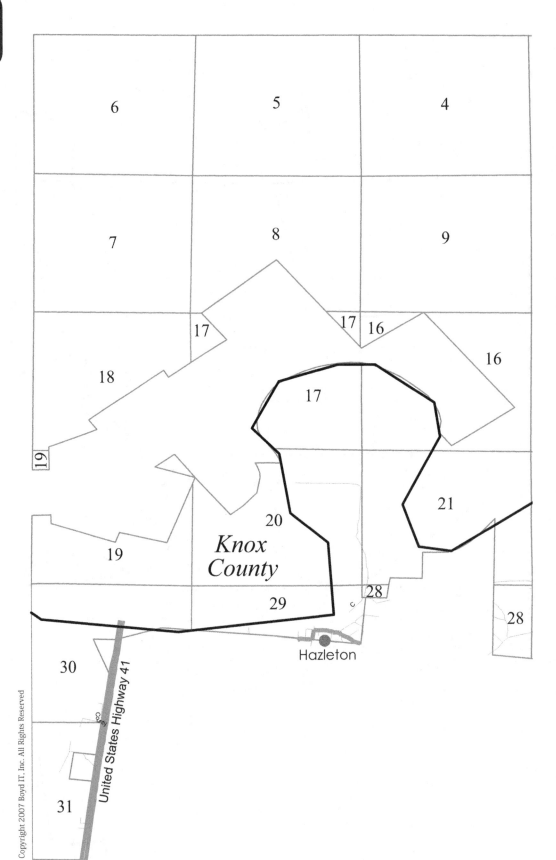

Road Map

T1-N R10-W
2nd PM Meridian

Map Group 2

Cities & Towns
Giro
Hazleton

Cemeteries
Barnett Cemetery
Phillips Cemetery

6

5

4

7

8

9

17

17   16

16

18

17

19

20

21

Knox County

19

28

29

28

Hazleton

30

31

United States Highway 41

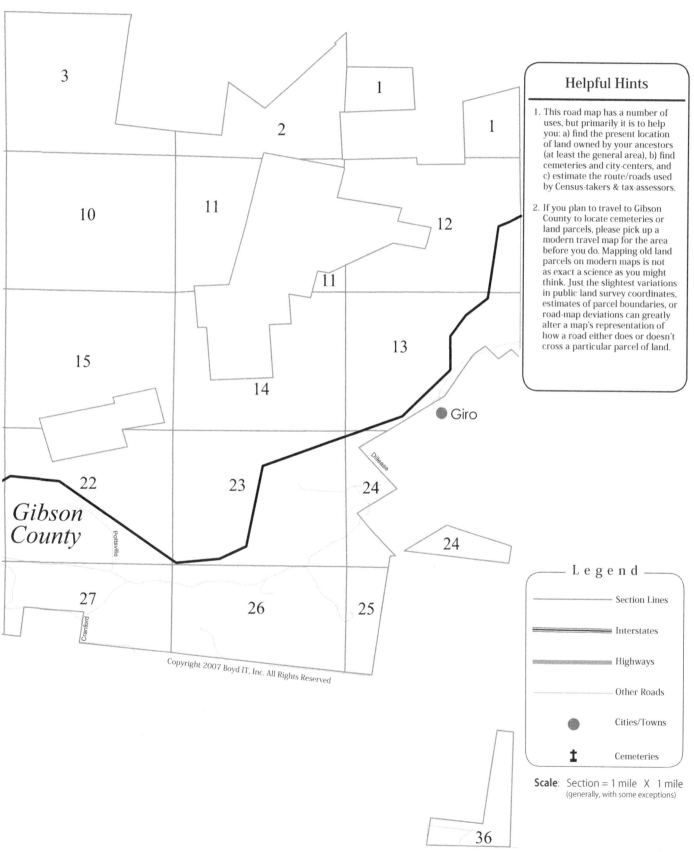

3

1

2

1

10

11

12

15

11

13

14

Giro

Dillease

22

23

24

Gibson County

Pottsville

24

27

26

25

Cranford

Copyright 2007 Boyd IT, Inc. All Rights Reserved

36

L e g e n d

Section Lines

Interstates

Highways

Other Roads

Cities/Towns

Cemeteries

Scale: Section = 1 mile X 1 mile
(generally, with some exceptions)

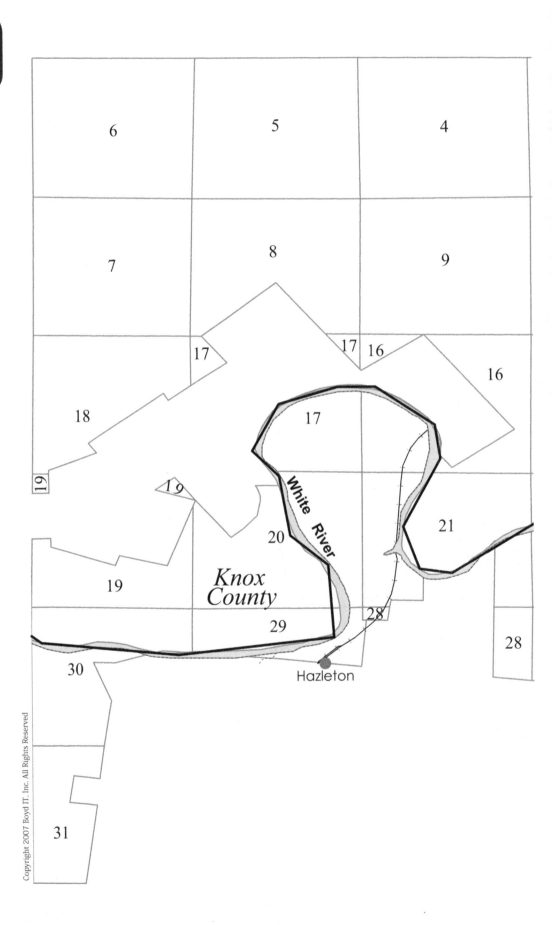

Historical Map

T1-N R10-W
2nd PM Meridian

Map Group 2

Cities & Towns
Giro
Hazleton

Cemeteries
Barnett Cemetery
Phillips Cemetery

6   5   4

7   8   9

17   17   16

18   16

17

19

19

White River

20   21

Knox
County

19

28

29

30   28

Hazleton

31

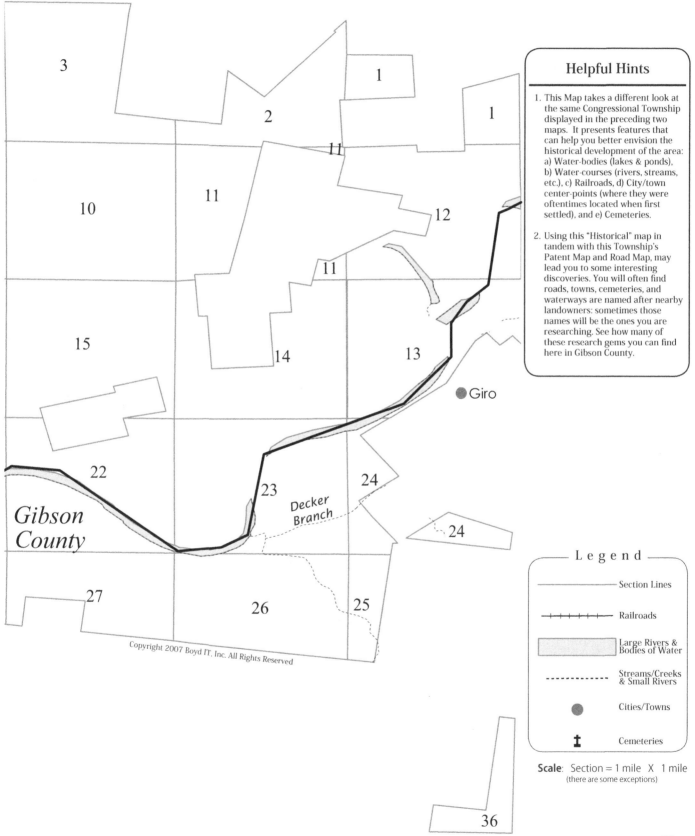

3

1

2

1

11

10

11

12

11

15

14

13

●Giro

22

23

24

Decker
Branch

24

Gibson
County

27

26

25

36

Helpful Hints

1. This Map takes a different look at the same Congressional Township displayed in the preceding two maps. It presents features that can help you better envision the historical development of the area: a) Water-bodies (lakes & ponds), b) Water-courses (rivers, streams, etc.), c) Railroads, d) City/town center-points (where they were oftentimes located when first settled), and e) Cemeteries.

2. Using this "Historical" map in tandem with this Township's Patent Map and Road Map, may lead you to some interesting discoveries. You will often find roads, towns, cemeteries, and waterways are named after nearby landowners: sometimes those names will be the ones you are researching. See how many of these research gems you can find here in Gibson County.

Legend

——————— Section Lines

+++++++ Railroads

▭ Large Rivers &
Bodies of Water

- - - - - Streams/Creeks
& Small Rivers

● Cities/Towns

☨ Cemeteries

Scale: Section = 1 mile X 1 mile
(there are some exceptions)

Map Group 3: Index to Land Patents

Township 1-South Range 12-West (2nd PM)

After you locate an individual in this Index, take note of the Section and Section Part then proceed to the Land Patent map on the pages immediately following. You should have no difficulty locating the corresponding parcel of land.

The "For More Info" Column will lead you to more information about the underlying Patents. See the *Legend* at right, and the "How to Use this Book" chapter, for more information.

```
                    LEGEND
          "For More Info . . . " column
A = Authority (Legislative Act, See Appendix "A")
B = Block or Lot (location in Section unknown)
C = Cancelled Patent
F = Fractional Section
G = Group (Multi-Patentee Patent, see Appendix "C")
V = Overlaps another Parcel
R = Re-Issued (Parcel patented more than once)

(A & G items require you to look in the Appendixes referred
to above. All other Letter-designations followed by a number
require you to locate line-items in this index that possess
the ID number found after the letter).
```

ID	Individual in Patent	Sec.	Sec. Part	Date Issued	Other Counties	For More Info . . .
111	BALENTINE, Harvey	33	NW	1837-20-03		A1 F
112	" "	28	N½S½	1838-22-05		A1 G3 F
115	BALLINTINE, Harvey	28	1	1835-28-10		A1 F
116	" "	28	2	1835-28-10		A1 F
113	" "	27	NWSW	1839-01-02		A1
114	" "	27	SWSW	1848-10-04		A1
117	BELL, Hiram	34	SWSW	1835-07-10		A1
128	BLACK, John	33	NWSE	1839-01-02		A1
129	BURGET, John	35	NENW	1837-18-03		A1
133	DIVEN, Joseph	33	NENE	1849-01-02		A1
134	" "	34	NWNW	1849-01-02		A1
149	GREATHOUSE, William	22	6	1838-07-09	Knox	A1 F
150	" "	23	N½	1838-07-09	Knox	A1
144	GWIN, Thomas	32		1823-04-08		A1 F
151	HAMILTON, William	36	E½NW	1844-01-08		A1
140	HATTON, Robert C	22	4	1835-05-09	Knox	A1 F
112	HINDE, T S	28	N½S½	1838-22-05		A1 G3 F
120	JOHNSON, Jacob	26	SWSE	1837-20-03		A1
118	" "	25	NWSW	1839-01-08		A1
119	" "	25	SESW	1844-01-08		A1
112	KAVANAUGH, B T	28	N½S½	1838-22-05		A1 G3 F
107	KENEIPP, Charles C	23	E½SW	1839-01-08	Knox	A1
146	KEY, Thomas	27	NWNE	1838-01-09		A1
145	" "	27	NENE	1839-01-02		A1
108	MELTON, Elijah	36	NWNW	1839-01-08		A1
130	MOCK, John	33	E½SE	1835-28-10		A1 F
152	MOORE, William	25	NESW	1841-10-08		A1
153	RAMSEY, William	13	E½S½	1826-01-07	Knox	A1 F
143	RUSSELL, Abraham	33	W½NE	1839-01-02		A1 G34
110	SHARP, Harris	34	NESW	1835-28-10		A1
124	SHARP, James	34	NWSW	1835-07-10		A1
125	" "	34	SESW	1835-10-09		A1
121	SHARP, James M	35	SENE	1837-15-03		A1 C
122	" "	35	SENW	1856-01-09		A1
131	SHARP, John	25	SWSW	1837-20-03		A1
154	SHARP, William	33	SENE	1837-30-03		A1
155	" "	34	SWNW	1840-01-10		A1
137	SMITH, Phillip	26	NESW	1837-15-03		A1
138	" "	26	SENW	1837-15-03		A1
126	SPROUL, James	28	N½	1829-02-07		A1 F
141	STEWART, Scoby	27	NWNW	1837-20-03		A1
142	" "	27	SWNW	1837-20-03		A1
143	" "	33	W½NE	1839-01-02		A1 G34
139	STILLWELL, Richard	13	S½N½	1839-01-02	Knox	A1 F
132	STILWELL, John	13	W½S½	1835-07-10	Knox	A1 F
136	TAYLOR, Mary	33	NWSW	1837-07-11		A1

ID	Individual in Patent	Sec.	Sec. Part	Date Issued	Other Counties	For More Info . . .
135	TAYLOR, Mary (Cont'd)	27	E½NW	1839-01-02		A1
148	TERRELL, James P	22	3	1832-10-04	Knox	A1 G35 F
123	" "	22	2	1835-10-09	Knox	A1 F
148	TERRELL, Walter	22	3	1832-10-04	Knox	A1 G35 F
147	" "	22	7	1839-01-02	Knox	A1 F
127	TOWNSEND, James	22	W½	1830-02-12	Knox	A1 F
109	WONZER, Ephraim	26	SESE	1837-20-03		A1

Patent Map

T1-S R12-W
2nd PM Meridian

Map Group 3

4

Township Statistics

Parcels Mapped	:	49
Number of Patents	:	47
Number of Individuals	:	35
Patentees Identified	:	35
Number of Surnames	:	30
Multi-Patentee Parcels	:	3
Oldest Patent Date	:	4/8/1823
Most Recent Patent	:	1/9/1856
Block/Lot Parcels	:	194
Parcels Re - Issued	:	0
Parcels that Overlap	:	0
Cities and Towns	:	2
Cemeteries	:	0

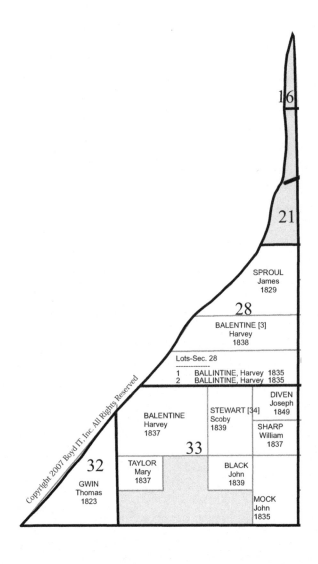

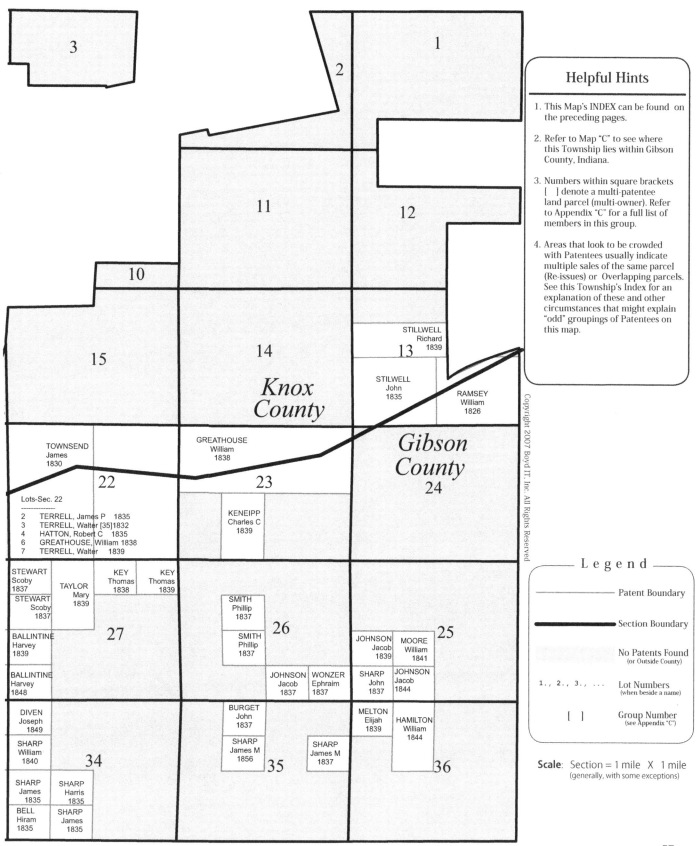

3

1

2

11

12

10

15

14

STILLWELL
Richard
1839

13

STILWELL
John
1835

RAMSEY
William
1826

Knox County

Gibson County
24

TOWNSEND
James
1830

GREATHOUSE
William
1838

22

23

Lots-Sec. 22
----
2   TERRELL, James P   1835
3   TERRELL, Walter [35]1832
4   HATTON, Robert C   1835
6   GREATHOUSE, William 1838
7   TERRELL, Walter   1839

KENEIPP
Charles C
1839

STEWART
Scoby
1837

TAYLOR
Mary
1839

KEY
Thomas
1838

KEY
Thomas
1839

STEWART
Scoby
1837

SMITH
Phillip
1837

26

BALLINTINE
Harvey
1839

27

SMITH
Phillip
1837

JOHNSON
Jacob
1839

MOORE
William
1841

25

BALLINTINE
Harvey
1848

JOHNSON
Jacob
1837

WONZER
Ephraim
1837

SHARP
John
1837

JOHNSON
Jacob
1844

DIVEN
Joseph
1849

BURGET
John
1837

MELTON
Elijah
1839

HAMILTON
William
1844

SHARP
William
1840

34

SHARP
James M
1856

35

SHARP
James M
1837

36

SHARP
James
1835

SHARP
Harris
1835

BELL
Hiram
1835

SHARP
James
1835

L e g e n d

———————— Patent Boundary

━━━━━━━ Section Boundary

No Patents Found
(or Outside County)

1., 2., 3., . . .   Lot Numbers
(when beside a name)

[   ]   Group Number
(see Appendix "C")

Scale: Section = 1 mile X 1 mile
(generally, with some exceptions)

Road Map

T1-S R12-W
2nd PM Meridian

Map Group 3

4

Cities & Towns
East Mount Carmel
White River

Cemeteries
None

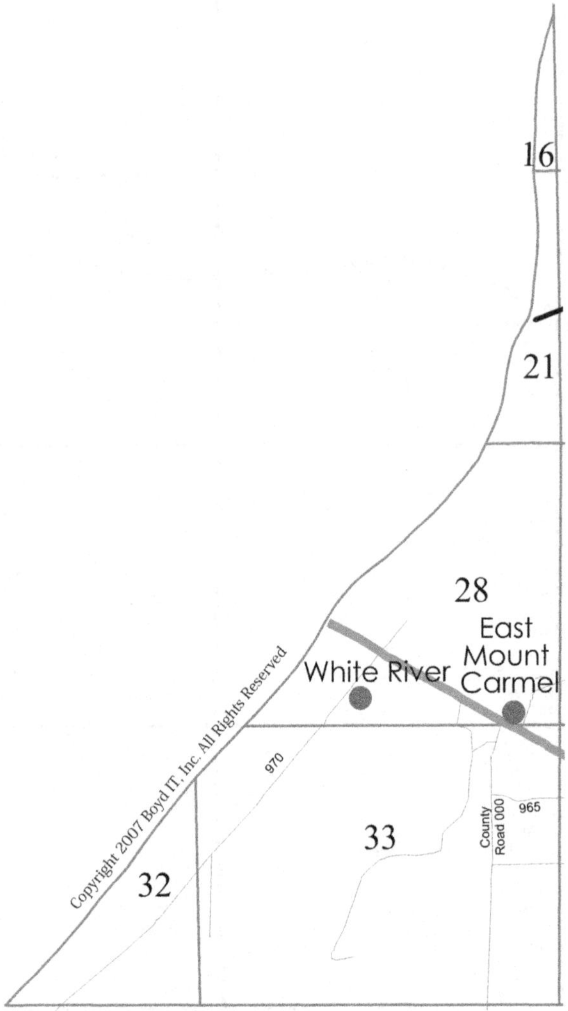

16

21

28
East
Mount
Carmel

White River

970

32

33

County
Road 000

965

58

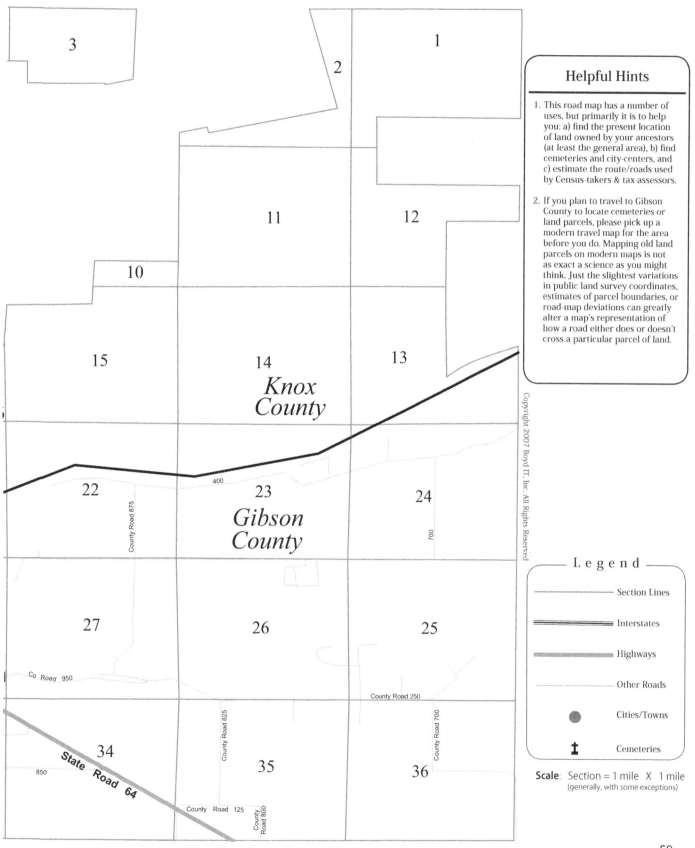

3

1

2

11

12

10

15

14

*Knox
County*

13

22

400

23

*Gibson
County*

24

County Road 875

700

27

26

25

Co Road 950

County Road 250

34

State Road 64

35

County Road 825

36

County Road 700

850

County Road 125

County Road 800

Legend

Section Lines

Interstates

Highways

Other Roads

Cities/Towns

Cemeteries

Scale: Section = 1 mile X 1 mile
(generally, with some exceptions)

59

Historical Map

T1-S R12-W
2nd PM Meridian

Map Group 3

4

Cities & Towns
East Mount Carmel
White River

Cemeteries
None

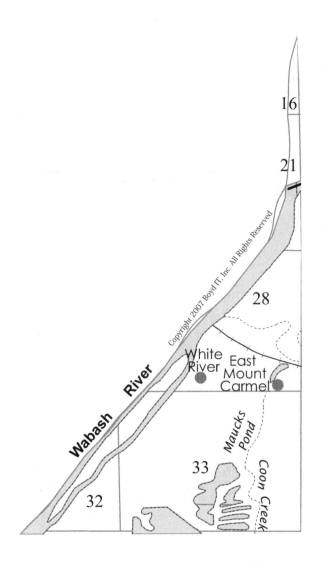

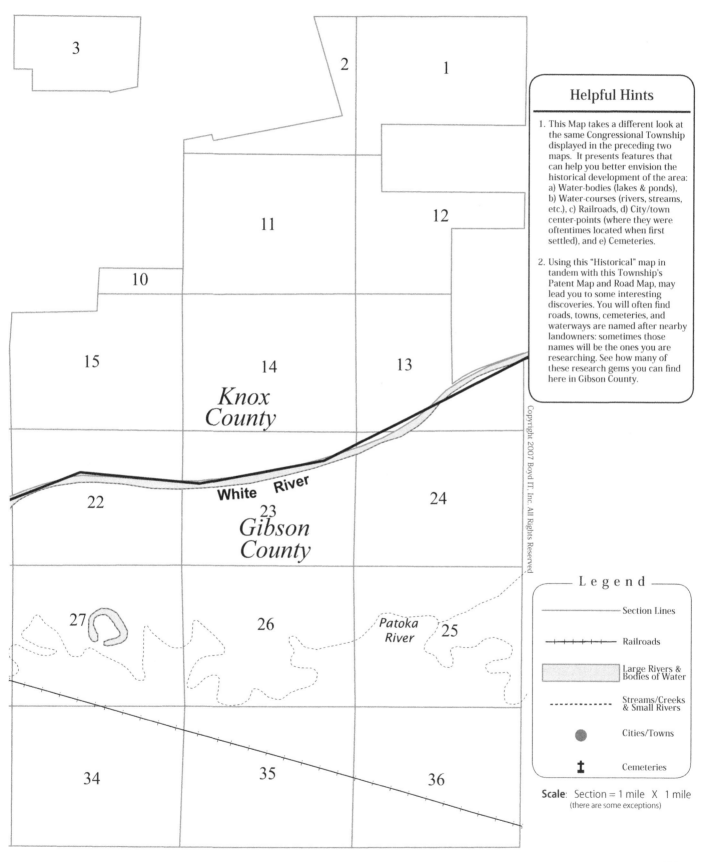

3

2

1

Helpful Hints

1. This Map takes a different look at
the same Congressional Township
displayed in the preceding two
maps. It presents features that
can help you better envision the
historical development of the area:
a) Water-bodies (lakes & ponds),
b) Water-courses (rivers, streams,
etc.), c) Railroads, d) City/town
center-points (where they were
oftentimes located when first
settled), and e) Cemeteries.

2. Using this "Historical" map in
tandem with this Township's
Patent Map and Road Map, may
lead you to some interesting
discoveries. You will often find
roads, towns, cemeteries, and
waterways are named after nearby
landowners: sometimes those
names will be the ones you are
researching. See how many of
these research gems you can find
here in Gibson County.

11

12

10

15

14

13

*Knox
County*

White   River

22

23
*Gibson
County*

24

Legend

27

26

*Patoka
River*

25

————— Section Lines

+++++ Railroads

▭ Large Rivers &
Bodies of Water

- - - - - Streams/Creeks
& Small Rivers

● Cities/Towns

✝ Cemeteries

34

35

36

Scale: Section = 1 mile X 1 mile
(there are some exceptions)

Map Group 4: Index to Land Patents

Township 1-South Range 11-West (2nd PM)

After you locate an individual in this Index, take note of the Section and Section Part then proceed to the Land Patent map on the pages immediately following. You should have no difficulty locating the corresponding parcel of land.

The "For More Info" Column will lead you to more information about the underlying Patents. See the *Legend* at right, and the "How to Use this Book" chapter, for more information.

ID	Individual in Patent	Sec.	Sec. Part	Date Issued	Other Counties	For More Info . . .
217	ADAMS, James	22	NENE	1835-09-05		A1
218	" "	22	NWNE	1835-09-05		A1
212	" "	15	E½NE	1835-10-01		A1
216	" "	15	SWNE	1835-10-01		A1
215	" "	15	SENW	1837-08-01		A1
213	" "	15	NENW	1838-09-05		A1
214	" "	15	NWNE	1838-09-05		A1
275	ALVIS, Thomas	21	NENW	1837-08-05		A1
249	BRATCHER, Meredith J	22	NESE	1840-10-01		A1
185	BRITTENHAM, Dyey	2	1	1837-11-07	Knox	A1 F
246	BRITTONHAM, Lucy	17	W½SW	1831-12-31	Knox	A1 F
221	BROWN, John	2		1837-08-05	Knox	A1 F
157	BRUNER, Abraham	17	E½SW	1831-12-31	Knox	A1
158	" "	23	SENE	1839-02-01		A1
234	BUCKNER, John T	18	4	1859-04-01	Knox	A1
297	BURTCH, William	21	SENW	1855-01-03		A1
298	" "	22	SWNE	1855-01-03		A1
182	CATLIN, Daniel	11	6	1839-08-01	Knox	A1 F
194	CHAPMAN, Ezra	7	5	1838-09-01	Knox	A1 F
193	" "	5	SWNW	1839-08-01	Knox	A1
196	CORNWELL, George	10	6	1855-01-03	Knox	A1
171	CULBERTSON, Andrew	23	E½NW	1829-07-02		A1
170	" "	17	S½NE	1837-03-20	Knox	A1
183	CURTIS, Daniel	7	2	1837-11-07	Knox	A1 F
301	DANIEL, William	10	W½W½	1837-11-07	Knox	A1 F
302	" "	9	1	1839-08-01	Knox	A1 F
303	" "	9	2	1839-08-01	Knox	A1 F
304	" "	9	NE	1839-08-01	Knox	A1 F
247	DAY, Mark	33	SWNW	1852-07-01		A1
296	DAY, Wiley	33	NWNW	1852-07-01		A1
164	DECKER, Abram	5	NWNE	1839-02-01	Knox	A1
222	DECKER, John	26	SWSW	1839-08-01		A1
223	" "	27	E½SW	1839-08-01		A1 G10
240	DEVIN, Joseph	8	8	1854-03-01	Knox	A1
239	" "	33	SENW	1856-06-03		A1
224	DOCKER, John	26	NWSW	1839-08-01		A1
290	EVANS, Thomas S	20	NENW	1837-08-05		A1 G15
289	" "	23	SWSW	1840-10-01		A1
179	EVINS, Charles	23	NWSW	1838-09-01		A1
159	FIELD, Abraham	1	4	1837-08-05	Knox	A1 F
161	" "	1	SESE	1837-08-05	Knox	A1
162	" "	1	W½NE	1837-08-05	Knox	A1 F
160	" "	1	NWSE	1848-05-10	Knox	A1 F
192	FIELD, Ezekiel	8	1	1838-09-01	Knox	A1 F
245	FIELD, Keen	1	5	1838-09-01	Knox	A1
276	FIELD, Thomas	12	NWNE	1838-09-01		A1

ID	Individual in Patent	Sec.	Sec. Part	Date Issued	Other Counties	For More Info . . .
163	FIELDS, Abraham	1	NW	1839-08-01	Knox	A1 F
258	FIELDS, Reuben	11	NW	1831-01-04	Knox	A1 F
273	FIELER, Stephen L	10	3	1839-08-01	Knox	A1 F
257	FILED, Reen W	1	SWSE	1858-08-30	Knox	A1
305	FRENCH, William	11	4	1845-05-01	Knox	A1 F
299	FULLERTON, William C	18	3	1837-11-07	Knox	A1 F
300	" "	7	SW	1839-02-01	Knox	A1 F
274	GERAULD, Sylvester J	23	SWNE	1853-04-15		A1
225	GORDON, John	12	W½SW	1832-04-10		A1 F
306	GREATHOUSE, William	20	E½NE	1838-09-01		A1
307	" "	21	W½NW	1838-09-01		A1
207	GRIGGS, Hugh M	15	NWSW	1835-10-07		A1
206	" "	11	1	1839-08-01	Knox	A1 F
264	HALL, Samuel	9	SWSE	1840-10-01	Knox	A1
211	HARNESS, Jackson	5	NENW	1837-11-07	Knox	A1
210	" "	5	NENE	1839-02-01	Knox	A1
180	HARRINGTON, Charles	27	SWSE	1839-08-01		A1
174	HARRISON, Assa	12	E½SW	1825-04-08		A1 F
176	HARRISON, Azza	12	SWSE	1835-10-01		A1
175	" "	12	NWSE	1839-02-01		A1
248	HERSHEY, Martha J	5	SWNE	1872-04-10	Knox	A1
308	HOWE, William	17	S½SE	1837-08-01	Knox	A1
198	HUMPHREYS, George	15	W½NW	1826-05-20		A1
197	" "	15	E½SW	1831-05-21		A1
200	" "	23	E½SE	1831-12-31		A1
199	" "	2	4	1837-11-07	Knox	A1 F
241	HUMPHREYS, Joseph	10	1	1837-03-20	Knox	A1 F
242	" "	2	2	1837-03-30	Knox	A1 F
243	" "	2	3	1837-03-30	Knox	A1 F
271	HUMPHREYS, Silas	11	N½	1837-03-20	Knox	A1 F
272	" "	2	SWSW	1837-11-07	Knox	A1 F
294	HUMPHREYS, Uriah	14	E½NE	1832-04-10		A1
292	" "	11	3	1838-09-01	Knox	A1 F
293	" "	11	NWSW	1838-09-01	Knox	A1 F
291	" "	10	E½SE	1839-08-01	Knox	A1 F
188	HURD, Elijah	5	SE	1830-12-02	Knox	A1 F
189	" "	9	N½	1830-12-02	Knox	A1 F R220
277	JACOBUS, Thomas	2	SENW	1837-11-07	Knox	A1 F
278	" "	5	SENE	1837-11-07	Knox	A1 F
309	JOHNSON, William	26	NESW	1835-10-28		A1
310	" "	26	SWNW	1840-10-01		A1
295	JONES, Wesley	27	SESE	1850-12-10		A1
169	KING, Alexander	33	NWSW	1852-07-01		A1
167	" "	32	NESE	1853-04-15		A1
168	" "	32	NWSE	1856-06-03		A1
226	LAGOW, John	29	SWSE	1852-07-01		A1
290	LANSDOWN, Abner	20	NENW	1837-08-05		A1 G15
227	LEACH, John	10	NE	1831-12-31	Knox	A1 F
228	LEECH, John	1	6	1837-11-07	Knox	A1 F
229	LUCAS, John	19	NENW	1835-10-07		A1
261	LUCAS, Robert	19	N½NE	1835-10-07		A1
209	LYNN, Isum	26	SWSE	1835-09-05		A1
208	" "	26	NWSE	1837-08-01		A1
219	LYNN, James	26	SESW	1835-10-07		A1
311	MADISON, William	17	W½	1858-08-30	Knox	A1 F
312	" "	18	1	1858-08-30	Knox	A1
313	" "	18	2	1858-08-30	Knox	A1
279	MANNING, Thomas	34	SENW	1837-03-20		A1
280	MARTIN, Thomas	23	NENE	1835-09-10		A1
281	" "	23	NWNE	1837-03-18		A1
315	MARTIN, William	12	E½SE	1831-01-04		A1 F
316	" "	12	SWNE	1839-08-01		A1
314	" "	1	7	1849-04-10	Knox	A1 F
181	MCCULLOM, Cornelius	20	W½NW	1821-08-20		A1
282	MCDANIEL, Thomas	28	SESW	1856-06-03		A1
283	MCMULLEN, Thomas	33	NESE	1849-08-01		A1
284	MCMULLIN, Thomas	33	SENE	1848-05-10		A1
285	" "	34	SESW	1848-05-10		A1
286	" "	34	SWNW	1848-05-10		A1
287	" "	34	W½SW	1848-05-10		A1
190	MEISENHELTER, Emanuel	8	3	1854-03-01	Knox	A1 G29
191	" "	8	4	1854-03-01	Knox	A1 G29
190	MEISENHELTER, Samuel	8	3	1854-03-01	Knox	A1 G29

ID	Individual in Patent	Sec.	Sec. Part	Date Issued	Other Counties	For More Info . . .
191	MEISENHELTER, Samuel (Cont'd)	8	4	1854-03-01	Knox	A1 G29
177	MILBURN, Cary A	8	5	1837-03-30	Knox	A1 F
178	" "	8	6	1837-03-30	Knox	A1 F
195	MILBURN, Felix	17	NW	1839-02-01	Knox	A1 F
230	MILBURN, John	8	9	1837-03-20	Knox	A1
231	"	8	NESW	1837-03-20	Knox	A1 F
232	MILLER, John	20	W½NE	1839-02-01		A1
256	MILLER, Peter S	1	NENE	1837-03-30	Knox	A1 F
223	MILN, William	27	E½SW	1839-08-01		A1 G10
253	MOONEY, Patrick	31	NWNW	1856-06-03		A1
236	MORRIS, John W	32	SENE	1852-07-01		A1
172	NIXON, Andrew	26	E½NW	1839-08-01		A1
265	OLMSTED, Samuel L	1	SESW	1838-09-07	Knox	A1
165	ORR, Adam	19	NWSW	1850-10-01		A1
259	PARRETT, Richard M	11	SWSW	1855-01-03	Knox	A1
254	PAYNE, Patrick	8	SESW	1837-03-18	Knox	A1 F
255	"	8	SWSE	1839-02-01	Knox	A1
288	PAYNE, Thomas	17	NWNE	1837-08-01	Knox	A1
250	PRICE, Mordicai	26	NWNW	1839-08-01		A1
251	PRINCE, Nathaniel	9	S½SW	1839-08-01	Knox	A1
220	PRITCHETT, Jeremiah	9	N½	1839-08-01	Knox	A1 F R189
166	PURCELL, Adam	10	2	1839-02-01	Knox	A1 F
266	PUTNAM, Samuel	7	1	1838-09-01	Knox	A1 F
267	" "	7	4	1838-09-01	Knox	A1
268	" "	7	E½SE	1838-09-01	Knox	A1 F
269	" "	8		1839-08-01	Knox	A1 F
233	RILEY, John	28	SENE	1848-05-10		A1
186	ROBERTS, Elias	33	N½NE	1849-02-01		A1
187	" "	33	SWNE	1849-04-10		A1
204	SHADLE, Henry	7	3	1839-02-01	Knox	A1 F
205	" "	7	6	1839-02-01	Knox	A1 F
244	SHIELDS, Joseph	5	S½SE	1854-08-23	Knox	A1 F
260	SLOAN, Richard	22	SENE	1838-09-05		A1
173	SPAIN, Archibald	14	W½NE	1831-12-31		A1
262	STEEN, Robert	17	N½SE	1837-11-07	Knox	A1
263	" "	23	SWNW	1837-11-07		A1
156	STEWART, Abel	23	NWNW	1835-10-07		A1
270	STEWART, Scoby	7		1838-09-01	Knox	A1 F
184	STORMONT, David	34	NENW	1849-02-01		A1
252	TURNER, Owen	12	E½NW	1844-08-01		A1
235	ULM, John	21	NWNE	1837-08-05		A1
201	VANDERHOOF, Haney	2	NENW	1838-09-01	Knox	A1 F
202	VANDERHOOF, Harvey	2	W½NW	1829-05-01	Knox	A1 F
203	VANDERHOOP, Harvey	2	W½NE	1839-02-01	Knox	A1
237	WISE, John	1		1837-11-07	Knox	A1 F
238	" "	2	E½NE	1837-11-07	Knox	A1 F
317	WITHERSPOON, William P	21	NENE	1850-10-01		A1
318	WOODHOUSE, William	5	W½SW	1839-08-01	Knox	A1 F

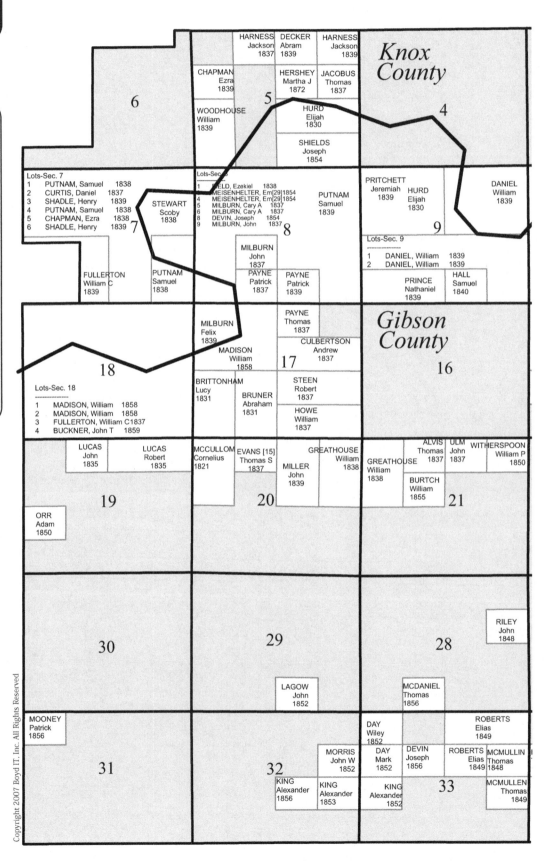

Patent Map

T1-S R11-W
2nd PM Meridian

Map Group 4

Township Statistics

Parcels Mapped	:	163
Number of Patents	:	147
Number of Individuals	:	108
Patentees Identified	:	107
Number of Surnames	:	88
Multi-Patentee Parcels	:	4
Oldest Patent Date	:	8/20/1821
Most Recent Patent	:	4/10/1872
Block/Lot Parcels	:	925
Parcels Re - Issued	:	1
Parcels that Overlap	:	0
Cities and Towns	:	1
Cemeteries	:	2

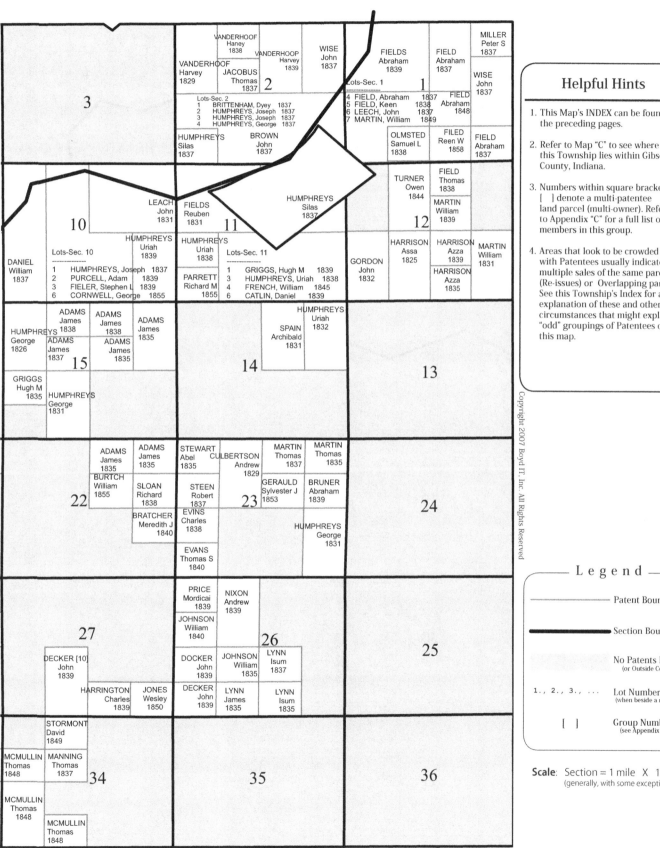

Helpful Hints

1. This Map's INDEX can be found on the preceding pages.

2. Refer to Map "C" to see where this Township lies within Gibson County, Indiana.

3. Numbers within square brackets [ ] denote a multi-patentee land parcel (multi-owner). Refer to Appendix "C" for a full list of members in this group.

4. Areas that look to be crowded with Patentees usually indicate multiple sales of the same parcel (Re-issues) or Overlapping parcels. See this Township's Index for an explanation of these and other circumstances that might explain "odd" groupings of Patentees on this map.

Legend

——————	Patent Boundary
▬▬▬▬▬	Section Boundary
	No Patents Found (or Outside County)
1., 2., 3., ...	Lot Numbers (when beside a name)
[ ]	Group Number (see Appendix "C")

Scale: Section = 1 mile X 1 mile (generally, with some exceptions)

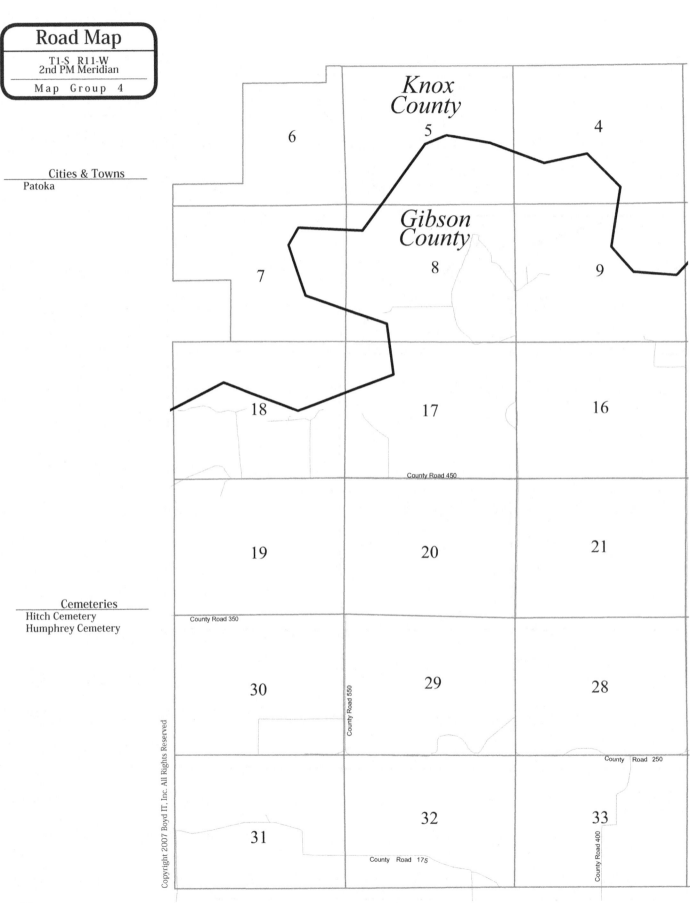

Road Map

T1-S R11-W
2nd PM Meridian

Map Group 4

Cities & Towns
Patoka

Knox County

Gibson County

Cemeteries
Hitch Cemetery
Humphrey Cemetery

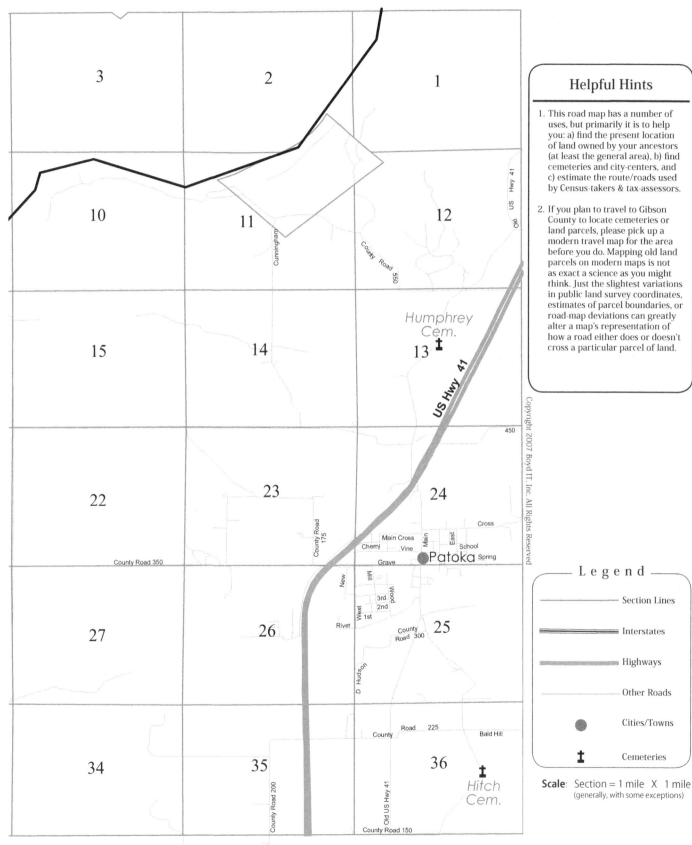

Helpful Hints

1. This road map has a number of uses, but primarily it is to help you: a) find the present location of land owned by your ancestors (at least the general area), b) find cemeteries and city-centers, and c) estimate the route/roads used by Census-takers & tax-assessors.

2. If you plan to travel to Gibson County to locate cemeteries or land parcels, please pick up a modern travel map for the area before you do. Mapping old land parcels on modern maps is not as exact a science as you might think. Just the slightest variations in public land survey coordinates, estimates of parcel boundaries, or road-map deviations can greatly alter a map's representation of how a road either does or doesn't cross a particular parcel of land.

Legend

————	Section Lines
══════	Interstates
▬▬▬▬	Highways
————	Other Roads
●	Cities/Towns
✝	Cemeteries

Scale: Section = 1 mile X 1 mile
(generally, with some exceptions)

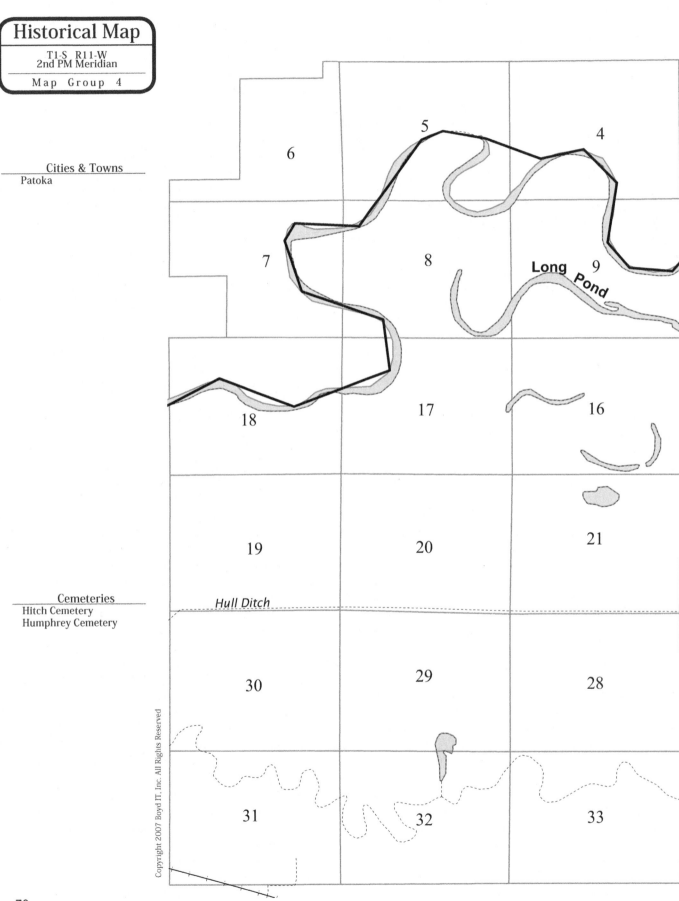

Historical Map

T1-S R11-W
2nd PM Meridian

Map Group 4

Cities & Towns
Patoka

Cemeteries
Hitch Cemetery
Humphrey Cemetery

6

5

4

7

8

Long Pond

9

18

17

16

19

20

21

Hull Ditch

30

29

28

31

32

33

Copyright 2007 Boyd IT, Inc. All Rights Reserved

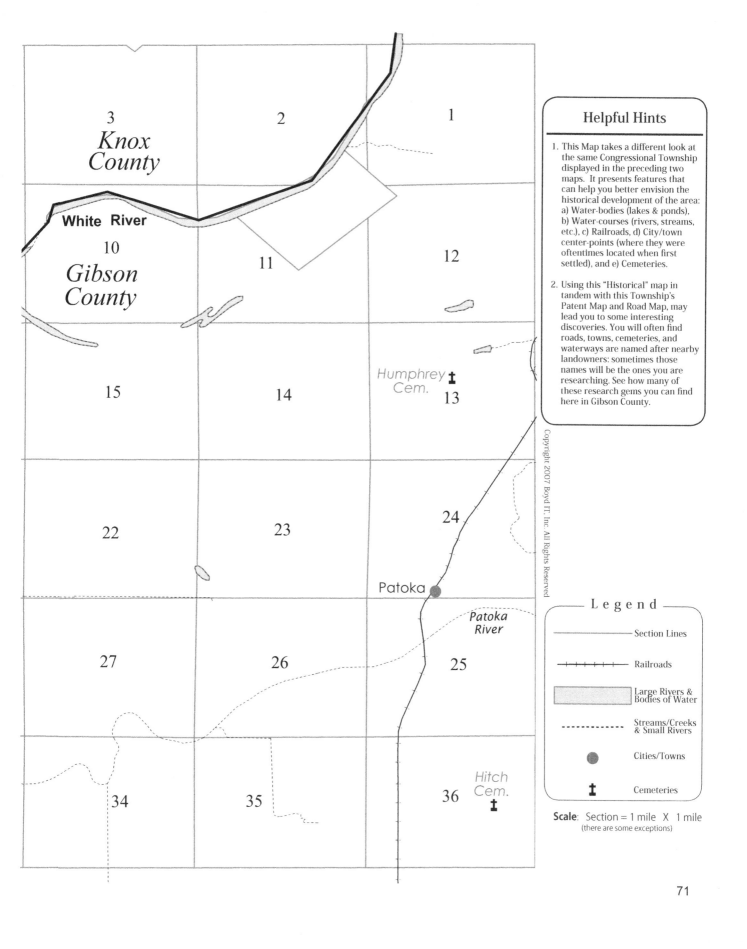

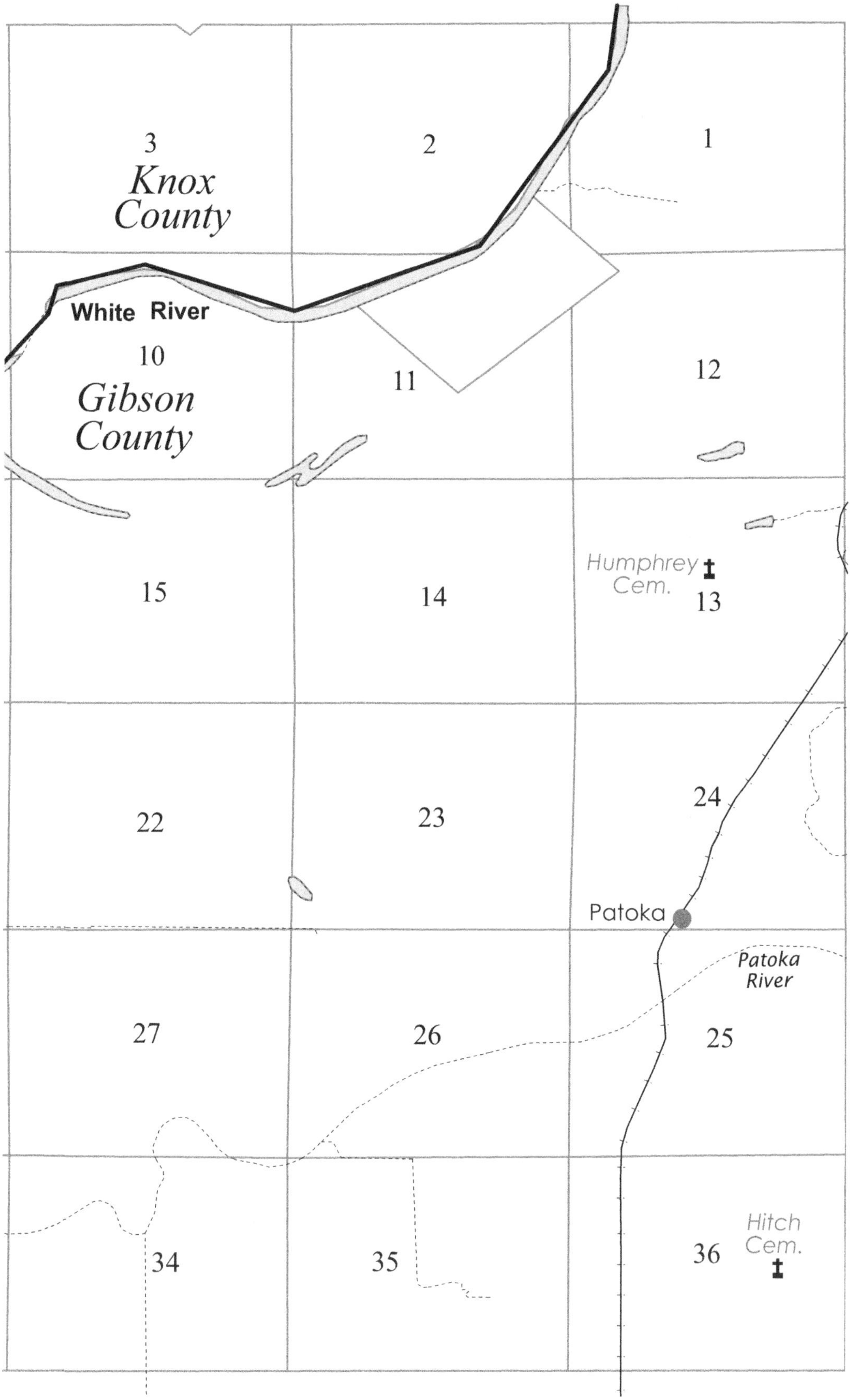
3
Knox County
2
1
White River
10
Gibson County
11
12
15
14
Humphrey Cem.
13
22
23
24
Patoka
27
26
Patoka River
25
34
35
36
Hitch Cem.

Helpful Hints

1. This Map takes a different look at the same Congressional Township displayed in the preceding two maps. It presents features that can help you better envision the historical development of the area: a) Water-bodies (lakes & ponds), b) Water-courses (rivers, streams, etc.), c) Railroads, d) City/town center-points (where they were oftentimes located when first settled), and e) Cemeteries.

2. Using this "Historical" map in tandem with this Township's Patent Map and Road Map, may lead you to some interesting discoveries. You will often find roads, towns, cemeteries, and waterways are named after nearby landowners: sometimes those names will be the ones you are researching. See how many of these research gems you can find here in Gibson County.

Legend

- Section Lines
- Railroads
- Large Rivers & Bodies of Water
- Streams/Creeks & Small Rivers
- Cities/Towns
- Cemeteries

Scale: Section = 1 mile X 1 mile
(there are some exceptions)

Map Group 5: Index to Land Patents

Township 1-South Range 10-West (2nd PM)

After you locate an individual in this Index, take note of the Section and Section Part then proceed to the Land Patent map on the pages immediately following. You should have no difficulty locating the corresponding parcel of land.

The "For More Info" Column will lead you to more information about the underlying Patents. See the *Legend* at right, and the "How to Use this Book" chapter, for more information.

```
                    LEGEND
            "For More Info . . . " column
A = Authority (Legislative Act, See Appendix "A")
B = Block or Lot (location in Section unknown)
C = Cancelled Patent
F = Fractional Section
G = Group (Multi-Patentee Patent, see Appendix "C")
V = Overlaps another Parcel
R = Re-Issued (Parcel patented more than once)

(A & G items require you to look in the Appendixes referred
to above. All other Letter-designations followed by a number
require you to locate line-items in this index that possess
the ID number found after the letter).
```

ID	Individual in Patent	Sec.	Sec. Part	Date Issued	Other Counties	For More Info . . .
388	AMOS, John	23	NENW	1841-05-25		A1
461	BALLENGER, William	1	S½S½	1824-08-09		A1 F
389	BERLIN, John	30	S½	1827-02-13		A1 F
372	BOSWELL, Henry	34	SWSE	1837-08-01		A1
373	" "	35	NWSW	1837-08-01		A1
379	BOSWELL, James	33	W½SW	1830-12-02		A1
427	BOSWELL, Nancy	33	E½SW	1830-12-02		A1
462	BOSWELL, William	33	SE	1829-05-01		A1
419	BROWN, Joseph R	31	S½NE	1829-04-02		A1 F
359	BROWNLEE, George	31	N½SE	1821-09-10		A1 F
360	" "	31	S½SE	1821-09-10		A1 F
361	" "	32	E½SE	1821-09-10		A1 F
362	" "	32	E½SW	1821-09-10		A1 F
363	" "	32	W½SE	1821-09-10		A1 F
364	" "	32	W½SW	1821-09-10		A1 F
431	BROWNLEE, Robert	28	NESW	1850-10-01		A1
330	CARITHERS, Andrew	34	NWSE	1839-08-01		A1
393	CARTER, John	27	SE	1821-10-01		A1
394	CHRISTY, John	34	E½SW	1839-08-01		A1
395	" "	34	W½NE	1839-08-01		A1
331	CRAWFORD, Andrew J	32	E½NW	1826-11-15		A1
332	" "	32	W½NE	1826-11-15		A1
333	" "	32	W½NW	1828-05-10		A1 F
452	CUNNINGHAM, Stewart	27	S½NW	1840-10-01		A1
430	DANIEL, Richard	34	E½SE	1823-08-04		A1
448	DAWSON, Shelton	36	NENW	1840-10-01		A1
450	DAWSON, Smith	36	SESW	1839-08-01		A1
396	DOSON, John	36	NESW	1838-09-07		A1
397	" "	36	SENW	1838-09-07		A1
445	DUNCAN, Shadrach	17	SESW	1841-12-10		A1
446	DUNCAN, Shadrack	20	NENW	1835-10-28		A1 F
447	" "	20	W½NW	1839-08-01		A1 F
398	ENNIS, John	12	3	1839-08-01		A1 F
432	FARR, Robert	33	NWNW	1835-10-15		A1
429	FIELDS, Reuben	6	1	1838-09-01		A1 F
400	FINNEY, John K	26	SWNW	1838-09-05		A1
375	GRIGGS, Hugh M	18	W½SW	1835-10-07		A1 F
365	GRIGSBY, George	36	SWSE	1839-02-01		A1
347	GRIGSLY, Demps	5	N½SW	1838-09-07		A1
386	GULLICK, John A	13	NWSW	1839-08-01		A1 F
387	" "	14	NESE	1839-08-01		A1 F
413	GULLICK, Jonathan	13	SWSW	1839-02-01		A1 F
414	" "	14	SESE	1839-02-01		A1 F
454	HARBISON, Thomas	35	SESE	1840-10-01		A1
399	HARGROVE, John	30	N½	1837-03-18		A1 F
421	HARGROVE, Linzey	20	S½SW	1838-09-01		A1 F

ID	Individual in Patent	Sec.	Sec. Part	Date Issued	Other Counties	For More Info . . .
422	HARGROVE, Linzey (Cont'd)	29	1	1841-05-25		A1 F
336	HARRISON, Azza	17	SE	1835-10-07		A1 F
377	HAVIN, Isaac	25	SESE	1840-10-01		A1
352	HEDGES, Elizabeth	6	S½	1829-07-02		A1 F
456	HOSACK, Thomas	36	NWNW	1835-10-15		A1
455	" "	35	E½NE	1838-09-07		A1
457	" "	36	SWNW	1838-09-07		A1
380	HUDELSON, James	28	W½NW	1837-03-18		A1 F
351	HUMPHREYS, Elijah	18	NE	1824-08-09		A1 F
369	HUMPHREYS, George	7		1824-08-09		A1 F
366	" "	17	N½	1835-10-28		A1 F
367	" "	17	NESW	1835-10-28		A1 F
368	" "	35	SESW	1837-08-05		A1
416	HUMPHREYS, Joseph	17	W½SW	1835-10-23		A1 F
463	KEY, William	18	NWSE	1835-10-28		A1 F
341	KIRK, Daniel	28	W½NE	1823-08-18		A1 F
348	KIRK, Dickson	14	W½SE	1839-02-01		A1
402	LANCE, John	35	SWSW	1835-09-05		A1 R474
401	" "	22	E½SE	1835-10-28		A1
464	LATHOM, William	31	W½	1826-11-15		A1 F
465	LEATHERS, William	29	2	1840-10-01		A1 F
449	LEMASTERS, Simeon	36	SWSW	1837-03-20		A1
466	LETHERS, William	29	SW	1835-10-01		A1 F
381	LYNN, James	31	N½NE	1829-05-01		A1 F
417	MARKLE, Joseph	13	SE	1839-08-01		A1 F
403	MARSHALL, John	23	SWNE	1838-09-05		A1
370	MCCARTNEY, Henry A	26	W½SE	1832-04-10		A1
371	" "	35	W½NE	1832-04-10		A1
418	MCKEMSON, Joseph	34	E½NE	1837-08-01		A1
376	MCMULLIN, Hugh	34	W½SW	1830-12-02		A1
382	MEKEMSON, James	26	SW	1825-04-08		A1
343	MILBURN, David	18	E½SW	1831-05-21		A1
344	" "	18	SWSE	1835-10-07		A1 F
345	" "	19	E½	1838-09-07		A1 F
346	" "	19	W½	1852-10-01		A1 F
451	MILLER, Smith	18	NW	1835-10-28		A1 F
384	MILLS, James	23	SENW	1835-09-05		A1
385	" "	23	SWNW	1835-09-05		A1
383	" "	23	NWSW	1837-08-01		A1
339	MITCHELL, Benniah G	1	6	1839-08-01		A1 F
349	MOORE, Edward	28	E½NW	1837-03-18		A1 F
390	MOORE, John C	22	SESW	1835-10-01		A1 F
391	" "	27	NENW	1837-11-07		A1
392	" "	27	W½NE	1839-08-01		A1
404	MUNFORD, John	33	E½NW	1826-05-20		A1
319	NIXON, Abraham	13	1	1839-02-01		A1
320	" "	13	5	1839-02-01		A1 F
434	NIXON, Robert	13	3	1835-10-28		A1 F
435	" "	14	NE	1835-10-28		A1 F
433	" "	13	2	1839-02-01		A1 F
321	PHILIPS, Alexander	15	3	1849-08-01		A1 F
436	PHILIPS, Robert	15	1	1837-08-05		A1 F
437	" "	15	2	1837-08-05		A1 F
322	PHILLIPS, Alexander	21	1	1837-08-05		A1 F
323	" "	21	2	1837-08-05		A1 F
324	" "	22	2	1837-08-05		A1 F
325	" "	22	3	1837-08-05		A1 F
438	PHILLIPS, Robert	22	W½SE	1829-05-01		A1
428	PIERCE, Nehemiah F	18	E½SE	1832-04-10		A1 F
329	PRICE, Amzi	12	4	1839-08-01		A1 F
467	PRICE, William	12	1	1839-08-01		A1 F
468	" "	12	2	1839-08-01		A1 F
423	REDBURN, Michael	36	SWNE	1837-08-05		A1
469	REDBURN, William	36	NWSE	1837-11-07		A1
470	" "	36	NWSW	1837-11-07		A1
439	RICK, Robert	14	SW	1837-08-05		A1 F
405	ROBINSON, John	12	S½	1835-10-23		A1 F
424	RODBURN, Michael	36	NWNE	1838-09-07		A1
444	SHANNON, Samuel	28	E½SE	1825-06-11		A1
378	SLAVEN, Isaac	35	NESE	1837-03-18		A1
440	SLAVEN, Robert	25	SWSW	1838-09-07		A1
335	SPAIN, Archibald	20	SENW	1839-08-01		A1 F
442	STEWART, Samuel A	29	E½NW	1831-12-31		A1 F

ID	Individual in Patent	Sec.	Sec. Part	Date Issued	Other Counties	For More Info . . .
443	STEWART, Samuel A (Cont'd)	29	NE	1835-10-23		A1 F
471	STORMENT, William	35	NWNW	1838-09-01		A1
441	TALES, Robert	22	SENE	1838-09-07		A1
472	TERRY, William	35	W½SE	1826-07-31		A1
374	THOMPSON, Henry	22	W½SW	1830-12-02		A1 F
406	TOMPSON, John	21	3	1835-10-28		A1 F
407	"	21	4	1835-10-28		A1 F
355	TOWNSEND, Erastus	28	W½SE	1828-05-05		A1
356	" "	33	E½NE	1828-05-05		A1
357	" "	33	W½NE	1829-07-02		A1
358	" "	27	SWSW	1835-10-28		A1 G36
354	TOWNSEND, Erastus D	28	W½SW	1831-12-31		A1
353	"	28	SESW	1835-09-05		A1
425	TOWNSEND, Milo	27	E½SW	1831-01-04		A1
358	" "	27	SWSW	1835-10-28		A1 G36
426	" "	34	E½NW	1837-08-05		A1
453	TOWNSEND, Susan	27	NWSW	1841-05-25		A1
326	TRIPPET, Alexander	21	N½S½	1835-10-15		A1 F
327	" "	27	NWNW	1835-10-28		A1
340	TRIPPET, Caleb	28	SENE	1840-10-01		A1
459	TRIPPET, Waitman	28	NENE	1835-10-28		A1 F
458	"	20	NE	1841-05-25		A1 F
328	TRIPPETT, Alexander	22	NESW	1838-09-05		A1
460	TRIPPETT, Waitman	21	S½S½	1835-10-23		A1 F
473	TURPIN, William	35	E½NW	1837-08-05		A1
474	" "	35	SWSW	1837-08-05		A1 R402
415	WALK, Jonathan	6	2	1835-10-01		A1 F
334	WHITE, Anson	27	E½NE	1831-06-01		A1
338	WHITSETT, Benjamin	34	SWNW	1848-05-10		A1
337	" "	34	NWNW	1848-06-01		A1
420	WILKS, Joseph	26	E½SE	1831-05-21		A1
350	WILLIAMS, Eli A	35	NESW	1835-10-28		A1
475	WRIGHT, William W	1	5	1841-05-25		A1 F
342	ZIMMERMAN, Daniel	33	SWNW	1837-11-07		A1
411	ZIMMERMAN, John	25	SWSE	1835-09-05		A1
412	" "	32	E½NE	1837-08-01		A1 F
408	" "	1	1	1839-02-01		A1 F
409	" "	1	2	1839-02-01		A1 F
410	" "	1	3	1839-08-01		A1 F

Patent Map

T1-S R10-W
2nd PM Meridian

Map Group 5

Township Statistics

Parcels Mapped	:	157
Number of Patents	:	145
Number of Individuals	:	105
Patentees Identified	:	106
Number of Surnames	:	80
Multi-Patentee Parcels	:	1
Oldest Patent Date	:	9/10/1821
Most Recent Patent	:	10/1/1852
Block/Lot Parcels	:	858
Parcels Re - Issued	:	1
Parcels that Overlap	:	0
Cities and Towns	:	1
Cemeteries	:	8

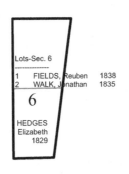

Lots-Sec. 6
----
1 FIELDS, Reuben 1838
2 WALK, Jonathan 1835

6

HEDGES
Elizabeth
1829

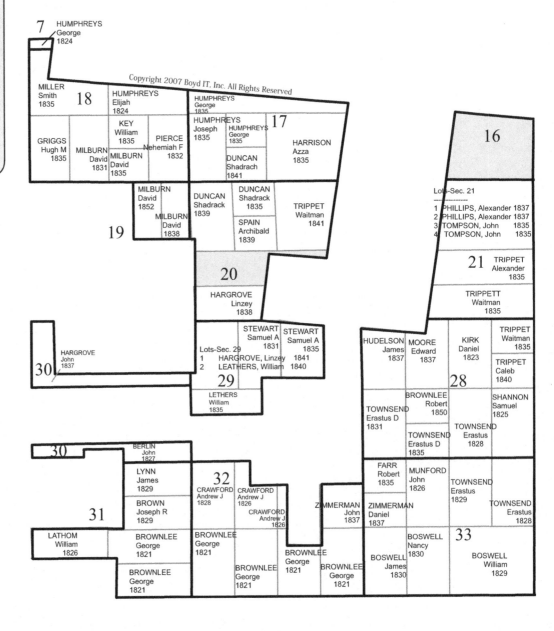

7 HUMPHREYS
George
1824

MILLER
Smith
1835   **18**

HUMPHREYS
Elijah
1824

HUMPHREYS
George
1835

17

GRIGGS
Hugh M
1835

MILBURN
David
1831

KEY
William
1835

MILBURN
David
1835

PIERCE
Nehemiah F
1832

HUMPHREYS
Joseph
1835

HUMPHREYS
George
1835

HARRISON
Azza
1835

DUNCAN
Shadrach
1841

16

MILBURN
David
1852

MILBURN
David
1838

MILBURN
David
1838

DUNCAN
Shadrack
1839

DUNCAN
Shadrack
1835

SPAIN
Archibald
1839

TRIPPET
Waitman
1841

Lots-Sec. 21
----
1 PHILLIPS, Alexander 1837
2 PHILLIPS, Alexander 1837
3 TOMPSON, John 1835
4 TOMPSON, John 1835

21 TRIPPET
Alexander
1835

19

20

HARGROVE
Linzey
1838

TRIPPETT
Waitman
1835

HARGROVE
John
1837

30

STEWART
Samuel A
1831

STEWART
Samuel A
1835

Lots-Sec. 29
----
1 HARGROVE, Linzey 1841
2 LEATHERS, William 1840

29

LETHERS
William
1835

HUDELSON
James
1837

MOORE
Edward
1837

KIRK
Daniel
1823

28

TRIPPET
Waitman
1835

TRIPPET
Caleb
1840

TOWNSEND
Erastus D
1831

BROWNLEE
Robert
1850

TOWNSEND
Erastus D
1835

TOWNSEND
Erastus
1828

SHANNON
Samuel
1825

BERLIN
John
1827

LYNN
James
1829

30

32

FARR
Robert
1835

MUNFORD
John
1826

TOWNSEND
Erastus
1829

BROWN
Joseph R
1829

CRAWFORD
Andrew J
1828

CRAWFORD
Andrew J
1826

CRAWFORD
Andrew J
1826

ZIMMERMAN
John
1837

ZIMMERMAN
Daniel
1837

TOWNSEND
Erastus
1828

31

LATHOM
William
1826

BROWNLEE
George
1821

BROWNLEE
George
1821

BROWNLEE
George
1821

BROWNLEE
George
1821

BROWNLEE
George
1821

BOSWELL
Nancy
1830

BOSWELL
James
1830

33

BOSWELL
William
1829

BROWNLEE
George
1821

Copyright 2007 Boyd IT, Inc. All Rights Reserved

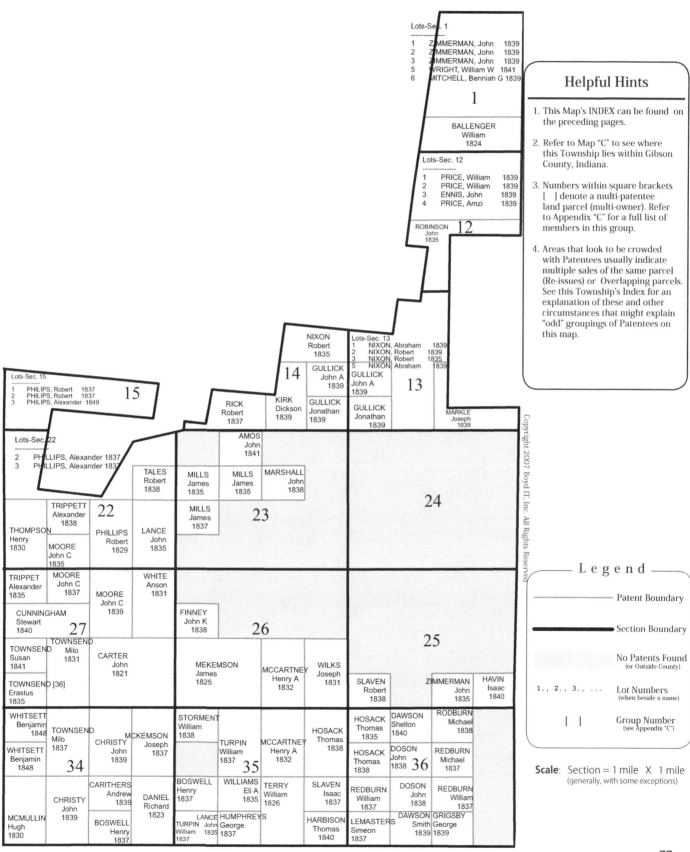

Lots-Sec. 1

1	ZIMMERMAN, John	1839
2	ZIMMERMAN, John	1839
3	ZIMMERMAN, John	1839
5	WRIGHT, William W	1841
6	MITCHELL, Benniah G	1839

1

BALLENGER
William
1824

Lots-Sec. 12

1	PRICE, William	1839
2	PRICE, William	1839
3	ENNIS, John	1839
4	PRICE, Amzi	1839

ROBINSON
John
1835

12

Helpful Hints

1. This Map's INDEX can be found on the preceding pages.

2. Refer to Map "C" to see where this Township lies within Gibson County, Indiana.

3. Numbers within square brackets [ ] denote a multi-patentee land parcel (multi-owner). Refer to Appendix "C" for a full list of members in this group.

4. Areas that look to be crowded with Patentees usually indicate multiple sales of the same parcel (Re-issues) or Overlapping parcels. See this Township's Index for an explanation of these and other circumstances that might explain "odd" groupings of Patentees on this map.

NIXON
Robert
1835

Lots-Sec. 13

1	NIXON, Abraham	1839
2	NIXON, Robert	1839
3	NIXON, Robert	1835
5	NIXON, Abraham	1839

14

GULLICK
John A
1839

GULLICK
John A
1839

13

Lots-Sec. 15

1	PHILIPS, Robert	1837
2	PHILIPS, Robert	1837
3	PHILIPS, Alexander	1849

15

RICK
Robert
1837

KIRK
Dickson
1839

GULLICK
Jonathan
1839

GULLICK
Jonathan
1839

MARKLE
Joseph
1839

Lots-Sec. 22

2	PHILLIPS, Alexander	1837
3	PHILLIPS, Alexander	1837

AMOS
John
1841

TALES
Robert
1838

MILLS
James
1835

MILLS
James
1835

MARSHALL
John
1838

24

TRIPPETT
Alexander
1838

22

MILLS
James
1837

23

THOMPSON
Henry
1830

MOORE
John C
1835

PHILLIPS
Robert
1829

LANCE
John
1835

TRIPPET
Alexander
1835

MOORE
John C
1837

WHITE
Anson
1831

MOORE
John C
1839

CUNNINGHAM
Stewart
1840

27

FINNEY
John K
1838

26

25

TOWNSEND
Susan
1841

TOWNSEND
Milo
1831

CARTER
John
1821

MEKEMSON
James
1825

MCCARTNEY
Henry A
1832

WILKS
Joseph
1831

TOWNSEND [36]
Erastus
1835

SLAVEN
Robert
1838

ZIMMERMAN
John
1835

HAVIN
Isaac
1840

WHITSETT
Benjamin
1848

TOWNSEND
Milo
1837

CHRISTY
John
1839

MCKEMSON
Joseph
1837

STORMENT
William
1838

TURPIN
William
1837

MCCARTNEY
Henry A
1832

HOSACK
Thomas
1838

HOSACK
Thomas
1835

DAWSON
Shelton
1840

RODBURN
Michael
1838

WHITSETT
Benjamin
1848

34

35

HOSACK
Thomas
1838

DOSON
John
1838

REDBURN
Michael
1837

36

CARITHERS
Andrew
1839

DANIEL
Richard
1823

BOSWELL
Henry
1837

WILLIAMS
Eli A
1835

TERRY
William
1826

SLAVEN
Isaac
1837

REDBURN
William
1837

DOSON
John
1838

REDBURN
William
1837

CHRISTY
John
1839

MCMULLIN
Hugh
1830

BOSWELL
Henry
1837

TURPIN
William
1837

LANCE John
1835

HUMPHREYS
George
1837

HARBISON
Thomas
1840

LEMASTERS
Simeon
1837

DAWSON
Smith
1839

GRIGSBY
George
1839

Legend

———————— Patent Boundary

▬▬▬▬▬▬▬▬ Section Boundary

No Patents Found
(or Outside County)

1., 2., 3., ... Lot Numbers
(when beside a name)

[ ] Group Number
(see Appendix "C")

Scale: Section = 1 mile X 1 mile
(generally, with some exceptions)

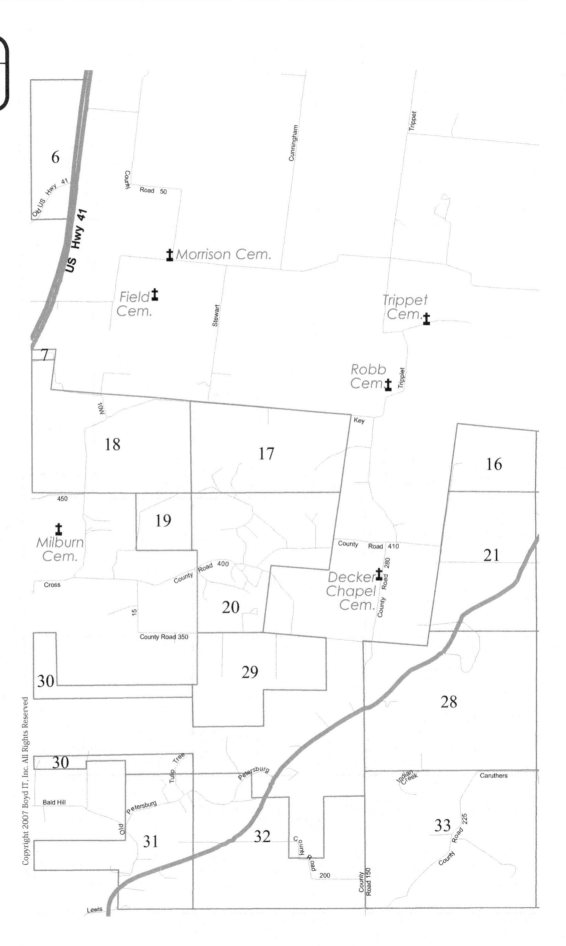

Road Map

T1-S R10-W
2nd PM Meridian

Map Group 5

Cities & Towns
Mount Olympus

Cemeteries
Armstrong Cemetery
Decker Chapel Cemetery
Field Cemetery
Kirk-McRoberts Cemetery
Milburn Cemetery
Morrison Cemetery
Robb Cemetery
Trippet Cemetery

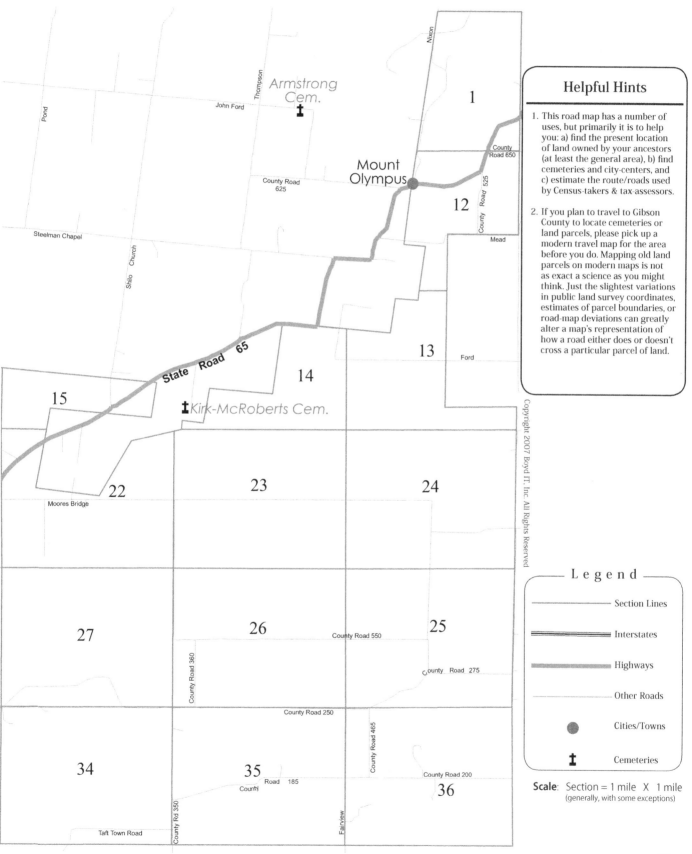

Helpful Hints

1. This road map has a number of uses, but primarily it is to help you: a) find the present location of land owned by your ancestors (at least the general area), b) find cemeteries and city-centers, and c) estimate the route/roads used by Census-takers & tax-assessors.

2. If you plan to travel to Gibson County to locate cemeteries or land parcels, please pick up a modern travel map for the area before you do. Mapping old land parcels on modern maps is not as exact a science as you might think. Just the slightest variations in public land survey coordinates, estimates of parcel boundaries, or road-map deviations can greatly alter a map's representation of how a road either does or doesn't cross a particular parcel of land.

Legend

———————	Section Lines
═══════════	Interstates
━━━━━━━━━	Highways
———————	Other Roads
●	Cities/Towns
✝	Cemeteries

Scale: Section = 1 mile X 1 mile
(generally, with some exceptions)

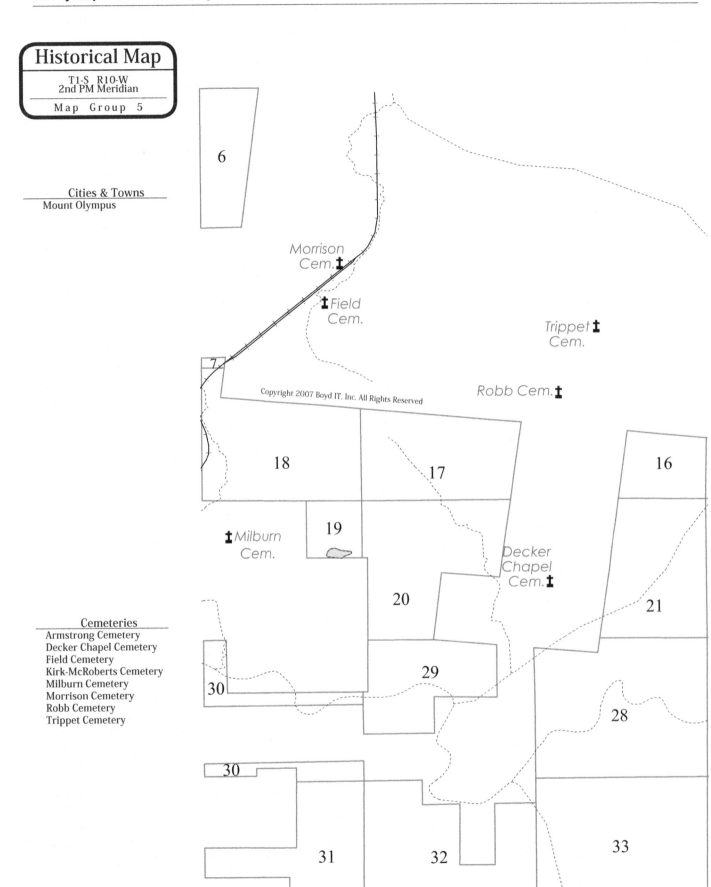

Historical Map

T1-S R10-W
2nd PM Meridian

Map Group 5

Cities & Towns
Mount Olympus

6

Morrison
Cem.

Field
Cem.

Trippet
Cem.

7

Robb Cem.

Copyright 2007 Boyd IT. Inc. All Rights Reserved

18

17

16

19

Milburn
Cem.

Decker
Chapel
Cem.

20

21

Cemeteries
Armstrong Cemetery
Decker Chapel Cemetery
Field Cemetery
Kirk-McRoberts Cemetery
Milburn Cemetery
Morrison Cemetery
Robb Cemetery
Trippet Cemetery

30

29

28

30

31

32

33

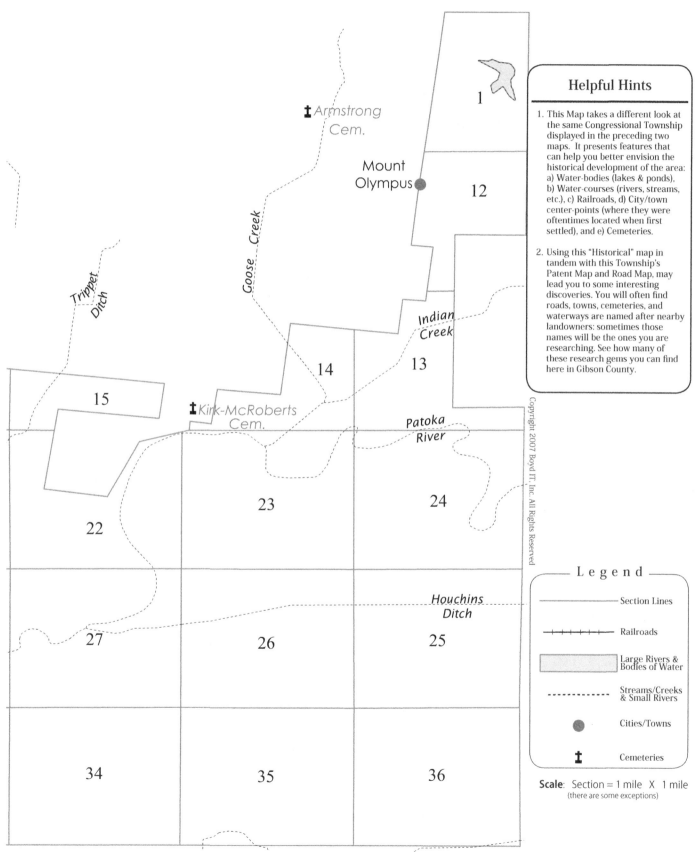

Helpful Hints

1. This Map takes a different look at the same Congressional Township displayed in the preceding two maps. It presents features that can help you better envision the historical development of the area: a) Water-bodies (lakes & ponds), b) Water-courses (rivers, streams, etc.), c) Railroads, d) City/town center-points (where they were oftentimes located when first settled), and e) Cemeteries.

2. Using this "Historical" map in tandem with this Township's Patent Map and Road Map, may lead you to some interesting discoveries. You will often find roads, towns, cemeteries, and waterways are named after nearby landowners: sometimes those names will be the ones you are researching. See how many of these research gems you can find here in Gibson County.

L e g e n d

——————— Section Lines

┼┼┼┼┼┼ Railroads

▭ Large Rivers & Bodies of Water

- - - - - - Streams/Creeks & Small Rivers

● Cities/Towns

☨ Cemeteries

Scale: Section = 1 mile X 1 mile
(there are some exceptions)

Map Group 6: Index to Land Patents

Township 1-South Range 9-West (2nd PM)

After you locate an individual in this Index, take note of the Section and Section Part then proceed to the Land Patent map on the pages immediately following. You should have no difficulty locating the corresponding parcel of land.

The "For More Info" Column will lead you to more information about the underlying Patents. See the *Legend* at right, and the "How to Use this Book" chapter, for more information.

```
                    LEGEND
        "For More Info . . . " column
A = Authority (Legislative Act, See Appendix "A")
B = Block or Lot (location in Section unknown)
C = Cancelled Patent
F = Fractional Section
G = Group (Multi-Patentee Patent, see Appendix "C")
V = Overlaps another Parcel
R = Re-Issued (Parcel patented more than once)

(A & G items require you to look in the Appendixes referred
to above. All other Letter-designations followed by a number
require you to locate line-items in this index that possess
the ID number found after the letter).
```

ID	Individual in Patent	Sec.	Sec. Part	Date Issued	Other Counties	For More Info . . .
517	BALDRIDGE, Samuel C	20	E½NW	1839-08-01		A1
492	BALLARD, James	6	W½SW	1839-08-01		A1
526	COLEMAN, William F	19	SWNE	1839-08-01		A1
484	COLVIN, Fielding	6	W½NE	1837-03-18		A1
483	" "	6	SESE	1840-10-01		A1
507	COLVIN, Richard	6	NENW	1837-03-20		A1
485	CRAW, Henry	30	SENW	1849-05-30		A1
487	CROW, Henry	30	NWNW	1837-03-18		A1
486	" "	30	NWNE	1837-08-05		A1
488	" "	31	NENE	1850-12-10		A1
498	CROW, Jason H	21	NENE	1848-05-01		A1
518	CUNINGHAM, Samuel	7	NESE	1840-10-01		A1
503	DILLON, Jonathan	17	NESW	1848-07-01		A1
491	GARDNER, Hugh W	17	W½SW	1837-11-07		A1
490	" "	17	SESW	1838-09-01		A1
499	GARDNER, John	29	NESW	1837-08-05		A1
479	GRIGSBY, Demps	32	E½SW	1837-03-30		A1
489	HARRIS, Hugh	17	NE	1839-02-01		A1
520	HART, Thomas	36	SENE	1875-01-15	Pike	A1
476	HARVEY, Andrew	7	SESE	1840-10-01		A1
494	HUSSEY, James	30	NENW	1839-08-01		A1
500	JONES, John	6	E½SW	1839-08-01		A1
501	JONES, John M	7	E½NE	1839-08-01		A1
521	JONES, Thomas	28	SESE	1835-09-10		A1
522	" "	33	NENE	1839-08-01		A1
525	JONES, Wiley	30	NENE	1835-10-28		A1
524	" "	28	W½NE	1837-03-20		A1
523	" "	28	NWSE	1837-08-05		A1
505	KIME, Michael	36	W½NW	1837-08-05	Pike	A1
480	KIRK, Edmond	20	NESW	1839-02-01		A1
481	KIRK, Edmund	21	W½SW	1837-08-05		A1
493	KIRK, James C	20	SESW	1837-08-05		A1
515	KIRK, Richard M	29	W½NE	1835-09-10		A1
512	" "	29	E½NE	1835-10-07		A1
514	" "	29	SENW	1835-10-07		A1
513	" "	29	NENW	1837-08-05		A1
516	" "	29	W½NW	1837-08-05		A1
508	" "	18	E½SE	1839-02-01		A1
509	" "	21	E½NW	1839-02-01		A1
510	" "	21	E½SW	1839-02-01		A1
511	" "	21	W½NE	1839-02-01		A1
528	KURTZ, William	30	SW	1855-01-03		A1
519	LEWIS, Stephen	6	SENW	1839-08-01		A1
504	MANIFOLD, Joseph	6	W½NW	1841-05-25		A1
477	MERKEL, Bernard	20	W½SW	1859-04-01		A1 R532
529	MOFFATT, William	17	NW	1839-02-01		A1

ID	Individual in Patent	Sec.	Sec. Part	Date Issued	Other Counties	For More Info . . .
478	ONEAL, Calvin	28	NESE	1835-10-15		A1
530	PAUL, William	19	E½NE	1839-08-01		A1
531	" "	20	W½NW	1839-08-01		A1
532	" "	20	W½SW	1839-08-01		A1 R477
495	PHILIPS, James N	7	SENW	1839-08-01		A1
533	PHILIPS, William	7	NWSE	1839-08-01		A1
527	PHILIPS, William H	18	NWSE	1839-08-01		A1
496	PHILLIPS, James N	19	NWNE	1839-08-01		A1
502	PHILLIPS, John	7	SWSE	1840-10-01		A1
534	PHILLIPS, William	18	SWSE	1837-08-05		A1
535	RICHARDSON, William	28	NENE	1835-10-01		A1
536	" "	28	SENE	1837-03-20		A1
537	ROUTT, William	21	SENE	1839-08-01		A1
482	SMITH, Elijah	28	NENW	1839-02-01		A1
497	TURNER, James	21	SE	1838-09-01		A1
538	TURPIN, William	35	SWNW	1837-08-05	Pike	A1
506	YAGER, Moses	6	NESE	1852-10-01		A1

Patent Map

T1-S R9-W
2nd PM Meridian

Map Group 6

Township Statistics

Parcels Mapped	:	63
Number of Patents	:	61
Number of Individuals	:	45
Patentees Identified	:	45
Number of Surnames	:	32
Multi-Patentee Parcels	:	0
Oldest Patent Date	:	9/10/1835
Most Recent Patent	:	1/15/1875
Block/Lot Parcels	:	0
Parcels Re - Issued	:	1
Parcels that Overlap	:	0
Cities and Towns	:	2
Cemeteries	:	2

3	2	1
10	11	12
15	14	13
22	23	24
27	26	25
34	TURPIN William 1837 35	KIME Michael 1837 36 HART Thomas 1875

Helpful Hints

1. This Map's INDEX can be found on the preceding pages.

2. Refer to Map "C" to see where this Township lies within Gibson County, Indiana.

3. Numbers within square brackets [ ] denote a multi-patentee land parcel (multi-owner). Refer to Appendix "C" for a full list of members in this group.

4. Areas that look to be crowded with Patentees usually indicate multiple sales of the same parcel (Re-issues) or Overlapping parcels. See this Township's Index for an explanation of these and other circumstances that might explain "odd" groupings of Patentees on this map.

Legend

——————— Patent Boundary

━━━━━━━ Section Boundary

No Patents Found
(or Outside County)

1., 2., 3., . . . Lot Numbers
(when beside a name)

[ ] Group Number
(see Appendix "C")

Scale: Section = 1 mile X 1 mile
(generally, with some exceptions)

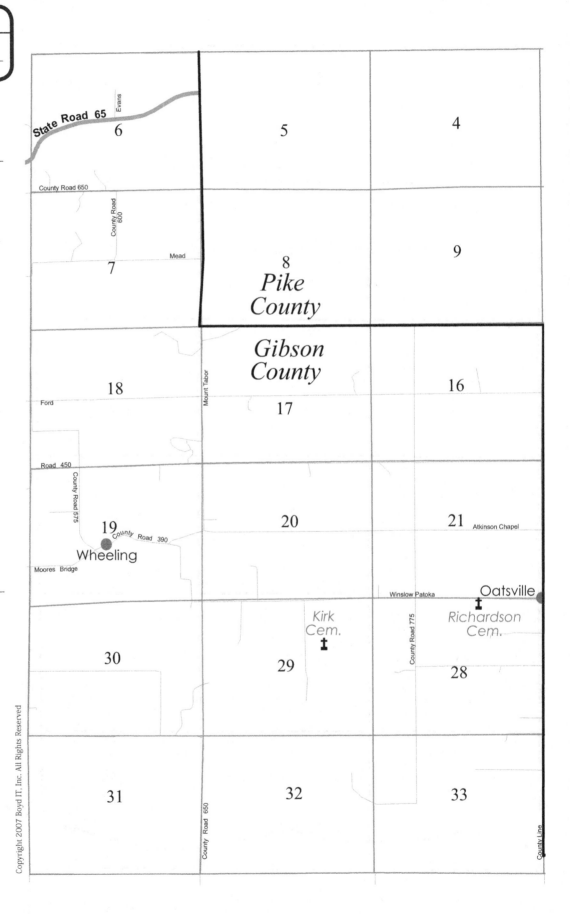

Road Map

T1-S R9-W
2nd PM Meridian

Map Group 6

__Cities & Towns__
Oatsville
Wheeling

__Cemeteries__
Kirk Cemetery
Richardson Cemetery

State Road 65

Evans

6

5

4

County Road 650

County Road 600

Mead

7

8

Pike County

9

Gibson County

18

Ford

Mount Tabor

17

16

Road 450

County Road 575

19

County Road 390

Wheeling

Moores Bridge

20

21

Atkinson Chapel

Winslow Patoka

Oatsville

Kirk Cem.

Richardson Cem.

County Road 775

30

29

28

31

County Road 650

32

33

County Line

3	2	1
10	11	12
15	14	13
22	23	24
27	26	25
34	35	36

Helpful Hints

1. This road map has a number of uses, but primarily it is to help you: a) find the present location of land owned by your ancestors (at least the general area), b) find cemeteries and city-centers, and c) estimate the route/roads used by Census-takers & tax-assessors.

2. If you plan to travel to Gibson County to locate cemeteries or land parcels, please pick up a modern travel map for the area before you do. Mapping old land parcels on modern maps is not as exact a science as you might think. Just the slightest variations in public land survey coordinates, estimates of parcel boundaries, or road-map deviations can greatly alter a map's representation of how a road either does or doesn't cross a particular parcel of land.

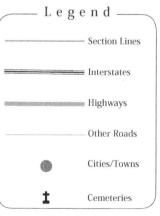

Legend

— Section Lines

Interstates

Highways

— Other Roads

● Cities/Towns

✝ Cemeteries

Scale: Section = 1 mile X 1 mile
(generally, with some exceptions)

Historical Map

T1-S R9-W
2nd PM Meridian

Map Group 6

Cities & Towns
Oatsville
Wheeling

6

5

4

7

8

9

*Pike
County*

*Gibson
County*

Indian Creek

18

17

16

Yellow
Creek

19

20

21

● Wheeling

Cemeteries
Kirk Cemetery
Richardson Cemetery

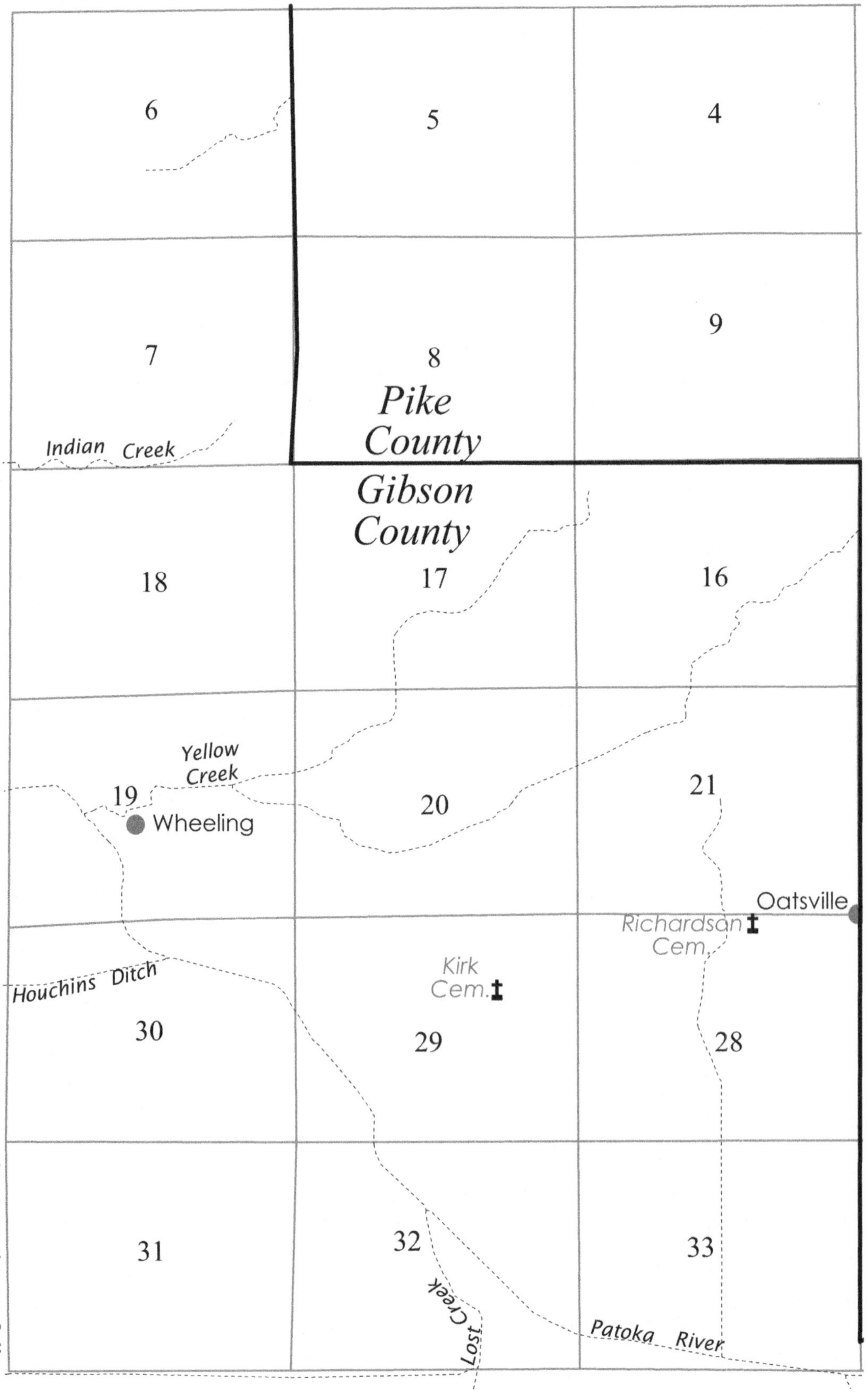

Oatsville

Richardson
Cem. ✝ ●

Kirk
Cem. ✝

Houchins Ditch

30

29

28

31

32

33

Lost Creek

Patoka River

3	2	1
10	11	12
15	14	13
22	23	24
27	26	25
34	35	36

Helpful Hints

1. This Map takes a different look at the same Congressional Township displayed in the preceding two maps. It presents features that can help you better envision the historical development of the area: a) Water-bodies (lakes & ponds), b) Water-courses (rivers, streams, etc.), c) Railroads, d) City/town center-points (where they were oftentimes located when first settled), and e) Cemeteries.

2. Using this "Historical" map in tandem with this Township's Patent Map and Road Map, may lead you to some interesting discoveries. You will often find roads, towns, cemeteries, and waterways are named after nearby landowners: sometimes those names will be the ones you are researching. See how many of these research gems you can find here in Gibson County.

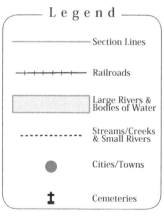

L e g e n d

———————— Section Lines

++++++++ Railroads

▭ Large Rivers & Bodies of Water

- - - - - - - Streams/Creeks & Small Rivers

● Cities/Towns

† Cemeteries

Scale: Section = 1 mile X 1 mile
(there are some exceptions)

Map Group 7: Index to Land Patents

Township 1-South Range 8-West (2nd PM)

After you locate an individual in this Index, take note of the Section and Section Part then proceed to the Land Patent map on the pages immediately following. You should have no difficulty locating the corresponding parcel of land.

The "For More Info" Column will lead you to more information about the underlying Patents. See the *Legend* at right, and the "How to Use this Book" chapter, for more information.

LEGEND
"For More Info . . ." column
A = Authority (Legislative Act, See Appendix "A")
B = Block or Lot (location in Section unknown)
C = Cancelled Patent
F = Fractional Section
G = Group (Multi-Patentee Patent, see Appendix "C")
V = Overlaps another Parcel
R = Re-Issued (Parcel patented more than once)
(A & G items require you to look in the Appendixes referred to above. All other Letter-designations followed by a number require you to locate line-items in this index that possess the ID number found after the letter).

ID	Individual in Patent	Sec.	Sec. Part	Date Issued	Other Counties	For More Info . . .
546	ATKINSON, James	32	NWNE	1839-02-01	Pike	A1
549	CLARK, William D	32	NESE	1841-12-10	Pike	A1
548	KNIGHT, John	31	NENE	1837-08-05	Pike	A1
547	MCADAMS, James	32	NWNW	1837-08-05	Pike	A1
539	PRATT, George W	31	NW	1839-02-01	Pike	A1 G31
540	" "	31	S½	1839-02-01	Pike	A1 G31
541	" "	31	SENE	1839-02-01	Pike	A1 G31
542	" "	31	W½NE	1839-02-01	Pike	A1 G31
544	" "	32	SWNE	1839-08-01	Pike	A1 G31
543	" "	32	E½NW	1843-08-09	Pike	A1 G31
545	" "	32	SWNW	1843-08-09	Pike	A1 G31
539	SULLIVAN, William	31	NW	1839-02-01	Pike	A1 G31
540	" "	31	S½	1839-02-01	Pike	A1 G31
541	" "	31	SENE	1839-02-01	Pike	A1 G31
542	" "	31	W½NE	1839-02-01	Pike	A1 G31
544	" "	32	SWNE	1839-08-01	Pike	A1 G31
543	" "	32	E½NW	1843-08-09	Pike	A1 G31
545	" "	32	SWNW	1843-08-09	Pike	A1 G31
539	THACHER, George M	31	NW	1839-02-01	Pike	A1 G31
540	" "	31	S½	1839-02-01	Pike	A1 G31
541	" "	31	SENE	1839-02-01	Pike	A1 G31
542	" "	31	W½NE	1839-02-01	Pike	A1 G31
544	" "	32	SWNE	1839-08-01	Pike	A1 G31
543	" "	32	E½NW	1843-08-09	Pike	A1 G31
545	" "	32	SWNW	1843-08-09	Pike	A1 G31

6	5
7	8
18	17
19	20
30	29

PRATT [31]
George W
1839

PRATT [31]
George W
1839

KNIGHT
John
1837

PRATT [31]
George W
1839

31

MCADAMS
James
1837

PRATT [31]
George W
1843

ATKINSON
James
1839

PRATT [31]
George W
1843

PRATT [31]
George W
1839

32

CLARK
William D
1841

PRATT [31]
George W
1839

Gibson County

Pike County

Patent Map

T1-S R8-W
2nd PM Meridian

Map Group 7

Township Statistics

Parcels Mapped	:	11
Number of Patents	:	7
Number of Individuals	:	7
Patentees Identified	:	5
Number of Surnames	:	7
Multi-Patentee Parcels	:	7
Oldest Patent Date	:	8/5/1837
Most Recent Patent	:	8/9/1843
Block/Lot Parcels	:	0
Parcels Re - Issued	:	0
Parcels that Overlap	:	0
Cities and Towns	:	0
Cemeteries	:	0

Note: the area contained in this map amounts to far less than a full Township. Therefore, its contents are completely on this single page (instead of a "normal" 2-page spread).

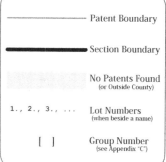

Legend

——————— Patent Boundary

——————— Section Boundary

No Patents Found
(or Outside County)

1., 2., 3., ...   Lot Numbers
(when beside a name)

[ ]   Group Number
(see Appendix "C")

Scale: Section = 1 mile X 1 mile
(generally, with some exceptions)

Road Map

T1-S R8-W
2nd PM Meridian

Map Group 7

Note: the area contained in this map amounts to far less than a full Township. Therefore, its contents are completely on this single page (instead of a "normal" 2-page spread).

Cities & Towns
None

Cemeteries
None

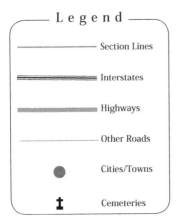

Legend

——— Section Lines

══ Interstates

━━ Highways

——— Other Roads

● Cities/Towns

✝ Cemeteries

Scale: Section = 1 mile X 1 mile
(generally, with some exceptions)

6	5
7	8
18	17
19	20
30	29
31	32

Pike County

Gibson County

6

5

7

8

18

17

19

20

30

29

Pike County

31

32

Gibson County

Patoka River

Historical Map

T1-S R8-W
2nd PM Meridian

Map Group 7

Note: the area contained in this map amounts to far less than a full Township. Therefore, its contents are completely on this single page (instead of a "normal" 2-page spread).

Cities & Towns
None

Cemeteries
None

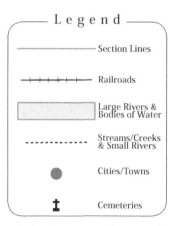

L e g e n d

——————— Section Lines

+—+—+—+—+ Railroads

Large Rivers & Bodies of Water

- - - - - - - Streams/Creeks & Small Rivers

● Cities/Towns

⚰ Cemeteries

Scale: Section = 1 mile X 1 mile
(there are some exceptions)

Map Group 8: Index to Land Patents

Township 2-South Range 14-West (2nd PM)

After you locate an individual in this Index, take note of the Section and Section Part then proceed to the Land Patent map on the pages immediately following. You should have no difficulty locating the corresponding parcel of land.

The "For More Info" Column will lead you to more information about the underlying Patents. See the *Legend* at right, and the "How to Use this Book" chapter, for more information.

```
                      LEGEND
            "For More Info . . . " column
A = Authority (Legislative Act, See Appendix "A")
B = Block or Lot (location in Section unknown)
C = Cancelled Patent
F = Fractional Section
G = Group  (Multi-Patentee Patent, see Appendix "C")
V = Overlaps another Parcel
R = Re-Issued (Parcel patented more than once)

(A & G items require you to look in the Appendixes referred
to above. All other Letter-designations followed by a number
require you to locate line-items in this index that possess
the ID number found after the letter).
```

ID	Individual in Patent	Sec.	Sec. Part	Date Issued	Other Counties	For More Info . . .
None						

We have not located any Federal Land
Patent records within the
Bureau of Land Management's database for

**Township 2-S Range 14-W
(Map Group 8)**

in **Gibson County.**

Accordingly, we have no
"Patent Map" for this township.

Nonetheless, we have included our
Road and Historical Maps, which
begin on the following page.

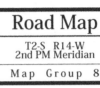

Road Map

T2-S R14-W
2nd PM Meridian

Map Group 8

Note: the area contained in this map amounts to far less than a full Township. Therefore, its contents are completely on this single page (instead of a "normal" 2-page spread).

Cities & Towns
None

Cemeteries
None

35

36

Legend

——————— Section Lines

═══════ Interstates

━━━━━━ Highways

——————— Other Roads

● Cities/Towns

† Cemeteries

Scale: Section = 1 mile X 1 mile
(generally, with some exceptions)

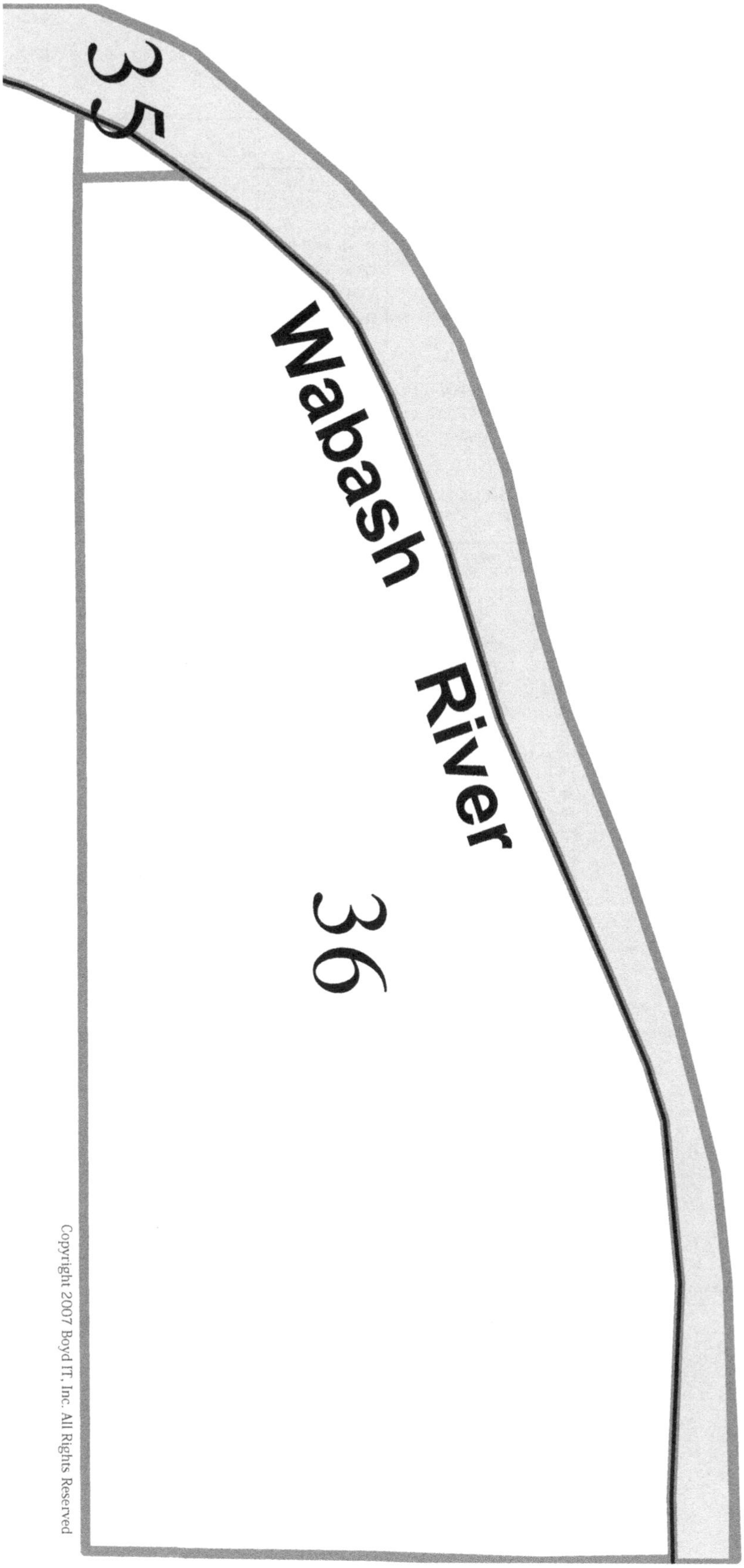

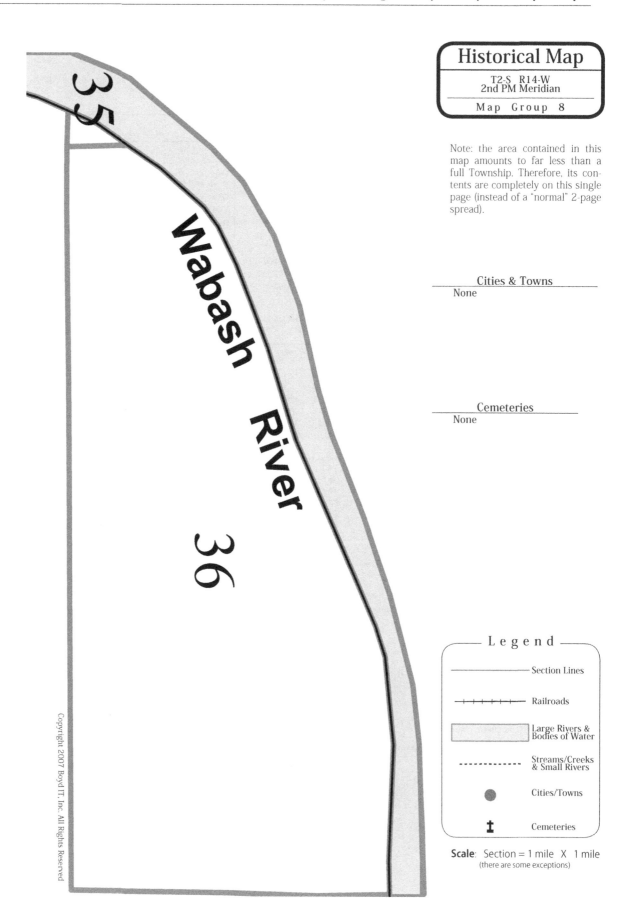

Historical Map

T2-S R14-W
2nd PM Meridian

Map Group 8

Note: the area contained in this map amounts to far less than a full Township. Therefore, its contents are completely on this single page (instead of a "normal" 2-page spread).

Cities & Towns

None

Cemeteries

None

Legend

Section Lines

Railroads

Large Rivers & Bodies of Water

Streams/Creeks & Small Rivers

Cities/Towns

Cemeteries

Scale: Section = 1 mile X 1 mile
(there are some exceptions)

Map Group 9: Index to Land Patents

Township 2-South Range 13-West (2nd PM)

After you locate an individual in this Index, take note of the Section and Section Part then proceed to the Land Patent map on the pages immediately following. You should have no difficulty locating the corresponding parcel of land.

The "For More Info" Column will lead you to more information about the underlying Patents. See the *Legend* at right, and the "How to Use this Book" chapter, for more information.

```
                          LEGEND
              "For More Info . . . " column
A = Authority (Legislative Act, See Appendix "A")
B = Block or Lot (location in Section unknown)
C = Cancelled Patent
F = Fractional Section
G = Group  (Multi-Patentee Patent, see Appendix "C")
V = Overlaps another Parcel
R = Re-Issued (Parcel patented more than once)

(A & G items require you to look in the Appendixes referred
to above. All other Letter-designations followed by a number
require you to locate line-items in this index that possess
the ID number found after the letter).
```

ID	Individual in Patent	Sec.	Sec. Part	Date Issued	Other Counties	For More Info . . .
589	ASHLEY, Thomas	32	S½S½	1831-21-05		A1 F
574	AULDRIDGE, John	1		1824-09-08		A1 F
568	BAKER, Ezra	14	1	1837-18-03		A1 F
562	" "	12	SW	1837-20-03		A1 F
565	" "	13	W½NE	1837-20-03		A1 F
566	" "	13	W½SW	1837-20-03		A1 F
569	" "	14	S½	1837-30-03		A1 F
564	" "	13	E½SW	1838-01-09		A1 F
561	" "	12		1852-01-10		A1
563	" "	13		1852-01-10		A1
567	" "	14		1852-01-10		A1
591	BARKER, William	35	7	1837-01-08		A1 F
590	" "	35	2	1837-18-03		A1 F
556	BENSON, David	23	SESE	1839-01-08		A1 F
570	BLACK, George	24	NENW	1840-01-10		A1
588	BLACK, Sarah	24	SWNW	1841-25-05		A1
551	BREEDLOVE, Abraham	23	3	1839-28-10		A1 F
584	BUMP, Martin	32	1	1837-15-03		A1 F
587	BUMP, Moses	31	SWSW	1837-01-08		A1 F
575	CASH, John	26	1	1839-01-09		A1 F
555	CROWLEY, Daniel	33	S½S½	1831-21-05		A1 F
552	" "	32	2	1835-28-10		A1 F
553	" "	33	4	1837-01-08		A1 F
554	" "	33	N½S½	1837-01-08		A1 F
550	DAVIS, Abijah	26	N½S½	1835-15-10		A1 F
578	ELDER, John R	26	8	1872-10-04		A1
576	HUGHES, John	12	N½N½	1837-05-08		A1 F
558	JORDAN, Eliba	35	3	1837-01-08		A1 F
573	JORDAN, Jefferson	26	7	1835-01-10		A1 F
577	JORDAN, John	35	6	1837-18-03		A1 F
582	JORDAN, Joshua	33	1	1839-01-08		A1 F
583	" "	33	3	1839-01-08		A1 F
593	LOVELLETT, William T	23	4	1839-01-08		A1 F
571	MCCURDY, George W	33	2	1875-??-01		A1
572	" "	35	5	1875-??-01		A1
581	MOWRER, Joseph	13	SENE	1837-20-03		A1 V563
559	PANLEY, Elijah	26	S½N½	1837-05-08		A1 F
592	PURCELL, William	23	1	1837-05-08		A1 F
585	SAWYER, Milo	12	1	1839-01-08		A1 F
586	" "	12	2	1839-01-08		A1 F
579	THOMPSON, John	23	W½SE	1837-05-08		A1 F
580	" "	26	2	1837-05-08		A1 F
557	WHITE, Elias	23	NESE	1839-01-02		A1 F
560	WONZER, Ephraim	23	2	1838-01-09		A1 F

Patent Map

T2-S R13-W
2nd PM Meridian

Map Group 9

Township Statistics

Parcels Mapped	:	44
Number of Patents	:	40
Number of Individuals	:	28
Patentees Identified	:	28
Number of Surnames	:	23
Multi-Patentee Parcels	:	0
Oldest Patent Date	:	9/8/1824
Most Recent Patent	:	10/4/1872
Block/Lot Parcels	:	653
Parcels Re - Issued	:	0
Parcels that Overlap	:	1
Cities and Towns	:	0
Cemeteries	:	0

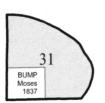

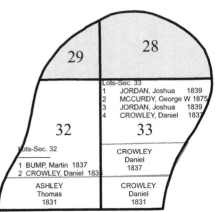

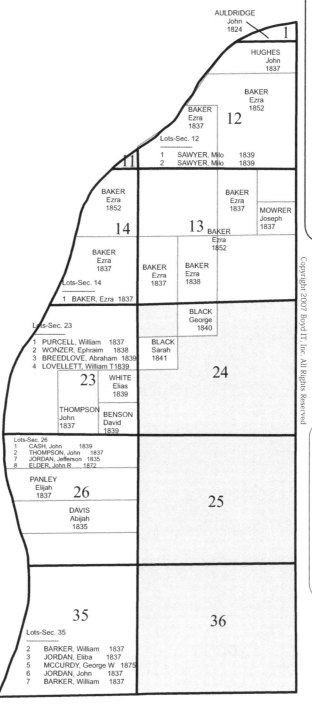

Helpful Hints

1. This Map's INDEX can be found on the preceding pages.

2. Refer to Map "C" to see where this Township lies within Gibson County, Indiana.

3. Numbers within square brackets [ ] denote a multi-patentee land parcel (multi-owner). Refer to Appendix "C" for a full list of members in this group.

4. Areas that look to be crowded with Patentees usually indicate multiple sales of the same parcel (Re-issues) or Overlapping parcels. See this Township's Index for an explanation of these and other circumstances that might explain "odd" groupings of Patentees on this map.

Legend

———— Patent Boundary

━━━━━● Section Boundary

No Patents Found
(or Outside County)

1., 2., 3., ... Lot Numbers
(when beside a name)

[ ] Group Number
(see Appendix "C")

Scale: Section = 1 mile X 1 mile
(generally, with some exceptions)

Road Map

T2-S R13-W
2nd PM Meridian

Map Group 9

Cities & Towns
None

Cemeteries
None

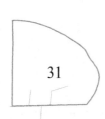

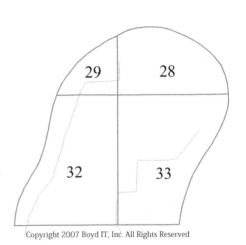

Helpful Hints

1. This road map has a number of uses, but primarily it is to help you: a) find the present location of land owned by your ancestors (at least the general area), b) find cemeteries and city-centers, and c) estimate the route/roads used by Census-takers & tax-assessors.

2. If you plan to travel to Gibson County to locate cemeteries or land parcels, please pick up a modern travel map for the area before you do. Mapping old land parcels on modern maps is not as exact a science as you might think. Just the slightest variations in public land survey coordinates, estimates of parcel boundaries, or road-map deviations can greatly alter a map's representation of how a road either does or doesn't cross a particular parcel of land.

1

12

11

14

13

County Road 1300

County Road 175

23

24

County Road 250

County Road 1500

26

25

County Road 350

35

36

Legend

————————	Section Lines
≡≡≡≡≡≡≡≡	Interstates
————————	Highways
————————	Other Roads
●	Cities/Towns
✝	Cemeteries

Scale: Section = 1 mile X 1 mile
(generally, with some exceptions)

Historical Map

T2-S R13-W
2nd PM Meridian

Map Group 9

<u>Cities & Towns</u>
None

<u>Cemeteries</u>
None

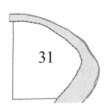

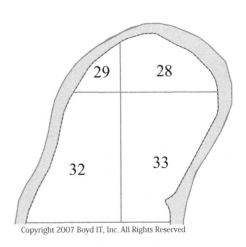

Helpful Hints

1. This Map takes a different look at the same Congressional Township displayed in the preceding two maps. It presents features that can help you better envision the historical development of the area: a) Water-bodies (lakes & ponds), b) Water-courses (rivers, streams, etc.), c) Railroads, d) City/town center-points (where they were oftentimes located when first settled), and e) Cemeteries.

2. Using this "Historical" map in tandem with this Township's Patent Map and Road Map, may lead you to some interesting discoveries. You will often find roads, towns, cemeteries, and waterways are named after nearby landowners: sometimes those names will be the ones you are researching. See how many of these research gems you can find here in Gibson County.

1

12

11

Coffee Bayou

14

13

Wabash River

23

24

26

25

Keniepe

35

36

Scott Ditch

L e g e n d

———— Section Lines

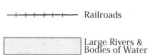 Railroads

 Large Rivers & Bodies of Water

- - - - - - - Streams/Creeks & Small Rivers

● Cities/Towns

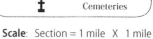 Cemeteries

Scale: Section = 1 mile X 1 mile
(there are some exceptions)

Map Group 10: Index to Land Patents

Township 2-South Range 12-West (2nd PM)

After you locate an individual in this Index, take note of the Section and Section Part then proceed to the Land Patent map on the pages immediately following. You should have no difficulty locating the corresponding parcel of land.

The "For More Info" Column will lead you to more information about the underlying Patents. See the *Legend* at right, and the "How to Use this Book" chapter, for more information.

```
                    LEGEND
            "For More Info . . . " column
A = Authority (Legislative Act, See Appendix "A")
B = Block or Lot (location in Section unknown)
C = Cancelled Patent
F = Fractional Section
G = Group  (Multi-Patentee Patent, see Appendix "C")
V = Overlaps another Parcel
R = Re-Issued (Parcel patented more than once)

(A & G items require you to look in the Appendixes referred
to above. All other Letter-designations followed by a number
require you to locate line-items in this index that possess
the ID number found after the letter).
```

ID	Individual in Patent	Sec.	Sec. Part	Date Issued	Other Counties	For More Info . . .
669	BAULDWIN, Wiley J	26	SWSW	1837-18-03		A1
670	" "	27	SESE	1837-20-03		A1
650	BEDELL, Moses	5	E½SE	1838-01-09		A1
651	" "	5	SWSE	1838-01-09		A1
602	BELLASS, Charles H	25	NWSW	1838-01-09		A1
608	BLACK, George	7	NWNE	1835-07-10		A1
645	BRADLEY, Lewis A	2	SE	1857-01-07		A1
671	BROWN, William H	36	SENE	1835-01-10		A1
658	CASEY, Samuel	26	SESW	1839-01-02		A1
654	CREEK, Pearson	17	SWNW	1858-30-08		A1
655	DENBO, Robert	24	NENE	1837-18-03		A1
656	" "	24	SWNE	1837-20-03		A1
620	DUNCAN, James F	21	NWNW	1841-25-05		A1
621	" "	21	SENW	1841-25-05		A1
618	EMISON, James	34	SE	1922-22-03		A1
619	" "	35	SW	1922-22-03		A1
605	FORBIS, Ezra	17	NWSW	1837-15-03		A1
606	" "	17	SWSE	1839-01-02		A1
634	FRAZER, John J	33	SENW	1837-07-11		A1
665	GWIN, Thomas	6		1823-24-07		A1 F
647	HARMON, Lewis	32	W½SE	1830-02-12		A1 R648
646	" "	32	SENE	1835-01-10		A1
648	" "	32	W½SE	1930-03-01		A1 R647
664	HARMON, Taylor	32	NESW	1839-01-02		A1
611	HARRIS, Gillam	24	SE	1945-09-11		A1 G22
623	HASKIN, James S	27	SWNE	1839-01-08		A1
632	HUGHES, John	5	4	1837-05-08		A1 F
633	" "	5	NESW	1837-05-08		A1 F
662	HUSE, Sarah	7	NENE	1837-07-11		A1
609	JACKSON, George	7	SESE	1837-15-03		A1
615	JOHNSON, Jacob	5	2	1837-15-03		A1
616	" "	5	SENE	1837-15-03		A1
614	" "	5	1	1837-20-03		A1 F
666	JOHNSON, Thomas M	36	SWNE	1835-10-09		A1
595	LANDSDOWN, Abner	3	NESW	1839-01-08		A1
631	LANSDOWN, Joel	3	SESW	1839-01-08		A1
607	LUCAS, Fielding	36	E½SE	1837-15-03		A1
599	LYNN, Andrew	9	NENE	1839-01-02		A1
644	MANCK, Julius	25	SENW	1839-01-02		A1
641	MAUCH, Joseph	25	N½NW	1837-18-03		A1
597	MAUCK, Abraham	17	SWSW	1837-07-11		A1
596	" "	17	SESE	1839-01-02		A1
659	MAUCK, Samuel	24	SENE	1835-05-09		A1
635	MCFADIN, John	27	NENE	1835-07-10		A1
598	MOCK, Abraham	25	E½NE	1829-02-07		A1
611	" "	24	SE	1945-09-11		A1 G22

ID	Individual in Patent	Sec.	Sec. Part	Date Issued	Other Counties	For More Info . . .
636	MOCK, John	3	NWNW	1835-28-10		A1
637	" "	4	NENE	1837-15-03		A1
638	MONTGOMERY, John	35	NE	1943-14-10		A1
652	MONTGOMERY, Moses	5	NENE	1835-01-10		A1 F
663	MONTGOMERY, Tandy B	36	NWNE	1837-20-03		A1
667	MONTGOMERY, Thomas	5	NW	1837-20-03		A1 F
617	MOWREY, Jacob	23	E½SW	1823-04-08		A1
603	MUSE, Daniel	7	SENE	1838-01-09		A1
668	MUSE, Thomas	7	NWNW	1837-07-11		A1
604	MUSIC, Ephraim	27	W½SW	1831-04-01		A1
653	OVERTON, Nathan	33	W½NW	1831-21-05		A1
601	REEVES, Barnes	26	E½NE	1831-04-01		A1
657	RICHARDS, Rowland B	4	E½SE	1839-01-02		A1
642	ROBERTS, Joseph	21	SWNE	1841-25-05		A1
639	RUTTER, John	35	SWNW	1838-01-09		A1
649	SELSOR, Milley	36	NENE	1837-05-08		A1
610	SHARP, George W	3	NWSE	1841-25-05		A1
612	SHARP, Harris	3	NENW	1838-07-09		A1
613	" "	3	SWNW	1841-25-05		A1
624	SHARP, James	3	W½NE	1840-01-10		A1
600	SMITH, Andrew	22	SESW	1844-01-08		A1
625	STEWART, James	25	NESW	1839-01-08		A1
626	" "	25	SESW	1839-01-08		A1
627	" "	25	SWSW	1839-01-08		A1
611	STORMONT, Robert	24	SE	1945-09-11		A1 G22
594	STRICKLAND, Aaron	8	SWSW	1838-01-09		A1
672	STRICKLAND, William R	5	3	1837-15-03		A1 F
673	" "	7	NENW	1838-01-09		A1
628	WARD, James	17	SESW	1839-01-08		A1
622	WATERS, James R	33	SWNE	1835-01-10		A1
660	WHITE, Samuel	7	NESE	1837-01-08		A1
661	" "	7	SWNE	1837-01-08		A1
640	WILLIAMS, Joseph J	27	SWNW	1837-05-08		A1
629	YAGER, Jeremiah V	21	NESW	1841-25-05		A1
630	" "	21	NWSE	1841-25-05		A1
643	YAGER, Joseph	27	SENE	1850-01-10		A1

Patent Map

T2-S R12-W
2nd PM Meridian

Map Group 10

Township Statistics

Parcels Mapped	:	80
Number of Patents	:	74
Number of Individuals	:	62
Patentees Identified	:	61
Number of Surnames	:	50
Multi-Patentee Parcels	:	1
Oldest Patent Date	:	4/8/1823
Most Recent Patent	:	9/11/1945
Block/Lot Parcels	:	133
Parcels Re - Issued	:	1
Parcels that Overlap	:	0
Cities and Towns	:	1
Cemeteries	:	0

Section 5:
MONTGOMERY Moses 1835
MONTGOMERY Thomas 1837
JOHNSON Jacob 1837
BEDELL Moses 1838
HUGHES John 1837

Lots-Sec. 5
1 JOHNSON, Jacob 1837
2 JOHNSON, Jacob 1837
3 STRICKLAND, William 1837
4 HUGHES, John 1837
BEDELL Moses 1838

Section 4:
MOCK John 1837
RICHARDS Rowland B 1839

Section 6:
GWIN Thomas 1823

Section 7:
MUSE Thomas 1837
STRICKLAND William R 1838
BLACK George 1835
HUSE Sarah 1837
WHITE Samuel 1837
MUSE Daniel 1838
WHITE Samuel 1837
JACKSON George 1837
STRICKLAND Aaron 1838

Section 9:
LYNN Andrew 1839

Section 18

Section 17:
CREEK Pearson 1858
FORBIS Ezra 1837
MAUCK Abraham 1837
WARD James 1839
FORBIS Ezra 1839
MAUCK Abraham 1839

Section 16

Section 19

Section 20

Section 21:
DUNCAN James F 1841
DUNCAN James F 1841
ROBERTS Joseph 1841
YAGER Jeremiah V 1841
YAGER Jeremiah V 1841

Section 30

Section 29

Section 28

Section 31

Section 32:
HARMON Taylor 1839
HARMON Lewis 1930
HARMON Lewis 1830

Section 33:
OVERTON Nathan 1831
HARMON Lewis 1835
FRAZER John J 1837
WATERS James R 1835

Section 3
MOCK John 1835
SHARP Harris 1838
SHARP James 1840
SHARP Harris 1841
LANDSDOWN Abner 1839
SHARP George W 1841
LANSDOWN Joel 1839

Section 2
BRADLEY Lewis A 1857

Section 1

Section 10

Section 11

Section 12

Section 15

Section 14

Section 13

Section 22
SMITH Andrew 1844

Section 23
MOWREY Jacob 1823

Section 24
DENBO Robert 1837
DENBO Robert 1837
MAUCK Samuel 1835
HARRIS [22] Gillam 1945

Section 27
WILLIAMS Joseph J 1837
HASKIN James S 1839
MCFADIN John 1835
YAGER Joseph 1850
MUSIC Ephraim 1831
BAULDWIN Wiley J 1837

Section 26
BAULDWIN Wiley J 1837
CASEY Samuel 1839
REEVES Barnes 1831

Section 25
MAUCH Joseph 1837
MANCK Julius 1839
BELLASS Charles H 1838
STEWART James 1839
STEWART James 1839
STEWART James 1839
MOCK Abraham 1829

Section 34

Section 35
RUTTER John 1838
EMISON James 1922

Section 36
MONTGOMERY John 1943
EMISON James 1922
MONTGOMERY Tandy B 1837
SELSOR Milley 1837
JOHNSON Thomas M 1835
BROWN William H 1835
LUCAS Fielding 1837

EMISON James 1922

Helpful Hints

1. This Map's INDEX can be found on the preceding pages.

2. Refer to Map "C" to see where this Township lies within Gibson County, Indiana.

3. Numbers within square brackets [ ] denote a multi-patentee land parcel (multi-owner). Refer to Appendix "C" for a full list of members in this group.

4. Areas that look to be crowded with Patentees usually indicate multiple sales of the same parcel (Re-issues) or Overlapping parcels. See this Township's Index for an explanation of these and other circumstances that might explain "odd" groupings of Patentees on this map.

Legend

———— Patent Boundary

▬▬▬▬ Section Boundary

No Patents Found (or Outside County)

1., 2., 3., ... Lot Numbers (when beside a name)

[ ] Group Number (see Appendix "C")

Scale: Section = 1 mile X 1 mile (generally, with some exceptions)

Road Map

T2-S R12-W
2nd PM Meridian

Map Group 10

Cities & Towns
Skelton

Cemeteries
None

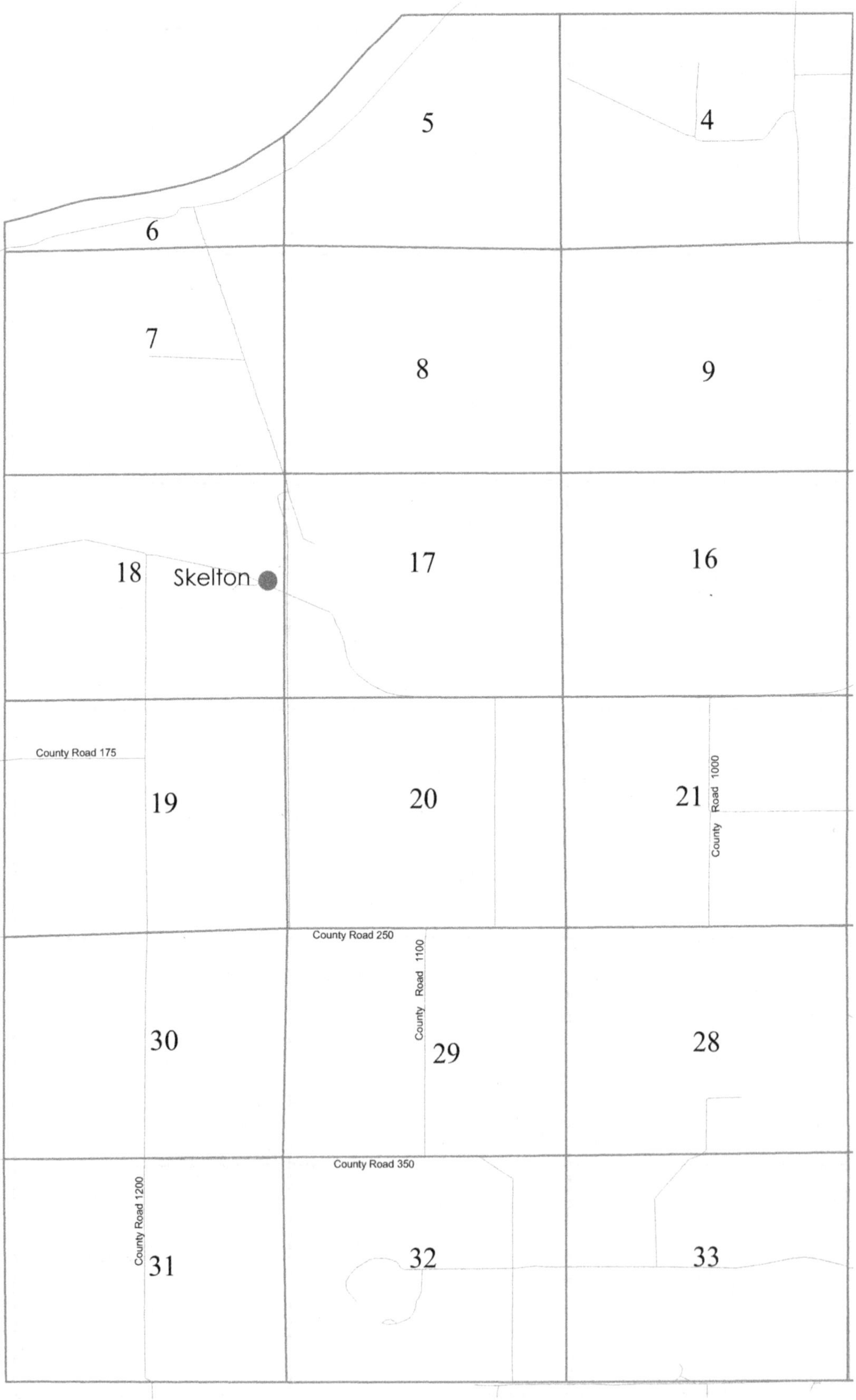

5

4

6

7

8

9

18

Skelton

17

16

County Road 175

19

20

21

County Road 1000

County Road 250

County Road 1100

30

29

28

County Road 350

County Road 1200

31

32

33

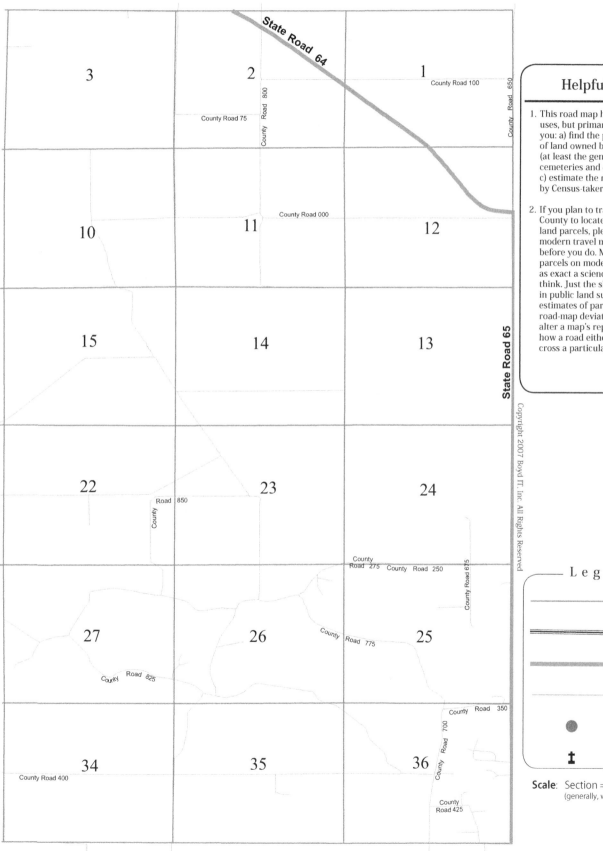

State Road 64

3

2

1

County Road 100

County Road 650

County Road 75

County Road 800

County Road 000

10

11

12

15

14

13

State Road 65

22

23

24

Road 850

County

County
Road 275   County Road 250

County Road 675

27

26

County Road 775   25

County Road 825

County Road 350

County Road 700

34

35

36

County Road 400

County
Road 425

Helpful Hints

1. This road map has a number of uses, but primarily it is to help you: a) find the present location of land owned by your ancestors (at least the general area), b) find cemeteries and city-centers, and c) estimate the route/roads used by Census-takers & tax-assessors.

2. If you plan to travel to Gibson County to locate cemeteries or land parcels, please pick up a modern travel map for the area before you do. Mapping old land parcels on modern maps is not as exact a science as you might think. Just the slightest variations in public land survey coordinates, estimates of parcel boundaries, or road-map deviations can greatly alter a map's representation of how a road either does or doesn't cross a particular parcel of land.

Legend

———— Section Lines

════ Interstates

▬▬▬ Highways

———— Other Roads

● Cities/Towns

⚓ Cemeteries

Scale: Section = 1 mile X 1 mile
(generally, with some exceptions)

111

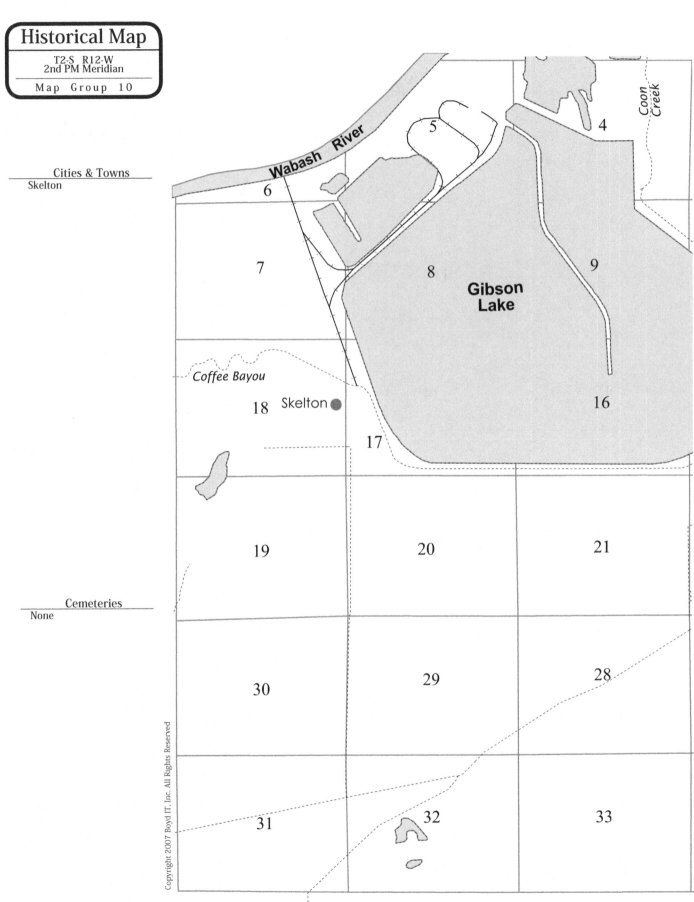

Historical Map

T2-S R12-W
2nd PM Meridian

Map Group 10

Cities & Towns
Skelton

Cemeteries
None

Wabash River

Coon Creek

5

4

6

7

8

Gibson Lake

9

Coffee Bayou

18   Skelton ●

17

16

19

20

21

30

29

28

31

32

33

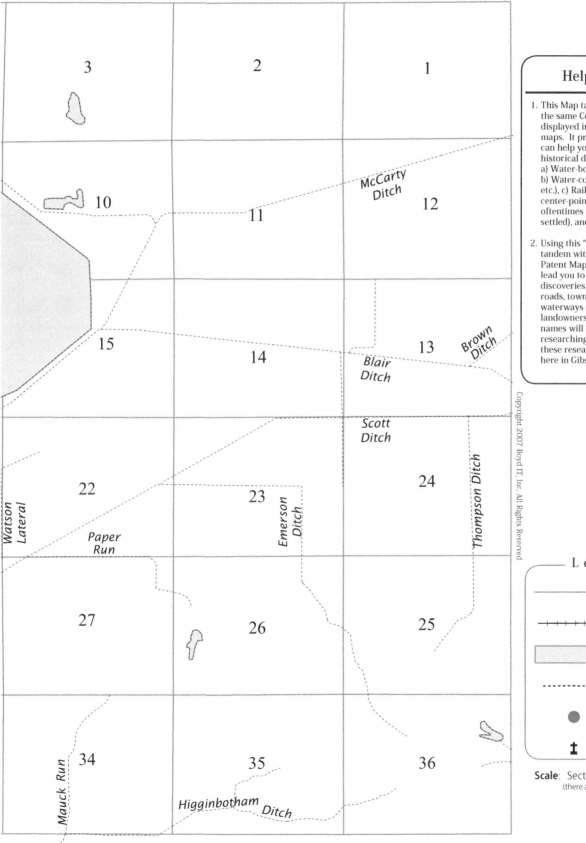

3

2

1

Helpful Hints

1. This Map takes a different look at the same Congressional Township displayed in the preceding two maps. It presents features that can help you better envision the historical development of the area: a) Water-bodies (lakes & ponds), b) Water-courses (rivers, streams, etc.), c) Railroads, d) City/town center-points (where they were oftentimes located when first settled), and e) Cemeteries.

2. Using this "Historical" map in tandem with this Township's Patent Map and Road Map, may lead you to some interesting discoveries. You will often find roads, towns, cemeteries, and waterways are named after nearby landowners: sometimes those names will be the ones you are researching. See how many of these research gems you can find here in Gibson County.

McCarty Ditch

10

11

12

15

14

13

Brown Ditch

Blair Ditch

Scott Ditch

22

23

Emerson Ditch

24

Thompson Ditch

Watson Lateral

Paper Run

27

26

25

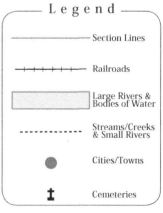

Legend

— Section Lines

—+—+—+— Railroads

▭ Large Rivers & Bodies of Water

------ Streams/Creeks & Small Rivers

● Cities/Towns

✝ Cemeteries

34

Mauck Run

35

36

Higginbotham Ditch

Scale: Section = 1 mile X 1 mile
(there are some exceptions)

Map Group 11: Index to Land Patents

Township 2-South Range 11-West (2nd PM)

After you locate an individual in this Index, take note of the Section and Section Part then proceed to the Land Patent map on the pages immediately following. You should have no difficulty locating the corresponding parcel of land.

The "For More Info" Column will lead you to more information about the underlying Patents. See the *Legend* at right, and the "How to Use this Book" chapter, for more information.

```
                    LEGEND
            "For More Info . . . " column
A = Authority (Legislative Act, See Appendix "A")
B = Block or Lot (location in Section unknown)
C = Cancelled Patent
F = Fractional Section
G = Group  (Multi-Patentee Patent, see Appendix "C")
V = Overlaps another Parcel
R = Re-Issued (Parcel patented more than once)

(A & G items require you to look in the Appendixes referred
to above. All other Letter-designations followed by a number
require you to locate line-items in this index that possess
the ID number found after the letter).
```

ID	Individual in Patent	Sec.	Sec. Part	Date Issued	Other Counties	For More Info . . .
None						

We have not located any Federal Land
Patent records within the
Bureau of Land Management's database for

**Township 2-S Range 11-W
(Map Group 11)**

in **Gibson County.**

Accordingly, we have no
"Patent Map" for this township.

Nonetheless, we have included our
Road and Historical Maps, which
begin on the following page.

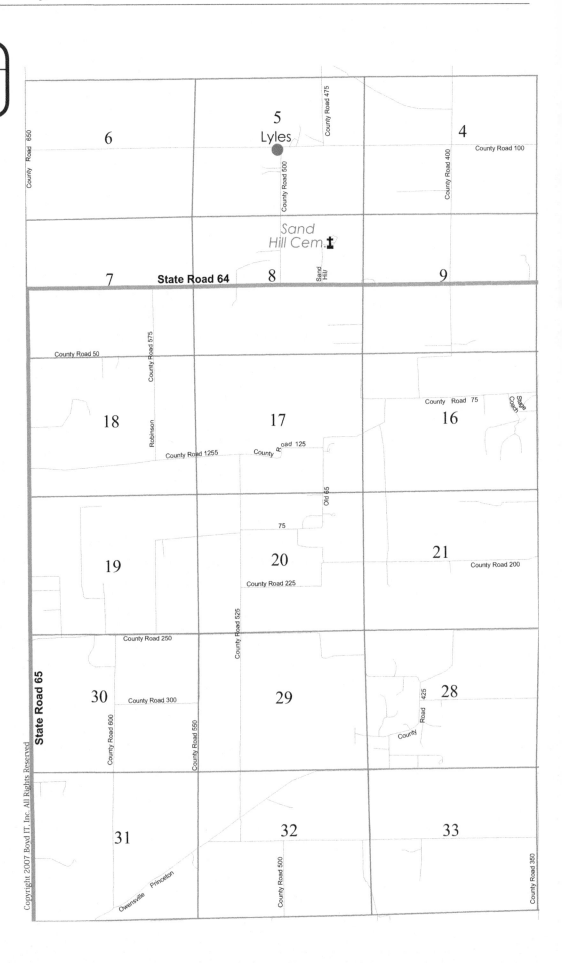

Road Map

T2-S R11-W
2nd PM Meridian

Map Group 11

Cities & Towns
King
Lyles

Cemeteries
Archer Cemetery
Sand Hill Cemetery

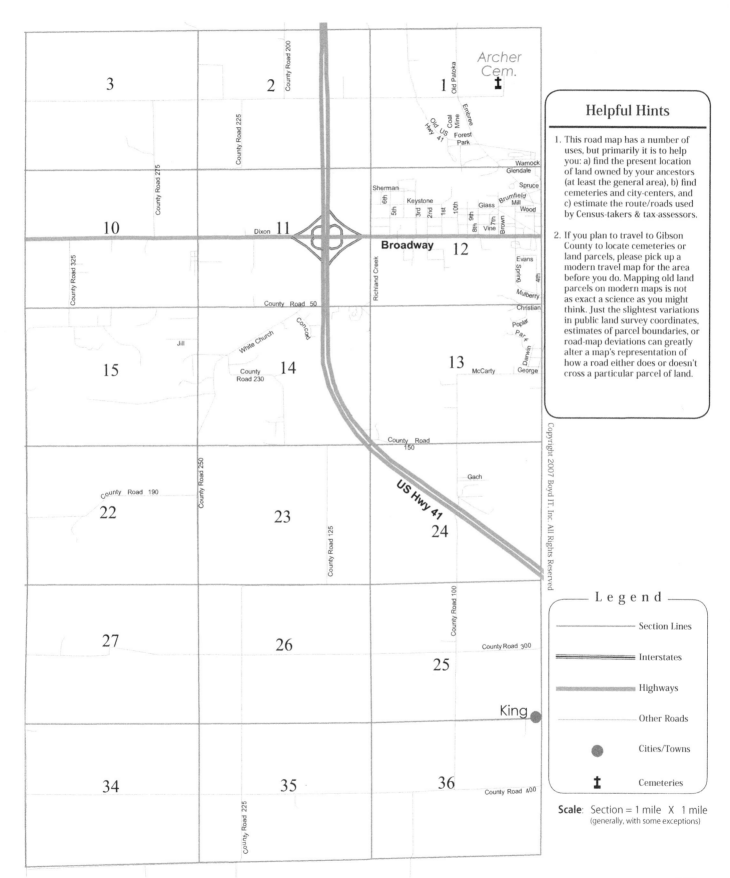

3

2

County Road 200

1

Old Patoka

Archer
Cem.

Embree

Coal
Mine

Old US
Hwy 41

Forest
Park

County Road 225

Wamock

Glendale

Spruce

Sherman

6th
5th

Keystone

3rd
2nd

1st
10th

Glass

Brumfield
Mill

County Road 275

9th

Wood

County Road 325

10

Dixon

11

8th

7th

Brown

Vine

12

Broadway

Evans

Spring

Richland Creek

4th

Mulberry

County Road 50

Christian

Poplar

Park

Jill

White Church

Concord

Darwin

George

15

County
Road 230

14

13

McCarty

County Road 250

County Road 150

County Road 190

Gach

County Road 125

22

23

US Hwy 41

24

County Road 100

27

26

County Road 300

25

King

34

35

36

County Road 400

County Road 225

Copyright 2007 Boyd IT. Inc. All Rights Reserved

Helpful Hints

1. This road map has a number of
uses, but primarily it is to help
you: a) find the present location
of land owned by your ancestors
(at least the general area), b) find
cemeteries and city-centers, and
c) estimate the route/roads used
by Census-takers & tax-assessors.

2. If you plan to travel to Gibson
County to locate cemeteries or
land parcels, please pick up a
modern travel map for the area
before you do. Mapping old land
parcels on modern maps is not
as exact a science as you might
think. Just the slightest variations
in public land survey coordinates,
estimates of parcel boundaries, or
road-map deviations can greatly
alter a map's representation of
how a road either does or doesn't
cross a particular parcel of land.

L e g e n d

———	Section Lines
═══	Interstates
━━━	Highways
———	Other Roads
●	Cities/Towns
†	Cemeteries

Scale: Section = 1 mile X 1 mile
(generally, with some exceptions)

Historical Map

T2-S R11-W
2nd PM Meridian

Map Group 11

Cities & Towns
King
Lyles

Cemeteries
Archer Cemetery
Sand Hill Cemetery

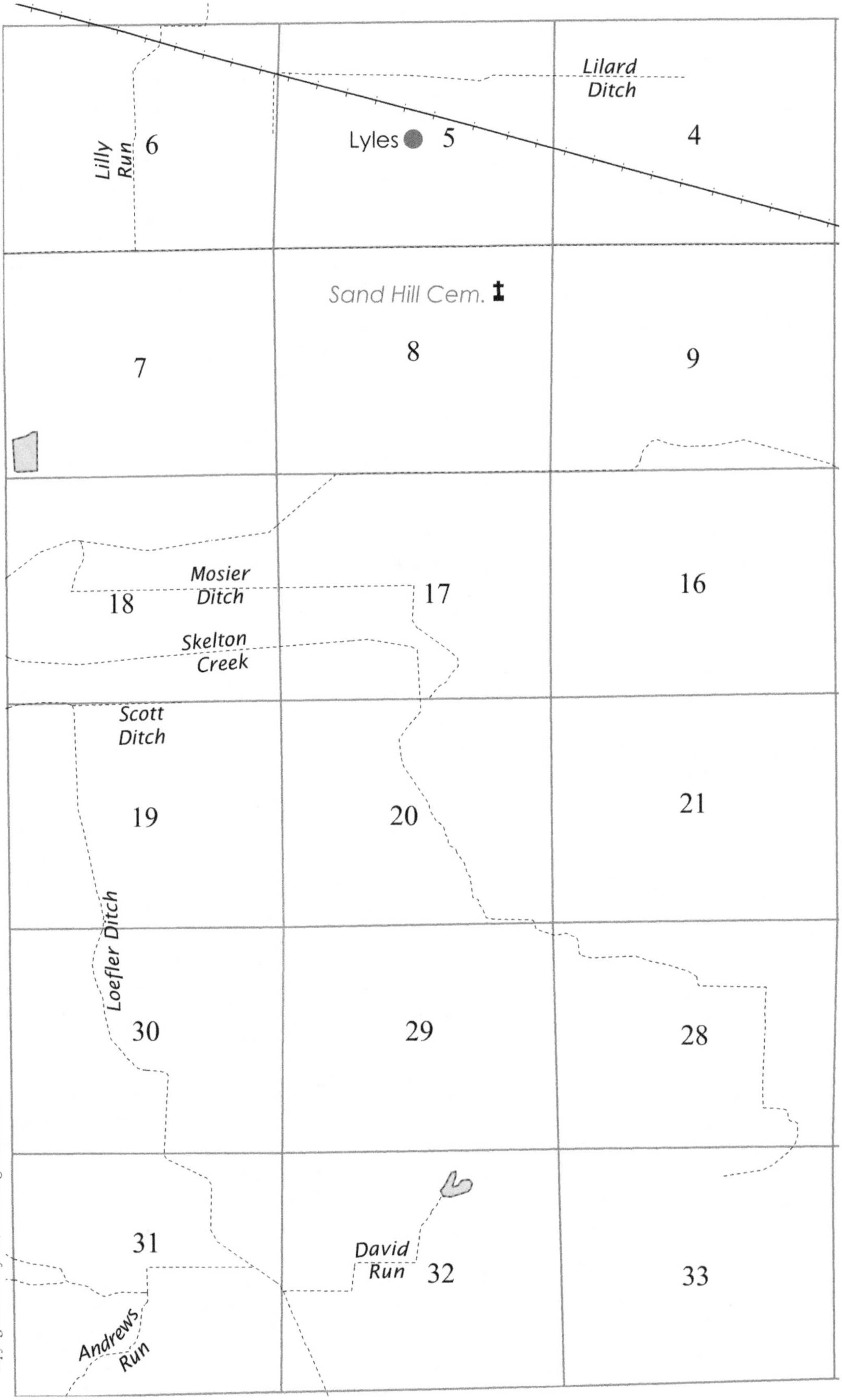

Lilard Ditch

Lilly Run

6

Lyles ● 5

4

Sand Hill Cem. ✝

7

8

9

Mosier Ditch

18

17

16

Skelton Creek

Scott Ditch

19

20

21

Loefler Ditch

30

29

28

31

David Run

32

33

Andrews Run

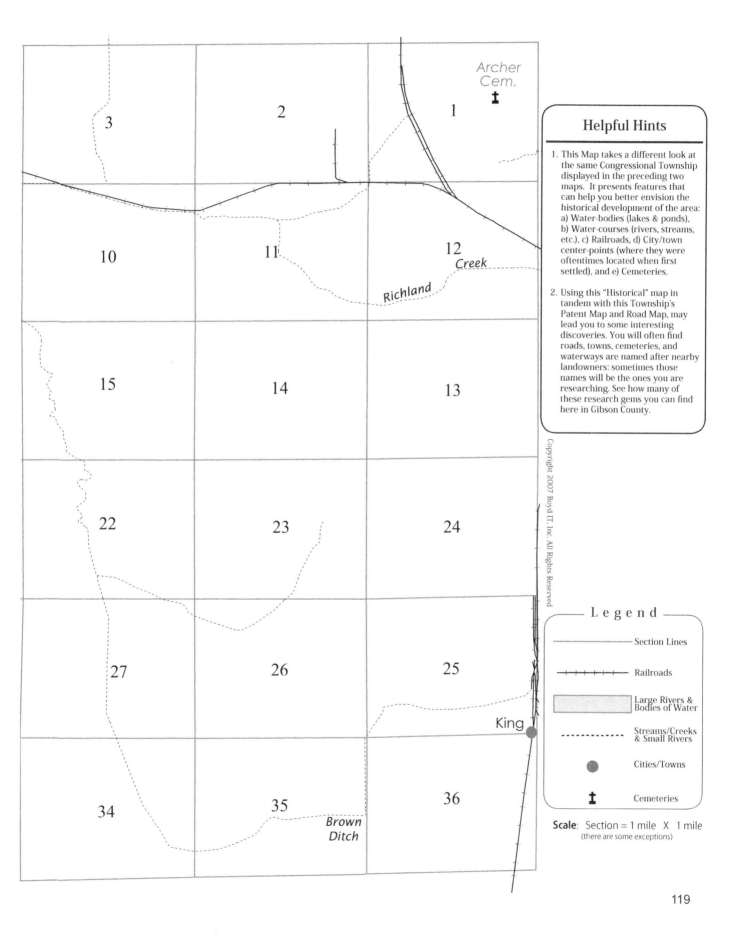

Archer
Cem.

3

2

1

10

11

12

Creek

Richland

15

14

13

22

23

24

27

26

25

King

34

35

36

Brown
Ditch

Helpful Hints

1. This Map takes a different look at
the same Congressional Township
displayed in the preceding two
maps. It presents features that
can help you better envision the
historical development of the area:
a) Water-bodies (lakes & ponds),
b) Water-courses (rivers, streams,
etc.), c) Railroads, d) City/town
center-points (where they were
oftentimes located when first
settled), and e) Cemeteries.

2. Using this "Historical" map in
tandem with this Township's
Patent Map and Road Map, may
lead you to some interesting
discoveries. You will often find
roads, towns, cemeteries, and
waterways are named after nearby
landowners: sometimes those
names will be the ones you are
researching. See how many of
these research gems you can find
here in Gibson County.

Legend

———————— Section Lines

+–+–+–+–+ Railroads

▭ Large Rivers &
Bodies of Water

- - - - - - Streams/Creeks
& Small Rivers

● Cities/Towns

‡ Cemeteries

Scale: Section = 1 mile X 1 mile
(there are some exceptions)

Map Group 12: Index to Land Patents

Township 2-South Range 10-West (2nd PM)

After you locate an individual in this Index, take note of the Section and Section Part then proceed to the Land Patent map on the pages immediately following. You should have no difficulty locating the corresponding parcel of land.

The "For More Info" Column will lead you to more information about the underlying Patents. See the *Legend* at right, and the "How to Use this Book" chapter, for more information.

ID	Individual in Patent	Sec.	Sec. Part	Date Issued	Other Counties	For More Info . . .
701	ASHMEAD, Hosea	22	SESE	1839-02-01		A1
823	BARBER, Sarah	13	SENE	1837-03-30		A1
834	BEAVIS, William	25	E½NE	1837-08-05		A1
744	BETTEOLFF, John L	22	NWSW	1837-08-01		A1
686	BIGHAM, Eli	21	NESE	1835-10-23		A1
687	"	21	SESE	1835-10-28		A1
711	BIGHAM, James	21	W½SE	1835-10-28		A1
745	BITTROLFF, John L	22	SWSW	1835-10-28		A1
812	BOICOURT, Samuel L	12	W½NW	1831-12-31		A1
835	BRAZELTON, William	30	E½NE	1829-04-10		A1
776	BROWN, Joseph R	14	SE	1837-11-07		A1
779	"	24	W½SE	1837-11-07		A1
777	"	24	E½NE	1839-02-01		A1
778	"	24	NWNE	1839-02-01		A1
795	CASBOLT, Polly	11	SWSW	1842-08-01		A1
799	CASBOLT, Robert	11	NESW	1839-08-01		A1
767	CHAMBERS, Joseph	29	SWSW	1835-09-05		A1
792	CHAMBERS, Norman	29	NWSW	1837-03-20		A1
731	CHRISTY, John	3	NENW	1839-08-01		A1
681	CLARK, Cornelius	27	NESW	1837-03-20		A1
790	CLARK, Matthew	11	E½NW	1838-09-07		A1
769	CROW, Joseph G	26	SWNE	1839-08-01		A1
734	DAVIDSON, John	3	E½NE	1835-09-05		A1
732	"	1	SWSE	1837-03-20		A1
733	"	12	NWNE	1837-03-20		A1
775	DAVIDSON, Joseph M	12	NENE	1837-08-05		A1
805	DAVIS, Samuel H	27	SESW	1837-03-20		A1
768	DAVISSON, Joseph	3	W½NE	1835-10-07		A1
713	DRAKE, James P	26	NWSE	1839-08-01		A1
714	"	31	NESW	1839-08-01		A1 C
715	"	34	E½SE	1839-08-01		A1
716	"	35	W½SW	1839-08-01		A1
689	EMBEE, Elisha	26	E½SE	1837-08-01		A1 G12
735	EWING, John	15	E½NW	1838-09-01		A1 G16
736	"	15	NE	1838-09-01		A1 G16
737	"	15	NWSE	1838-09-01		A1 G16
704	FERRIS, Isaac	1	NW	1819-02-03		A2
705	"	28	SW	1819-10-13		A2
706	"	32	NE	1819-10-13		A2
738	FISHER, John	27	NWNW	1839-08-01		A1
796	FISHER, Purnell	9	SENW	1835-09-10		A1
739	FRENCH, John	33	SWSW	1839-08-01		A1
824	GEISE, Sophia	27	NENW	1839-08-01		A1
836	GUIREY, William G	12	SWSE	1841-05-25		A1
729	HALL, Job H	35	NWNE	1839-02-01		A1
730	"	35	SESW	1839-02-01		A1

ID	Individual in Patent	Sec.	Sec. Part	Date Issued	Other Counties	For More Info . . .
810	HALL, Samuel	4	E½SE	1831-01-04		A1
811	" "	4	NWSE	1835-09-05		A1
689	" "	26	E½SE	1837-08-01		A1 G12
742	HARGROVE, John	23	SWNE	1839-08-01		A1
791	HARGROVE, Nicholas J	26	SENE	1837-08-05		A1
743	HARTEN, John K	14	SENW	1849-04-10		A1
712	HARTIN, James	23	NENE	1839-08-01		A1
783	HARTIN, Margaret	1	NWSE	1839-02-01		A1
690	HASSELBRINK, Frederick	27	NWSW	1839-08-01		A1
691	" "	28	NESE	1839-08-01		A1
721	HOGE, James W	21	NENW	1839-02-01		A1
837	HOGUE, William H	21	NWSW	1835-10-07		A1
699	HOPKINS, Henry	7	SW	1914-08-27		A1
852	HOWE, Willis	4	SWSE	1838-09-01		A1 G24
707	HUDSPETH, Isaac	31	E½NE	1831-12-31		A1
708	" "	31	W½NE	1831-12-31		A1
693	HUMPHREYS, George	2	SWNE	1835-10-07		A1
798	HUSSEY, Richard	12	W½SW	1831-05-21		A1
797	" "	12	NESW	1837-03-30		A1
854	HUSSEY, Zachariah	11	SESE	1839-08-01		A1
674	HUTHER, Adam	27	W½NE	1835-10-28		A1
692	HUTHER, Frederick	22	SWSE	1835-10-28		A1
830	JOHNSTON, Thomas	12	SESE	1845-05-01		A1
800	KINGSBURY, Robert	30	W½NE	1829-04-10		A1
852	KIRKMAN, Joseph Jackson	4	SWSE	1838-09-01		A1 G24
700	KLUSMANN, Henry	28	E½NE	1840-10-01		A1
747	LAGOW, John	9	SESE	1839-02-01		A1
746	" "	2	NWNE	1850-12-10		A1
813	LAWRENCE, Samuel	2	W½SE	1835-10-15		A1
814	" "	24	N½NW	1837-03-20		A1
838	LAWRENCE, William	1	E½SE	1835-09-10		A1
840	" "	12	SENW	1837-03-20		A1
839	" "	12	NENW	1837-08-05		A1
841	LOSE, William	23	NWSW	1838-09-01		A1
842	MARTIN, William	12	NESE	1839-02-01		A1
843	" "	12	SESW	1839-02-01		A1
760	MAXAM, John S	22	SENE	1835-10-28		A1
680	MCCARTY, Chaney	33	SWSE	1837-08-05		A1
748	MCCRAY, John	25	W½NW	1829-05-01		A1
749	" "	26	NENE	1837-08-05		A1
784	MCHISSICK, Martin	12	NWSE	1839-02-01		A1
785	" "	12	SWNE	1839-02-01		A1
676	MCWILLIAMS, Alexander	10	E½SW	1839-02-01		A1
677	" "	10	SWSE	1839-02-01		A1
678	" "	10	SWSW	1839-12-04		A1
684	MCWILLIAMS, David C	10	NWSE	1838-09-05		A1
751	MCWILLIAMS, John	9	NESE	1835-10-23		A1
750	" "	10	NWSW	1837-11-07		A1
735	MILBURN, Robert	15	E½NW	1838-09-01		A1 G16
736	" "	15	NE	1838-09-01		A1 G16
737	" "	15	NWSE	1838-09-01		A1 G16
803	" "	26	W½NW	1840-10-01		A1
815	MITCHELL, Samuel	27	SWSW	1835-10-23		A1
816	" "	28	SESE	1835-10-23		A1
825	MITCHELL, Stacy	32	E½SE	1823-07-24		A1
826	" "	33	NWSE	1835-10-07		A1
817	MURPHEY, Samuel	13	SWNE	1835-10-01		A1
702	MURPHY, Hugh	14	NENW	1841-05-25		A1
698	ONEAL, Harvey	21	SENW	1835-10-28		A1
754	ORR, John	10	E½NW	1835-10-07		A1
756	" "	20	W½SE	1835-10-07		A1
755	" "	10	E½SE	1840-10-01		A1
757	" "	28	NW	1840-10-01		A1
758	" "	28	W½NE	1840-10-01		A1
759	" "	29	E½NE	1840-10-01		A1
703	PARKINSON, Hugh	29	W½NE	1839-08-01		A1
685	PINNEY, Edwin	15	E½SE	1839-08-01		A1
694	PRATT, George W	26	SW	1839-08-01		A1 G31
695	" "	35	W½NW	1839-08-01		A1 G31
741	RATZE, John G	32	NWSE	1837-03-18		A1
740	" "	28	SWSE	1837-08-01		A1
774	REAVIS, Joseph L	25	NWNE	1838-09-01		A1
773	" "	25	NESW	1839-08-01		A1

ID	Individual in Patent	Sec.	Sec. Part	Date Issued	Other Counties	For More Info . . .
786	REAVIS, Martin	36	SESE	1837-11-07		A1
829	REAVIS, Tabitha	25	SWNE	1837-08-01		A1
828	" "	25	SESW	1839-08-01		A1
846	REAVIS, William	36	SWSE	1839-08-01		A1
847	" "	23	E½SE	1840-10-01		A1 G32
844	" "	36	NWNE	1852-07-01		A1
845	" "	36	SESW	1852-07-01		A1
787	RENNIS, Martin	36	NESE	1838-09-07		A1
675	REVES, Alexander D	25	SWSW	1839-08-01		A1
831	REVES, Tobitha	25	NWSW	1837-08-01		A1
709	REYNOLDS, Isaac	15	SWSW	1838-09-01		A1
770	REYNOLDS, Joseph H	20	NESE	1835-10-01		A1
771	" "	20	SESE	1837-03-20		A1
772	" "	23	W½SE	1839-08-01		A1
847	" "	23	E½SE	1840-10-01		A1 G32
782	ROBB, Lewis	22	NENE	1839-02-01		A1
848	ROWE, William	11	NWSW	1839-08-01		A1
780	RUTLEDGE, Joseph	24	SW	1839-02-01		A1
788	SCHMOLL, Martin	23	E½SW	1839-08-01		A1
789	" "	23	SWSW	1839-08-01		A1
806	SHANNON, Samuel H	21	W½NE	1835-10-01		A1
808	" "	22	SWNW	1835-10-23		A1
807	" "	22	NWNW	1837-08-01		A1
809	" "	27	SESE	1839-02-01		A1
717	SKELTON, James	35	E½NE	1839-08-01		A1
793	SMITH, Nuttall	27	NENE	1835-10-23		A1
832	SMITH, Wiatt	23	NWNE	1838-09-01		A1
833	SMITH, Wiley	27	SENE	1837-11-07		A1
853	SMITH, Wyett	21	NESW	1835-10-07		A1
682	SPENCER, Daniel	24	SENW	1835-10-15		A1
683	" "	24	SWNE	1837-08-01		A1
781	SPENCER, Lemuel T	24	SWNW	1837-08-01		A1
761	SPROWL, John	10	SENE	1838-09-01		A1
752	SPROWL, John O	10	NENE	1837-03-18		A1
753	" "	11	W½NW	1838-09-01		A1
762	STERNS, John	21	S½SW	1838-09-01		A1
718	STORMON, James	3	NESW	1835-09-05		A1
719	" "	3	SWSW	1835-09-05		A1
720	STORMONT, James	3	SESW	1837-08-01		A1
804	STORMONT, Robert	9	W½SE	1835-10-23		A1
849	STORMONT, William	9	NENW	1835-10-23		A1
710	STRICKLAND, Isaac	26	SWSE	1839-02-01		A1
827	STRICKLAND, Stephen	34	E½NW	1831-06-01		A1
694	SULLIVAN, William	26	SW	1839-08-01		A1 G31
695	" "	35	W½NW	1839-08-01		A1 G31
694	THACHER, George M	26	SW	1839-08-01		A1 G31
695	" "	35	W½NW	1839-08-01		A1 G31
763	WALKER, John T	26	E½NW	1848-05-10		A1
764	" "	26	NWNE	1848-05-10		A1
696	WELLER, George	27	SENW	1838-09-01		A1
697	" "	27	SWNW	1838-09-01		A1
722	WHEELER, James	33	NWSW	1837-03-18		A1
766	WHEELER, Johnson	35	SESE	1839-02-01		A1
765	" "	28	NWSE	1839-08-01		A1
794	WHEELER, Payton	32	SWSE	1837-08-01		A1
818	WHEELER, Samuel	34	NWNW	1837-03-20		A1
819	" "	34	SWNW	1837-03-20		A1
679	WHITSETT, Benjamin	3	NWSW	1837-11-07		A1
820	WHITSETT, Samuel	3	SENW	1839-02-01		A1
822	WHITSITT, Samuel	4	W½NE	1830-12-02		A1 C
821	" "	13	NWNE	1848-05-10		A1
688	WILLIAMS, Eli	23	SENE	1840-10-01		A1
728	WILLIAMS, Jese L	35	E½NW	1839-02-01		A1
723	WILSON, James	13	NESW	1835-10-01		A1
724	" "	13	SESW	1837-03-20		A1
801	WILSON, Robert M	13	E½SE	1835-10-23		A1
802	" "	13	SWSE	1837-03-20		A1
850	WILSON, William	13	NWSE	1835-10-23		A1
726	WOOD, James	22	NWSE	1835-10-28		A1
725	" "	22	NESE	1837-03-18		A1
727	" "	27	W½SE	1837-08-01		A1
851	WOOD, William	27	NESE	1838-09-01		A1

Patent Map

T2-S R10-W
2nd PM Meridian

Map Group 12

Township Statistics

Parcels Mapped	:	181
Number of Patents	:	170
Number of Individuals	:	124
Patentees Identified	:	122
Number of Surnames	:	88
Multi-Patentee Parcels	:	8
Oldest Patent Date	:	2/3/1819
Most Recent Patent	:	8/27/1914
Block/Lot Parcels	:	0
Parcels Re - Issued	:	0
Parcels that Overlap	:	0
Cities and Towns	:	3
Cemeteries	:	4

6

5

4

WHITSITT
Samuel
1830

HALL
Samuel
1835

HALL
Samuel
1831

HOWE [24]
Willis
1838

7

HOPKINS
Henry
1914

8

9

STORMONT
William
1835

FISHER
Purnell
1835

MCWILLIAMS
John
1835

STORMONT
Robert
1835

LAGOW
John
1839

18

17

16

19

20

21

HOGE
James W
1839

SHANNON
Samuel H
1835

ONEAL
Harvey
1835

ORR
John
1835

REYNOLDS
Joseph H
1835

HOGUE
William H
1835

SMITH
Wyett
1835

BIGHAM
James
1835

BIGHAM
Eli
1835

REYNOLDS
Joseph H
1837

STERNS
John
1838

BIGHAM
Eli
1835

30

29

28

KINGSBURY
Robert
1829

BRAZELTON
William
1829

CHAMBERS
Norman
1837

CHAMBERS
Joseph
1835

PARKINSON
Hugh
1839

ORR
John
1840

ORR
John
1840

ORR
John
1840

KLUSMANN
Henry
1840

WHEELER
Johnson
1839

HASSELBRINK
Frederick
1839

FERRIS
Isaac
1819

RATZE
John G
1837

MITCHELL
Samuel
1835

31

32

33

HUDSPETH
Isaac
1831

HUDSPETH
Isaac
1831

DRAKE
James P
1839

FERRIS
Isaac
1819

RATZE
John G
1837

WHEELER
Payton
1837

MITCHELL
Stacy
1823

WHEELER
James
1837

FRENCH
John
1839

MITCHELL
Stacy
1835

MCCARTY
Chaney
1837

Section 3
CHRISTY John 1839
DAVISSON Joseph 1835
DAVIDSON John 1835
WHITSETT Samuel 1839
WHITSETT Benjamin 1837
STORMON James 1835
STORMON James 1835
STORMONT James 1837
3

Section 2
LAGOW John 1850
HUMPHREYS George 1835
LAWRENCE Samuel 1835
2

Section 1
FERRIS Isaac 1819
HARTIN Margaret 1839
LAWRENCE William 1835
DAVIDSON John 1837
1

Section 10
ORR John 1835
SPROWL John O 1837
SPROWL John 1838
MCWILLIAMS John 1837
MCWILLIAMS David C 1838
MCWILLIAMS Alexander 1839
ORR John 1840
MCWILLIAMS Alexander 1839
MCWILLIAMS Alexander 1839
10

Section 11
SPROWL John O 1838
CLARK Matthew 1838
ROWE William 1839
CASBOLT Robert 1839
CASBOLT Polly 1842
HUSSEY Zachariah 1839
11

Section 12
BOICOURT Samuel L 1831
LAWRENCE William 1837
DAVIDSON John 1837
DAVIDSON Joseph M 1837
LAWRENCE William 1837
MCHISSICK Martin 1839
HUSSEY Richard 1831
HUSSEY Richard 1837
MCHISSICK Martin 1839
MARTIN William 1837
MARTIN William 1839
GUIREY William G 1841
JOHNSTON Thomas 1845
12

Section 15
EWING [16] John 1838
EWING [16] John 1838
EWING [16] John 1838
PINNEY Edwin 1839
REYNOLDS Isaac 1838
15

Section 14
MURPHY Hugh 1841
HARTEN John K 1849
BROWN Joseph R 1837
14

Section 13
WHITSITT Samuel 1848
MURPHEY Samuel 1835
BARBER Sarah 1837
WILSON James 1835
WILSON William 1835
WILSON James 1837
WILSON Robert M 1837
WILSON Robert M 1835
13

Section 22
SHANNON Samuel H 1837
SHANNON Samuel H 1835
ROBB Lewis 1839
MAXAM John S 1835
BETTEOLFF John L 1837
BITTROLFF John L 1835
WOOD James 1835
WOOD James 1837
HUTHER Frederick 1835
ASHMEAD Hosea 1839
22

Section 23
LOSE William 1838
SCHMOLL Martin 1839
SCHMOLL Martin 1839
SMITH Wiatt 1838
HARGROVE John 1839
HARTIN James 1839
WILLIAMS Eli 1840
REYNOLDS Joseph H 1839
REAVIS [32] William 1840
23

Section 24
LAWRENCE Samuel 1837
SPENCER Lemuel T 1837
SPENCER Daniel 1835
SPENCER Daniel 1837
RUTLEDGE Joseph 1839
BROWN Joseph R 1839
BROWN Joseph R 1839
BROWN Joseph R 1837
24

Section 27
FISHER John 1839
GEISE Sophia 1839
SMITH Nuttall 1835
HUTHER Adam 1835
WELLER George 1838
WELLER George 1838
SMITH Wiley 1837
HASSELBRINK Frederick 1839
CLARK Cornelius 1837
WOOD William 1838
MITCHELL Samuel 1835
DAVIS Samuel H 1837
WOOD James 1837
SHANNON Samuel H 1839
27

Section 26
MILBURN Robert 1840
WALKER John T 1848
WALKER John T 1848
CROW Joseph G 1839
HARGROVE Nicholas J 1837
PRATT [31] George W 1839
DRAKE James P 1839
EMBEE [12]
STRICKLAND Isaac 1839
Elisha 1837
26

Section 25
MCCRAY John 1837
MCCRAY John 1829
REAVIS Joseph L 1838
REAVIS Tabitha 1837
BEAVIS William 1837
REVES Tobitha 1837
REAVIS Joseph L 1839
REVES Alexander D 1839
REAVIS Tabitha 1839
25

Section 34
WHEELER Samuel 1837
STRICKLAND Stephen 1831
WHEELER Samuel 1837
34

Section 35
PRATT [31] George W 1839
HALL Job H 1839
SKELTON James 1839
WILLIAMS Jese L 1839
DRAKE James P 1839
HALL Job H 1839
WHEELER Johnson 1839
35

Section 36
REAVIS William 1852
RENNIS Martin 1838
REAVIS William 1852
REAVIS William 1839
REAVIS Martin 1837
36

Legend
—— Patent Boundary
━━ Section Boundary
No Patents Found (or Outside County)
1., 2., 3., ... Lot Numbers (when beside a name)
[ ] Group Number (see Appendix "C")

Scale: Section = 1 mile X 1 mile (generally, with some exceptions)

Road Map

T2-S R10-W
2nd PM Meridian

Map Group 12

Cities & Towns
Baldwin Heights
Douglas
Princeton

Cemeteries
Maple Hill Cemetery
Odd Fellows Cemetery
Saint Josephs Cemetery
Warnock Cemetery

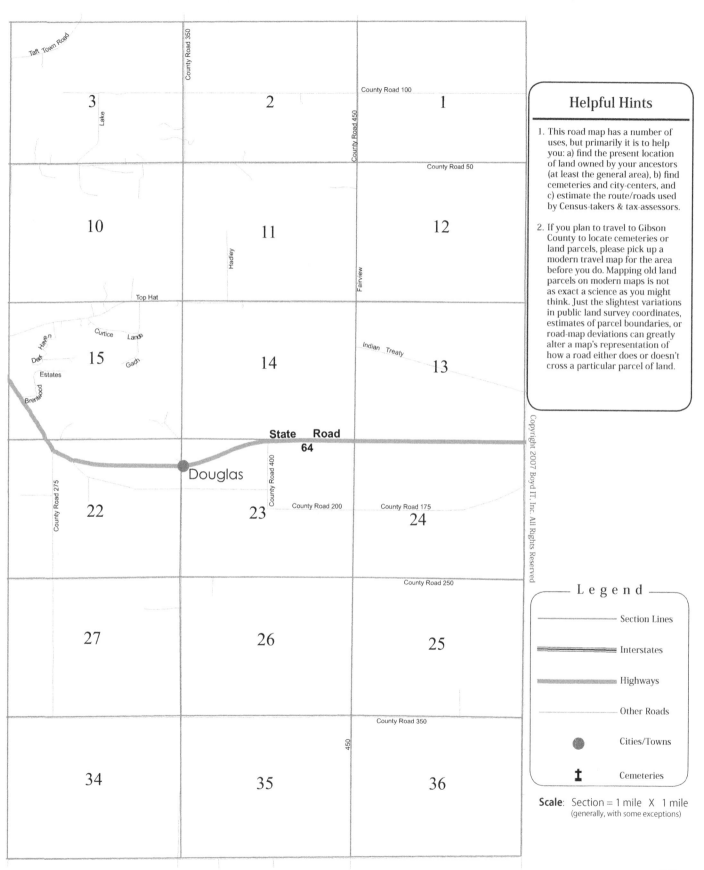

Helpful Hints

1. This road map has a number of uses, but primarily it is to help you: a) find the present location of land owned by your ancestors (at least the general area), b) find cemeteries and city-centers, and c) estimate the route/roads used by Census-takers & tax-assessors.

2. If you plan to travel to Gibson County to locate cemeteries or land parcels, please pick up a modern travel map for the area before you do. Mapping old land parcels on modern maps is not as exact a science as you might think. Just the slightest variations in public land survey coordinates, estimates of parcel boundaries, or road-map deviations can greatly alter a map's representation of how a road either does or doesn't cross a particular parcel of land.

Legend

— Section Lines

═ Interstates

━ Highways

— Other Roads

● Cities/Towns

✝ Cemeteries

Scale: Section = 1 mile X 1 mile
(generally, with some exceptions)

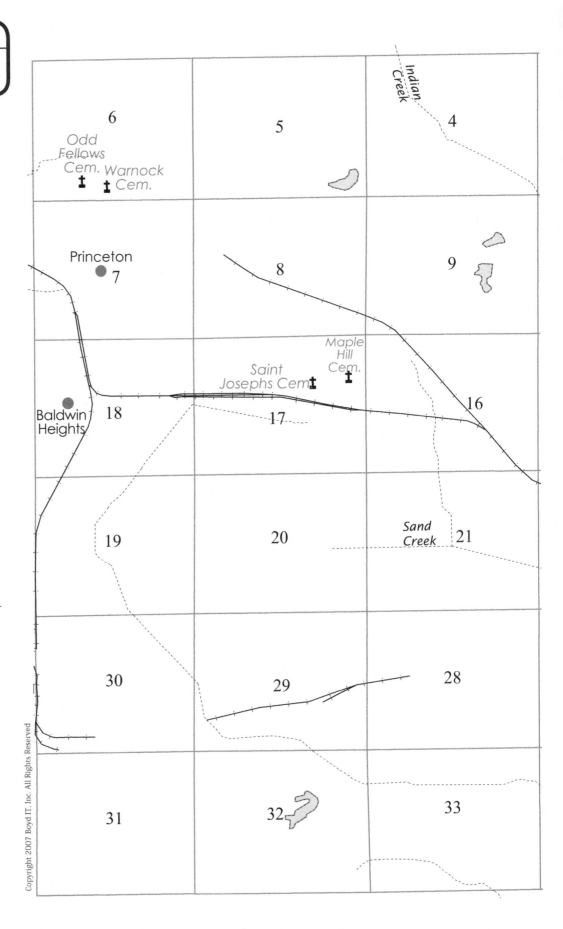

Historical Map

T2-S R10-W
2nd PM Meridian

Map Group 12

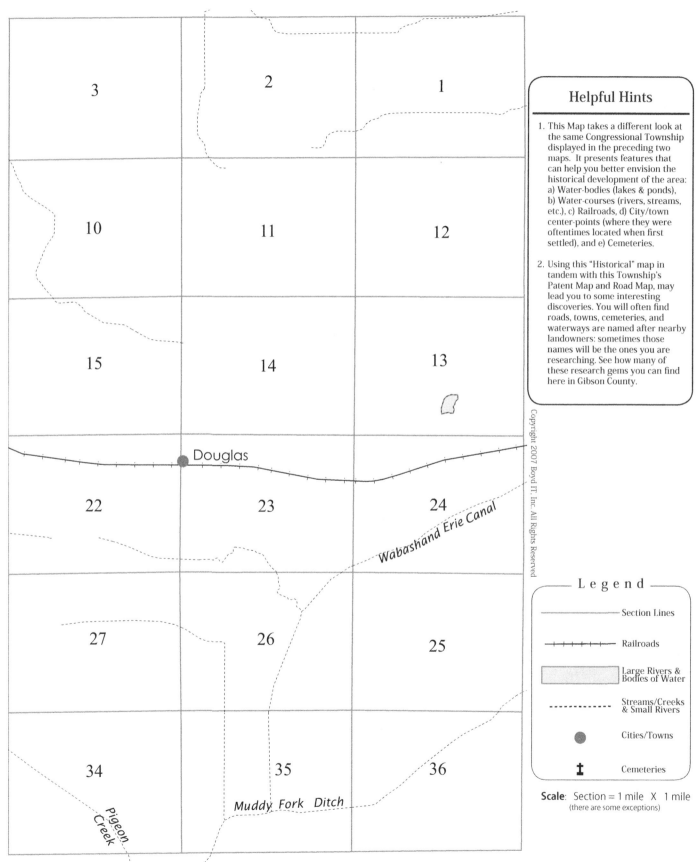

3

2

1

10

11

12

15

14

13

Helpful Hints

1. This Map takes a different look at the same Congressional Township displayed in the preceding two maps. It presents features that can help you better envision the historical development of the area: a) Water-bodies (lakes & ponds), b) Water-courses (rivers, streams, etc.), c) Railroads, d) City/town center-points (where they were oftentimes located when first settled), and e) Cemeteries.

2. Using this "Historical" map in tandem with this Township's Patent Map and Road Map, may lead you to some interesting discoveries. You will often find roads, towns, cemeteries, and waterways are named after nearby landowners: sometimes those names will be the ones you are researching. See how many of these research gems you can find here in Gibson County.

Douglas

22

23

24

Wabash and Erie Canal

27

26

25

34

35

36

Muddy Fork Ditch

Pigeon Creek

L e g e n d

————————	Section Lines
+++++++	Railroads
▭	Large Rivers & Bodies of Water
- - - - - - -	Streams/Creeks & Small Rivers
●	Cities/Towns
✝	Cemeteries

Scale: Section = 1 mile X 1 mile
(there are some exceptions)

Map Group 13: Index to Land Patents

Township 2-South Range 9-West (2nd PM)

After you locate an individual in this Index, take note of the Section and Section Part then proceed to the Land Patent map on the pages immediately following. You should have no difficulty locating the corresponding parcel of land.

The "For More Info" Column will lead you to more information about the underlying Patents. See the *Legend* at right, and the "How to Use this Book" chapter, for more information.

```
┌─────────────────────────────────────────────────────┐
│                    LEGEND                            │
│        "For More Info . . . " column                 │
│ ─────────────────────────────────────────────────── │
│ A = Authority (Legislative Act, See Appendix "A")    │
│ B = Block or Lot (location in Section unknown)       │
│ C = Cancelled Patent                                 │
│ F = Fractional Section                               │
│ G = Group  (Multi-Patentee Patent, see Appendix "C") │
│ V = Overlaps another Parcel                          │
│ R = Re-Issued (Parcel patented more than once)       │
│                                                      │
│ (A & G items require you to look in the Appendixes referred │
│ to above. All other Letter-designations followed by a number │
│ require you to locate line-items in this index that possess  │
│ the ID number found after the letter).               │
└─────────────────────────────────────────────────────┘
```

ID	Individual in Patent	Sec.	Sec. Part	Date Issued	Other Counties	For More Info . . .
872	BARBER, David	32	NWNW	1839-02-01		A1
966	BARBER, Nancy	7	SWSE	1838-09-01		A1
948	BARRETT, John W	34	NWNW	1839-02-01		A1
962	BARRETT, Lucinda	28	NESE	1839-08-01		A1
961	" "	27	SWSW	1841-08-10		A1
978	BARRETT, Samuel G	28	SENE	1852-10-01		A1
1003	BARRETT, William	33	NENE	1835-10-07		A1
1002	" "	28	SESE	1837-08-05		A1
1005	BARRETT, William C	27	NWSW	1850-10-01		A1
906	BEASLEY, Hardy	19	E½SE	1835-10-28		A1
991	BEASLEY, Thomas	29	W½SE	1839-02-01		A1
992	" "	29	W½SW	1839-02-01		A1
993	" "	32	NWNE	1840-10-01		A1
1004	BEAVIS, William	19	W½NW	1837-08-05		A1
877	BIGHAM, Eli	10	E½SE	1839-08-01		A1
896	BORLAND, Francis	12	SW	1839-08-01		A1
898	" "	13	E½SW	1839-08-01		A1
899	" "	13	NW	1839-08-01		A1
900	" "	13	W½NE	1839-08-01		A1
901	" "	13	W½SE	1839-08-01		A1
902	" "	13	W½SW	1839-08-01		A1
895	" "	11	E½NE	1840-10-01		A1
897	" "	12	W½NW	1840-10-01		A1
870	BOSWELL, Craven	4	SESW	1835-10-07		A1
967	BREEDLOVE, Nathan	28	NENW	1840-10-01		A1
869	BROWN, Commodore P	20	NWSE	1850-12-10		A1
958	BROWN, Joseph R	18	SWSE	1837-11-07		A1
996	BURCHFIELD, Thomas	19	S½NE	1835-10-28		A1 C R928
994	" "	17	SWSW	1837-03-15		A1
995	" "	19	NWSE	1837-08-05		A1
925	COCKRUM, James W	13	E½NE	1837-08-05		A1
924	" "	1	E½SE	1837-11-07		A1
953	COCKRUM, Jordan P	30	S½SE	1839-02-01		A1
907	COLEMAN, Henry	24	NENW	1850-10-01		A1
908	COLEMAN, Henry F	9	NENW	1835-10-01		A1
879	COULTER, Elijah	36	E½SE	1839-08-01		A1
934	COX, John	21	SWSW	1835-10-07		A1
933	" "	21	NWSW	1837-11-07		A1
950	CURRY, Jonathan	18	NWSE	1837-03-30		A1
949	" "	18	NESE	1838-09-01		A1
951	" "	28	E½SW	1839-02-01		A1
952	" "	28	W½SE	1839-02-01		A1
935	DAVIS, John	29	NENW	1841-05-25		A1
910	DEVIN, James	29	E½SW	1831-12-31		A1
911	" "	31	W½NE	1831-12-31		A1
857	DILL, Alexander	17	SENE	1849-05-30		A1

ID	Individual in Patent	Sec.	Sec. Part	Date Issued	Other Counties	For More Info . . .
988	DILL, Solomon	14	SENE	1848-05-01		A1
989	" "	2	SESW	1852-07-01	Pike	A1
1007	DILL, William	26	NWNW	1848-05-01		A1
1008	" "	26	SWNW	1849-05-30		A1
1006	" "	26	NENW	1850-12-10		A1
926	DORRELL, James W	19	NENE	1835-10-07		A1
927	" "	19	NWNE	1835-10-07		A1
928	" "	19	S½NE	1838-11-28		A1 R996
913	DOWNEY, James M	21	N½NW	1849-04-10		A1
954	DUFF, Joseph M	21	SENW	1852-07-01		A1
858	DUNCAN, Andrew	21	E½SW	1840-10-01		A1
859	" "	21	SWNW	1840-10-01		A1
1031	DUNCAN, William S	14	SESE	1841-05-25		A1
1032	" "	24	NWNW	1841-05-25		A1
984	EGGLESTON, Seth C	17	NESW	1839-08-01		A1
985	" "	17	SESW	1839-08-01		A1
868	ELWYNE, Charles J	14	NWNE	1848-07-01		A1
882	EMBREE, Elisha	11	E½SW	1837-11-07		A1
883	" "	11	W½SE	1837-11-07		A1
884	" "	9	E½SW	1837-11-07		A1
885	" "	9	W½SE	1837-11-07		A1
881	" "	10	SWNE	1839-08-01		A1
1009	EMBREE, William	6	W½NW	1838-09-07		A1
888	FARMER, Farris	22	SENE	1848-05-01		A1
892	FARMER, Fleming	4	SWSW	1835-10-01		A1
891	" "	4	NESW	1840-10-01		A1
889	" "	10	NWSW	1848-05-10		A1
890	" "	10	SWSW	1850-12-10		A1
893	FARMER, Forris	14	SWSW	1841-05-25		A1
894	" "	22	NENE	1850-12-10		A1
937	FARMER, John	34	NESE	1837-03-20		A1
938	" "	34	NWSE	1839-02-01		A1
939	" "	35	W½NW	1839-08-01		A1
936	" "	34	E½NW	1841-05-25		A1
1010	FARMER, William	4	NWSW	1837-03-18		A1
912	FINNEY, James	9	NWSW	1840-10-01		A1
1011	FOSTER, William	19	E½NW	1837-08-01		A1
1012	" "	19	S½SW	1837-08-01		A1
1015	GRIFFITH, William	11	SESE	1842-08-01		A1
1016	" "	14	NENE	1842-08-01		A1
861	GUDGEL, Andrew	25	W½SW	1848-07-01		A1
860	" "	25	NESW	1850-12-10		A1
979	HALL, Samuel	34	NESW	1849-02-01		A1
1018	HAMILTON, William	28	W½NW	1840-10-01		A1
1019	" "	29	E½NE	1840-10-01		A1
856	HARPER, Adam B	35	W½NE	1839-08-01		A1
880	HARPER, Elijah W	35	NENE	1850-10-01		A1 R878
940	HARPER, John	11	NWNW	1840-10-01		A1
972	HARPER, Robert	26	SWNE	1839-02-01		A1
970	" "	23	W½SW	1839-08-01		A1
971	" "	26	SENE	1839-08-01		A1 V931
998	HARPER, Thomas	11	SENW	1841-05-25		A1
999	" "	11	SWNE	1850-10-01		A1
1020	HARPER, William	26	SENW	1850-12-10		A1
1017	HARPER, William H	36	SENW	1839-08-01		A1
904	HEDRICK, George	30	SENE	1856-06-03		A1
941	HOGE, John	17	W½NE	1839-08-01		A1
905	HUMPHREYS, George	6	SESW	1837-03-30		A1
1021	JARREL, William	14	NESE	1841-05-25		A1
875	JOHNSON, David	5	SWNE	1835-10-07		A1
874	" "	5	NESW	1837-03-18		A1
873	" "	5	E½NW	1841-05-25		A1
876	" "	5	W½NW	1850-12-10		A1
960	JOHNSON, Lewis	7	SESE	1835-09-10		A1
1022	KEERTZ, William	9	SWNE	1856-06-03		A1
931	KILLPATRICK, John B	26	E½NE	1841-05-25		A1 V971
1023	LATHAN, William	8	E½SE	1837-08-05		A1
1024	LAWRENCE, William	6	W½SW	1835-09-10		A1
986	LEMASTERS, Simeon	7	NWNE	1837-08-01		A1
987	" "	8	E½SW	1840-10-01		A1
909	LOVEBAUGH, Jacob	28	5	1838-09-01		A1
997	LOYD, Thomas C	31	SWSW	1837-08-01		A1
903	MANNING, Francis M	20	SWSE	1850-12-10		A1

ID	Individual in Patent	Sec.	Sec. Part	Date Issued	Other Counties	For More Info . . .
1025	MANNING, William	21	SWNE	1839-08-01		A1
916	MCCLELLAN, James	8	E½NE	1840-10-01		A1
917	"	"	8	SWNE	1840-10-01		A1
915	"	"	7	NESE	1852-07-01		A1
955	MCCLELLAN, Joseph	18	NE	1835-10-15		A1
956	"	"	8	SWSW	1838-09-07		A1
918	MCCONELL, James	32	SESE	1841-05-25		A1
943	MCCONNEL, John	18	SWSW	1837-03-18		A1
942	"	"	18	E½SW	1837-03-20		A1
973	MCCONNELL, Robert	36	E½SW	1838-09-05		A1
974	"	"	36	W½SE	1838-09-05		A1
878	MCCULLOCH, Elihu	35	NENE	1839-02-01		A1 R880
930	MCCULLOCH, Jane P	35	E½SE	1839-02-01		A1
963	MCCULLOCH, Margaret	36	W½SW	1839-02-01		A1
980	MCDILL, Samuel	26	SW	1839-08-01		A1
871	MILLS, Daniel	18	NWSW	1835-09-10		A1
864	MINIS, Calvin	14	NWSE	1845-06-01		A1
865	"	"	14	SWNE	1849-05-26		A1 R866
866	"	"	14	SWNE	1849-11-12		A1 R865
867	MINNIS, Calvin	23	NESW	1841-05-25		A1
919	MINNIS, James	23	SWNW	1841-05-25		A1
1000	MINNIS, Thomas	23	SENW	1838-09-07		A1
981	MOORE, Samuel	5	SENE	1837-03-18		A1
982	PARKER, Sanford R	15	NENE	1848-05-10		A1
983	"	"	15	NWNE	1850-10-01		A1
944	PERKINS, John	18	SESE	1851-02-01		A1
855	POTTER, Absalom	10	N½NE	1839-02-01		A1
959	POTTER, Josephus	2	SWSW	1850-12-10	Pike	A1
1001	POTTER, Thomas	3	SE	1838-09-07	Pike	A1
990	REAVIS, Tabitha	31	SESW	1839-02-01		A1
1026	REAVIS, William	19	N½SW	1837-03-15		A1
1028	"	"	30	E½NW	1837-08-01		A1
1027	"	"	19	SWSE	1837-11-07		A1
1029	"	"	30	W½SW	1839-02-01		A1
1030	"	"	33	W½SW	1850-12-10		A1
975	ROWE, Robert	10	E½NW	1839-02-01		A1
921	SKELSON, James	31	NESW	1837-08-01		A1
922	SKELTEN, James	31	SENW	1838-09-07		A1
923	SKELTON, James	31	W½NW	1826-07-31		A1
1034	SKELTON, William	33	SENE	1850-12-10		A1
1033	"	"	22	NWNE	1852-07-01		A1
976	STEEL, Robert	26	NWNE	1839-08-01		A1
977	"	"	35	NENW	1839-08-01		A1
957	STERETT, Joseph P	33	E½SW	1844-08-01		A1
947	TAYLOR, John	9	SWNW	1839-08-01		A1
1013	TAYLOR, William G	8	E½NW	1826-07-31		A1
1014	"	"	8	NWNE	1835-10-01		A1
965	TERRY, Miles	9	NWNW	1835-10-01		A1
964	"	"	5	W½SW	1839-08-01		A1
968	TRUITT, Purnel	7	NESW	1839-02-01		A1
969	TRUITT, Purnell	7	NWSW	1835-10-28		A1
920	WALLACE, James S	22	SWNE	1848-07-01		A1
946	WALLACE, John T	23	SWNE	1848-05-01		A1
945	"	"	23	NWNE	1850-12-10		A1
932	WHITE, John C	35	SENW	1850-12-10		A1
862	WILSON, Ann	28	W½SW	1839-02-01		A1
863	"	"	29	E½SE	1839-02-01		A1
886	WILSON, Ellen	33	E½NW	1839-02-01		A1
887	"	"	33	W½NE	1839-02-01		A1
929	WILSON, James	32	E½NW	1839-02-01		A1
914	WILSON, James M	18	S½NW	1837-11-07		A1
1035	WILSON, William	32	SWNE	1840-10-01		A1
1036	WOOD, William	30	NENE	1848-05-10		A1
1037	"	"	30	SWNE	1850-12-10		A1

Patent Map

T2-S R9-W
2nd PM Meridian

Map Group 13

Township Statistics

Parcels Mapped	:	183
Number of Patents	:	173
Number of Individuals	:	114
Patentees Identified	:	114
Number of Surnames	:	73
Multi-Patentee Parcels	:	0
Oldest Patent Date	:	7/31/1826
Most Recent Patent	:	6/3/1856
Block/Lot Parcels	:	14
Parcels Re - Issued	:	3
Parcels that Overlap	:	2
Cities and Towns	:	3
Cemeteries	:	1

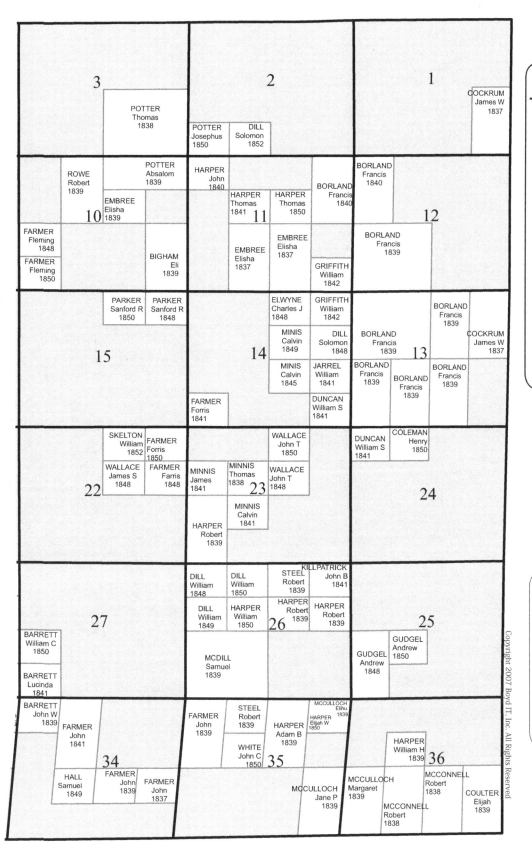

3

POTTER
Thomas
1838

POTTER
Josephus
1850

DILL
Solomon
1852

2

1

COCKRUM
James W
1837

ROWE
Robert
1839

POTTER
Absalom
1839

EMBREE
Elisha
1839

10

FARMER
Fleming
1848

FARMER
Fleming
1850

BIGHAM
Eli
1839

HARPER
John
1840

HARPER
Thomas
1841

11

HARPER
Thomas
1850

EMBREE
Elisha
1837

EMBREE
Elisha
1837

BORLAND
Francis
1840

BORLAND
Francis
1840

GRIFFITH
William
1842

BORLAND
Francis
1840

BORLAND
Francis
1839

12

PARKER
Sanford R
1850

PARKER
Sanford R
1848

15

14

ELWYNE
Charles J
1848

MINIS
Calvin
1849

MINIS
Calvin
1845

FARMER
Forris
1841

GRIFFITH
William
1842

DILL
Solomon
1848

JARREL
William
1841

DUNCAN
William S
1841

BORLAND
Francis
1839

BORLAND
Francis
1839

13

BORLAND
Francis
1839

BORLAND
Francis
1839

BORLAND
Francis
1839

COCKRUM
James W
1837

SKELTON
William
1852

FARMER
Forris
1850

WALLACE
James S
1848

FARMER
Farris
1848

22

MINNIS
James
1841

HARPER
Robert
1839

MINNIS
Thomas
1838

23

MINNIS
Calvin
1841

WALLACE
John T
1850

WALLACE
John T
1848

DUNCAN
William S
1841

COLEMAN
Henry
1850

24

27

BARRETT
William C
1850

BARRETT
Lucinda
1841

DILL
William
1848

DILL
William
1849

MCDILL
Samuel
1839

DILL
William
1850

HARPER
William
1850

STEEL
Robert
1839

KILLPATRICK
John B
1841

HARPER
Robert
1839

HARPER
Robert
1839

26

25

GUDGEL
Andrew
1848

GUDGEL
Andrew
1850

BARRETT
John W
1839

FARMER
John
1841

34

HALL
Samuel
1849

FARMER
John
1839

FARMER
John
1837

FARMER
John
1839

STEEL
Robert
1839

WHITE
John C
1850

35

MCCULLOCH
Elihu
1839

HARPER
Elijah W
1850

HARPER
Adam B
1839

MCCULLOCH
Jane P
1839

MCCULLOCH
Margaret
1839

HARPER
William H
1839

36

MCCONNELL
Robert
1838

MCCONNELL
Robert
1838

COULTER
Elijah
1839

Helpful Hints

1. This Map's INDEX can be found on the preceding pages.

2. Refer to Map "C" to see where this Township lies within Gibson County, Indiana.

3. Numbers within square brackets [ ] denote a multi-patentee land parcel (multi-owner). Refer to Appendix "C" for a full list of members in this group.

4. Areas that look to be crowded with Patentees usually indicate multiple sales of the same parcel (Re-issues) or Overlapping parcels. See this Township's Index for an explanation of these and other circumstances that might explain "odd" groupings of Patentees on this map.

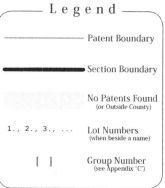

Legend

———— Patent Boundary

▬▬▬ Section Boundary

No Patents Found
(or Outside County)

1., 2., 3., ... Lot Numbers
(when beside a name)

[ ] Group Number
(see Appendix "C")

Scale: Section = 1 mile X 1 mile
(generally, with some exceptions)

Road Map

T2-S R9-W
2nd PM Meridian

Map Group 13

Cities & Towns
Francisco
Gudgel
Oak Hill

Cemeteries
Meade Cemetery

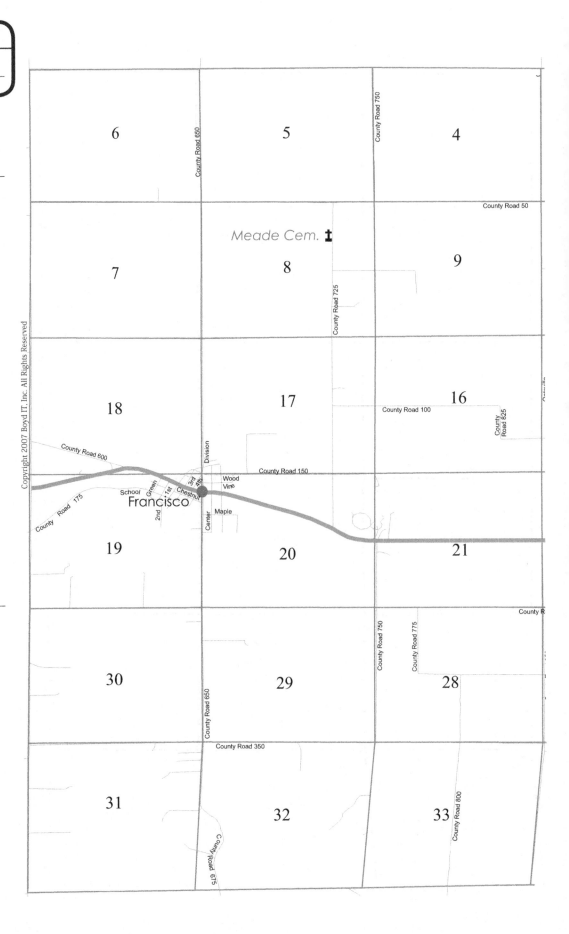

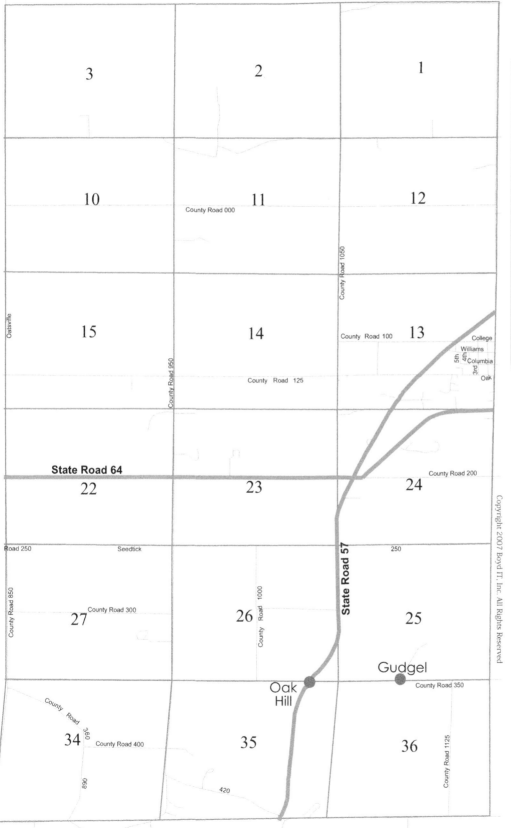

3

2

1

10

County Road 000

11

12

County Road 1050

15

Oatsville

14

County Road 100

13

College

Williams

5th
4th
3rd

Columbia

Oak

County Road 950

County Road 125

State Road 64

22

23

County Road 200

24

Road 250

Seedtick

250

State Road 57

County Road 850

County Road 300

27

County Road 1000

26

25

Gudgel

Oak
Hill

County Road 350

County Road

County Road 400

360

34

968

420

35

County 1125

36

Copyright 2007 Boyd IT, Inc. All Rights Reserved

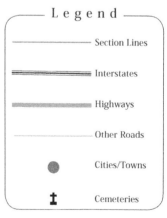

Helpful Hints

1. This road map has a number of uses, but primarily it is to help you: a) find the present location of land owned by your ancestors (at least the general area), b) find cemeteries and city-centers, and c) estimate the route/roads used by Census-takers & tax-assessors.

2. If you plan to travel to Gibson County to locate cemeteries or land parcels, please pick up a modern travel map for the area before you do. Mapping old land parcels on modern maps is not as exact a science as you might think. Just the slightest variations in public land survey coordinates, estimates of parcel boundaries, or road-map deviations can greatly alter a map's representation of how a road either does or doesn't cross a particular parcel of land.

L e g e n d

——————— Section Lines

═══════ Interstates

━━━━━━ Highways

——————— Other Roads

● Cities/Towns

✝ Cemeteries

Scale: Section = 1 mile X 1 mile
(generally, with some exceptions)

Historical Map

T2-S R9-W
2nd PM Meridian

Map Group 13

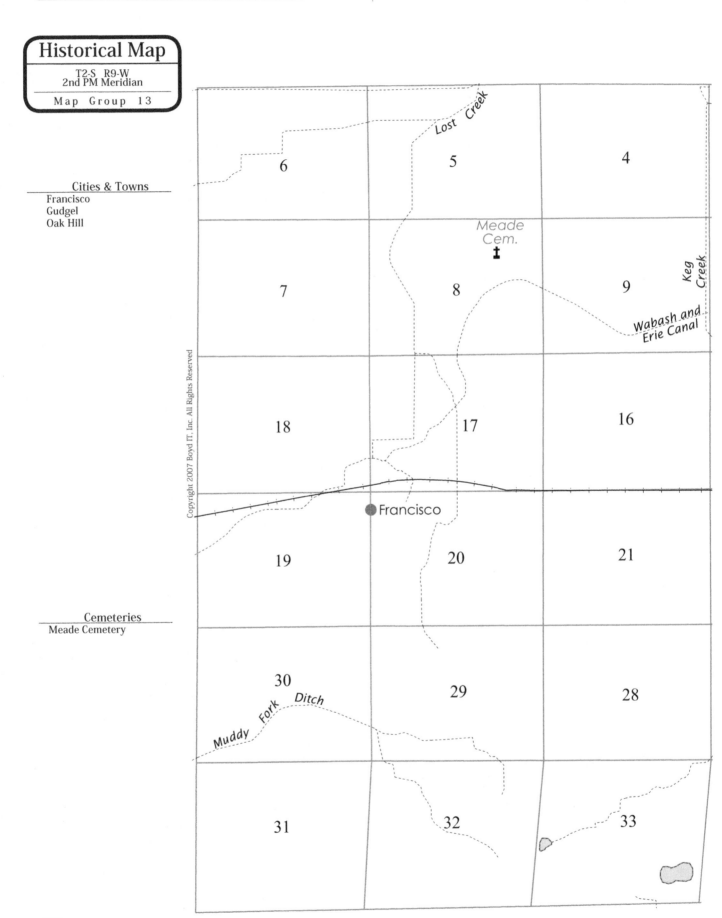

Cities & Towns

Francisco
Gudgel
Oak Hill

Cemeteries

Meade Cemetery

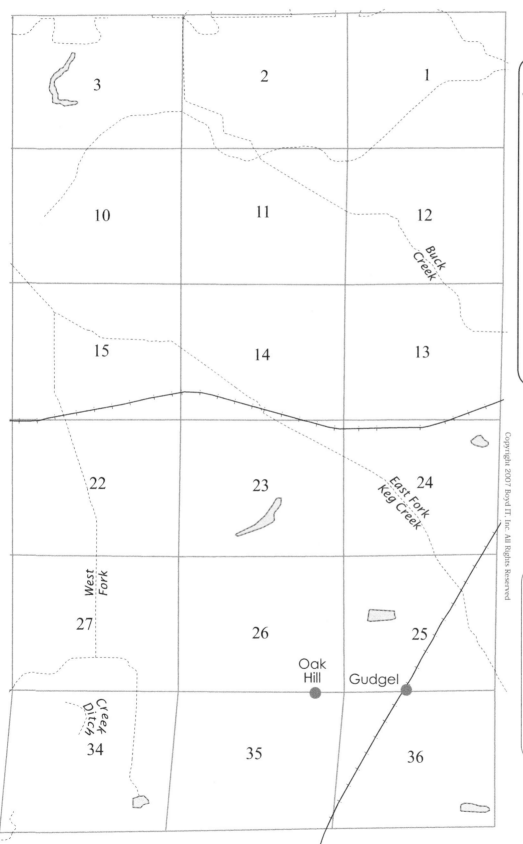

Helpful Hints

1. This Map takes a different look at the same Congressional Township displayed in the preceding two maps. It presents features that can help you better envision the historical development of the area: a) Water-bodies (lakes & ponds), b) Water-courses (rivers, streams, etc.), c) Railroads, d) City/town center-points (where they were oftentimes located when first settled), and e) Cemeteries.

2. Using this "Historical" map in tandem with this Township's Patent Map and Road Map, may lead you to some interesting discoveries. You will often find roads, towns, cemeteries, and waterways are named after nearby landowners: sometimes those names will be the ones you are researching. See how many of these research gems you can find here in Gibson County.

Legend

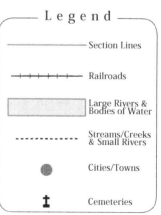

——————— Section Lines

+++++++ Railroads

▭ Large Rivers & Bodies of Water

- - - - - - Streams/Creeks & Small Rivers

● Cities/Towns

⚓ Cemeteries

Scale: Section = 1 mile X 1 mile
(there are some exceptions)

Map Group 14: Index to Land Patents

Township 2-South Range 8-West (2nd PM)

After you locate an individual in this Index, take note of the Section and Section Part then proceed to the Land Patent map on the pages immediately following. You should have no difficulty locating the corresponding parcel of land.

The "For More Info" Column will lead you to more information about the underlying Patents. See the *Legend* at right, and the "How to Use this Book" chapter, for more information.

```
                    LEGEND
         "For More Info . . . " column
A = Authority (Legislative Act, See Appendix "A")
B = Block or Lot (location in Section unknown)
C = Cancelled Patent
F = Fractional Section
G = Group  (Multi-Patentee Patent, see Appendix "C")
V = Overlaps another Parcel
R = Re-Issued (Parcel patented more than once)

(A & G items require you to look in the Appendixes referred
to above. All other Letter-designations followed by a number
require you to locate line-items in this index that possess
the ID number found after the letter).
```

ID	Individual in Patent	Sec.	Sec. Part	Date Issued	Other Counties	For More Info . . .
1042	BARNES, David	6	NWNW	1837-11-07		A1
1093	BARRETT, Richard M	18	SESW	1835-10-15		A1
1094	BELL, Thomas	32	E½SE	1841-05-25		A1
1084	BROWN, Joseph R	5	E½SE	1837-08-05		A1
1085	"	7	E½NE	1837-08-05		A1
1086	"	8	W½NW	1837-08-05		A1
1039	CARPENTER, Alvin B	5	W½SW	1840-10-01		A1 G4
1039	CARPENTER, Willard	5	W½SW	1840-10-01		A1 G4
1041	COCKRUM, Columbus	6	S½NW	1837-11-07		A1
1067	COCKRUM, James W	17	W½NE	1830-12-02		A1
1070	"	18	W½NE	1837-08-01		A1
1066	"	17	NWSW	1837-08-05		A1
1068	"	18	NESE	1837-08-05		A1
1069	"	18	NESW	1837-08-05		A1
1071	"	18	W½SW	1837-08-05		A1
1076	"	7	E½SE	1837-08-05		A1
1077	"	8	SWSW	1837-08-05		A1
1073	"	6	NENW	1837-11-07		A1
1074	"	6	SW	1837-11-07		A1
1075	"	6	W½SE	1837-11-07		A1
1072	"	6	E½SE	1839-02-01		A1
1091	COLEMAN, Page	5	SENE	1837-08-05		A1
1095	COLLINS, Thomas	30	NENE	1850-12-10		A1
1096	"	30	NWNE	1850-12-10		A1
1099	CRAVENS, William	31	NWNE	1837-11-07		A1
1098	"	31	NENW	1839-08-01		A1
1100	CRAVINS, William	32	NWNE	1848-05-10		A1
1058	CRAWFORD, Holly	19	SENE	1850-12-10		A1
1057	"	19	NENE	1852-07-01		A1
1092	DILL, Philemon	32	SWSW	1839-02-01		A1
1046	EMBNER, Elisha	17	E½SW	1837-08-05		A1
1047	"	18	E½NE	1837-08-05		A1
1048	"	18	W½SE	1837-08-05		A1
1049	EMBREE, Elisha	19	E½SE	1837-08-05		A1
1050	"	8	NENE	1837-08-05		A1
1061	FARMER, Isaac	31	SWSE	1839-08-01		A1
1043	FARRIS, David	29	SESE	1849-04-10		A1
1087	HARGROVE, Marstew G	17	SWSW	1839-08-01		A1
1088	HARGROVE, Martin G	17	W½NW	1837-08-01		A1
1102	HARGROVE, William	17	SENW	1837-03-18		A1
1101	"	17	NENW	1839-02-01		A1
1103	"	17	W½SE	1839-08-01		A1
1062	HARGROW, Jacob W	8	SESE	1854-03-01		A1
1107	HOWE, Willis	29	NWSE	1838-09-01		A1
1078	JOHNSON, John N	19	SW	1840-10-01		A1
1040	KELL, Archibald	31	NENE	1839-08-01		A1

ID	Individual in Patent	Sec.	Sec. Part	Date Issued	Other Counties	For More Info . . .
1063	KELL, James	30	NWSW	1848-05-10		A1
1090	KELL, Matthew	30	SESW	1838-09-07		A1
1089	" "	30	NESW	1839-08-01		A1
1104	KURTZ, William	5	NWNE	1855-01-03		A1
1056	LATHORN, Harrison	8	NWSW	1837-08-05		A1
1038	LOOMIS, Albert	30	SENE	1848-07-01		A1
1044	MASON, David	29	SESW	1841-05-25		A1
1045	" "	29	SWSE	1841-05-25		A1
1064	MASON, James	29	NESW	1841-08-10		A1
1065	MINNIS, James	32	SWNE	1850-12-10		A1
1082	MONTGOMERY, Joseph H	8	NESE	1837-08-05		A1
1083	" "	8	SENE	1837-08-05		A1
1079	NICHOL, John	19	W½NE	1840-10-01		A1
1105	NOFOET, William	30	SWNE	1848-07-01		A1
1053	PRATT, George W	6	NE	1839-02-01		A1 G31
1054	" "	7	W½NE	1839-08-01		A1 G31
1055	" "	7	W½SE	1839-08-01		A1 G31
1106	REYNOLDS, William	31	SW	1839-08-01		A1
1053	SULLIVAN, William	6	NE	1839-02-01		A1 G31
1054	" "	7	W½NE	1839-08-01		A1 G31
1055	" "	7	W½SE	1839-08-01		A1 G31
1053	THACHER, George M	6	NE	1839-02-01		A1 G31
1054	" "	7	W½NE	1839-08-01		A1 G31
1055	" "	7	W½SE	1839-08-01		A1 G31
1051	WATT, George M	31	E½SE	1840-10-01		A1
1052	" "	32	NWSW	1840-10-01		A1
1059	WATT, Hugh	32	E½SW	1840-10-01		A1
1060	" "	32	W½SE	1840-10-01		A1
1097	WATT, Thomas	29	E½NW	1841-05-25		A1
1080	WHEELER, Johnson	32	NENE	1849-04-10		A1
1081	" "	32	SENE	1850-12-10		A1

Patent Map

T2-S R8-W
2nd PM Meridian

Map Group 14

Township Statistics

Parcels Mapped	:	70
Number of Patents	:	61
Number of Individuals	:	44
Patentees Identified	:	41
Number of Surnames	:	35
Multi-Patentee Parcels	:	4
Oldest Patent Date	:	12/2/1830
Most Recent Patent	:	1/3/1855
Block/Lot Parcels	:	0
Parcels Re - Issued	:	0
Parcels that Overlap	:	0
Cities and Towns	:	3
Cemeteries	:	1

Note: the area contained in this map amounts to far less than a full Township. Therefore, its contents are completely on this single page (instead of a "normal" 2-page spread).

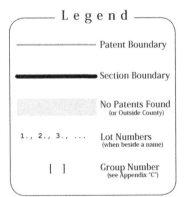

Legend

——————	Patent Boundary
▬▬▬▬▬	Section Boundary
(shaded)	No Patents Found (or Outside County)
1., 2., 3., ...	Lot Numbers (when beside a name)
[ ]	Group Number (see Appendix "C")

Scale: Section = 1 mile X 1 mile
(generally, with some exceptions)

Section 6
BARNES David 1837
COCKRUM James W 1837
PRATT [31] George W 1839
COCKRUM Columbus 1837
COCKRUM James W 1837
COCKRUM James W 1839
COCKRUM James W 1837

Section 5
KURTZ William 1855
CARPENTER [4] Alvin B 1840

Section 4
COLEMAN Page 1837
BROWN Joseph R 1837

Section 7
PRATT [31] George W 1839
BROWN Joseph R 1837
PRATT [31] George W 1839
COCKRUM James W 1837

Section 8
BROWN Joseph R 1837
LATHORN Harrison 1837
COCKRUM James W 1837
EMBREE Elisha 1837
MONTGOMERY Joseph H 1837
MONTGOMERY Joseph H 1837
HARGROW Jacob W 1854

Section 9

Section 18
COCKRUM James W 1837
EMBNER Elisha 1837
COCKRUM James W 1837
BARRETT Richard M 1835
EMBNER Elisha 1837
COCKRUM James W 1837

Section 17
HARGROVE William 1839
HARGROVE Martin G 1837
HARGROVE William 1837
COCKRUM James W 1830
COCKRUM James W 1837
EMBNER Elisha 1837
HARGROVE Marstew G 1839
HARGROVE William 1839

Section 16

Section 19
NICHOL John 1840
CRAWFORD Holly 1852
CRAWFORD Holly 1850
JOHNSON John N 1840
EMBREE Elisha 1837

Section 20
Gibson County

Section 21
Pike County

Section 30
COLLINS Thomas 1850
COLLINS Thomas 1850
NOFOET William 1848
LOOMIS Albert 1848
KELL James 1848
KELL Matthew 1839
KELL Matthew 1838

Section 29
WATT Thomas 1841
MASON James 1841
HOWE Willis 1838
MASON David 1841
MASON David 1841
FARRIS David 1849

Section 28

Section 31
CRAVENS William 1839
CRAVENS William 1837
KELL Archibald 1839
REYNOLDS William 1839
FARMER Isaac 1839
WATT George M 1840

Section 32
WATT George M 1840
DILL Philemon 1839
WATT Hugh 1840
WATT Hugh 1840
CRAVINS William 1848
WHEELER Johnson 1849
MINNIS James 1850
WHEELER Johnson 1850
BELL Thomas 1841

Section 33

142

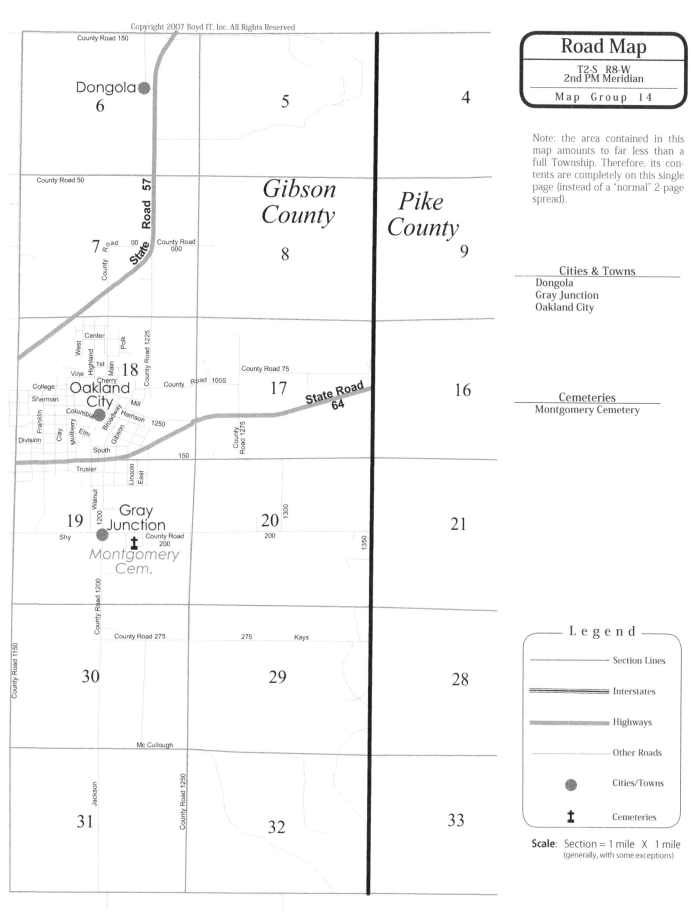

Road Map

T2-S R8-W
2nd PM Meridian

Map Group 14

Note: the area contained in this map amounts to far less than a full Township. Therefore, its contents are completely on this single page (instead of a "normal" 2-page spread).

Cities & Towns
Dongola
Gray Junction
Oakland City

Cemeteries
Montgomery Cemetery

Legend

——————— Section Lines

═══════ Interstates

━━━━━━ Highways

——————— Other Roads

● Cities/Towns

✝ Cemeteries

Scale: Section = 1 mile X 1 mile
(generally, with some exceptions)

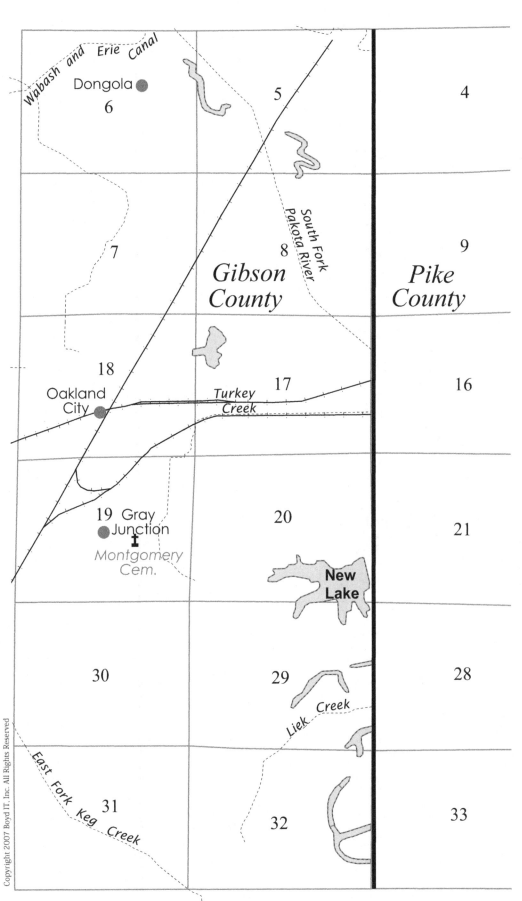

Historical Map

T2-S R8-W
2nd PM Meridian

Map Group 14

Note: the area contained in this map amounts to far less than a full Township. Therefore, its contents are completely on this single page (instead of a "normal" 2-page spread).

Cities & Towns
Dongola
Gray Junction
Oakland City

Cemeteries
Montgomery Cemetery

Legend

——————— Section Lines

+‑+‑+‑+‑+‑ Railroads

▭ Large Rivers & Bodies of Water

-------------- Streams/Creeks & Small Rivers

● Cities/Towns

✝ Cemeteries

Scale: Section = 1 mile X 1 mile
(there are some exceptions)

Wabash and Erie Canal

Dongola ●
6

5

4

South Fork Pakota River

7

8

Gibson County

9

Pike County

18

Oakland City ●

Turkey Creek

17

16

19 Gray Junction ●
✝
Montgomery Cem.

20

New Lake

21

30

29

Liek Creek

28

East Fork Keg Creek

31

32

33

Map Group 15: Index to Land Patents

Township 3-South Range 14-West (2nd PM)

After you locate an individual in this Index, take note of the Section and Section Part then proceed to the Land Patent map on the pages immediately following. You should have no difficulty locating the corresponding parcel of land.

The "For More Info" Column will lead you to more information about the underlying Patents. See the *Legend* at right, and the "How to Use this Book" chapter, for more information.

```
                    LEGEND
          "For More Info . . . " column
A = Authority (Legislative Act, See Appendix "A")
B = Block or Lot (location in Section unknown)
C = Cancelled Patent
F = Fractional Section
G = Group  (Multi-Patentee Patent, see Appendix "C")
V = Overlaps another Parcel
R = Re-Issued (Parcel patented more than once)

(A & G items require you to look in the Appendixes referred
to above. All other Letter-designations followed by a number
require you to locate line-items in this index that possess
the ID number found after the letter).
```

ID	Individual in Patent	Sec.	Sec. Part	Date Issued	Other Counties	For More Info . . .
1154	BARNETT, Thomas	13	NENE	1837-03-15		A1 F
1153	"	12	5	1837-08-01		A1 F
1156	BOREN, Uriah E	25	NESW	1837-03-30		A1
1159	BURTON, William L	25	NWSW	1837-03-30		A1
1123	CARBAUGH, Jacob	13	E½SW	1830-12-02		A1 R1124
1124	"	13	E½SW	1940-02-23		A1 R1123
1140	CARBAUGH, John	14	SW	1835-10-07		A1 C F
1137	"	14	3	1837-08-01		A1 F
1141	"	26	NENW	1839-08-01		A1 F
1138	"	14	4	1940-11-25		A1
1139	"	14	5	1940-11-25		A1
1110	CARPENTER, Alvin B	23	SW	1839-08-01		A1 F
1111	"	23	W½SE	1839-08-01		A1
1112	CLARK, Andrew	13	SENE	1837-03-18		A1
1108	COOPER, A J	12	N½NW	1841-05-25		A1 F
1125	CROWLEY, James	12	4	1838-09-01		A1
1114	FLOWER, George	13	E½SE	1821-08-20		A1
1115	"	13	W½SE	1821-08-20		A1
1116	"	13	W½SW	1821-08-20		A1
1128	GRAY, James	27	E½SE	1838-09-01		A1 G18 F
1129	"	27	NE	1838-09-01		A1 G18 F
1126	"	26	SENW	1839-08-01		A1 G18
1127	"	26	W½SW	1839-08-01		A1 G18
1148	GRAYSON, Napolean	11	1	1839-08-01		A1 F
1149	"	11	2	1839-08-01		A1 F
1113	GRIFFEN, Caleb H	24	NESE	1838-09-01		A1
1143	HARMAN, John	27	4	1837-03-20		A1 F
1151	HARMON, Robert	23	2	1838-09-01		A1
1152	"	23	NW	1838-09-01		A1 F
1157	HUDSON, William	27	3	1837-11-07		A1 F
1158	"	27	NESW	1837-11-07		A1 F
1135	RACHELS, John B	25	S½SE	1838-09-01		A1 V1144
1136	"	25	SESW	1838-09-01		A1
1155	SCOTT, Thomas	14	1	1857-07-01		A1
1142	STEPHENS, John D	26	SWSE	1841-05-25		A1
1121	THOMAS, Isaac	25	NWSE	1835-10-01		A1 V1144
1130	TWEEDLE, James	12	3	1839-02-01		A1 F
1131	"	12	6	1839-02-01		A1 F
1134	"	13	W½NE	1839-02-01		A1
1132	"	12	SENE	1839-08-01		A1 F
1133	"	13	NW	1839-08-01		A1
1109	VAUGHN, Abel	27	NWSE	1838-09-01		A1
1128	WALDEN, Robert D	27	E½SE	1838-09-01		A1 G18 F
1129	"	27	NE	1838-09-01		A1 G18 F
1150	"	27	SWSE	1839-02-01		A1
1126	"	26	SENW	1839-08-01		A1 G18

ID	Individual in Patent	Sec.	Sec. Part	Date Issued	Other Counties	For More Info . . .
1127	WALDEN, Robert D (Cont'd)	26	W½SW	1839-08-01		A1 G18
1144	WALLER, John	25	W½SE	1838-09-01		A1 V1121, 1135
1160	WARD, William	14	2	1857-07-01		A1
1120	WEBB, George	28	N½	1831-05-21		A1 F
1117	" "	21		1835-09-10		A1 F
1118	" "	28	1	1837-08-05		A1
1119	" "	28	2	1837-08-05		A1
1146	WHITE, John	25	NESE	1835-10-07		A1
1145	" "	25	E½NE	1838-09-01		A1
1147	WILKINS, John	24	E½NW	1830-12-02		A1
1161	WILKINS, William	24	NWNW	1839-08-01		A1
1122	WILLIAMS, Isaac	26	W½NW	1835-10-01		A1 F

Patent Map

T3-S R14-W
2nd PM Meridian

Map Group 15

Township Statistics

Parcels Mapped	:	54
Number of Patents	:	46
Number of Individuals	:	30
Patentees Identified	:	30
Number of Surnames	:	28
Multi-Patentee Parcels	:	4
Oldest Patent Date	:	8/20/1821
Most Recent Patent	:	11/25/1940
Block/Lot Parcels	:	481
Parcels Re - Issued	:	1
Parcels that Overlap	:	3
Cities and Towns	:	0
Cemeteries	:	0

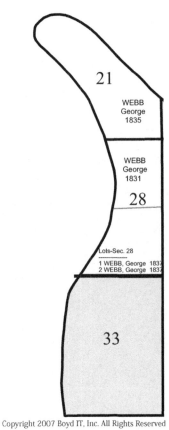

21

WEBB
George
1835

WEBB
George
1831

28

Lots-Sec. 28
1 WEBB, George 1837
2 WEBB, George 1837

33

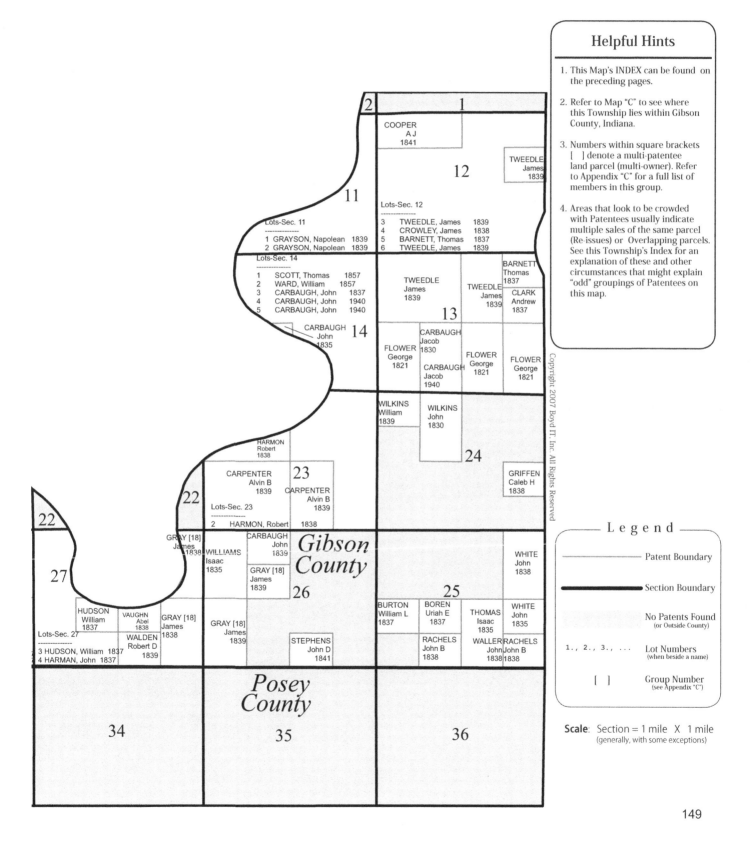

Helpful Hints

1. This Map's INDEX can be found on the preceding pages.

2. Refer to Map "C" to see where this Township lies within Gibson County, Indiana.

3. Numbers within square brackets [ ] denote a multi-patentee land parcel (multi-owner). Refer to Appendix "C" for a full list of members in this group.

4. Areas that look to be crowded with Patentees usually indicate multiple sales of the same parcel (Re-issues) or Overlapping parcels. See this Township's Index for an explanation of these and other circumstances that might explain "odd" groupings of Patentees on this map.

Legend

———————	Patent Boundary
━━━━━━━	Section Boundary
	No Patents Found (or Outside County)
1., 2., 3., ...	Lot Numbers (when beside a name)
[ ]	Group Number (see Appendix "C")

Scale: Section = 1 mile X 1 mile (generally, with some exceptions)

Section 1

Section 2

COOPER A J 1841

12

TWEEDLE James 1839

11

Lots-Sec. 12
----
3 TWEEDLE, James 1839
4 CROWLEY, James 1838
5 BARNETT, Thomas 1837
6 TWEEDLE, James 1839

Lots-Sec. 11
----
1 GRAYSON, Napolean 1839
2 GRAYSON, Napolean 1839

Lots-Sec. 14
----
1 SCOTT, Thomas 1857
2 WARD, William 1857
3 CARBAUGH, John 1837
4 CARBAUGH, John 1940
5 CARBAUGH, John 1940

BARNETT Thomas 1837

TWEEDLE James 1839

TWEEDLE James 1839

CLARK Andrew 1837

CARBAUGH John 1835

14

13

FLOWER George 1821

CARBAUGH Jacob 1830

CARBAUGH Jacob 1940

FLOWER George 1821

FLOWER George 1821

WILKINS William 1839

WILKINS John 1830

HARMON Robert 1838

24

CARPENTER Alvin B 1839

23

CARPENTER Alvin B 1839

Lots-Sec. 23
----
2 HARMON, Robert 1838

GRIFFEN Caleb H 1838

22

GRAY [18] James 1838

CARBAUGH John 1839

Gibson County

WILLIAMS Isaac 1835

GRAY [18] James 1839

22

26

WHITE John 1838

27

HUDSON William 1837

VAUGHN Abel 1838

GRAY [18] James 1838

WALDEN Robert D 1839

GRAY [18] James 1839

25

BURTON William L 1837

BOREN Uriah E 1837

THOMAS Isaac 1835

WHITE John 1835

Lots-Sec. 27
----
3 HUDSON, William 1837
4 HARMAN, John 1837

STEPHENS John D 1841

RACHELS John B 1838

WALLER John 1838

RACHELS John B 1838

Posey County

34

35

36

Road Map

T3-S R14-W
2nd PM Meridian

Map Group 15

Cities & Towns
None

Cemeteries
None

21

28

33

Helpful Hints

1. This road map has a number of uses, but primarily it is to help you: a) find the present location of land owned by your ancestors (at least the general area), b) find cemeteries and city-centers, and c) estimate the route/roads used by Census-takers & tax-assessors.

2. If you plan to travel to Gibson County to locate cemeteries or land parcels, please pick up a modern travel map for the area before you do. Mapping old land parcels on modern maps is not as exact a science as you might think. Just the slightest variations in public land survey coordinates, estimates of parcel boundaries, or road-map deviations can greatly alter a map's representation of how a road either does or doesn't cross a particular parcel of land.

2

1

12

11

14

13

County Road 1875

24

23

22

22

County Road 725

County Road 2150

26

25

Gibson County

27

Posey County

34

35

36

Legend

———————	Section Lines
≡≡≡≡≡≡≡	Interstates
▬▬▬▬▬▬	Highways
———————	Other Roads
●	Cities/Towns
⚰	Cemeteries

Scale: Section = 1 mile X 1 mile
(generally, with some exceptions)

Historical Map

T3-S R14-W
2nd PM Meridian

Map Group 15

Cities & Towns
None

Cemeteries
None

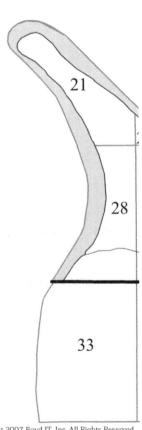

21

28

33

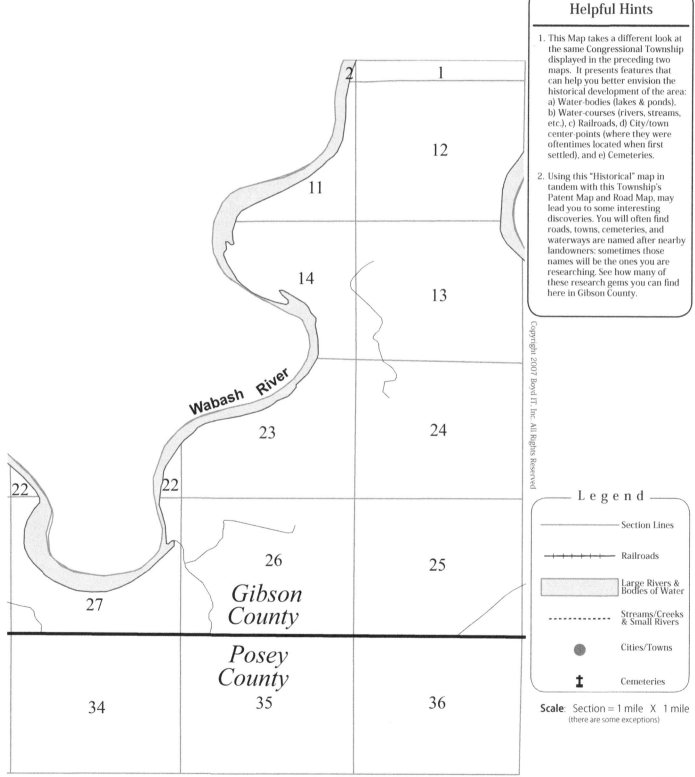

Helpful Hints

1. This Map takes a different look at the same Congressional Township displayed in the preceding two maps. It presents features that can help you better envision the historical development of the area: a) Water-bodies (lakes & ponds), b) Water-courses (rivers, streams, etc.), c) Railroads, d) City/town center-points (where they were oftentimes located when first settled), and e) Cemeteries.

2. Using this "Historical" map in tandem with this Township's Patent Map and Road Map, may lead you to some interesting discoveries. You will often find roads, towns, cemeteries, and waterways are named after nearby landowners: sometimes those names will be the ones you are researching. See how many of these research gems you can find here in Gibson County.

2

1

12

11

14

13

Wabash River

23

24

22

22

26

25

Gibson
County

27

Posey
County

34

35

36

Legend

——————— Section Lines

+—+—+—+—+ Railroads

▭ Large Rivers &
Bodies of Water

- - - - - - - Streams/Creeks
& Small Rivers

● Cities/Towns

‡ Cemeteries

Scale: Section = 1 mile X 1 mile
(there are some exceptions)

Map Group 16: Index to Land Patents

Township 3-South Range 13-West (2nd PM)

After you locate an individual in this Index, take note of the Section and Section Part then proceed to the Land Patent map on the pages immediately following. You should have no difficulty locating the corresponding parcel of land.

The "For More Info" Column will lead you to more information about the underlying Patents. See the *Legend* at right, and the "How to Use this Book" chapter, for more information.

```
┌─────────────────────────────────────────────────────────┐
│                      LEGEND                             │
│          "For More Info . . . " column                  │
│ A = Authority (Legislative Act, See Appendix "A")       │
│ B = Block or Lot (location in Section unknown)          │
│ C = Cancelled Patent                                    │
│ F = Fractional Section                                  │
│ G = Group  (Multi-Patentee Patent, see Appendix "C")    │
│ V = Overlaps another Parcel                             │
│ R = Re-Issued (Parcel patented more than once)          │
│                                                         │
│ (A & G items require you to look in the Appendixes referred │
│ to above. All other Letter-designations followed by a number │
│ require you to locate line-items in this index that possess │
│ the ID number found after the letter).                  │
└─────────────────────────────────────────────────────────┘
```

ID	Individual in Patent	Sec.	Sec. Part	Date Issued	Other Counties	For More Info . . .
1239	ASHLEY, Thomas	20	NWSW	1838-09-01		A1
1240	" "	29	SWSW	1839-02-01		A1
1241	" "	30	SESE	1839-02-01		A1
1238	" "	19	NESE	1841-05-25		A1
1202	BARKER, Jesse	11	NWSW	1835-10-01		A1 F
1201	" "	10	1	1835-10-28		A1 F
1203	" "	11	S½NW	1839-02-01		A1 F
1242	BARNETT, Thomas	18	NESW	1839-08-01		A1
1166	BENNETT, Benjamin	30	NENE	1835-10-23		A1 C
1177	BENNETT, George W	28	SWNW	1835-09-10		A1 C
1249	BISHOP, William L	8	2	1857-07-01		A1
1194	CALVIN, James	18	SWSE	1835-10-15		A1 C F
1230	CARTWRIGHT, Presley	18	NENE	1838-09-01		A1 F
1231	" "	18	W½NE	1838-09-01		A1 F
1186	CASSELBERRY, Isaac S	5	E½	1838-09-01		A1 F
1173	CLARK, George L	30	N½SE	1857-07-01		A1
1174	" "	30	NE	1857-07-01		A1
1175	" "	30	NESW	1857-07-01		A1
1180	CONNER, Henry H	24	SWSE	1839-02-01		A1
1178	CREEK, Gillison	25	SESE	1839-08-01		A1
1235	CREEK, Rumzy B	24	SESE	1839-02-01		A1
1243	CREEK, Washington	21	SESE	1839-08-01		A1
1196	CROWLEY, James	18	W½SW	1830-12-02		A1 F
1195	" "	18	W½NW	1835-10-07		A1 F
1245	DAUGHERTY, William	30	NWSW	1858-08-30		A1
1204	DAVIS, Joel	15	NWNW	1835-10-28		A1 G7
1205	DAVIS, John	19	NESW	1835-10-07		A1 F
1206	" "	19	SENW	1838-09-01		A1
1232	DAVIS, Redwine	25	NENE	1850-12-10		A1
1246	DAVIS, William	30	SWSE	1841-05-25		A1
1182	DENBY, Henry H	8	1	1837-11-07		A1 F
1183	" "	8	3	1837-11-07		A1 F
1181	" "	7	3	1838-09-07		A1 F
1207	FIFER, John	18	E½SE	1835-10-15		A1 C F
1208	" "	20	E½SW	1839-02-01		A1
1209	" "	29	N½NW	1839-02-01		A1
1236	GARRETT, Stephen	25	SESW	1840-10-01		A1
1216	GARTON, Joseph	25	NESE	1839-08-01		A1
1225	GUTHRIE, Peter	19	SESE	1835-10-01		A1
1226	" "	20	SWSW	1835-10-15		A1
1237	HENING, Stephen	18	E½NW	1835-10-28		A1 F
1210	HEPNER, John H	19	NWSE	1857-07-01		A1
1211	" "	19	SWSE	1857-07-01		A1
1184	HUNT, Henry	15	NWSW	1838-09-01		A1
1215	HUNT, Jordan	9	1	1837-03-20		A1 F
1162	JORDAN, Absalom	15	NENW	1838-09-07		A1

ID	Individual in Patent	Sec.	Sec. Part	Date Issued	Other Counties	For More Info . . .
1163	JORDAN, Alfred	17	NWNE	1837-03-15		A1
1172	JORDAN, Elilea	11	N½NW	1839-08-01		A1 F
1192	JORDAN, Jacob P	4		1835-09-05		A1 F
1193	" "	9	N½N½	1837-08-01		A1 F
1212	JORDAN, John	2	W½	1835-10-01		A1 F
1220	JORDAN, Joshua	9	E½SW	1831-01-04		A1 F
1221	" "	9	S½N½	1837-03-15		A1 F
1233	JORDAN, River	7	4	1837-11-07		A1 F
1224	JORDEN, Mary	20	SWNE	1838-09-01		A1
1164	JORDON, Alfred	17	E½NW	1830-12-02		A1
1222	JORDON, Joshua	9	2	1835-10-28		A1 F
1234	JORDON, River	17	W½NW	1826-05-20		A1
1248	KINCHELOE, William H	6		1839-08-01		A1 F
1250	LEMAR, Young	7	W½	1839-08-01		A1 F
1197	MOUTRAY, James	19	NWSW	1835-10-07		A1
1217	NEWSUM, Joseph	25	SWSE	1841-05-25		A1
1191	OGLESBY, Jacob	25	NWSE	1839-08-01		A1
1176	OVERTON, George	21	SWNW	1840-10-01		A1
1189	PADEN, Jacob A	14	SESW	1841-05-25		A1
1190	" "	14	SWSE	1841-05-25		A1
1167	PIERCE, Chauncey	21	E½SE	1839-08-01		A1
1223	REEDER, Joshua	30	SWSW	1839-08-01		A1
1179	SIMPSON, Greenberry	25	NESW	1840-10-01		A1
1171	SMITH, David	21	W½SW	1832-04-10		A1
1170	" "	20	NESE	1835-10-07		A1
1229	SMITH, Peter	21	NWSE	1835-10-23		A1
1228	" "	10	3	1835-10-28		A1 F
1227	" "	10	2	1839-08-01		A1 F
1247	SUMNERS, William G	23	NWNE	1839-08-01		A1
1185	SUMPTER, Henry	30	SENE	1835-10-15		A1 C
1213	THOMAS, John	29	SESW	1840-10-01		A1
1200	TWEEDLE, James	21	W½NE	1831-12-31		A1
1199	" "	21	SWSE	1839-02-01		A1
1198	" "	19	NENW	1839-08-01		A1
1218	WALDEN, Joseph	12	SE	1857-07-01		A1
1244	WATERS, William A	19	S½SW	1839-02-01		A1
1204	WATTS, Asa	15	NWNW	1835-10-28		A1 G7
1165	" "	10	4	1837-08-01		A1 F
1214	WILKINS, John	19	W½NW	1830-12-02		A1
1169	WILLIAMS, Daniel	30	SWNW	1835-09-10		A1
1168	" "	30	NWNW	1838-09-01		A1
1187	WILLIAMS, Isaac	30	NENW	1838-09-01		A1
1188	" "	30	SESW	1855-01-03		A1
1219	WILLIAMS, Joseph	30	SENW	1838-09-01		A1

Patent Map

T3-S R13-W
2nd PM Meridian

Map Group 16

Township Statistics

Parcels Mapped	:	89
Number of Patents	:	86
Number of Individuals	:	63
Patentees Identified	:	63
Number of Surnames	:	45
Multi-Patentee Parcels	:	1
Oldest Patent Date	:	5/20/1826
Most Recent Patent	:	8/30/1858
Block/Lot Parcels	:	374
Parcels Re - Issued	:	0
Parcels that Overlap	:	0
Cities and Towns	:	3
Cemeteries	:	0

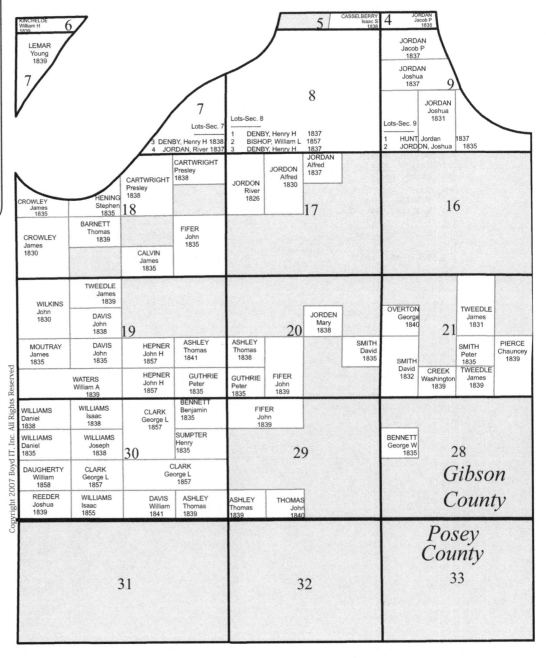

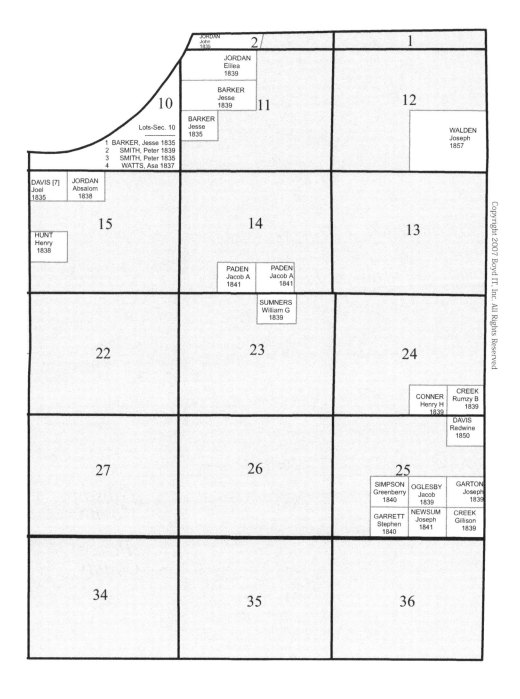

1. This Map's INDEX can be found on the preceding pages.

2. Refer to Map "C" to see where this Township lies within Gibson County, Indiana.

3. Numbers within square brackets [ ] denote a multi-patentee land parcel (multi-owner). Refer to Appendix "C" for a full list of members in this group.

4. Areas that look to be crowded with Patentees usually indicate multiple sales of the same parcel (Re-issues) or Overlapping parcels. See this Township's Index for an explanation of these and other circumstances that might explain "odd" groupings of Patentees on this map.

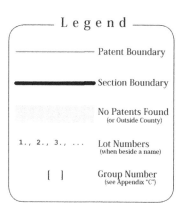

Legend

——— Patent Boundary

▬▬▬ Section Boundary

No Patents Found
(or Outside County)

1., 2., 3., ... Lot Numbers
(when beside a name)

[ ] Group Number
(see Appendix "C")

Scale: Section = 1 mile X 1 mile
(generally, with some exceptions)

Road Map

T3-S R13-W
2nd PM Meridian

Map Group 16

Cities & Towns
Crawleyville
Hickory Ridge
Jimtown

Cemeteries
None

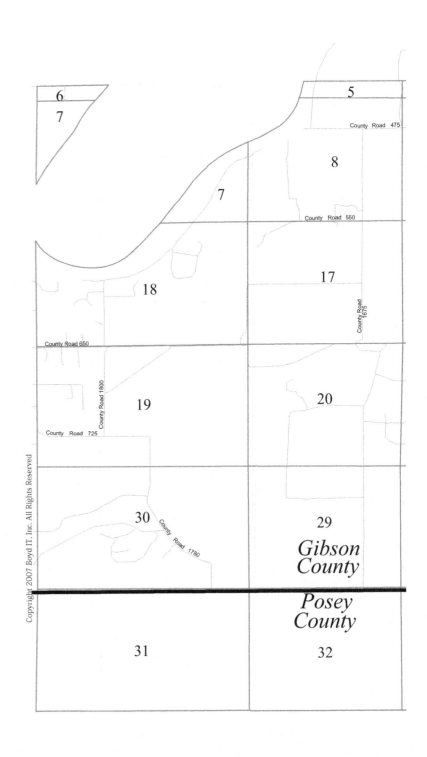

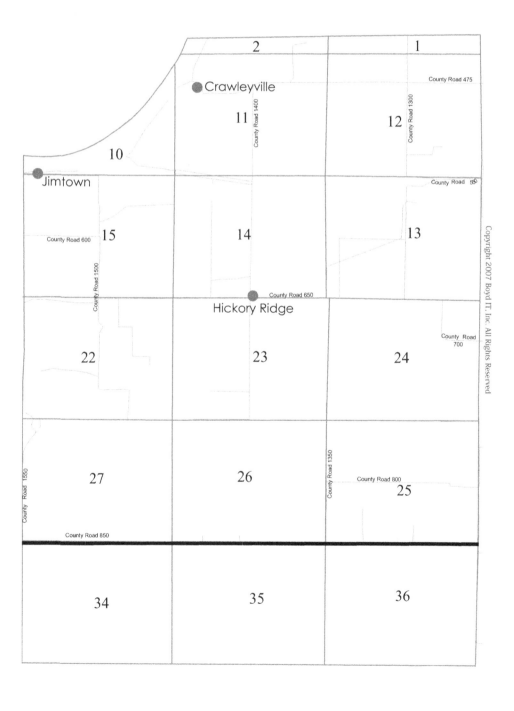

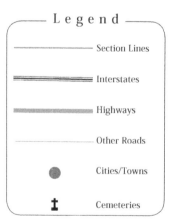

Copyright 2007 Boyd IT, Inc. All Rights Reserved

Helpful Hints

1. This road map has a number of uses, but primarily it is to help you: a) find the present location of land owned by your ancestors (at least the general area), b) find cemeteries and city-centers, and c) estimate the route/roads used by Census-takers & tax-assessors.

2. If you plan to travel to Gibson County to locate cemeteries or land parcels, please pick up a modern travel map for the area before you do. Mapping old land parcels on modern maps is not as exact a science as you might think. Just the slightest variations in public land survey coordinates, estimates of parcel boundaries, or road-map deviations can greatly alter a map's representation of how a road either does or doesn't cross a particular parcel of land.

Legend

————	Section Lines
══════	Interstates
——————	Highways
————	Other Roads
●	Cities/Towns
✝	Cemeteries

Scale: Section = 1 mile X 1 mile
(generally, with some exceptions)

Historical Map

T3-S R13-W
2nd PM Meridian

Map Group 16

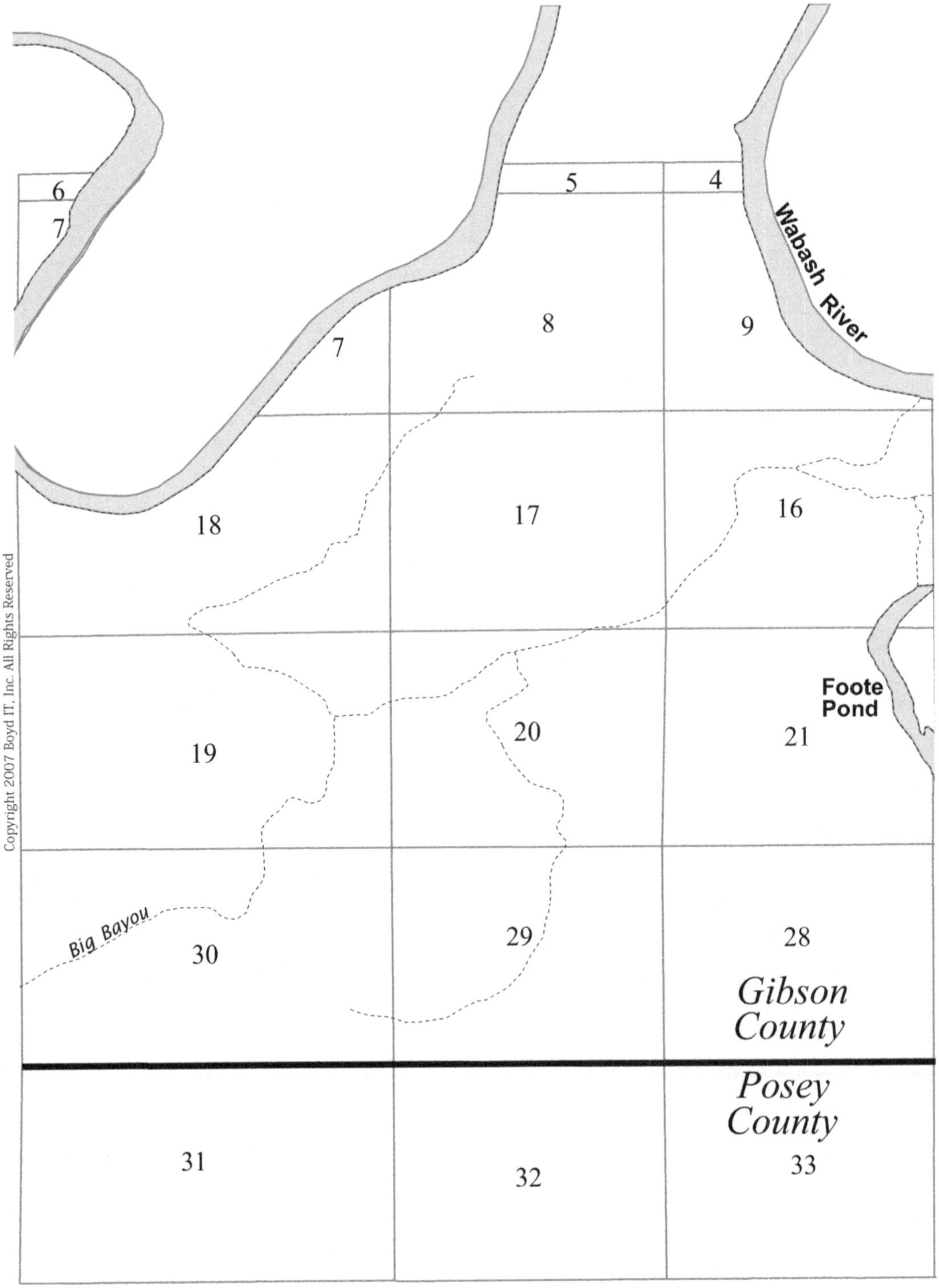

Cities & Towns

- Crawleyville
- Hickory Ridge
- Jimtown

Cemeteries

None

6
7
5
4
Wabash River
8
9
7
18
17
16
19
20
21
Foote Pond
Big Bayou
30
29
28
Gibson County
Posey County
31
32
33

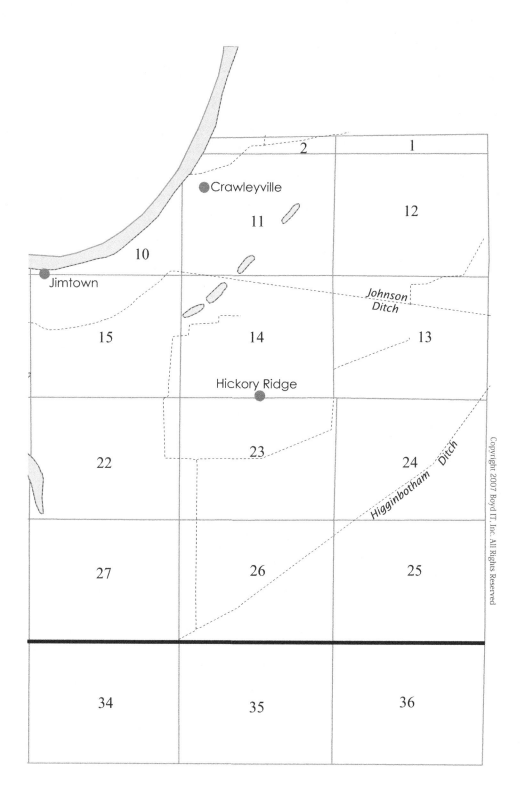

2

1

● Crawleyville

11

12

10

● Jimtown

Johnson Ditch

15

14

13

Hickory Ridge ●

23

22

24

Higginbotham Ditch

27

26

25

34

35

36

Helpful Hints

1. This Map takes a different look at the same Congressional Township displayed in the preceding two maps. It presents features that can help you better envision the historical development of the area: a) Water-bodies (lakes & ponds), b) Water-courses (rivers, streams, etc.), c) Railroads, d) City/town center-points (where they were oftentimes located when first settled), and e) Cemeteries.

2. Using this "Historical" map in tandem with this Township's Patent Map and Road Map, may lead you to some interesting discoveries. You will often find roads, towns, cemeteries, and waterways are named after nearby landowners: sometimes those names will be the ones you are researching. See how many of these research gems you can find here in Gibson County.

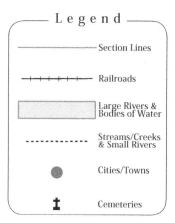

L e g e n d

——————— Section Lines

+–+–+–+–+ Railroads

Large Rivers & Bodies of Water

- - - - - - - Streams/Creeks & Small Rivers

● Cities/Towns

‡ Cemeteries

Scale: Section = 1 mile X 1 mile
(there are some exceptions)

Map Group 17: Index to Land Patents

Township 3-South Range 12-West (2nd PM)

After you locate an individual in this Index, take note of the Section and Section Part then proceed to the Land Patent map on the pages immediately following. You should have no difficulty locating the corresponding parcel of land.

The "For More Info" Column will lead you to more information about the underlying Patents. See the *Legend* at right, and the "How to Use this Book" chapter, for more information.

```
                    LEGEND
          "For More Info . . . " column
A = Authority (Legislative Act, See Appendix "A")
B = Block or Lot (location in Section unknown)
C = Cancelled Patent
F = Fractional Section
G = Group (Multi-Patentee Patent, see Appendix "C")
V = Overlaps another Parcel
R = Re-Issued (Parcel patented more than once)

(A & G items require you to look in the Appendixes referred
to above. All other Letter-designations followed by a number
require you to locate line-items in this index that possess
the ID number found after the letter).
```

ID	Individual in Patent	Sec.	Sec. Part	Date Issued	Other Counties	For More Info . . .
1292	ASH, James	21	SENW	1848-05-10		A1
1293	" "	21	W½NW	1848-05-10		A1
1294	AULDREDGE, James	20	NESW	1839-08-01		A1
1315	AULDRIDGE, John	17	SWNW	1839-02-01		A1
1358	AULDRIDGE, Thomas R	20	SENW	1839-02-01		A1
1253	BAIRD, Andrew	29	NENE	1850-10-01		A1
1281	BALDWIN, Green B	9	SENW	1835-09-10		A1
1280	" "	9	NESW	1835-10-15		A1
1355	BALDWIN, Telitha	8	SESE	1839-02-01		A1
1309	CASH, Jeremiah	15	NWNW	1835-10-28		A1
1363	CHALMERS, William	18	NESW	1839-02-01		A1
1346	CHURCH, Samuel	29	NWSW	1852-10-01		A1
1288	CREEK, Isom	19	SWSW	1837-08-05		A1
1289	CREEK, Jacob	20	NWSW	1837-11-07		A1
1316	CREEK, John	30	NENE	1838-09-01		A1
1341	CREEK, Pearson	19	SWSE	1839-08-01		A1
1360	CREEK, Washington	19	NWSW	1839-08-01		A1
1317	CROCKETT, John	18	NENE	1840-10-01		A1 G5
1275	CROSS, Fetherton	8	E½NW	1831-05-21		A1
1311	DAVIS, Jesse	33	SWNW	1835-10-23		A1
1310	"	32	SWNE	1837-08-05		A1
1313	DAVIS, Joel	32	SWNW	1837-03-20		A1
1314	"	32	NWNW	1837-08-01		A1 G6
1343	DAVIS, Robert C	31	E½NE	1831-06-01		A1
1344	" "	32	NWSW	1837-08-05		A1
1373	DAVIS, William R	32	NESE	1835-10-01		A1
1314	" "	32	NWNW	1837-08-01		A1 G6
1374	" "	31	SWSE	1837-08-05		A1 G8
1372	" "	29	SWNW	1852-10-01		A1
1296	EATON, James	31	NW	1823-07-24		A1
1255	FORREST, Benjamin	17	W½SW	1839-08-01		A1
1286	FRAZER, Hiram J	9	SWSW	1837-11-07		A1
1320	FRAZER, John J	9	SESW	1837-11-07		A1
1252	GARRET, Amos	20	SWNW	1839-08-01		A1
1268	GARRET, Eli	8	NENE	1838-09-07		A1
1284	GARRET, Henry	8	W½SE	1831-12-08		A1
1283	" "	8	SWNW	1835-09-05		A1
1282	" "	8	NWSW	1835-09-10		A1
1350	GARRET, Shubal	9	W½NE	1829-05-01		A1
1349	" "	9	SENE	1838-09-07		A1
1356	GARRET, Thomas	20	NWNW	1852-10-01		A1
1297	GARRETT, James	8	NWNE	1838-09-01		A1
1351	GARRETT, Shubel	9	NENE	1835-10-07		A1
1364	GARRETT, William	18	SE	1838-09-01		A1
1319	GARTEN, John	33	SESW	1835-09-10		A1
1318	" "	33	NESW	1835-10-15		A1

ID	Individual in Patent	Sec.	Sec. Part	Date Issued	Other Counties	For More Info . . .
1329	GARTON, Joseph	30	SENE	1839-08-01		A1
1337	GOODWIN, Moses	32	SENW	1838-09-01		A1
1290	GREEK, Jacob	19	NWSE	1835-10-15		A1
1262	GRIER, Charles	21	SWNE	1837-03-20		A1
1261	``	21	NWNE	1837-08-05		A1
1254	GWIN, Baily W	9	NENW	1840-10-01		A1
1317	HALL, Samuel	18	NENE	1840-10-01		A1 G5
1365	HAMER, William	24	SW	1916-07-03		A1 G20
1259	HARMON, Bennett	8	NESE	1838-09-01		A1
1332	HARMON, Lewis	5	W½SE	1831-12-31		A1
1333	``	``	9	NWSW	1837-11-07		A1
1334	``	``	9	SWNW	1837-11-07		A1
1354	HARMON, Syrack	8	SENE	1837-11-07		A1 R1327
1335	HARRISS, Morgan	28	SENW	1837-03-20		A1
1336	``	29	NESE	1837-03-20		A1
1331	HOBBS, Lawson E	28	NWNW	1852-07-01		A1
1367	HUNTER, William	28	W½SE	1831-06-01		A1
1366	``	``	28	SWNW	1838-09-05		A1
1277	JOHNSON, George	33	SWSW	1835-10-01		A1
1374	``	``	31	SWSE	1837-08-05		A1 G8
1321	JOHNSON, John	33	NWSE	1835-09-10		A1
1322	``	``	33	SWSE	1835-10-23		A1
1357	JOHNSON, Thomas	5	W½NW	1831-05-21		A1
1368	JOHNSON, William	33	NWSW	1835-09-10		A1
1298	JORDAN, James	9	E½SE	1831-12-31		A1
1300	``	``	9	SWSE	1835-10-07		A1
1299	``	``	9	NWSE	1835-10-23		A1
1266	KNOLES, Eddy	29	SESE	1835-10-23		A1
1269	KNOLES, Eli	33	NWNW	1835-10-07		A1
1353	KNOLES, Solomon	29	SWSE	1837-03-18		A1
1352	``	``	29	NWSE	1841-05-25		A1
1369	KNOLES, William	28	E½SW	1831-06-01		A1
1370	``	``	28	SWNE	1835-10-23		A1
1276	LUCAS, Fielding	1	W½NE	1823-08-04		A1
1340	LUCAS, Oliver	1	NENE	1835-09-10		A1
1361	MARVELL, Wiley	32	W½SE	1832-04-10		A1
1345	MCCRARY, Robert	1	SENE	1837-03-15		A1
1323	MCFADEN, John	7	E½SE	1838-09-01		A1
1301	MCGARY, James	2	SW	1923-11-17		A1 G26
1301	MCGARY, Jesse	2	SW	1923-11-17		A1 G26
1301	MCGARY, John	2	SW	1923-11-17		A1 G26
1267	MCREYNOLDS, Edward	33	E½SE	1832-04-10		A1
1371	MOOTRY, William	20	NENW	1852-10-01		A1
1365	MOUNCE, Smith	24	SW	1916-07-03		A1 G20
1338	MURPHEY, Noah	29	E½NW	1852-10-01		A1
1339	``	``	29	W½NE	1852-10-01		A1
1291	PADEN, Jacob	21	E½SW	1829-05-01		A1
1302	PRICE, James	29	NESW	1838-09-01		A1
1303	``	``	29	SWSW	1839-02-01		A1
1324	PRICE, John	32	NWNE	1839-08-01		A1
1326	REDMAN, John	28	NWNE	1835-10-23		A1
1325	``	``	28	NENW	1837-03-30		A1
1317	ROBBISON, Henry	18	NENE	1840-10-01		A1 G5
1327	ROBINSON, John	8	SENE	1838-09-01		A1 R1354
1359	ROBINSON, Thomas	18	SESW	1840-10-01		A1
1270	SAULMAN, Elijah	31	NWSE	1837-08-01		A1
1271	SAULMON, Elijah	30	SESE	1839-08-01		A1
1285	SAULMON, Heritage	32	SESE	1835-10-15		A1
1295	SHARP, James E	10	W½SW	1835-10-07		A1
1272	SIMPSON, Ephraim	19	SENW	1837-03-18		A1
1273	``	``	19	SWNW	1839-08-01		A1
1274	SIMPSON, Ephriam	19	NWNW	1852-10-01		A1
1304	SIMPSON, James	6	SENE	1837-03-30		A1
1328	SIMPSON, John	9	NWNW	1839-08-01		A1
1342	SIMPSON, Richard	5	E½SW	1824-08-09		A1
1375	SIMPSON, William	19	E½SW	1837-03-30		A1
1376	``	``	19	NENW	1839-02-01		A1
1305	SKELTON, James	18	NWNE	1838-09-01		A1
1306	``	``	7	SWSE	1838-09-01		A1
1251	SMITH, Adam	32	SWSW	1837-08-05		A1
1377	STEEL, William	5	W½SW	1835-10-07		A1
1307	TARRET, James	20	SWSW	1838-09-01		A1
1308	``	``	29	NWNW	1838-09-01		A1

ID	Individual in Patent	Sec.	Sec. Part	Date Issued	Other Counties	For More Info . . .
1330	WASSON, Joseph	22	E½NW	1830-12-02		A1
1312	WELBORN, Jesse Y	17	NENW	1835-10-01		A1
1260	WESTFALL, Calvin	29	SENE	1850-10-01		A1
1287	WESTFALL, Hiram	21	NENW	1837-08-05		A1
1265	WHEELER, David	15	SWNW	1835-10-07		A1
1347	WHEELER, Samuel	20	SESW	1852-07-01		A1
1348	" "	20	SWSE	1852-10-01		A1
1263	WIGGINS, Charles S	21	NWSW	1852-10-01		A1
1257	WILLIAMS, Benjamin	30	NWNW	1837-03-20		A1
1256	" "	29	SESW	1838-09-01		A1
1258	" "	32	NENW	1838-09-01		A1
1279	WILLIAMS, George	31	SWNE	1835-10-15		A1
1278	" "	31	NWNE	1837-11-07		A1
1362	WILLIAMS, Wiliam	30	SWNW	1838-09-07		A1
1264	WILLY, Clement	30	NESE	1838-09-01		A1

Patent Map

T3-S R12-W
2nd PM Meridian

Map Group 17

Township Statistics

Parcels Mapped	:	127
Number of Patents	:	122
Number of Individuals	:	100
Patentees Identified	:	97
Number of Surnames	:	61
Multi-Patentee Parcels	:	5
Oldest Patent Date	:	7/24/1823
Most Recent Patent	:	11/17/1923
Block/Lot Parcels	:	0
Parcels Re - Issued	:	1
Parcels that Overlap	:	0
Cities and Towns	:	4
Cemeteries	:	7

6

SIMPSON
James
1837

JOHNSON
Thomas
1831

5

SIMPSON
Richard
1824

HARMON
Lewis
1831

STEEL
William
1835

4

7

GARRET
Henry
1835

MCFADEN
John
1838

SKELTON
James
1838

SKELTON
James
1838

CROCKETT [5]
John
1840

CROSS
Fetherton
1831

GARRET
Henry
1835

8

GARRET
James
1838

GARRET
Eli
1838

GARRET
Henry
1831

HARMON
Syrack
1837 ROBINSON
John
1838

GARRET
Henry
1835

HARMON
Bennett
1838

SIMPSON
John
1839

GWIN
Baily W
1840

HARMON
Lewis
1837

BALDWIN
Green B
1835

GARRET
Shubal
1829

GARRETT
Shubel
1835

GARRET
Shubal
1838

9

HARMON
Lewis
1837

BALDWIN
Green B
1835

JORDAN
James
1835

JORDAN
James
1831

BALDWIN
Telitha
1839

FRAZER
Hiram J
1837

FRAZER
John J
1837

JORDAN
James
1835

WELBORN
Jesse Y
1835

AULDRIDGE
John
1839

CHALMERS
William
1839

18

ROBINSON
Thomas
1840

GARRETT
William
1838

FORREST
Benjamin
1839

17

16

SIMPSON
Ephriam
1852

SIMPSON
William
1839

SIMPSON
Ephraim
1839

SIMPSON
Ephraim
1837

19

CREEK
Washington
1839

SIMPSON
William
1837

GREEK
Jacob
1835

CREEK
Isom
1837

CREEK
Pearson
1839

GARRET
Thomas
1852

GARRET
Amos
1839

CREEK
Jacob
1837

TARRET
James
1838

MOOTRY
William
1852

AULDRIDGE
Thomas R
1839

AULDREDGE
James
1839

WHEELER
Samuel
1852

20

WHEELER
Samuel
1852

WESTFALL
Hiram
1837

ASH
James
1848

ASH
James
1848

GRIER
Charles
1837

GRIER
Charles
1837

21

WIGGINS
Charles S
1852

PADEN
Jacob
1829

WILLIAMS
Benjamin
1837

WILLIAMS
Wiliam
1838

30

CREEK
John
1838

GARTON
Joseph
1839

WILLY
Clement
1838

SAULMON
Elijah
1839

TARRET
James
1838

DAVIS
William R
1852

CHURCH
Samuel
1852

PRICE
James
1839

MURPHEY
Noah
1852

MURPHEY
Noah
1852

29

PRICE
James
1838

WILLIAMS
Benjamin
1838

BAIRD
Andrew
1850

WESTFALL
Calvin
1850

KNOLES
Solomon
1841

HARRISS
Morgan
1837

KNOLES
Solomon
1837

KNOLES
Eddy
1835

HOBBS
Lawson E
1852

HUNTER
William
1838

KNOLES
William
1831

REDMAN
John
1835

REDMAN
John
1837

HARRISS
Morgan
1837

KNOLES
William
1835

28

HUNTER
William
1831

EATON
James
1823

WILLIAMS
George
1837

WILLIAMS
George
1835

SAULMAN
Elijah
1837

DAVIS [8]
William R
1837

31

DAVIS
Robert C
1831

DAVIS
Robert C
1837

SMITH
Adam
1837

DAVIS [6]
Joel
1837

DAVIS
Joel
1837

GOODWIN
Moses
1838

WILLIAMS
Benjamin
1838

32

MARVELL
Wiley
1832

PRICE
John
1839

DAVIS
Jesse
1837

DAVIS
William R
1835

SAULMON
Heritage
1835

KNOLES
Eli
1835

DAVIS
Jesse
1835

JOHNSON
William
1835

JOHNSON
George
1835

33

GARTEN
John
1835

GARTEN
John
1835

JOHNSON
John
1835

MCREYNOLDS
Edward
1832

JOHNSON
John
1835

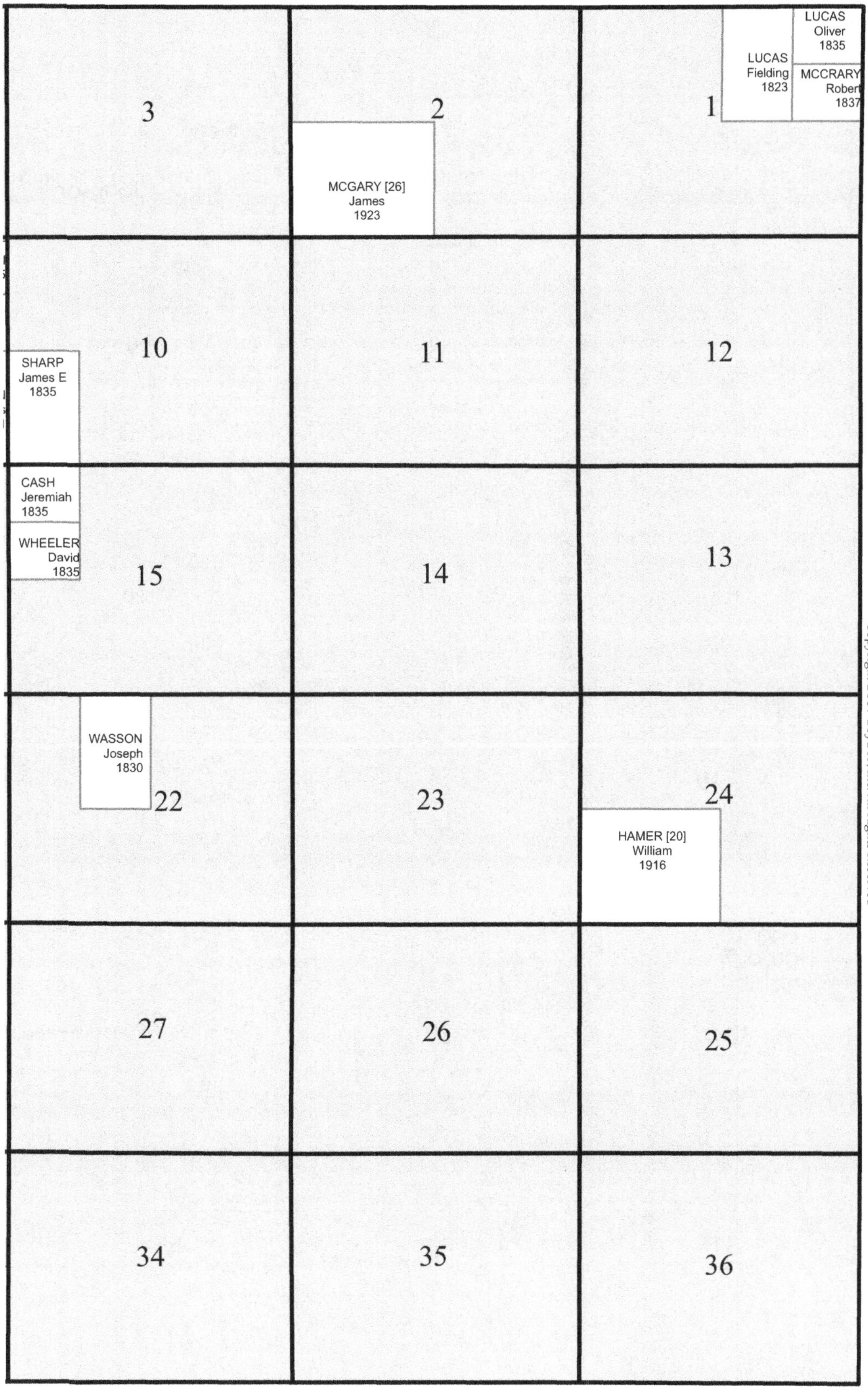

| | | LUCAS Oliver 1835 |
| 3 | 2 | LUCAS Fielding 1823 | 1 | MCCRARY Robert 1837 |

MCGARY [26] James 1923

SHARP James E 1835

| 10 | 11 | 12 |

CASH Jeremiah 1835

WHEELER David 1835

| 15 | 14 | 13 |

WASSON Joseph 1830

| 22 | 23 | 24 |

HAMER [20] William 1916

| 27 | 26 | 25 |

| 34 | 35 | 36 |

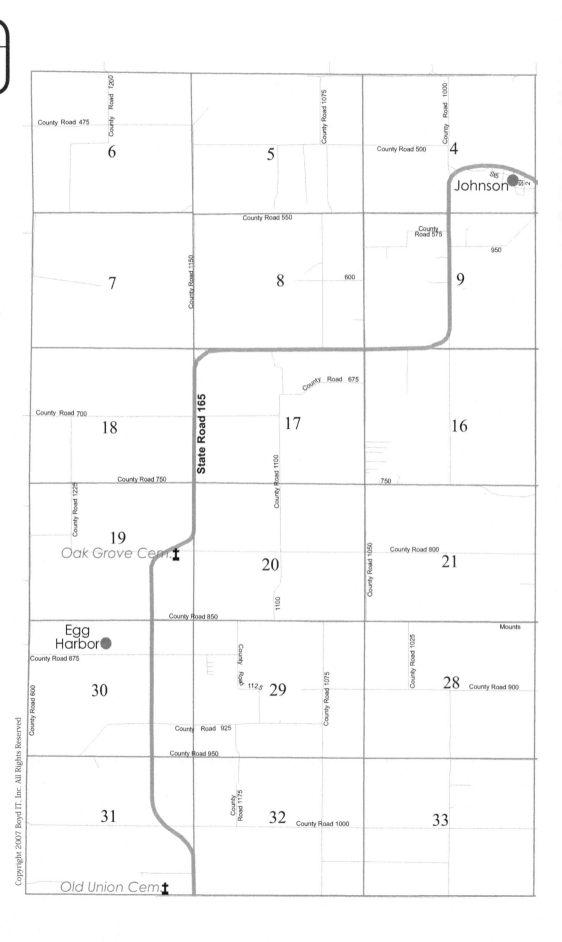

Road Map

T3-S R12-W
2nd PM Meridian

Map Group 17

Cities & Towns
Egg Harbor
Johnson
Mounts
Owensville

Cemeteries
Benson Cemetery
Knowles Cemetery
Mauck Cemetery
Oak Grove Cemetery
Old Union Cemetery
Skelton Cemetery
Wilson Cemetery

✝ *Mauck Cem.*

3

2

1

North
Short
2nd
Warehouse
Clark
Main
3rd
Mill

State Road 168

Skelton Cem. ✝

Warrick
Elm
1st
Owensville

10

County Road 600

11

County Road 850

12

County Road 650

County Road 700

County Road 750

15

14

13

State Road 65

22

23

24

Benson Cem. ✝

● Mounts

27

26

25

County Road 900

County Road 950 ✝

Wilson Cem.

34

Antioch Church

35

Cedar Grove

36

County Road 1000

Knowles Cem. ✝

Helpful Hints

1. This road map has a number of uses, but primarily it is to help you: a) find the present location of land owned by your ancestors (at least the general area), b) find cemeteries and city-centers, and c) estimate the route/roads used by Census-takers & tax-assessors.

2. If you plan to travel to Gibson County to locate cemeteries or land parcels, please pick up a modern travel map for the area before you do. Mapping old land parcels on modern maps is not as exact a science as you might think. Just the slightest variations in public land survey coordinates, estimates of parcel boundaries, or road-map deviations can greatly alter a map's representation of how a road either does or doesn't cross a particular parcel of land.

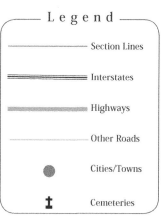

L e g e n d

——————— Section Lines

═══════ Interstates

━━━━━━ Highways

——————— Other Roads

● Cities/Towns

✝ Cemeteries

Scale: Section = 1 mile X 1 mile
(generally, with some exceptions)

Historical Map

T3-S R12-W
2nd PM Meridian

Map Group 17

Cities & Towns
Egg Harbor
Johnson
Mounts
Owensville

Cemeteries
Benson Cemetery
Knowles Cemetery
Mauck Cemetery
Oak Grove Cemetery
Old Union Cemetery
Skelton Cemetery
Wilson Cemetery

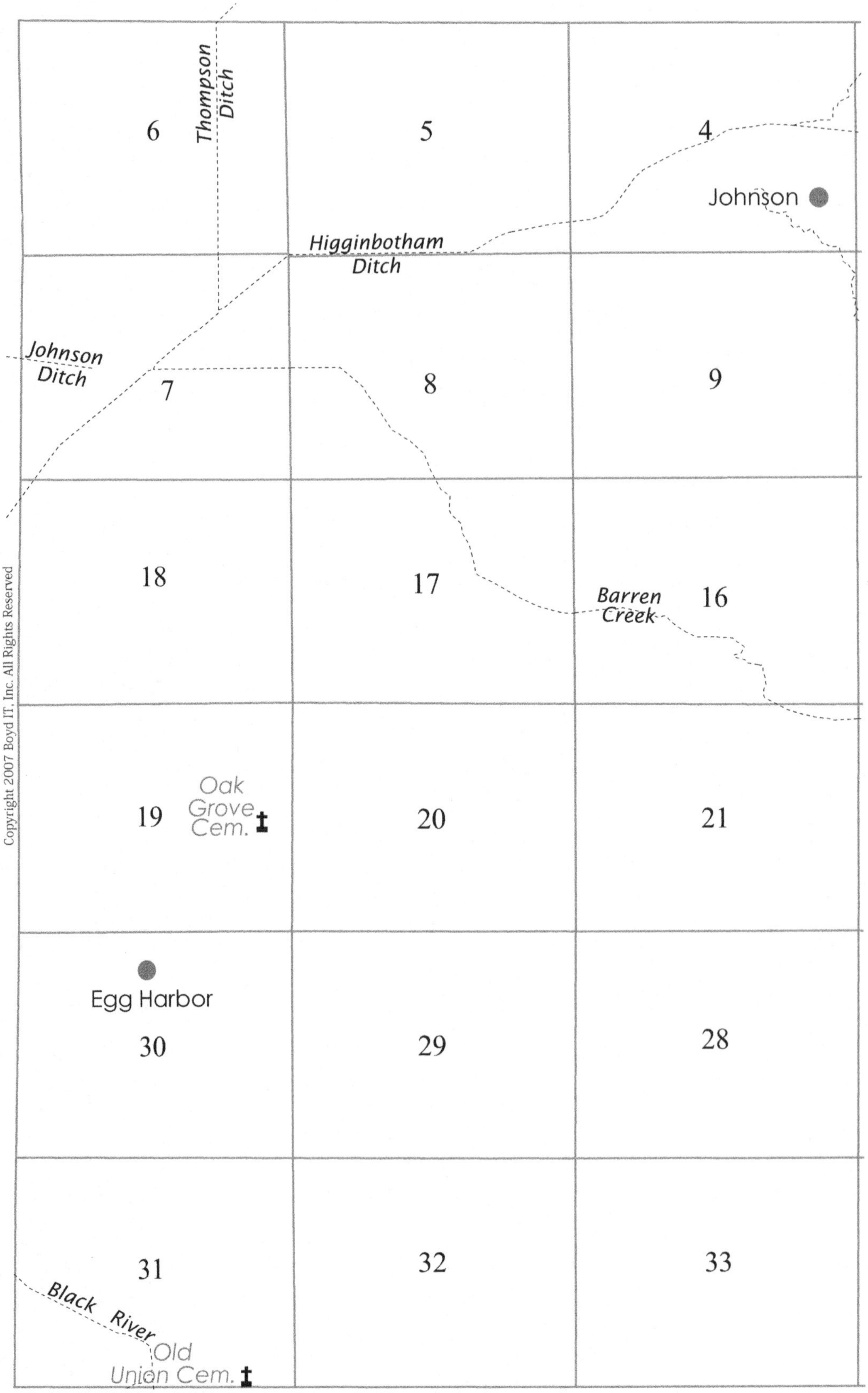

Thompson Ditch

6

5

4

Johnson ●

Higginbotham Ditch

Johnson Ditch

7

8

9

18

17

Barren Creek

16

19

Oak Grove Cem. ✝

20

21

● Egg Harbor

30

29

28

31

32

33

Black River

Old Union Cem. ✝

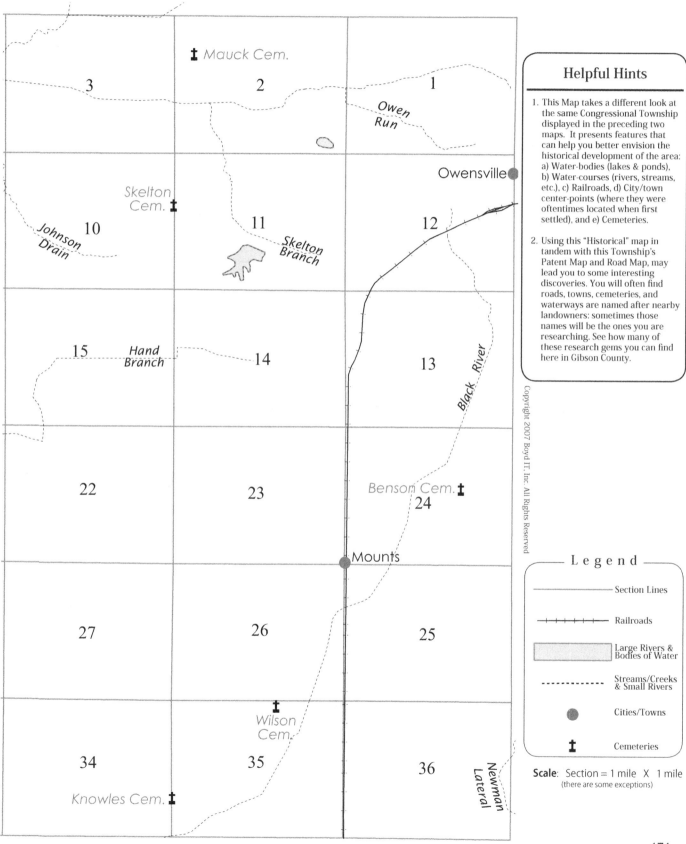

Mauck Cem.

3

2

1

Owen Run

Owensville

Skelton Cem.

Johnson Drain

10

11

Skelton Branch

12

15

Hand Branch

14

13

Black River

22

23

Benson Cem.

24

Mounts

27

26

25

Wilson Cem.

34

35

36

Newman Lateral

Knowles Cem.

Helpful Hints

1. This Map takes a different look at the same Congressional Township displayed in the preceding two maps. It presents features that can help you better envision the historical development of the area: a) Water-bodies (lakes & ponds), b) Water-courses (rivers, streams, etc.), c) Railroads, d) City/town center-points (where they were oftentimes located when first settled), and e) Cemeteries.

2. Using this "Historical" map in tandem with this Township's Patent Map and Road Map, may lead you to some interesting discoveries. You will often find roads, towns, cemeteries, and waterways are named after nearby landowners: sometimes those names will be the ones you are researching. See how many of these research gems you can find here in Gibson County.

Legend

——————	Section Lines
+++++++	Railroads
▭	Large Rivers & Bodies of Water
- - - - - -	Streams/Creeks & Small Rivers
●	Cities/Towns
✝	Cemeteries

Scale: Section = 1 mile X 1 mile
(there are some exceptions)

Map Group 18: Index to Land Patents

Township 3-South Range 11-West (2nd PM)

After you locate an individual in this Index, take note of the Section and Section Part then proceed to the Land Patent map on the pages immediately following. You should have no difficulty locating the corresponding parcel of land.

The "For More Info" Column will lead you to more information about the underlying Patents. See the *Legend* at right, and the "How to Use this Book" chapter, for more information.

LEGEND
"For More Info . . . " column

A = Authority (Legislative Act, See Appendix "A")
B = Block or Lot (location in Section unknown)
C = Cancelled Patent
F = Fractional Section
G = Group (Multi-Patentee Patent, see Appendix "C")
V = Overlaps another Parcel
R = Re-Issued (Parcel patented more than once)

(A & G items require you to look in the Appendixes referred to above. All other Letter-designations followed by a number require you to locate line-items in this index that possess the ID number found after the letter).

ID	Individual in Patent	Sec.	Sec. Part	Date Issued	Other Counties	For More Info . . .
1566	ADAMS, Samuel	25	SENE	1837-03-18		A1
1608	ALSOP, Willis	4	NWSE	1835-10-15		A1
1607	" "	4	NESE	1837-03-20		A1
1497	AMES, John	12	W½SW	1848-05-10		A1 G1
1498	AYERS, John	1	E½NE	1837-03-18		A1
1424	BARKER, Elias	11	NWNW	1835-10-01		A1
1425	" "	2	SWSW	1837-03-18		A1
1494	BARKER, Jesse	11	NESW	1839-02-01		A1
1499	BARKER, John	11	NENW	1837-03-18		A1
1500	" "	2	SESW	1837-03-18		A1
1497	BARLOW, John	12	W½SW	1848-05-10		A1 G1
1446	BELOAT, George W	27	E½NW	1837-03-18		A1
1477	BELOAT, James	10	NWSW	1852-07-01		A1
1478	" "	10	SWSW	1856-06-03		A1
1502	BLYTHE, John C	29	NWNE	1839-02-01		A1
1430	BOREN, Evans	34	SESE	1839-08-01		A1
1509	BOREN, John M	28	SWSW	1837-03-15		A1
1395	BROTHERS, David	24	E½NW	1835-10-01		A1
1396	" "	33	W½NE	1837-03-20		A1
1460	BROTHERS, Hudson B	14	NESE	1837-08-05		A1
1476	BROTHERS, James B	22	E½NE	1831-12-31		A1
1475	" "	1	NESW	1844-08-01		A1
1505	BROTHERS, John H	15	W½SE	1837-03-30		A1
1584	BROTHERS, William	26	NWSE	1838-09-01		A1
1479	BRUMFIELD, James	36	E½NW	1838-09-01		A1
1501	BYRN, John	4	E½NE	1831-06-01		A1
1419	CHAFFIN, Edwin	28	E½SW	1837-03-15		A1
1420	" "	33	E½NW	1837-03-15		A1
1421	" "	33	W½SE	1837-03-20		A1
1533	CLARK, Joseph	36	SE	1839-08-01		A1
1380	CONNER, Alexander	12	E½NE	1831-06-01		A1
1381	" "	13	E½SE	1838-09-01		A1
1544	DAY, Levi	2	NWNE	1839-02-01		A1 G9
1544	DAY, Marcrum	2	NWNE	1839-02-01		A1 G9
1503	DEPRIEST, John	3	W½SW	1835-10-07		A1
1379	DOUGLASS, Albert W	17	SWSE	1837-03-30		A1
1465	DOUGLASS, Isaac P	14	W½SW	1831-06-01		A1
1466	" "	22	W½NE	1832-04-10		A1
1464	" "	11	SESE	1835-09-10		A1
1467	" "	27	E½SE	1837-08-01		A1
1468	" "	27	SENE	1839-08-01		A1
1495	DOUGLASS, Jesse	21	E½NE	1831-12-08		A1
1508	DOUGLASS, John J	11	SWSE	1835-10-07		A1
1507	" "	11	SESW	1837-03-20		A1
1382	DOWNING, Alexander R	23	W½NW	1831-05-21		A1
1539	DUNCAN, Joshua	34	W½NE	1837-08-05		A1

ID	Individual in Patent	Sec.	Sec. Part	Date Issued	Other Counties	For More Info . . .
1540	DUNCAN, Joshua (Cont'd)	35	N½SE	1840-10-01		A1
1586	EMBREE, William	31	E½NW	1837-03-18		A1
1534	FIELD, Joseph	3	N½NW	1831-06-01		A1 V1471
1416	FIELDS, Edmund	17	W½NE	1835-10-23		A1
1417	"	8	S½SW	1837-03-18		A1
1480	FURGUSON, James	11	SENW	1839-02-01		A1
1575	GOOCH, Thomas M	36	E½SW	1839-08-01		A1
1576	"	36	SWSW	1839-08-01		A1
1590	GUDGEL, William	9	SWSE	1835-10-01		A1
1589	"	9	NWSE	1837-03-18		A1
1438	HALBROOK, George	12	E½SW	1837-03-18		A1
1393	HALBROOKS, Dansy	1	SWSW	1837-08-01		A1
1394	"	12	NWNW	1837-08-01		A1
1592	HALBROOKS, William	13	E½NW	1838-09-01		A1
1546	HARDY, Luke E	10	NWSE	1837-03-30		A1
1434	HAWKINS, Franklin	15	NENE	1835-10-01		A1
1435	"	20	NENW	1838-09-01		A1
1454	HAWKINS, Henry	22	NWSE	1837-03-20		A1
1455	"	22	SESW	1837-03-20		A1
1567	HAWKINS, Samuel	17	NWSE	1835-10-23		A1
1574	HAWKINS, Thomas	15	SWNW	1835-10-01		A1
1573	HEAD, Stephen	21	SESE	1839-02-01		A1
1591	HILL, William H	2	SWNW	1844-08-01		A1
1390	HOLCOM, Benjamin	35	S½SE	1838-09-01		A1
1431	HOPKINS, Ezekiel	1	NESE	1839-02-01		A1
1413	HUGHES, Devenport	15	NENE	1838-09-01		A1
1414	"	15	NWNE	1838-09-01		A1
1506	HULL, John	8	N½SW	1835-10-28		A1
1456	JOHNSON, Henry	3	SENW	1840-10-01		A1
1463	KENNERLY, Isaac	34	W½SE	1831-12-31		A1
1462	"	34	NESE	1839-02-01		A1
1483	KITCHEN, James	35	SWNE	1837-03-20		A1
1481	"	34	NESW	1837-08-05		A1
1482	"	34	SENE	1839-02-01		A1
1484	"	35	SWSW	1840-10-01		A1
1541	KITCHEN, Joshua	35	NESW	1838-09-01		A1
1389	KNOLES, Archibald	29	E½SE	1835-10-23		A1
1388	"	28	NWSW	1837-03-18		A1
1422	KNOLES, Eli	29	SENE	1838-09-01		A1
1423	"	29	SWNE	1838-09-01		A1
1496	KNOLES, Jesse	14	NWSE	1835-10-23		A1
1593	LAW, William	13	W½SW	1835-09-10		A1
1594	LEGRANGE, William	11	NWNE	1839-02-01		A1
1472	LEWIS, Isam	4	SWSE	1837-03-18		A1
1418	LOCKWOOD, Edward B	24	NESE	1835-10-23		A1
1426	MARVEL, Elisha	35	NWNE	1837-03-20		A1
1439	MARVEL, George	25	SW	1837-03-20		A1
1556	MARVEL, Painter	29	SWNW	1835-10-23		A1
1555	"	29	E½NW	1837-03-20		A1
1582	MARVEL, Thomas W	25	W½NE	1837-03-20		A1
1545	MCCRARY, Logan	7	NENW	1840-10-01		A1
1562	MCCRARY, Robert	6	W½NW	1831-12-31		A1
1561	"	6	E½NW	1837-08-01		A1
1485	MCDOWELL, James L	35	SESW	1840-10-01		A1
1563	MCGAREY, Robert	4	SESE	1839-08-01		A1
1557	MCGARY, Patsy	11	SWSW	1839-08-01		A1
1564	MCGARY, Robert	15	NWNW	1839-08-01		A1
1504	MCGREGOR, John G	27	SWNE	1839-08-01		A1
1596	MCINTIRE, William	1	SESE	1837-03-30		A1
1595	"	1	NWSE	1838-09-01		A1
1486	MCKIDDY, James	17	SENE	1835-09-05		A1
1461	MCMULLIN, Hugh	1	NWSW	1849-08-01		A1
1578	MCMULLIN, Thomas	2	NWSE	1848-05-10		A1
1579	"	2	SESE	1848-05-10		A1
1580	"	2	SWNE	1848-05-10		A1
1577	"	2	NESW	1856-06-03		A1
1581	"	2	SWSE	1856-06-03		A1
1378	MILLER, Adam	4	W½NE	1826-11-15		A1
1401	MILLER, David	27	NWSE	1839-02-01		A1
1402	"	27	SWSE	1839-02-01		A1
1399	"	23	NENW	1839-08-01		A1
1400	"	23	NWNE	1839-08-01		A1
1514	MILLER, John	35	SWNW	1837-08-01		A1

ID	Individual in Patent	Sec.	Sec. Part	Date Issued	Other Counties	For More Info . . .
1512	MILLER, John (Cont'd)	35	NWSW	1838-09-01		A1
1513	" "	35	SENW	1838-09-01		A1
1597	MILLER, William	35	NWNW	1837-08-01		A1
1598	MINTON, William	15	SWSW	1837-03-20		A1
1515	MONTGOMERY, John	3	SESW	1835-10-07		A1
1516	" "	3	SWSE	1837-03-20		A1
1552	MONTGOMERY, Nathan	10	NWNE	1839-02-01		A1
1599	MONTGOMERY, William	20	NWNE	1839-02-01		A1
1600	" "	20	SWNW	1839-02-01		A1
1609	MONTGOMERY, Willis S	9	SWNE	1837-03-18		A1
1610	MONTGOMERY, Willis Smith	9	SENE	1837-03-20		A1
1427	MORRIS, Elisha	35	NENW	1838-09-01		A1
1437	MOUNTS, Garrard	29	SWSW	1835-09-05		A1
1436	" "	29	NWSW	1835-10-01		A1
1549	MOUNTS, Montgomery	10	SENW	1837-03-20		A1
1550	" "	10	SWNE	1837-03-20		A1
1451	NEWSOM, Harrison	30	E½SW	1832-06-06		A1
1452	NEWSUM, Harrison	29	NWNW	1835-10-01		A1
1572	ORR, Simon	2	NENE	1849-04-10		A1
1440	PEARCE, George	12	NWNE	1837-03-18		A1
1442	PIERCE, George	12	SWNE	1835-10-01		A1
1441	" "	12	NENW	1838-09-01		A1
1447	POE, Greenup	15	NWSW	1837-03-20		A1
1612	PRITCHETT, Wright	9	SESE	1837-03-15		A1
1611	" "	9	NWNE	1837-03-20		A1
1474	PRIVETT, Jacob	34	NENE	1839-08-01		A1
1415	REDMAN, Durham C	10	SENE	1856-06-03		A1
1565	REDMAN, Robert	20	SENW	1838-09-01		A1
1457	REEL, Henry	24	S½SW	1837-03-18		A1
1458	" "	36	NWSW	1839-08-01		A1
1536	REEL, Joseph N	24	SWSE	1839-02-01		A1 R1470
1403	ROBB, David	14	E½SW	1835-09-05		A1
1404	" "	14	SENW	1835-09-05		A1
1405	" "	15	SENE	1835-09-05		A1
1406	" "	22	SWSE	1839-02-01		A1
1407	" "	26	E½SE	1839-02-01		A1
1473	ROBERTSON, Isham	21	W½SE	1821-10-01		A1
1408	ROBINSON, David	1	SESW	1837-08-01		A1
1409	" "	1	SWSE	1837-08-01		A1
1588	ROBINSON, William F	34	W½SW	1830-12-02		A1
1587	" "	34	SESW	1835-10-01		A1
1383	ROSBOROUGH, Alexander	14	E½NE	1835-10-23		A1
1487	ROSBOROUGH, James	24	W½NW	1835-10-23		A1
1432	RUTLEDGE, Ezekiel	15	NESE	1837-03-20		A1
1433	" "	15	SESE	1839-08-01		A1
1530	RUTLEDGE, Johnson	17	NENE	1835-09-05		A1
1531	" "	27	NENE	1841-05-25		A1
1603	RUTLEDGE, William	28	W½NE	1837-03-15		A1
1602	" "	27	NWNE	1839-08-01		A1
1488	SCOTT, James	26	SWSE	1837-03-15		A1
1537	SCOTT, Joseph	17	E½SE	1831-12-31		A1
1538	" "	20	SWNE	1837-03-15		A1
1547	SHERWOOD, Marcus	13	W½SE	1835-10-15		A1
1459	SIDES, Henry	23	SWNE	1835-10-28		A1
1490	SIDES, James	22	NESE	1837-03-20		A1
1491	" "	22	SESE	1839-02-01		A1
1489	" "	15	SWNE	1844-08-01		A1
1387	SILLAVEN, Andrew	3	NESE	1837-03-18		A1
1386	" "	2	NWSW	1837-11-07		A1
1569	SILLAVEN, Samuel	3	W½NE	1829-07-02		A1
1568	" "	3	NENE	1835-09-05		A1
1518	SIMPSON, John	14	SWNW	1835-09-05		A1
1517	" "	10	NENW	1837-03-18		A1
1453	SMITH, Harrison	3	NESW	1841-05-25		A1
1469	SMITH, Isaac	32	E½NE	1832-06-06		A1
1520	SMITH, John	29	SWSE	1835-10-23		A1
1521	" "	3	NWSE	1837-03-18		A1
1519	" "	29	NWSE	1838-09-01		A1
1548	SMITH, Martin	11	SWNW	1839-02-01		A1
1604	SMITH, William	20	NWNW	1835-09-10		A1
1523	STEWART, John W	23	SENW	1835-10-01		A1
1524	" "	27	W½NW	1835-10-07		A1
1570	STONE, Silas S	2	NESE	1835-10-28		A1

ID	Individual in Patent	Sec.	Sec. Part	Date Issued	Other Counties	For More Info . . .
1571	STONE, Silas S (Cont'd)	2	SENE	1835-10-28		A1
1385	THOMAS, Andrew J	15	SESW	1837-03-15		A1
1384	" "	10	SESW	1839-08-01		A1
1412	THOMAS, David	22	W½SW	1831-12-31		A1
1410	" "	21	NESE	1835-10-07		A1
1411	" "	22	NESW	1837-03-15		A1
1429	THOMAS, Ephraim	10	SESE	1856-06-03		A1
1492	THOMAS, James	1	W½NW	1850-12-10		A1
1448	THOMPSON, Greenup	10	NESW	1839-08-01		A1
1449	" "	10	SWNW	1840-10-01		A1
1450	" "	9	NESE	1840-10-01		A1
1443	TRIBBLE, George	36	NWNE	1837-03-30		A1
1444	TRIBLE, George	36	E½NE	1824-08-09		A1
1445	" "	36	SWNE	1839-02-01		A1
1522	TRIBLE, John	36	W½NW	1830-12-02		A1
1583	WALLACE, Washington	1	W½NE	1839-02-01		A1
1428	WALTERS, Enoch	13	E½SW	1838-09-01		A1
1560	WALTERS, Reuben	13	W½NW	1839-08-01		A1
1558	" "	11	NESE	1856-06-03		A1
1559	" "	11	SENE	1856-06-03		A1
1470	WATTERS, Isaac	24	SWSE	1838-09-01		A1 R1536
1613	WEED, Zenas M	14	N½NW	1840-10-01		A1
1493	WEST, James	29	NENE	1838-09-01		A1
1392	WHITING, Charles	23	NENE	1835-10-01		A1
1391	" "	14	SESE	1835-10-07		A1
1606	WILKINSON, William	31	W½SW	1830-12-02		A1
1605	" "	31	E½SW	1835-10-23		A1
1543	WILSON, Joshua	31	W½NE	1835-10-07		A1
1542	" "	31	E½NE	1835-10-23		A1
1585	WILSON, William C	7	SENW	1835-09-05		A1
1510	WITHERSPOON, John M	10	NWNW	1835-10-15		A1
1511	" "	9	NENE	1839-02-01		A1
1551	WITHERSPOON, Moses C	2	NWNW	1835-10-01		A1
1601	WITHERSPOON, William P	3	SENE	1837-08-05		A1
1397	WOODS, David L	2	NENW	1837-03-20		A1
1398	" "	2	SENW	1837-03-20		A1
1471	WOODS, Isaac	3	NENW	1835-10-01		A1 V1534
1525	WOODS, John	11	NWSE	1839-02-01		A1
1526	" "	11	SWNE	1839-02-01		A1
1535	WOODS, Joseph M	24	N½SW	1841-05-25		A1
1527	WRIGHT, John	1	E½NW	1839-02-01		A1
1528	" "	10	SWSE	1845-05-01		A1
1532	WRIGHT, Jonathan	11	NWSW	1840-10-01		A1
1529	YAGER, John	30	E½NE	1831-12-31		A1
1553	YAGER, Nicholas	5	E½SW	1835-10-15		A1
1554	YEAGER, Nickolas	6	W½NE	1837-08-01		A1

Patent Map

T3-S R11-W
2nd PM Meridian

Map Group 18

Township Statistics

Parcels Mapped	:	236
Number of Patents	:	221
Number of Individuals	:	157
Patentees Identified	:	155
Number of Surnames	:	98
Multi-Patentee Parcels	:	2
Oldest Patent Date	:	10/1/1821
Most Recent Patent	:	6/3/1856
Block/Lot Parcels	:	0
Parcels Re - Issued	:	1
Parcels that Overlap	:	2
Cities and Towns	:	3
Cemeteries	:	3

Section 6: MCCRARY Robert 1831; MCCRARY Robert 1837; YEAGER Nickolas 1837

Section 5: YAGER Nicholas 1835

Section 4: MILLER Adam 1826; BYRN John 1831; ALSOP Willis 1835; ALSOP Willis 1837; LEWIS Isam 1837; MCGAREY Robert 1839

Section 7: MCCRARY Logan 1840; WILSON William C 1835

Section 8: HULL John 1835; FIELDS Edmund 1837

Section 9: WITHERSPOON John M 1839; PRITCHETT Wright 1837; MONTGOMERY Willis S 1837; MONTGOMERY Willis Smith 1837; GUDGEL William 1837; THOMPSON Greenup 1840; GUDGEL William 1835; PRITCHETT Wright 1837

Section 18

Section 17: FIELDS Edmund 1835; RUTLEDGE Johnson 1835; MCKIDDY James 1835; HAWKINS Samuel 1835; SCOTT Joseph 1831; DOUGLASS Albert W 1837

Section 16

Section 19

Section 20: SMITH William 1835; HAWKINS Franklin 1838; MONTGOMERY William 1839; MONTGOMERY William 1839; REDMAN Robert 1838; SCOTT Joseph 1837

Section 21: DOUGLASS Jesse 1831; ROBERTSON Isham 1821; THOMAS David 1835; HEAD Stephen 1839

Section 30: YAGER John 1831; NEWSOM Harrison 1832

Section 29: NEWSUM Harrison 1835; MARVEL Painter 1835; MARVEL Painter 1837; BLYTHE John C 1839; WEST James 1838; KNOLES Eli 1838; KNOLES Eli 1838; MOUNTS Garrard 1835; SMITH John 1838; MOUNTS Garrard 1835; SMITH John 1835; KNOLES Archibald 1835

Section 28: KNOLES Archibald 1837; CHAFFIN Edwin 1837; BOREN John M 1837; RUTLEDGE William 1837

Section 31: EMBREE William 1837; WILSON Joshua 1835; WILSON Joshua 1835; WILKINSON William 1830; WILKINSON William 1835

Section 32: SMITH Isaac 1832

Section 33: CHAFFIN Edwin 1837; BROTHERS David 1837; CHAFFIN Edwin 1837

Section 3
FIELD Joseph 1831
WOODS Isaac 1835
SILLAVEN Samuel 1829
SILLAVEN Samuel 1835
JOHNSON Henry 1840
WITHERSPOON William P 1837
DEPRIEST John 1835
SMITH Harrison 1841
SMITH John 1837
SILLAVEN Andrew 1837
MONTGOMERY John 1835
MONTGOMERY John 1837

Section 2
WITHERSPOON Moses C 1835
WOODS David L 1837
DAY [9] Levi 1839
ORR Simon 1849
HILL William H 1844
WOODS David L 1837
MCMULLIN Thomas 1848
STONE Silas S 1835
SILLAVEN Andrew 1837
MCMULLIN Thomas 1856
MCMULLIN Thomas 1848
STONE Silas S 1835
BARKER Elias 1837
BARKER John 1837
MCMULLIN Thomas 1856
MCMULLIN Thomas 1848

Section 1
THOMAS James 1850
WRIGHT John 1839
WALLACE Washington 1839
AYERS John 1837
MCMULLIN Hugh 1849
BROTHERS James B 1844
MCINTIRE William 1838
HOPKINS Ezekiel 1839
HALBROOKS Dansy 1837
ROBINSON David 1837
ROBINSON David 1837
MCINTIRE William 1837

Section 10
WITHERSPOON John M 1835
SIMPSON John 1837
MONTGOMERY Nathan 1839
THOMPSON Greenup 1840
MOUNTS Montgomery 1837
MOUNTS Montgomery 1837
REDMAN Durham C 1856
BELOAT James 1852
THOMPSON Greenup 1839
HARDY Luke E 1837
BELOAT James 1856
THOMAS Andrew J 1839
WRIGHT John 1845
THOMAS Ephraim 1856

Section 11
BARKER Elias 1835
BARKER John 1837
LEGRANGE William 1839
SMITH Martin 1839
FURGUSON James 1839
WOODS John 1839
WALTERS Reuben 1856
WRIGHT Jonathan 1840
BARKER Jesse 1839
WOODS John 1839
WALTERS Reuben 1856
MCGARY Patsy 1839
DOUGLASS John J 1837
DOUGLASS John J 1835
DOUGLASS Isaac P 1835

Section 12
HALBROOKS Dansy 1837
PIERCE George 1838
PEARCE George 1837
CONNER Alexander 1831
PIERCE George 1835
AMES [1] John 1848
HALBROOK George 1837

Section 15
MCGARY Robert 1839
HAWKINS Franklin 1835
HUGHES Devenport 1838
HUGHES Devenport 1838
HAWKINS Thomas 1835
SIDES James 1844
ROBB David 1835
POE Greenup 1837
BROTHERS John H 1837
RUTLEDGE Ezekiel 1837
MINTON William 1837
THOMAS Andrew J 1837
RUTLEDGE Ezekiel 1839

Section 14
WEED Zenas M 1840
ROSBOROUGH Alexander 1835
SIMPSON John 1835
ROBB David 1835
DOUGLASS Isaac P 1831
ROBB David 1835
KNOLES Jesse 1835
BROTHERS Hudson B 1837
WHITING Charles 1835

Section 13
WALTERS Reuben 1839
HALBROOKS William 1838
LAW William 1835
WALTERS Enoch 1838
SHERWOOD Marcus 1835
CONNER Alexander 1838

Section 22
DOUGLASS Isaac P 1832
BROTHERS James B 1831
THOMAS David 1837
HAWKINS Henry 1837
SIDES James 1837
THOMAS David 1831
HAWKINS Henry 1837
ROBB David 1839
SIDES James 1839

Section 23
DOWNING Alexander R 1831
MILLER David 1839
MILLER David 1839
WHITING Charles 1835
STEWART John W 1835
SIDES Henry 1835

Section 24
BROTHERS David 1835
ROSBOROUGH James 1835
WOODS Joseph M 1841
LOCKWOOD Edward B 1835
REEL Henry 1837
WATTERS Isaac 1838
REEL Joseph N 1839

Section 27
STEWART John W 1835
BELOAT George W 1837
RUTLEDGE William 1839
RUTLEDGE Johnson 1841
MCGREGOR John G 1839
DOUGLASS Isaac P 1839
MILLER David 1839
DOUGLASS Isaac P 1837
MILLER David 1839

Section 26
BROTHERS William 1838
ROBB David 1839
SCOTT James 1837

Section 25
MARVEL Thomas W 1837
ADAMS Samuel 1837
MARVEL George 1837

Section 34
DUNCAN Joshua 1837
PRIVETT Jacob 1839
KITCHEN James 1839
ROBINSON William F 1830
KITCHEN James 1837
KENNERLY Isaac 1839
KENNERLY Isaac 1831
ROBINSON William F 1835
BOREN Evans 1839

Section 35
MILLER William 1837
MORRIS Elisha 1838
MARVEL Elisha 1837
MILLER John 1837
MILLER John 1838
KITCHEN James 1837
MILLER John 1838
KITCHEN Joshua 1838
DUNCAN Joshua 1840
KITCHEN James 1840
MCDOWELL James L 1840
HOLCOM Benjamin 1838

Section 36
TRIBLE John 1830
BRUMFIELD James 1838
TRIBBLE George 1837
TRIBLE George 1824
TRIBLE George 1839
REEL Henry 1839
GOOCH Thomas M 1839
CLARK Joseph 1839
GOOCH Thomas M 1839

Helpful Hints

1. This Map's INDEX can be found on the preceding pages.

2. Refer to Map "C" to see where this Township lies within Gibson County, Indiana.

3. Numbers within square brackets [ ] denote a multi-patentee land parcel (multi-owner). Refer to Appendix "C" for a full list of members in this group.

4. Areas that look to be crowded with Patentees usually indicate multiple sales of the same parcel (Re-issues) or Overlapping parcels. See this Township's Index for an explanation of these and other circumstances that might explain "odd" groupings of Patentees on this map.

Legend

— Patent Boundary

▬ Section Boundary

No Patents Found (or Outside County)

1., 2., 3., ... Lot Numbers (when beside a name)

[ ] Group Number (see Appendix "C")

Scale: Section = 1 mile X 1 mile (generally, with some exceptions)

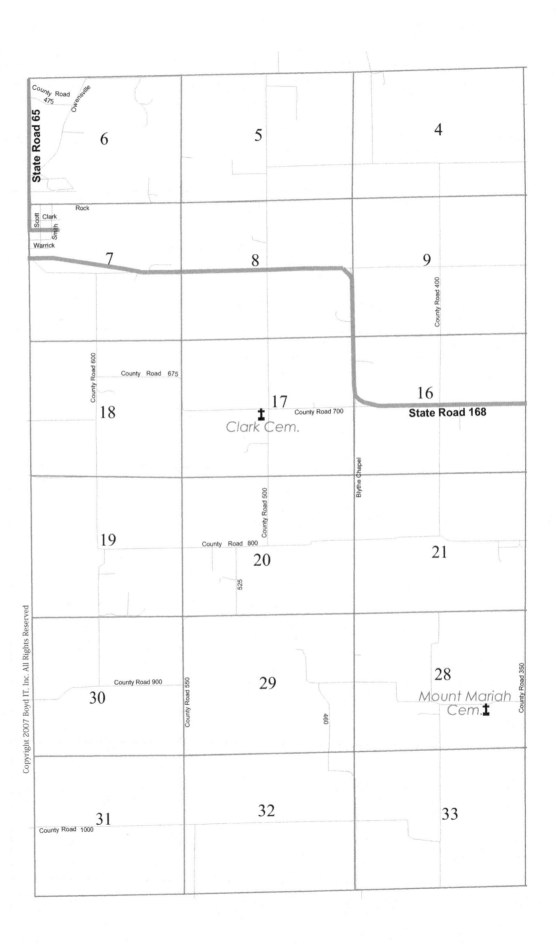

Road Map

T3-S R11-W
2nd PM Meridian

Map Group 18

Cities & Towns
Durham
Fort Branch
McGary

Cemeteries
Clark Cemetery
Durham Cemetery
Mount Mariah Cemetery

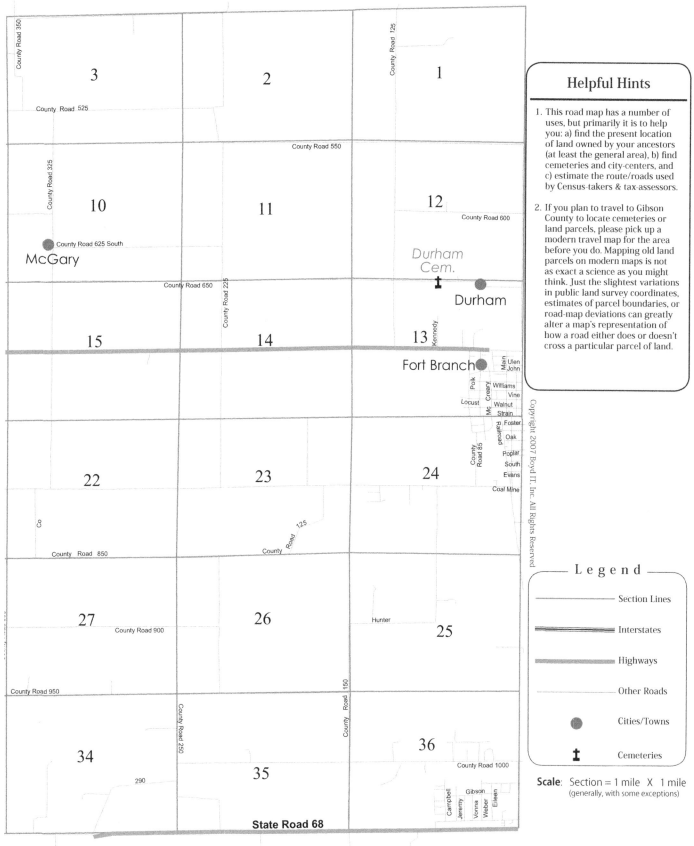

Helpful Hints

1. This road map has a number of uses, but primarily it is to help you: a) find the present location of land owned by your ancestors (at least the general area), b) find cemeteries and city-centers, and c) estimate the route/roads used by Census-takers & tax-assessors.

2. If you plan to travel to Gibson County to locate cemeteries or land parcels, please pick up a modern travel map for the area before you do. Mapping old land parcels on modern maps is not as exact a science as you might think. Just the slightest variations in public land survey coordinates, estimates of parcel boundaries, or road-map deviations can greatly alter a map's representation of how a road either does or doesn't cross a particular parcel of land.

Legend

————	Section Lines
══════	Interstates
▬▬▬▬	Highways
————	Other Roads
●	Cities/Towns
✝	Cemeteries

Scale: Section = 1 mile X 1 mile
(generally, with some exceptions)

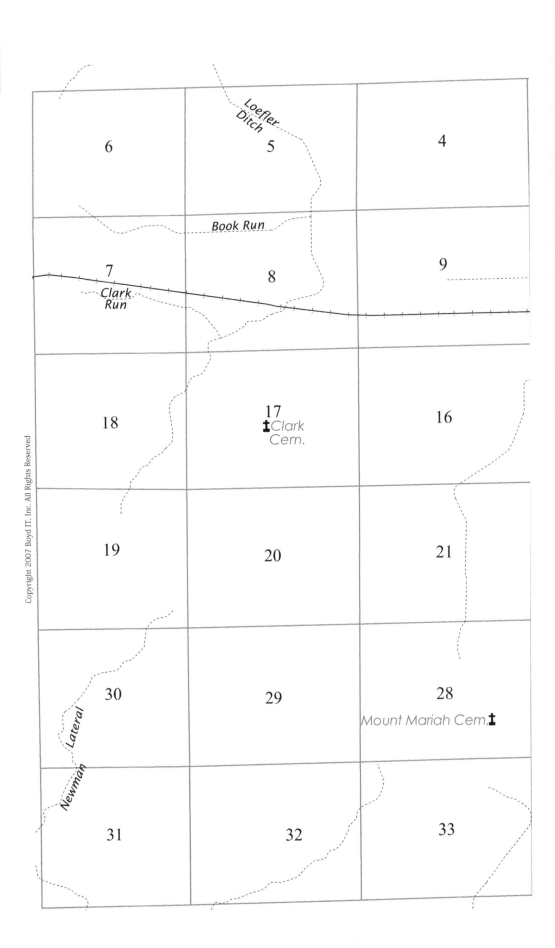

Historical Map

T3-S R11-W
2nd PM Meridian

Map Group 18

Cities & Towns
Durham
Fort Branch
McGary

Cemeteries
Clark Cemetery
Durham Cemetery
Mount Mariah Cemetery

Loefler Ditch

6　　5　　4

Book Run

7　　8　　9

Clark Run

18　　17 ✝*Clark Cem.*　16

19　　20　　21

Lateral

30　　29　　28

Mount Mariah Cem. ✝

Newman

31　　32　　33

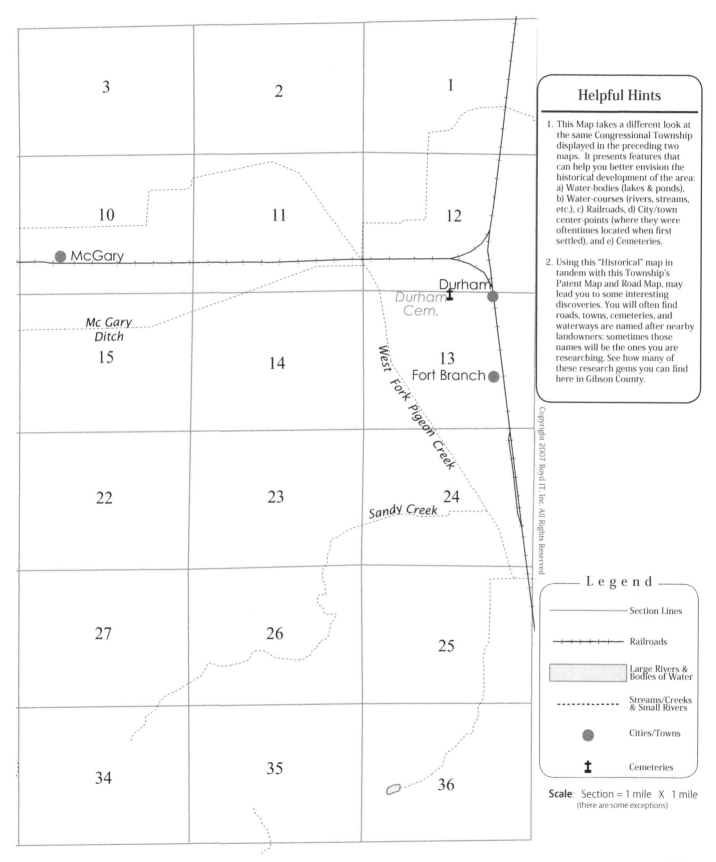

3

2

1

Helpful Hints

1. This Map takes a different look at the same Congressional Township displayed in the preceding two maps. It presents features that can help you better envision the historical development of the area: a) Water-bodies (lakes & ponds), b) Water-courses (rivers, streams, etc.), c) Railroads, d) City/town center-points (where they were oftentimes located when first settled), and e) Cemeteries.

2. Using this "Historical" map in tandem with this Township's Patent Map and Road Map, may lead you to some interesting discoveries. You will often find roads, towns, cemeteries, and waterways are named after nearby landowners: sometimes those names will be the ones you are researching. See how many of these research gems you can find here in Gibson County.

10

11

12

McGary

Durham

Durham
Cem.

Mc Gary
Ditch

15

14

West Fork Pigeon Creek

13
Fort Branch

22

23

24

Sandy Creek

Legend

—————— Section Lines

+++++++ Railroads

Large Rivers &
Bodies of Water

- - - - - Streams/Creeks
& Small Rivers

● Cities/Towns

✝ Cemeteries

27

26

25

34

35

36

Scale: Section = 1 mile X 1 mile
(there are some exceptions)

Map Group 19: Index to Land Patents

Township 3-South Range 10-West (2nd PM)

After you locate an individual in this Index, take note of the Section and Section Part then proceed to the Land Patent map on the pages immediately following. You should have no difficulty locating the corresponding parcel of land.

The "For More Info" Column will lead you to more information about the underlying Patents. See the *Legend* at right, and the "How to Use this Book" chapter, for more information.

ID	Individual in Patent	Sec.	Sec. Part	Date Issued	Other Counties	For More Info . . .
1756	ADAMS, John S	18	SWSW	1835-10-28		A1
1757	" "	30	NESW	1839-02-01		A1
1804	ADAMS, Samuel	30	W½SW	1837-03-18		A1
1677	AMORY, Francis	1	W½NE	1839-02-01		A1 G2
1678	" "	2	E½SW	1839-02-01		A1 G2
1679	" "	2	NENE	1839-02-01		A1 G2 R1736
1672	" "	10	E½SE	1839-08-01		A1
1673	" "	11	W½SW	1839-08-01		A1
1674	" "	15	E½NE	1839-08-01		A1
1675	" "	25	SWNE	1839-08-01		A1
1676	" "	3	E½NE	1839-08-01		A1
1677	AMORY, George W	1	W½NE	1839-02-01		A1 G2
1678	" "	2	E½SW	1839-02-01		A1 G2
1679	" "	2	NENE	1839-02-01		A1 G2 R1736
1698	ARBURN, Henry	35	NENW	1849-05-30		A1
1638	AYERS, David	21	E½SW	1835-10-01		A1
1639	" "	21	SWSW	1835-10-15		A1
1640	AYRES, David	5	SESW	1839-02-01		A1
1614	BROKAW, Abraham	6	E½NE	1837-08-05		A1
1787	BROKAW, Peter	17	SWNW	1837-03-20		A1
1786	" "	17	SENW	1838-09-01		A1
1688	BURRUCKER, George M	9	SENW	1840-10-01		A1
1684	CIDELS, George	8	E½SE	1835-10-01		A1
1685	" "	9	SWSW	1838-09-01		A1
1774	COMPTON, Kenneth	12	SWSW	1850-12-10		A1
1616	CONNER, Alexander	17	NWNW	1835-10-23		A1
1617	" "	18	NENE	1835-10-23		A1
1618	" "	8	NWNW	1848-05-01		A1
1622	CONNOR, Alexander	6	E½SE	1831-01-04		A1
1621	" "	5	W½SW	1837-03-18		A1
1619	" "	17	E½SW	1838-09-05		A1
1620	" "	20	NWNE	1838-09-05		A1
1808	CORY, Samuel	32	SENW	1838-09-05		A1
1807	" "	30	SWSE	1839-02-01		A1
1680	DAVIDSON, Frederick	18	W½NW	1831-12-31		A1
1722	DAVIS, James H	11	SWNW	1850-12-10		A1
1630	DAY, Benjamin J	29	NENW	1858-08-30		A1
1631	" "	29	W½NW	1858-08-30		A1
1745	DEPRIEST, John	3	SWSW	1835-10-01		A1
1744	" "	3	NWSW	1838-09-01		A1
1832	DEPRIEST, William	3	NWNE	1837-08-01		A1
1833	" "	4	E½NW	1837-08-01		A1
1729	DRAKE, James P	2	NWSW	1839-08-01		A1
1730	" "	2	SENW	1839-08-01		A1
1666	EMBREE, Elisha	10	W½SW	1837-08-01		A1 G13
1663	" "	2	SWSW	1837-08-01		A1

ID	Individual in Patent	Sec.	Sec. Part	Date Issued	Other Counties	For More Info . . .
1661	EMBREE, Elisha (Cont'd)	15	E½NW	1837-08-05		A1
1662	" "	15	W½NE	1837-08-05		A1
1665	" "	9	E½SE	1837-08-05		A1
1659	" "	10	W½SE	1837-11-07		A1
1664	" "	27	W½NW	1837-11-07		A1
1657	" "	10	E½NE	1839-02-01		A1
1658	" "	10	W½NE	1839-02-01		A1
1660	" "	11	NWNW	1839-02-01		A1
1834	EMBREE, William	5	SE	1837-11-07		A1
1835	" "	9	NWNW	1838-09-01		A1
1809	ENLOW, Samuel	20	SESE	1845-06-01		A1 R1646
1800	ERVIN, Robert	21	NENW	1838-09-01		A1
1799	" "	21	NE	1839-02-01		A1
1801	" "	21	NWSE	1839-02-01		A1
1625	ESTES, Bartlet B	5	SWNE	1839-02-01		A1
1669	ESTES, Ellenor	5	SENE	1837-03-20		A1
1712	FALLS, Hume	8	SWNW	1848-05-01		A1
1623	FOSTER, Amasa D	7	E½NE	1837-03-18		A1
1747	FREEMAN, John G	22	NWSW	1838-09-01		A1
1746	" "	22	NENW	1839-08-01		A1
1823	GEDNEY, Thomas	18	W½NE	1831-12-31		A1
1802	GOORLEY, Robert	29	NENE	1837-08-01		A1
1741	GRAHAM, John A	26	W½NW	1838-09-01		A1
1777	GRANT, Luke	36	SWSE	1849-04-10		A1
1681	GRAPER, Frederick	33	NWNE	1856-06-03		A1
1831	GRUNDER, Vendelin	29	SENW	1844-08-01		A1
1837	HALBROOKS, William	18	W½SE	1831-06-01		A1
1836	" "	18	NWSW	1835-10-23		A1
1653	HALCOMBE, Elihu	34	W½SW	1831-01-04		A1
1666	HALL, Samuel	10	W½SW	1837-08-01		A1 G13
1810	" "	26	SESW	1849-04-10		A1
1857	HALL, Zachariah	4	NWNW	1840-10-01		A1
1838	HANNAH, William	1	SENW	1839-02-01		A1
1839	" "	13	NENW	1839-08-01		A1
1840	" "	13	NWNE	1839-08-01		A1 G21
1626	HAYHURST, Benjamin	12	NWSE	1841-05-25		A1
1627	" "	12	NWSW	1841-05-25		A1
1628	" "	12	SWNE	1841-05-25		A1
1629	" "	12	SWNW	1841-05-25		A1
1701	HOLCOM, Hosea	22	W½NE	1839-02-01		A1 G23
1699	HOLCOMB, Henry	26	SWSW	1841-05-25		A1
1702	HOLCOMB, Hosea	36	W½SW	1837-03-15		A1
1816	HOLCOMB, Silas M	35	SWNW	1848-06-01		A1
1815	" "	35	SENW	1850-12-10		A1
1654	HOLCOMBE, Elihu	33	NESE	1837-08-01		A1
1655	" "	33	SWNE	1837-11-07		A1
1656	" "	35	SESE	1837-11-07		A1
1705	HOLCOMBE, Hosea	28	E½NE	1835-09-05		A1
1710	" "	35	NESE	1835-09-10		A1
1706	" "	28	W½NE	1837-08-01		A1
1707	" "	33	SESE	1837-11-07		A1
1708	" "	34	NESE	1837-11-07		A1
1703	" "	15	W½SE	1839-08-01		A1
1704	" "	22	SWSW	1839-08-01		A1
1709	" "	35	E½NE	1839-08-01		A1
1817	HOLCOMBE, Silas M	34	SESE	1841-05-25		A1
1783	HOLLIS, Othuiel	17	W½SE	1838-09-01		A1
1700	HOPKINS, Hiram A	30	NENE	1840-10-01		A1
1645	HOSACK, David	29	SENE	1839-08-01		A1
1647	HOSICK, David	30	SESE	1837-08-05		A1
1646	" "	20	SESE	1837-11-07		A1 R1809
1701	HOWE, Willis	22	W½NE	1839-02-01		A1 G23
1855	" "	9	SESW	1839-02-01		A1
1856	" "	9	SWSE	1839-02-01		A1
1713	HUDSPETH, Isaac	8	W½SE	1831-01-04		A1
1753	HUGO, John R	2	NWSE	1839-08-01		A1
1796	INGRAM, Richard	17	NESE	1835-10-28		A1
1797	" "	18	NESE	1837-03-20		A1
1798	" "	18	SENE	1839-08-01		A1
1714	KENNERLY, Isaac	13	W½NW	1839-02-01		A1
1750	KENT, John	8	NWSW	1840-10-01		A1
1687	KESTER, George	33	NWNW	1845-06-01		A1
1686	" "	32	NWNE	1849-04-10		A1

ID	Individual in Patent	Sec.	Sec. Part	Date Issued	Other Counties	For More Info . . .
1632	KEYS, Charles	29	SWNE	1841-05-25		A1
1723	KING, James H	34	SENW	1837-11-07		A1
1785	KING, Patrick W	20	SWSW	1840-10-01		A1
1784	" "	20	SESW	1841-05-25		A1
1727	KNEREMER, James	13	NWSW	1841-08-10		A1
1670	KNOX, Enoch	18	SESE	1837-11-07		A1
1841	KURTZ, William	34	NWNE	1854-01-03		A1
1751	LEPRIEST, John	3	E½SW	1837-08-05		A1
1752	LININGER, John	29	E½SW	1841-05-25		A1
1652	LOCKWOOD, Edward B	19	W½SW	1837-03-18		A1
1822	LOCKWOOD, Stephen U	19	NWNW	1838-09-01		A1
1689	MANNING, George	2	NESE	1838-09-05		A1
1690	" "	2	SWNE	1839-02-01		A1
1789	MANNING, Reuben	12	NENE	1839-02-01		A1
1682	MAYER, George A	14	NENE	1839-02-01		A1
1683	" "	14	NWNE	1839-02-01		A1
1763	MAYHALL, Jonas	1	E½SW	1838-09-05		A1
1764	" "	1	NWSW	1838-09-05		A1
1742	MCCULLOUGH, John A	21	SWNW	1837-11-07		A1
1743	MCCULLOUGH, John A	20	NENW	1841-05-25		A1
1775	MCDONALD, Lewis A	27	SWSW	1848-05-10		A1
1811	MCDONALD, Samuel	34	NENE	1848-05-10		A1
1643	MCGARRAH, David D	33	E½NE	1837-11-07		A1
1644	" "	33	NWSE	1837-11-07		A1
1642	" "	32	NWNW	1838-09-01		A1
1641	" "	31	SENE	1839-08-01		A1
1769	MCGARRAH, Joseph	31	NENE	1838-09-01		A1
1770	" "	32	NENE	1839-02-01		A1
1767	" "	20	SENW	1841-05-25		A1
1768	" "	20	W½NW	1841-05-25		A1
1633	MCKEE, Daniel A	24	N½NE	1848-05-01		A1
1634	" "	24	SWNE	1849-04-10		A1
1805	MILLS, Samuel C	25	NWNE	1838-09-01		A1 G30
1806	" "	25	NWNW	1838-09-01		A1 G30
1842	MOFFATT, William	28	E½SW	1839-02-01		A1
1843	" "	28	NW	1839-02-01		A1
1844	MURFITT, William	27	SESW	1850-10-01		A1
1840	MYERS, James	13	NWNE	1839-08-01		A1 G21
1812	MYERS, Samuel	28	SESE	1840-10-01		A1
1749	NEELY, John J	5	W½NW	1828-05-05		A1
1776	NEIPERT, Lewis	10	SESW	1850-12-10		A1
1824	NICKELS, Thomas	8	SWSW	1838-09-05		A1
1731	PIERCE, James	8	SESE	1837-08-01		A1
1780	RALSTON, Martha	30	NENW	1854-03-02		A1
1818	REAVIS, Solomon	20	NENE	1839-02-01		A1
1819	" "	21	NWNW	1839-02-01		A1
1847	REAVIS, William	30	SESW	1850-10-01		A1
1846	" "	11	NESW	1850-12-10		A1
1849	REED, William	32	NWSW	1838-09-05		A1
1848	" "	28	W½SW	1839-02-01		A1
1715	REYNOLDS, Isaac	4	NESW	1838-09-01		A1
1754	RICKEY, John	9	NESW	1838-09-07		A1
1755	" "	9	NWSE	1838-09-07		A1
1758	SAIBART, John	31	E½SE	1840-10-01		A1
1732	SCANTLIN, James	31	W½NE	1839-08-01		A1
1748	SCHONK, John H	17	NENW	1837-03-18		A1
1803	SHANNON, Robert	15	E½SW	1839-02-01		A1
1850	SHAW, William	11	E½NW	1839-08-01		A1
1851	" "	2	SWSE	1839-08-01		A1
1759	SHERRY, John	36	SESE	1841-05-25		A1
1692	SIDLE, George	8	NESW	1837-08-01		A1
1691	" "	35	W½NE	1848-05-10		A1
1693	SIDLES, George	14	SESE	1850-12-10		A1
1805	SKELTON, Jacob	25	NWNE	1838-09-01		A1 G30
1806	" "	25	NWNW	1838-09-01		A1 G30
1733	SKELTON, James	36	NESW	1849-04-10		A1
1852	SKELTON, William	13	SWNE	1838-09-01		A1
1636	SMITH, Daniel	32	E½SW	1835-10-15		A1
1825	SMITH, Thomas	26	NESW	1850-12-10		A1
1615	SPAIN, Abraham	32	SESE	1837-08-05		A1
1779	SPAIN, Macklin	32	SWSE	1838-09-01		A1
1778	" "	29	W½SE	1840-10-01		A1
1724	SPEAR, James H	5	NENW	1837-08-01		A1

ID	Individual in Patent	Sec.	Sec. Part	Date Issued	Other Counties	For More Info . . .
1719	SPEER, Jacob	5	NESW	1837-03-20		A1
1720	" "	5	SENW	1837-03-20		A1
1781	STALLINGS, Moses	35	NWNW	1841-05-25		A1
1790	STALLINGS, Reuben	34	SENE	1839-02-01		A1
1772	STEPHENS, Joshua W	13	E½NE	1839-02-01		A1
1773	" "	13	E½SE	1839-02-01		A1
1667	STOCKLAND, Elisha	2	SENE	1838-09-07		A1
1637	STRICKLAND, Daniel	14	NWSE	1849-04-10		A1
1648	STRICKLAND, David	25	NENE	1848-05-10		A1
1668	STRICKLAND, Elisha	1	SWNW	1837-08-01		A1
1716	STRICKLAND, Isaac	12	NENW	1837-08-05		A1
1734	STRICKLAND, James	12	NWNE	1838-09-01		A1
1736	" "	2	NENE	1838-09-01		A1 R1679
1735	" "	13	SESW	1850-12-10		A1
1820	STRICKLAND, Stephen	12	NWNW	1838-09-05		A1
1821	" "	2	NWNW	1839-02-01		A1 V1765
1853	STUNKLE, William	34	SWNE	1856-06-03		A1
1788	SUMNER, Philip	8	E½NE	1821-08-20		A1
1650	TAYLOR, David	32	NWSE	1838-09-01		A1
1649	" "	14	S½NE	1839-08-01		A1
1717	TAYLOR, Isaac	13	NESW	1840-10-01		A1
1854	TAYLOR, William	13	NWSE	1839-08-01		A1
1826	TRIBLE, Thomas	31	NWNW	1839-08-01		A1
1635	TUCKER, Daniel B	7	E½SE	1835-10-15		A1
1738	VICKERS, James	1	SENE	1837-03-20		A1
1737	" "	1	NENE	1838-09-01		A1
1739	WALLACE, James	22	SESW	1856-06-03		A1
1782	WALLIS, Nicholas	21	S½SE	1837-08-01		A1
1828	WALLIS, Thomas	21	SENW	1837-03-20		A1
1827	" "	20	NESE	1839-08-01		A1
1791	WALTERS, Reuben	19	E½NW	1831-06-01		A1
1792	" "	19	E½SW	1831-06-01		A1
1794	" "	19	W½NE	1831-12-31		A1
1793	" "	19	SWNW	1835-10-23		A1
1795	" "	20	NESW	1837-08-01		A1
1718	WATTERS, Isaac	20	NWSW	1838-09-01		A1
1760	WHEELER, John	5	NENE	1835-10-15		A1
1813	WHEELER, Samuel	1	NWNW	1838-09-05		A1
1671	WHITE, Ezekiel	32	SWNW	1835-10-15		A1
1728	WHITE, James M	30	NWSE	1837-03-18		A1
1694	WILLIAMS, George	31	E½SW	1840-10-01		A1
1695	" "	31	W½SE	1840-10-01		A1
1696	" "	31	W½SW	1840-10-01		A1
1814	WILLIAMS, Samuel	20	S½NE	1839-02-01		A1
1829	WILLIAMS, Thomas	17	SESE	1837-03-18		A1
1830	" "	21	NWSW	1840-10-01		A1
1761	WIRE, John	24	SENE	1849-04-10		A1
1740	WOOD, James	9	SWNW	1838-09-07		A1
1651	WOODS, Dickson	8	W½NE	1837-11-07		A1
1697	WOODS, Hamilton	8	NENW	1837-03-20		A1
1711	WOODS, Hugh	5	NWNE	1837-03-20		A1
1721	WOODS, James C	4	SWNW	1838-09-01		A1
1725	WOODS, James H	4	SESW	1837-08-01		A1
1726	" "	9	NENW	1839-02-01		A1
1762	WOODS, John	15	SWSW	1838-09-05		A1
1771	WOODS, Joseph	9	NENE	1837-08-05		A1
1766	WOODS, Joseph H	9	NWNE	1839-02-01		A1
1845	WOODS, William P	4	W½SW	1839-08-01		A1
1624	YIERLING, Barbara	9	NWSW	1838-09-01		A1
1765	YOUNG, Jonathan	2	W½NW	1839-02-01		A1 V1821

Patent Map

T3-S R10-W
2nd PM Meridian

Map Group 19

Township Statistics

Parcels Mapped	:	244
Number of Patents	:	226
Number of Individuals	:	156
Patentees Identified	:	156
Number of Surnames	:	113
Multi-Patentee Parcels	:	8
Oldest Patent Date	:	8/20/1821
Most Recent Patent	:	8/30/1858
Block/Lot Parcels	:	0
Parcels Re - Issued	:	2
Parcels that Overlap	:	2
Cities and Towns	:	2
Cemeteries	:	2

Section 6
BROKAW Abraham 1837
NEELY John J 1828
CONNOR Alexander 1831
CONNOR Alexander 1837

Section 5
SPEAR James H 1837
SPEER Jacob 1837
WOODS Hugh 1837
WHEELER John 1835
ESTES Bartlet B 1839
ESTES Ellenor 1837
SPEER Jacob 1837
AYRES David 1839
EMBREE William 1837

Section 4
HALL Zachariah 1840
DEPRIEST William 1837
WOODS James C 1838
REYNOLDS Isaac 1838
WOODS William P 1839
WOODS James H 1837

Section 7
FOSTER Amasa D 1837
TUCKER Daniel B 1835

Section 8
CONNER Alexander 1848
WOODS Hamilton 1837
FALLS Hume 1848
WOODS Dickson 1837
SUMNER Philip 1821
KENT John 1840
SIDLE George 1837
HUDSPETH Isaac 1831
CIDELS George 1835
NICKELS Thomas 1838
PIERCE James 1837

Section 9
EMBREE William 1838
WOODS James H 1839
WOODS Joseph H 1839
WOODS Joseph 1837
WOOD James 1838
BURRUCKER George M 1840
YIERLING Barbara 1838
RICKEY John 1838
RICKEY John 1838
EMBREE Elisha 1837
CIDELS George 1838
HOWE Willis 1839
HOWE Willis 1839

Section 18
DAVIDSON Frederick 1831
GEDNEY Thomas 1831
HALBROOKS William 1835
HALBROOKS William 1831
ADAMS John S 1835

Section 17
CONNER Alexander 1835
CONNER Alexander 1835
SCHONK John H 1837
INGRAM Richard 1839
BROKAW Peter 1837
BROKAW Peter 1838
INGRAM Richard 1837
CONNOR Alexander 1838
HOLLIS Othuiel 1838
INGRAM Richard 1835
WILLIAMS Thomas 1837
KNOX Enoch 1837

Section 16

Section 19
LOCKWOOD Stephen U 1838
WALTERS Reuben 1835
WALTERS Reuben 1831
WALTERS Reuben 1831
LOCKWOOD Edward B 1837
WALTERS Reuben 1831

Section 20
MCCULLOUGH John A 1841
MCGARRAH Joseph 1841
CONNOR Alexander 1838
MCGARRAH Joseph 1841
WILLIAMS Samuel 1839
WATTERS Isaac 1838
WALTERS Reuben 1837
WALLIS Thomas 1839
KING Patrick W 1840
KING Patrick W 1841
HOSICK David 1837
ENLOW Samuel 1845

Section 21
REAVIS Solomon 1839
REAVIS Solomon 1839
ERVIN Robert 1838
ERVIN Robert 1839
MCCCULLOUGH John A 1837
WALLIS Thomas 1837
WILLIAMS Thomas 1840
AYERS David 1835
ERVIN Robert 1839
AYERS David 1835
WALLIS Nicholas 1837

Section 30
RALSTON Martha 1854
HOPKINS Hiram A 1840
ADAMS Samuel 1837
ADAMS John S 1839
WHITE James M 1837
REAVIS William 1850
CORY Samuel 1839
HOSICK David 1837

Section 29
DAY Benjamin J 1858
DAY Benjamin J 1858
GOORLEY Robert 1837
GRUNDER Vendelin 1844
KEYS Charles 1841
HOSACK David 1839
LININGER John 1841
SPAIN Macklin 1840

Section 28
MOFFATT William 1839
HOLCOMBE Hosea 1835
HOLCOMBE Hosea 1837
REED William 1839
MOFFATT William 1839
MYERS Samuel 1840

Section 31
TRIBLE Thomas 1839
SCANTLIN James 1839
MCGARRAH Joseph 1838
MCGARRAH David D 1839
WILLIAMS George 1840
WILLIAMS George 1840
WILLIAMS George 1840
SAIBART John 1840

Section 32
MCGARRAH David D 1838
WHITE Ezekiel 1835
CORY Samuel 1838
KESTER George 1849
MCGARRAH Joseph 1839
REED William 1838
SMITH Daniel 1835
TAYLOR David 1838
SPAIN Macklin 1838
SPAIN Abraham 1837

Section 33
KESTER George 1845
GRAPER Frederick 1856
MCGARRAH David D 1837
HOLCOMBE Elihu 1837
HOLCOMBE Elihu 1837
MCGARRAH David D 1837
HOLCOMBE Hosea 1837

Section 3

DEPRIEST William 1837

AMORY Francis 1839

3

DEPRIEST John 1838

LEPRIEST John 1837

DEPRIEST John 1835

Section 2

STRICKLAND Stephen 1839

YOUNG Jonathan 1839

DRAKE James P 1839

MANNING George 1839

STOCKLAND Elisha 1838

DRAKE James P 1839

AMORY [2] Francis 1839

HUGO John R 1839

MANNING George 1838

2

EMBREE Elisha 1837

SHAW William 1839

Section 1

STRICKLAND James 1838 AMORY [2] Francis 1839

WHEELER Samuel 1838

AMORY [2] Francis 1839

VICKERS James 1838

STRICKLAND Elisha 1837

HANNAH William 1839

VICKERS James 1837

MAYHALL Jonas 1838

MAYHALL Jonas 1838

1

Section 10

EMBREE Elisha 1839

EMBREE Elisha 1839

10

EMBREE [13] Elisha 1837

EMBREE Elisha 1837

NEIPERT Lewis 1850

Section 11

EMBREE Elisha 1839

DAVIS James H 1850

SHAW William 1839

11

AMORY Francis 1839

REAVIS William 1850

Section 12

STRICKLAND Stephen 1838

STRICKLAND Isaac 1837

STRICKLAND James 1838

MANNING Reuben 1839

HAYHURST Benjamin 1841

HAYHURST Benjamin 1841

12

HAYHURST Benjamin 1841

HAYHURST Benjamin 1841

COMPTON Kenneth 1850

Section 15

EMBREE Elisha 1837

EMBREE Elisha 1837

AMORY Francis 1839

15

WOODS John 1838

SHANNON Robert 1839

HOLCOMBE Hosea 1839

Section 14

MAYER George A 1839

MAYER George A 1839

TAYLOR David 1839

14

STRICKLAND Daniel 1849

SIDLES George 1850

Section 13

HANNAH William 1839

HANNAH [21] William 1839

STEPHENS Joshua W 1839

KENNERLY Isaac 1839

SKELTON William 1838

13

KNEREMER James 1841

TAYLOR Isaac 1840

TAYLOR William 1839

STEPHENS Joshua W 1839

STRICKLAND James 1850

Section 22

FREEMAN John G 1839

HOLCOM [23] Hosea 1839

22

FREEMAN John G 1838

HOLCOMBE Hosea 1839

WALLACE James 1856

Section 23

23

Section 24

MCKEE Daniel A 1848

MCKEE Daniel A 1849

WIRE John 1849

24

Section 27

EMBREE Elisha 1837

27

MCDONALD Lewis A 1848

MURFITT William 1850

Section 26

GRAHAM John A 1838

26

SMITH Thomas 1850

HOLCOMB Henry 1841

HALL Samuel 1849

Section 25

MILLS [30] Samuel C 1838

MILLS [30] Samuel C 1838

STRICKLAND David 1848

AMORY Francis 1839

25

Section 34

KURTZ William 1854

MCDONALD Samuel 1848

KING James H 1837

STUNKLE William 1856

STALLINGS Reuben 1839

34

HOLCOMBE Hosea 1837

HOLCOMBE Silas M 1841

Section 35

STALLINGS Moses 1841

ARBURN Henry 1849

SIDLE George 1848

HOLCOMBE Hosea 1839

HOLCOMB Silas M 1848

HOLCOMB Silas M 1850

35

HOLCOMBE Hosea 1835

HOLCOMBE Elihu 1837

Section 36

HOLCOMB Hosea 1837

SKELTON James 1849

36

SHERRY John 1841

GRANT Luke 1849

HALCOMBE Elihu 1831

Helpful Hints

1. This Map's INDEX can be found on the preceding pages.

2. Refer to Map "C" to see where this Township lies within Gibson County, Indiana.

3. Numbers within square brackets [ ] denote a multi-patentee land parcel (multi-owner). Refer to Appendix "C" for a full list of members in this group.

4. Areas that look to be crowded with Patentees usually indicate multiple sales of the same parcel (Re-issues) or Overlapping parcels. See this Township's Index for an explanation of these and other circumstances that might explain "odd" groupings of Patentees on this map.

Legend

———— Patent Boundary

▬▬▬▬ Section Boundary

No Patents Found (or Outside County)

1., 2., 3., ... Lot Numbers (when beside a name)

[ ] Group Number (see Appendix "C")

Scale: Section = 1 mile X 1 mile (generally, with some exceptions)

Road Map

T3-S R10-W
2nd PM Meridian

Map Group 19

Cities & Towns
Fort Gibson (historical)
Haubstadt

Cemeteries
Stunkel Cemetery
Walnut Hill Cemetery

6

Tulip Tree

5

County Road 100

County Road 175

County Road 475

4

County Road 240

County Road 500

County Road 550

Walnut Hill Cem.

7

County Road 600

8

9

County Road 650

18

17

16

Sinclair

Tretter Park

Locust

Walters

Willard

Hull

Walnut

Eastview

Mulberry

Center

Poplar

Lincoln

Hilcrest

Sunrise

Comanche

Apache

County Road 750

County Road 200

County Road 800

19

20

21

30

29

County Road 100

28

County Road 900

County Road 925

Keister

Road 975

County

US Hwy 41

County Road 990

32

33

County
Road 1000

31

Main

Race

Gibson

3rd

5th Haub

1st

4th

2nd

6th

Elm

Plum

Haubstadt

State Road 68

County Road 50

County Road 1025

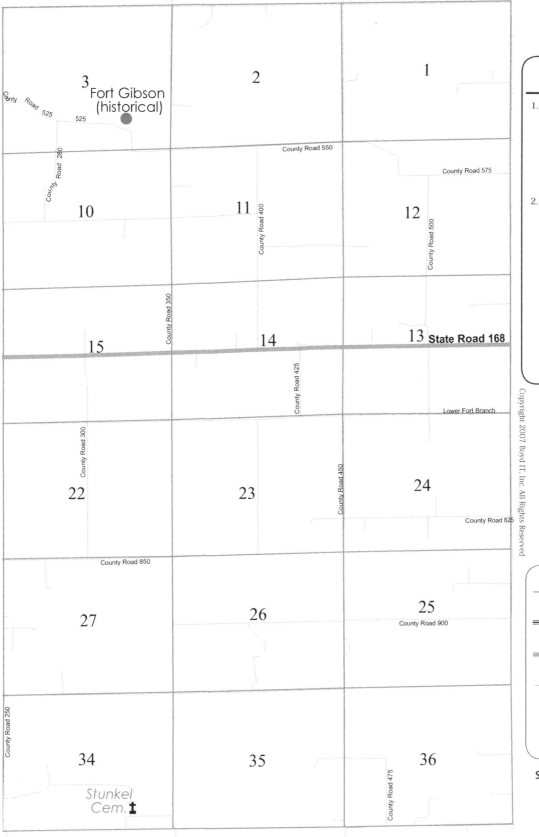

County Road 525

525

3 Fort Gibson (historical)

County Road 280

2

1

County Road 550

County Road 575

10

11

County Road 400

12

County Road 500

County Road 350

15

14

13 **State Road 168**

County Road 425

Lower Fort Branch

County Road 300

22

23

County Road 450

24

County Road 825

County Road 850

27

26

25

County Road 900

County Road 250

34

35

36

County Road 475

Stunkel Cem.

Helpful Hints

1. This road map has a number of uses, but primarily it is to help you: a) find the present location of land owned by your ancestors (at least the general area), b) find cemeteries and city-centers, and c) estimate the route/roads used by Census-takers & tax-assessors.

2. If you plan to travel to Gibson County to locate cemeteries or land parcels, please pick up a modern travel map for the area before you do. Mapping old land parcels on modern maps is not as exact a science as you might think. Just the slightest variations in public land survey coordinates, estimates of parcel boundaries, or road-map deviations can greatly alter a map's representation of how a road either does or doesn't cross a particular parcel of land.

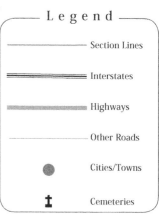

L e g e n d

———————— Section Lines

════════════ Interstates

━━━━━━━━ Highways

———————— Other Roads

● Cities/Towns

✝ Cemeteries

Scale: Section = 1 mile X 1 mile
(generally, with some exceptions)

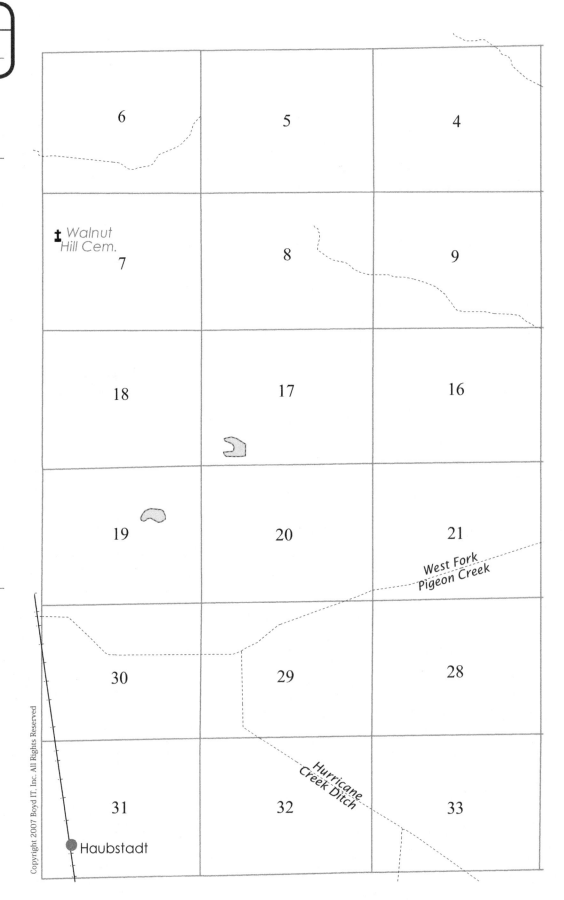

Historical Map

T3-S R10-W
2nd PM Meridian

Map Group 19

Cities & Towns
Fort Gibson (historical)
Haubstadt

Cemeteries
Stunkel Cemetery
Walnut Hill Cemetery

Copyright 2007 Boyd IT. Inc. All Rights Reserved

6　　5　　4

‡ *Walnut
Hill Cem.*
7　　8　　9

18　　17　　16

19　　20　　21

West Fork
Pigeon Creek

30　　29　　28

Hurricane
Creek Ditch

31　　32　　33

● Haubstadt

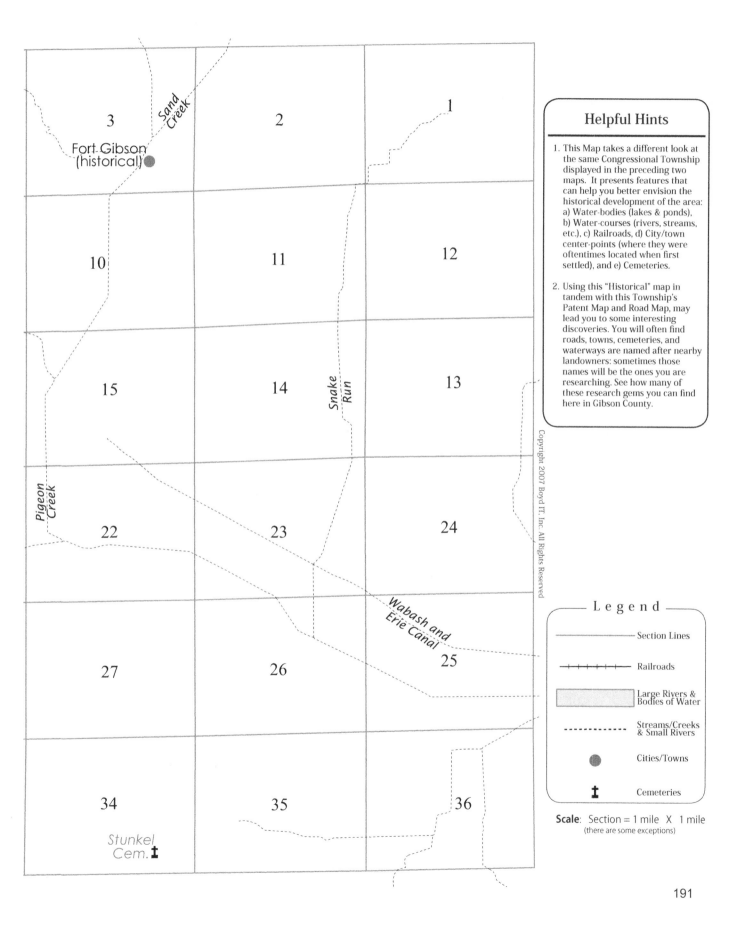

Helpful Hints

1. This Map takes a different look at the same Congressional Township displayed in the preceding two maps. It presents features that can help you better envision the historical development of the area: a) Water-bodies (lakes & ponds), b) Water-courses (rivers, streams, etc.), c) Railroads, d) City/town center-points (where they were oftentimes located when first settled), and e) Cemeteries.

2. Using this "Historical" map in tandem with this Township's Patent Map and Road Map, may lead you to some interesting discoveries. You will often find roads, towns, cemeteries, and waterways are named after nearby landowners: sometimes those names will be the ones you are researching. See how many of these research gems you can find here in Gibson County.

Legend

———————	Section Lines
┼┼┼┼┼┼	Railroads
▭	Large Rivers & Bodies of Water
- - - - - - -	Streams/Creeks & Small Rivers
●	Cities/Towns
✝	Cemeteries

Scale: Section = 1 mile X 1 mile
(there are some exceptions)

Map Group 20: Index to Land Patents

Township 3-South Range 9-West (2nd PM)

After you locate an individual in this Index, take note of the Section and Section Part then proceed to the Land Patent map on the pages immediately following. You should have no difficulty locating the corresponding parcel of land.

The "For More Info" Column will lead you to more information about the underlying Patents. See the *Legend* at right, and the "How to Use this Book" chapter, for more information.

```
┌─────────────────────────────────────────────────────┐
│                    LEGEND                            │
│         "For More Info . . . " column                │
├─────────────────────────────────────────────────────┤
│ A = Authority (Legislative Act, See Appendix "A")    │
│ B = Block or Lot (location in Section unknown)       │
│ C = Cancelled Patent                                 │
│ F = Fractional Section                               │
│ G = Group  (Multi-Patentee Patent, see Appendix "C") │
│ V = Overlaps another Parcel                          │
│ R = Re-Issued (Parcel patented more than once)       │
│                                                      │
│ (A & G items require you to look in the Appendixes   │
│ referred to above. All other Letter-designations     │
│ followed by a number require you to locate line-items│
│ in this index that possess the ID number found after │
│ the letter).                                         │
└─────────────────────────────────────────────────────┘
```

ID	Individual in Patent	Sec.	Sec. Part	Date Issued	Other Counties	For More Info . . .
1903	AMORY, Francis	18	SWSW	1839-02-01		A1 G2
1904	" "	18	W½NW	1839-02-01		A1 G2
1905	" "	6	NENE	1839-02-01		A1 G2
1906	" "	6	NESE	1839-02-01		A1 G2
1903	AMORY, George W	18	SWSW	1839-02-01		A1 G2
1904	" "	18	W½NW	1839-02-01		A1 G2
1905	" "	6	NENE	1839-02-01		A1 G2
1906	" "	6	NESE	1839-02-01		A1 G2
1920	BASS, Howell	28	NWNW	1841-05-25		A1
1989	BASS, Jordan	28	SWNW	1849-08-01		A1
1990	BEASLEY, Joseph	6	E½SW	1837-11-07		A1
1991	" "	6	SWNE	1839-08-01		A1
2047	BOOKER, William	11	NWNE	1840-10-01		A1
2044	BOYCE, William A	27	SWSE	1838-09-01		A1
2045	" "	34	SWSW	1839-02-01		A1
2013	BRADSHAW, Robert	36	SESW	1835-10-28		A1
1868	BURTON, Amos	2	W½NE	1840-10-01		A1
1870	" "	9	SWNE	1840-10-01		A1
1871	" "	9	W½SE	1840-10-01		A1
1869	" "	9	SENW	1841-05-25		A1
1875	BURTON, Basel	9	E½SW	1840-10-01		A1
1876	BURTON, Benjamin	10	N½NW	1848-05-01		A1
1880	BURTON, David	4	SW	1840-10-01		A1
1916	COFFMAN, Henry J	27	E½SW	1840-10-01		A1
1917	" "	27	NWSW	1840-10-01		A1
1918	" "	29	SWSW	1840-10-01		A1
2040	CRISWELL, Thomas A	33	NESE	1849-02-01		A1
2048	DEPRIEST, William	19	NWNE	1848-05-01		A1
1929	DEVIN, James	3	E½SW	1839-02-01		A1
1930	" "	3	SWNE	1839-02-01		A1
1931	" "	3	W½SE	1839-02-01		A1
1952	FRENCH, James W	8	NESE	1844-08-01		A1
1909	GALLOWAY, George	2	NW	1840-10-01		A1
1907	" "	11	E½SW	1841-05-25		A1
1908	" "	11	W½SE	1841-05-25		A1
2026	HALL, Samuel	17	NWSE	1848-07-01		A1
1862	HARBISON, Adam	25	SWNE	1841-05-25		A1
1884	HARBISON, David M	25	E½NE	1841-05-25		A1
2041	HARBISON, Thomas	4	SENE	1839-02-01		A1
2027	HENDERSON, Samuel	5	NESW	1839-02-01		A1
2001	HOESELE, Landalin	20	SESW	1845-05-01		A1
1864	HOLCOMB, Alexander	13	W½NE	1840-10-01		A1
1863	" "	13	E½NW	1841-05-25		A1
1865	" "	14	E½SE	1851-02-01		A1
1957	INGRAM, John	29	NESW	1852-07-01		A1
1955	INGRUM, Jesse	22	SESW	1850-12-10		A1

ID	Individual in Patent	Sec.	Sec. Part	Date Issued	Other Counties	For More Info . . .
1959	KELL, John	12	E½SW	1839-08-01		A1
1958	" "	12	E½SE	1841-05-25		A1
1935	KILLPATRICK, James M	13	E½SE	1840-10-01		A1
1936	" "	13	W½SE	1840-10-01		A1
1960	KILLPATRICK, John	23	SWSE	1838-09-01		A1
1956	KILLPATRICK, John B	26	W½NE	1840-10-01		A1
1996	KILLPATRICK, Josiah	28	W½NE	1839-02-01		A1
1997	" "	35	SENE	1839-02-01		A1
1995	" "	27	NWSE	1839-08-01		A1
1999	" "	36	NESW	1839-08-01		A1
1998	" "	36	NENW	1840-10-01		A1
2000	" "	36	NWNE	1841-05-25		A1
2024	KINCADE, Samuel A	23	NESE	1841-08-10		A1
1877	MANAHAN, Charles C	2	NESW	1840-10-01		A1
1878	" "	2	W½SE	1840-10-01		A1
2002	MARINER, Littleton B	8	NENE	1850-12-10		A1
1888	MARTIN, David	12	NWNW	1835-10-15		A1
1886	" "	1	SESE	1837-03-20		A1
1887	" "	1	W½SW	1838-09-01		A1
1889	" "	12	W½SE	1839-08-01		A1
1890	" "	13	E½NE	1839-08-01		A1
1885	" "	1	E½SW	1840-10-01		A1
1891	" "	15	S½NE	1840-10-01		A1
1919	MARTIN, Henry	13	SW	1839-08-01		A1
1965	MARTIN, John	10	SWSE	1835-10-15		A1
1964	" "	10	NWSE	1838-09-01		A1
1963	" "	10	E½SE	1840-10-01		A1
1962	" "	10	E½NE	1841-05-25		A1
2010	MARTIN, Reuben	1	SWSE	1840-10-01		A1
1874	MASON, Andrew	8	W½SE	1844-08-01		A1
2008	MASON, Reason	2	SESW	1840-10-01		A1
2009	" "	2	SWSW	1841-05-25		A1
2050	MASON, William J	8	SESE	1848-05-01		A1
2049	" "	17	NENE	1849-02-01		A1
1988	MAYHALL, Jonas	6	SESE	1837-11-07		A1
1986	" "	18	SE	1838-09-05		A1
1987	" "	27	NW	1838-09-05		A1
1934	MCCLEARY, James L	17	SESE	1845-05-01		A1
2051	MCCLEARY, William	17	E½NW	1826-05-20		A1
2053	" "	17	W½NE	1837-11-07		A1
2052	" "	17	NWNW	1838-09-05		A1
2054	" "	18	W½NE	1838-09-05		A1
1966	MCCLELLAND, John	5	E½NE	1852-07-01		A1
2042	MCCRORY, Thomas	2	SESE	1838-09-07		A1
1901	MCCULLOCH, Elihu	1	NWNW	1839-02-01		A1
1954	MCCULLOCH, Jane P	2	NENE	1839-08-01		A1
1882	MCCULLOH, David E	15	SWNW	1839-08-01		A1
1883	" "	15	W½SW	1848-06-01		A1
2028	MCCULLOUGH, Samuel	11	NENE	1838-09-07		A1
2030	" "	2	NESE	1839-02-01		A1
2031	" "	3	E½NW	1839-02-01		A1
2029	" "	11	SENE	1846-02-19		A1
2032	" "	33	NWNW	1848-05-10		A1
2055	MCCULLOUGH, William	27	S½NE	1839-08-01		A1
2003	MCDILL, Morris L	36	W½SW	1838-09-07		A1
2033	MCDILL, Samuel	35	NENE	1840-10-01		A1
1881	MCGARRAH, David D	5	SESW	1835-10-01		A1
2056	MCGARRAH, William	26	NWSW	1839-08-01		A1
1911	MCGREGER, George	15	NENE	1835-10-15		A1
1910	" "	12	SWNW	1838-09-01		A1
1912	" "	15	NWNE	1838-09-01		A1
1913	MCGREGOR, George	11	W½SW	1841-05-25		A1
2071	MCGREW, Wilson	7	NE	1837-08-05		A1
2072	" "	7	NENW	1852-07-01		A1
1937	MCMILLAN, James	36	SENE	1840-10-01		A1
1969	MCMILLAN, John	36	SENW	1835-10-28		A1
1967	" "	25	W½SW	1838-09-01		A1
1970	" "	36	SWNW	1839-02-01		A1
1968	" "	26	E½SE	1839-08-01		A1
1938	MCMILLEN, James	36	SWNE	1839-08-01		A1
1921	MCMULLIN, Hugh	28	SW	1848-05-10		A1 G28
1923	" "	33	E½NW	1848-05-10		A1 G28
1922	" "	32	NENE	1848-07-01		A1 G28

ID	Individual in Patent	Sec.	Sec. Part	Date Issued	Other Counties	For More Info . . .
1924	MCMULLIN, Hugh (Cont'd)	33	SWNW	1848-07-01		A1 G28
1921	MCMULLIN, Thomas	28	SW	1848-05-10		A1 G28
1923	" "	33	E½NW	1848-05-10		A1 G28
1922	" "	32	NENE	1848-07-01		A1 G28
1924	" "	33	SWNW	1848-07-01		A1 G28
2035	MEEK, Samuel	20	NWSW	1850-10-01		A1
2034	" "	20	NESW	1852-07-01		A1
1971	MORRIS, John	31	E½SE	1839-08-01		A1
1972	" "	32	N½SW	1839-08-01		A1 V2058
1973	" "	32	SWNW	1839-08-01		A1
2014	MURPHY, Robert C	1	SWNW	1841-05-25		A1
2015	" "	12	W½NE	1841-05-25		A1
2016	" "	2	SENE	1841-05-25		A1
2057	NEWMAN, William	31	SENE	1840-10-01		A1
2058	" "	32	E½SW	1840-10-01		A1 V1972
1892	NULL, David	11	NW	1840-10-01		A1
1894	" "	4	NW	1840-10-01		A1
1895	" "	9	E½SE	1841-05-25		A1
1896	" "	9	NENW	1848-06-01		A1
1897	" "	9	W½SW	1848-06-01		A1
1893	" "	13	SWNW	1849-04-10		A1
1939	ORIN, James	23	SESE	1841-08-10		A1
1940	" "	24	E½SE	1841-08-10		A1
1941	" "	24	SW	1841-08-10		A1
1942	" "	24	W½SE	1841-08-10		A1
1943	" "	25	E½SW	1841-08-10		A1
1944	" "	25	NW	1841-08-10		A1
1945	" "	25	NWNE	1841-08-10		A1
1946	" "	25	W½SE	1841-08-10		A1
1899	REAVIS, Elias	7	SESW	1835-09-10		A1
2063	REAVIS, William	6	W½SE	1837-11-07		A1
2061	" "	6	N½NW	1839-02-01		A1
2062	" "	6	NWNE	1839-08-01		A1
2059	" "	20	NENE	1850-12-10		A1
2060	" "	22	NESW	1852-10-01		A1
2043	RICE, Washington	19	NENE	1848-05-01		A1
2012	SAXTON, Robert A	35	NENW	1839-08-01		A1
1879	SHANNER, Charles T	19	SWSW	1856-06-03		A1
2017	SHELTON, Robert	7	NWSE	1837-03-15		A1
2064	SHIELDS, William	17	W½SW	1844-08-01		A1
1974	SIMPSON, John	36	SE	1839-02-01		A1
2046	SIMPSON, William B	35	NWNE	1841-12-10		A1
1925	SINZICK, Jacob	31	NWNW	1841-12-10		A1
1900	SKELTON, Elias	14	N½NW	1856-06-03		A1
1927	SKELTON, Jacob	8	W½NW	1839-02-01		A1 G33
1926	" "	8	NWSW	1839-08-01		A1
1928	SKELTON, Jacob W	20	SWSW	1849-04-10		A1
1947	SKELTON, James	5	NWSE	1839-02-01		A1
1976	SKELTON, John	8	W½NE	1837-11-07		A1
1975	" "	8	SENE	1840-10-01		A1
1977	" "	9	SWNW	1841-05-25		A1
2007	SKELTON, Ralph	5	SWSE	1839-09-01		A1
2018	SKELTON, Robert	7	SWSE	1839-04-01		A1
2065	SKELTON, William	7	SENW	1838-09-01		A1
2019	SPEAR, Robert	26	E½SW	1840-10-01		A1
2020	" "	26	NW	1840-10-01		A1
2021	" "	26	W½SE	1840-10-01		A1
2022	" "	27	E½SE	1840-10-01		A1
1872	STEEL, Andrew H	14	NWSE	1839-08-01		A1
1873	" "	14	SENW	1839-08-01		A1
1948	STEEL, James	3	SWNW	1837-08-01		A1
1950	" "	4	NENE	1839-02-01		A1
1951	" "	4	SESE	1839-02-01		A1
1949	" "	3	W½SW	1841-08-10		A1
1978	STEEL, John	14	W½NE	1831-05-21		A1
2023	STEEL, Robert	3	NWNW	1839-02-01		A1
1992	STEPHENS, Joshua W	18	E½NW	1839-02-01		A1
1993	" "	18	E½SW	1839-02-01		A1
1994	" "	28	E½NW	1839-02-01		A1
1927	" "	8	W½NW	1839-02-01		A1 G33
2066	STERETT, William	4	NESE	1840-10-01		A1
2067	" "	4	W½NE	1840-10-01		A1
2068	" "	4	W½SE	1840-10-01		A1

ID	Individual in Patent	Sec.	Sec. Part	Date Issued	Other Counties	For More Info . . .
2070	SWANEY, William W	13	NWNW	1850-10-01		A1
1902	TAYLOR, Ephraim	26	SWSW	1838-09-01		A1
2038	TAYLOR, Stephen S	19	NWSW	1856-06-03		A1
2069	TAYLOR, William	18	NWSW	1837-11-07		A1
1953	TRENCH, James W	9	NWNW	1850-12-10		A1
1914	VICKERS, Grandison	6	SENW	1838-09-01		A1
1915	"	6	SWNW	1838-09-07		A1
2037	VICKERS, Stacy	6	W½SW	1839-02-01		A1
2039	VON PRICE, STEPHEN	33	SESE	1848-07-01		A1
2011	WEST, Riley W	22	SWSW	1850-12-10		A1
1979	WHEATON, John	31	E½SW	1839-08-01		A1
1980	"	31	W½SE	1839-08-01		A1
2036	WHITNEY, Solon	30	SWSW	1840-10-01		A1
1860	WILSON, Aaron	5	E½NW	1839-02-01		A1
1861	"	5	W½NE	1839-02-01		A1
1858	"	21	SESW	1839-08-01		A1
1859	"	21	SWSE	1839-08-01		A1
1866	WILSON, Allen	18	NENE	1839-08-01		A1
1867	"	7	E½SE	1839-08-01		A1
1898	WILSON, David	36	NENE	1841-05-25		A1
1981	WILSON, John	5	W½NW	1838-09-07		A1
1982	"	6	SENE	1838-09-07		A1
1984	WIRE, John	8	SWSW	1845-06-01		A1
1983	"	17	SWNW	1850-12-10		A1
2005	WISE, Peter P	17	SWSE	1850-12-10		A1
2006	"	20	NWNE	1851-02-01		A1
2025	WOOD, Samuel H	11	E½SE	1840-10-01		A1
1932	WOODS, James H	19	SENE	1848-05-01		A1
1933	"	19	SWNE	1850-10-01		A1
1985	WOODS, John	7	NESW	1839-02-01		A1
1961	WOODS, John L	7	NWSW	1837-11-07		A1
2004	WOODS, Patrick E	19	NESW	1850-12-10		A1

Patent Map

T3-S R9-W
2nd PM Meridian

Map Group 20

Township Statistics

Parcels Mapped	:	215
Number of Patents	:	198
Number of Individuals	:	117
Patentees Identified	:	116
Number of Surnames	:	74
Multi-Patentee Parcels	:	9
Oldest Patent Date	:	5/20/1826
Most Recent Patent	:	6/3/1856
Block/Lot Parcels	:	0
Parcels Re - Issued	:	0
Parcels that Overlap	:	2
Cities and Towns	:	3
Cemeteries	:	2

Section 6
- REAVIS William 1839
- REAVIS William 1839
- AMORY [2] Francis 1839
- WILSON John 1838
- WILSON Aaron 1839
- VICKERS Grandison 1838
- VICKERS Grandison 1838
- BEASLEY Joseph 1839
- WILSON John 1838
- VICKERS Stacy 1839
- BEASLEY Joseph 1837
- REAVIS William 1837
- AMORY [2] Francis 1839
- MAYHALL Jonas 1837

Section 5
- MCCLELLAND John 1852
- WILSON Aaron 1839
- WILSON Aaron 1839
- HENDERSON Samuel 1839
- SKELTON James 1839
- MCGARRAH David D 1835
- SKELTON Ralph 1839

Section 4
- STEEL James 1839
- STERETT William 1840
- HARBISON Thomas 1839
- NULL David 1840
- BURTON David 1840
- STERETT William 1840
- STERETT William 1840
- STEEL James 1839

Section 7
- MCGREW Wilson 1852
- MCGREW Wilson 1837
- SKELTON William 1838
- WOODS John L 1837
- WOODS John 1839
- SHELTON Robert 1837
- WILSON Allen 1839
- REAVIS Elias 1835
- SKELTON Robert 1839

Section 8
- SKELTON [33] Jacob 1839
- SKELTON Jacob 1839
- WIRE John 1845
- SKELTON John 1837
- MARINER Littleton B 1850
- SKELTON John 1840
- MASON Andrew 1844
- FRENCH James W 1844
- MASON William J 1848
- TRENCH James W 1850
- SKELTON John 1841
- NULL David 1848

Section 9
- NULL David 1848
- BURTON Amos 1841
- BURTON Basel 1840
- NULL David 1848
- BURTON Amos 1840
- BURTON Amos 1840
- NULL David 1841

Section 18
- AMORY [2] Francis 1839
- MCCLEARY William 1838
- WILSON Allen 1839
- STEPHENS Joshua W 1839
- TAYLOR William 1837
- STEPHENS Joshua W 1839
- AMORY [2] Francis 1839
- MAYHALL Jonas 1838

Section 17
- MCCLEARY William 1838
- WIRE John 1850
- MCCLEARY William 1837
- MCCLEARY William 1826
- SHIELDS William 1844
- MASON William J 1849
- HALL Samuel 1848
- WISE Peter P 1850
- MCCLEARY James L 1845

Section 16

Section 19
- DEPRIEST William 1848
- RICE Washington 1848
- WOODS James H 1850
- WOODS James H 1848
- TAYLOR Stephen S 1856
- WOODS Patrick E 1850
- SHANNER Charles T 1856

Section 20
- WISE Peter P 1851
- REAVIS William 1850
- MEEK Samuel 1850
- MEEK Samuel 1852
- SKELTON Jacob W 1849
- HOESELE Landalin 1845

Section 21
- WILSON Aaron 1839
- WILSON Aaron 1839

Section 30
- WHITNEY Solon 1840
- SINZICK Jacob 1841

Section 29
- INGRAM John 1852
- COFFMAN Henry J 1840

Section 28
- BASS Howell 1841
- KILLPATRICK Josiah 1839
- BASS Jordan 1849
- STEPHENS Joshua W 1839
- MCMULLIN [28] Hugh 1848

Section 31
- WHEATON John 1839
- WHEATON John 1839
- NEWMAN William 1840
- MORRIS John 1839

Section 32
- MORRIS John 1839
- MORRIS John 1839
- NEWMAN William 1840

Section 33
- MCMULLIN [28] Hugh 1848
- MCCULLOUGH Samuel 1848
- MCMULLIN [28] Hugh 1848
- MCMULLIN Hugh 1848
- MCMULLIN [28] Hugh 1848
- CRISWELL Thomas A 1849
- PRICE Stephen Von 1848

STEEL Robert 1839		MCCULLOCH Jane P 1839	MCCULLOCH Elihu 1839
MCCULLOUGH Samuel 1839	BURTON Amos 1840		
STEEL James 1837	DEVIN James 1839	GALLOWAY George 1840	MURPHY Robert C 1841	MURPHY Robert C 1841	
3	**2**	**1**
		MANAHAN Charles C 1840	MCCULLOUGH Samuel 1839		MARTIN David 1840	
STEEL James 1841	DEVIN James 1839	DEVIN James 1839	MASON Reason 1841	MASON Reason 1840	MANAHAN Charles C 1840	MCCRORY Thomas 1838	MARTIN David 1838	MARTIN Reuben 1840	MARTIN David 1837
BURTON Benjamin 1848		MARTIN John 1841	NULL David 1840	BOOKER William 1840	MCCULLOUGH Samuel 1838	MARTIN David 1835	MURPHY Robert C 1841
				MCCULLOUGH Samuel 1846	MCGREGER George 1838	
10	**11**	**12**
	MARTIN John 1838	MARTIN John 1840	GALLOWAY George 1841	GALLOWAY George 1841	WOOD Samuel H 1840	KELL John 1839	KELL John 1841
	MARTIN John 1835	MCGREGOR George 1841			MARTIN David 1839	
	MCGREGER George 1838	MCGREGER George 1835	SKELTON Elias 1856	STEEL John 1831	SWANEY William W 1850	HOLCOMB Alexander 1840	MARTIN David 1839
MCCULLOH David E 1839	MARTIN David 1840		STEEL Andrew H 1839	**14**	NULL David 1849	HOLCOMB Alexander 1841	**13**
MCCULLOH David E 1848	**15**			STEEL Andrew H 1839			KILLPATRICK James M 1840
			HOLCOMB Alexander 1851	MARTIN Henry 1839	KILLPATRICK James M 1840	
22	**23**	**24**
	REAVIS William 1852			KINCADE Samuel A 1841	ORIN James 1841		ORIN James 1841	ORIN James 1841
WEST Riley W 1850	INGRUM Jesse 1850		KILLPATRICK John 1838	ORIN James 1841			
			KILLPATRICK John B 1840		ORIN James 1841	ORIN James 1841	
MAYHALL Jonas 1838		SPEAR Robert 1840				HARBISON Adam 1841	HARBISON David M 1841
27	MCCULLOUGH William 1839	**26**		**25**	
COFFMAN Henry J 1840	KILLPATRICK Josiah 1839	SPEAR Robert 1840	MCGARRAH William 1839	SPEAR Robert 1840	SPEAR Robert 1840	MCMILLAN John 1839		ORIN James 1841	ORIN James 1841
COFFMAN Henry J 1840	BOYCE William A 1838		TAYLOR Ephraim 1838			MCMILLAN John 1838		
			SAXTON Robert A 1839	SIMPSON William B 1841	MCDILL Samuel 1840		KILLPATRICK Josiah 1840	KILLPATRICK Josiah 1841	WILSON David 1841
					KILLPATRICK Josiah 1839	MCMILLAN John 1839	MCMILLAN John 1835	MCMILLEN James 1839	MCMILLAN James 1840
34	**35**	**36**
					MCDILL Morris L 1838	KILLPATRICK Josiah 1839	SIMPSON John 1839
					BRADSHAW Robert 1835	
BOYCE William A 1839						

Helpful Hints

1. This Map's INDEX can be found on the preceding pages.

2. Refer to Map "C" to see where this Township lies within Gibson County, Indiana.

3. Numbers within square brackets [ ] denote a multi-patentee land parcel (multi-owner). Refer to Appendix "C" for a full list of members in this group.

4. Areas that look to be crowded with Patentees usually indicate multiple sales of the same parcel (Re-issues) or Overlapping parcels. See this Township's Index for an explanation of these and other circumstances that might explain "odd" groupings of Patentees on this map.

Legend

— Patent Boundary

━ Section Boundary

No Patents Found (or Outside County)

1., 2., 3., ... Lot Numbers (when beside a name)

[ ] Group Number (see Appendix "C")

Scale: Section = 1 mile X 1 mile (generally, with some exceptions)

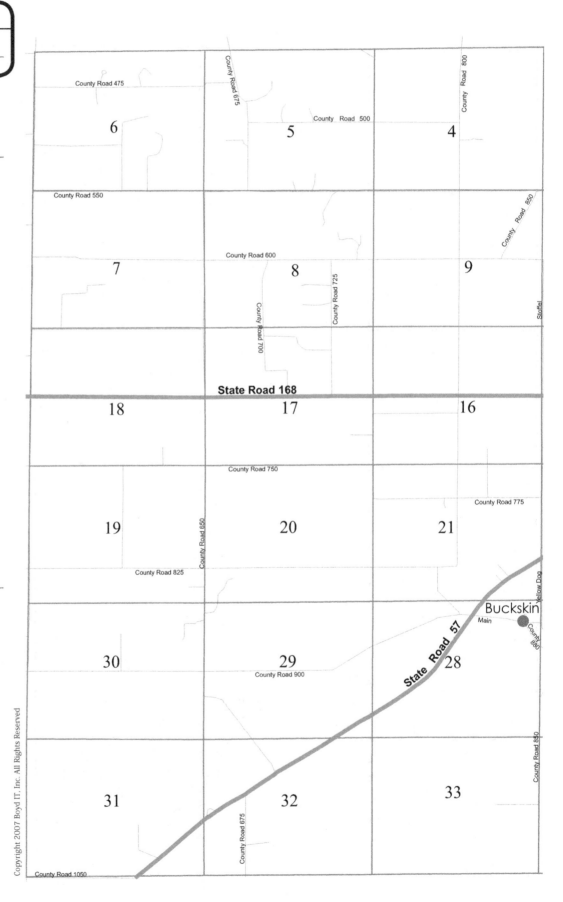

Road Map

T3-S R9-W
2nd PM Meridian

Map Group 20

Cities & Towns
Buckskin
Mackey
Somerville

Cemeteries
Albright Cemetery
Townsley Cemetery

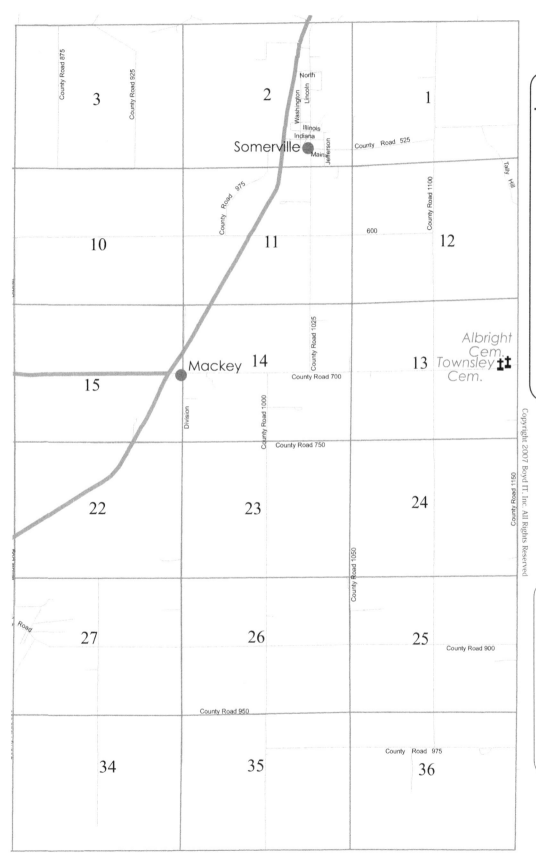

Helpful Hints

1. This road map has a number of uses, but primarily it is to help you: a) find the present location of land owned by your ancestors (at least the general area), b) find cemeteries and city-centers, and c) estimate the route/roads used by Census-takers & tax-assessors.

2. If you plan to travel to Gibson County to locate cemeteries or land parcels, please pick up a modern travel map for the area before you do. Mapping old land parcels on modern maps is not as exact a science as you might think. Just the slightest variations in public land survey coordinates, estimates of parcel boundaries, or road-map deviations can greatly alter a map's representation of how a road either does or doesn't cross a particular parcel of land.

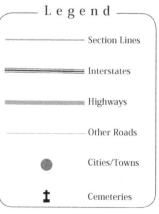

Legend

——————— Section Lines

══════════ Interstates

▬▬▬▬▬▬ Highways

——————— Other Roads

● Cities/Towns

‡ Cemeteries

Scale: Section = 1 mile X 1 mile
(generally, with some exceptions)

Historical Map

T3-S R9-W
2nd PM Meridian

Map Group 20

Cities & Towns
Buckskin
Mackey
Somerville

Cemeteries
Albright Cemetery
Townsley Cemetery

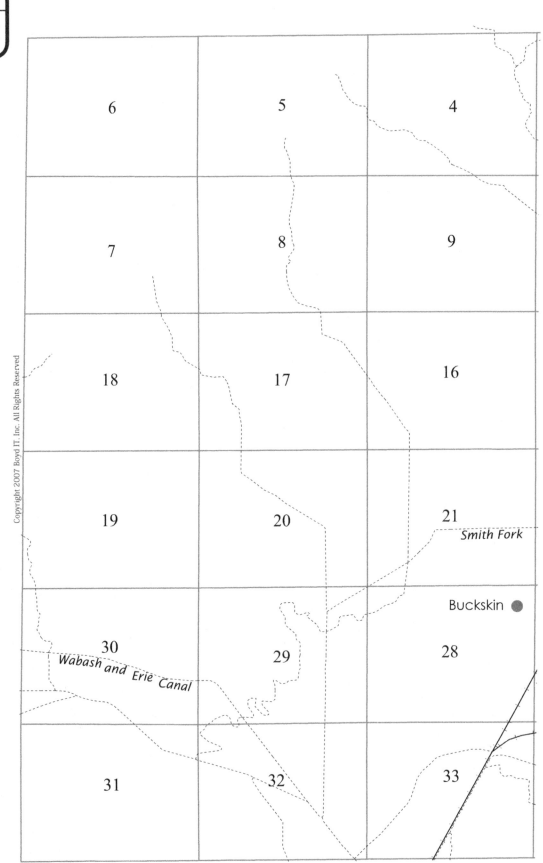

6

5

4

7

8

9

18

17

16

19

20

21

Smith Fork

Buckskin ●

30

Wabash and Erie Canal

29

28

31

32

33

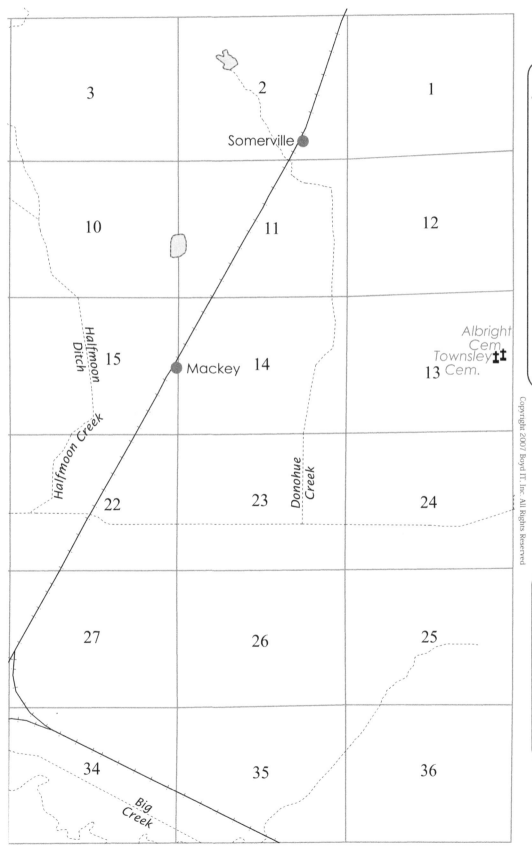

3

2

1

Somerville ●

10

11

12

Halfmoon
Ditch

15   ● Mackey   14

Albright
Cem
Townsley ‡‡
13 Cem.

Halfmoon Creek

22

23

Donohue
Creek

24

27

26

25

34

35

36

Big
Creek

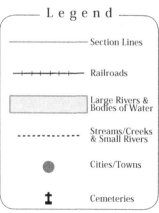

Helpful Hints

1. This Map takes a different look at the same Congressional Township displayed in the preceding two maps. It presents features that can help you better envision the historical development of the area: a) Water-bodies (lakes & ponds), b) Water-courses (rivers, streams, etc.), c) Railroads, d) City/town center-points (where they were oftentimes located when first settled), and e) Cemeteries.

2. Using this "Historical" map in tandem with this Township's Patent Map and Road Map, may lead you to some interesting discoveries. You will often find roads, towns, cemeteries, and waterways are named after nearby landowners: sometimes those names will be the ones you are researching. See how many of these research gems you can find here in Gibson County.

Legend

——————— Section Lines

+—+—+—+—+ Railroads

▭ Large Rivers & Bodies of Water

- - - - - - Streams/Creeks & Small Rivers

● Cities/Towns

‡ Cemeteries

Scale: Section = 1 mile X 1 mile
(there are some exceptions)

Map Group 21: Index to Land Patents

Township 3-South Range 8-West (2nd PM)

After you locate an individual in this Index, take note of the Section and Section Part then proceed to the Land Patent map on the pages immediately following. You should have no difficulty locating the corresponding parcel of land.

The "For More Info" Column will lead you to more information about the underlying Patents. See the *Legend* at right, and the "How to Use this Book" chapter, for more information.

	LEGEND
	"For More Info . . . " column
A =	Authority (Legislative Act, See Appendix "A")
B =	Block or Lot (location in Section unknown)
C =	Cancelled Patent
F =	Fractional Section
G =	Group (Multi-Patentee Patent, see Appendix "C")
V =	Overlaps another Parcel
R =	Re-Issued (Parcel patented more than once)

(A & G items require you to look in the Appendixes referred to above. All other Letter-designations followed by a number require you to locate line-items in this index that possess the ID number found after the letter).

ID	Individual in Patent	Sec.	Sec. Part	Date Issued	Other Counties	For More Info . . .
2104	BALDWIN, Reuben	8	E½SW	1841-05-25		A1
2076	BARKER, Andrew J	32	SENW	1837-03-20		A1
2122	BELL, Thomas	17	SESW	1839-02-01		A1
2124	" "	20	E½NW	1839-02-01		A1
2123	" "	19	SWSE	1840-10-01		A1
2125	" "	29	NWNW	1840-10-01		A1
2126	" "	5	E½SW	1840-10-01	Pike	A1
2127	" "	7	E½SE	1840-10-01		A1
2128	" "	7	SWSE	1840-10-01		A1
2129	" "	8	W½SW	1840-10-01		A1
2073	BLACK, Agness	32	SWSE	1840-10-01		A1
2119	EDRINGTON, Silas	30	W½NW	1824-08-09		A1
2130	EWING, Thomas	8	NENW	1839-02-01		A1 G17
2084	FARMER, Forris	6	NENE	1840-10-01		A1
2079	FARRIS, David	7	NWSE	1837-11-07		A1
2130	GOORLEY, Robert	8	NENW	1839-02-01		A1 G17
2132	HARBISON, William	31	E½NE	1840-10-01		A1
2133	" "	31	W½SE	1840-10-01		A1
2134	" "	32	W½NE	1840-10-01		A1
2135	" "	32	W½SW	1840-10-01		A1
2074	HOLCOMB, Alexander	8	NWSE	1839-02-01		A1
2075	" "	8	SWNE	1839-02-01		A1
2118	HOWE, Sanford	5	SWSE	1838-09-01	Pike	A1
2130	HUMMER, William	8	NENW	1839-02-01		A1 G17
2092	KELL, John	8	NWNW	1840-10-01		A1
2103	KELL, Matthew	7	NENE	1839-08-01		A1
2094	KILLPATRICK, John	30	E½NE	1831-12-31		A1
2095	" "	30	W½NE	1838-09-01		A1
2093	" "	19	SESE	1839-08-01		A1
2102	KILLPATRICK, Josiah	30	E½NW	1839-08-01		A1
2131	KILLPATRICK, Thomas	29	SWNW	1841-05-25		A1
2083	KIRK, Elizabeth	32	NWSE	1840-10-01		A1
2091	KIRKPATRICK, James K	32	E½SE	1840-10-01		A1
2136	LYNN, William	17	NWNE	1839-02-01		A1
2137	" "	8	SWSE	1839-02-01		A1
2085	MARTIN, Henry	17	NESW	1839-02-01		A1
2087	" "	7	E½SW	1839-08-01		A1
2086	" "	19	NWNE	1841-05-25		A1
2097	MCCLELLAND, John	6	E½SE	1839-08-01		A1
2096	" "	5	NE	1841-05-25	Pike	A1
2105	MCCONNEL, Robert	6	W½NE	1838-09-07		A1
2117	MCDILL, Samuel	30	W½SW	1839-08-01		A1
2077	MCGREGER, Andrew	18	SESW	1835-10-15		A1
2098	MCGREGER, John	7	SENE	1835-10-07		A1
2099	" "	8	SWNW	1835-10-07		A1
2109	MCGREGER, Robert	7	NWNE	1835-10-07		A1

ID	Individual in Patent	Sec.	Sec. Part	Date Issued	Other Counties	For More Info . . .
2108	MCGREGER, Robert (Cont'd)	6	SWSE	1838-09-01		A1
2106	" "	18	NESW	1841-05-25		A1
2107	" "	5	W½SW	1841-05-25	Pike	A1
2110	MCGREGOR, Robert	8	SENW	1839-02-01		A1
2078	MINNIS, Calvin	18	SE	1821-08-28		A1
2111	PATTERSON, Robert	6	SW	1838-09-05		A1
2139	RAINEY, William	32	NENW	1840-10-01		A1
2140	" "	32	W½NW	1840-10-01		A1
2138	" "	31	NENW	1844-08-01		A1
2088	SIMPSON, Hugh	31	E½SE	1835-10-28		A1
2120	SIMPSON, Solomon	30	NESE	1841-12-10		A1
2121	" "	31	SENW	1850-12-10		A1
2142	SIMPSON, William	30	W½SE	1829-04-10		A1
2143	" "	31	W½NE	1829-04-10		A1
2141	" "	30	SESE	1839-08-01		A1
2112	SPEAR, Robert	29	E½NE	1841-05-25		A1
2113	" "	29	E½NW	1841-05-25		A1
2114	" "	29	NESE	1841-05-25		A1
2115	" "	29	W½NE	1841-05-25		A1
2116	" "	29	W½SE	1841-05-25		A1
2089	WATT, Hugh	5	N½NW	1840-10-01	Pike	A1
2090	" "	6	NWSE	1840-10-01		A1
2080	WILSON, David	19	W½SW	1840-10-01		A1
2081	" "	30	E½SW	1840-10-01		A1
2082	" "	31	NWNW	1841-05-25		A1
2100	WILSON, Joseph	6	NW	1839-08-01		A1
2101	" "	7	W½SW	1839-08-01		A1
2144	WILSON, Zacheus	7	NW	1839-08-01		A1

Patent Map

T3-S R8-W
2nd PM Meridian

Map Group 21

Township Statistics

Parcels Mapped	:	72
Number of Patents	:	67
Number of Individuals	:	40
Patentees Identified	:	38
Number of Surnames	:	31
Multi-Patentee Parcels	:	1
Oldest Patent Date	:	8/28/1821
Most Recent Patent	:	12/10/1850
Block/Lot Parcels	:	0
Parcels Re - Issued	:	0
Parcels that Overlap	:	0
Cities and Towns	:	0
Cemeteries	:	2

Note: the area contained in this map amounts to far less than a full Township. Therefore, its contents are completely on this single page (instead of a "normal" 2-page spread).

Legend

— Patent Boundary

━ Section Boundary

No Patents Found (or Outside County)

1., 2., 3., ... Lot Numbers (when beside a name)

[ ] Group Number (see Appendix "C")

Scale: Section = 1 mile X 1 mile (generally, with some exceptions)

Section 6

WILSON Joseph 1839
MCCONNEL Robert 1838
FARMER Forris 1840
PATTERSON Robert 1838
WATT Hugh 1840
MCCLELLAND John 1839
MCGREGER Robert 1838

Section 5

WATT Hugh 1840
MCCLELLAND John 1841
MCGREGER Robert 1841
BELL Thomas 1840
HOWE Sanford 1838

Section 4

Section 7

WILSON Zacheus 1839
MCGREGER Robert 1835
KELL Matthew 1839
MCGREGER John 1835
WILSON Joseph 1839
MARTIN Henry 1839
FARRIS David 1837
BELL Thomas 1840
BELL Thomas 1840

Section 8

KELL John 1840
EWING [17] Thomas 1839
MCGREGER John 1835
MCGREGOR Robert 1839
HOLCOMB Alexander 1839
BALDWIN Reuben 1841
HOLCOMB Alexander 1839
LYNN William 1839

Section 9

LYNN William 1839

Pike County

Section 16

Section 18

MCGREGER Robert 1841
MCGREGER Andrew 1835
MINNIS Calvin 1821

Section 17

MARTIN Henry 1839
BELL Thomas 1839

Gibson County

Section 19

MARTIN Henry 1841
WILSON David 1840
BELL Thomas 1840
KILLPATRICK John 1839

Section 20

BELL Thomas 1839

Warrick County

Section 21

Section 30

EDRINGTON Silas 1824
KILLPATRICK John 1838
KILLPATRICK Josiah 1839
KILLPATRICK John 1831
WILSON David 1840
MCDILL Samuel 1839
SIMPSON Solomon 1841
SIMPSON William 1829
SIMPSON William 1839

Section 29

BELL Thomas 1840
SPEAR Robert 1841
KILLPATRICK Thomas 1841
SPEAR Robert 1841
SPEAR Robert 1841
SPEAR Robert 1841
SPEAR Robert 1841

Section 28

Section 31

WILSON David 1841
RAINEY William 1844
SIMPSON Solomon 1850
SIMPSON William 1829
HARBISON William 1840
HARBISON William 1840
SIMPSON Hugh 1835

Section 32

RAINEY William 1840
RAINEY William 1840
HARBISON William 1840
BARKER Andrew J 1837
KIRK Elizabeth 1840
HARBISON William 1840
BLACK Agness 1840
KIRKPATRICK James K 1840

Section 33

6

Jackson

5

County Road 1300

4

County Road 525

Road Map
T3-S R8-W
2nd PM Meridian
Map Group 21

Note: the area contained in this map amounts to far less than a full Township. Therefore, its contents are completely on this single page (instead of a "normal" 2-page spread).

Gibson County

Pike County

7

Tally   Hill

8

9

Cities & Towns
None

18

Mackey
Spurgeon

17

16

Cemeteries
Eden Cemetery
Kilpatrick Cemetery

Warrick County

19

County Road 1200

County Road 1250

20

Beckley

21

County Road 850

Kilpatrick Cem. ✝

Eden Cem. ✝

30

County Road 1150

County Road 1225

29

County Road 1300

28

Legend

Section Lines

Interstates

Highways

Other Roads

● Cities/Towns

✝ Cemeteries

County   Road   950

31

County Road 1000

32

County Road 1325

County Road 1025

33

Scale: Section = 1 mile X 1 mile
(generally, with some exceptions)

Historical Map

T3-S R8-W
2nd PM Meridian

Map Group 21

Note: the area contained in this map amounts to far less than a full Township. Therefore, its contents are completely on this single page (instead of a "normal" 2-page spread).

Cities & Towns
None

Cemeteries
Eden Cemetery
Kilpatrick Cemetery

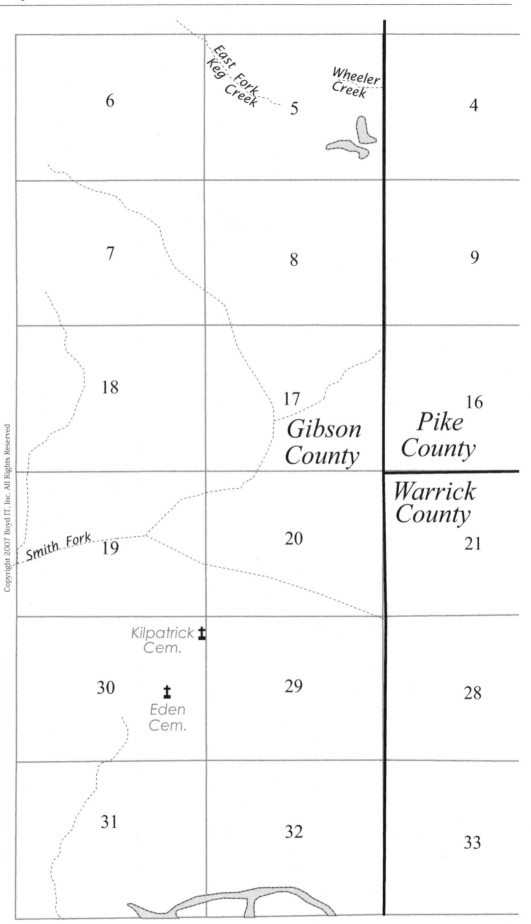

East Fork Keg Creek

Wheeler Creek

6	5	4
7	8	9
18	17	16

Gibson County

Pike County

Warrick County

19	20	21
30	29	28
31	32	33

Smith Fork

Kilpatrick Cem.

Eden Cem.

Legend

— Section Lines

+–+–+ Railroads

Large Rivers & Bodies of Water

----- Streams/Creeks & Small Rivers

● Cities/Towns

✝ Cemeteries

Scale: Section = 1 mile X 1 mile
(there are some exceptions)

Map Group 22: Index to Land Patents

Township 4-South Range 11-West (2nd PM)

After you locate an individual in this Index, take note of the Section and Section Part then proceed to the Land Patent map on the pages immediately following. You should have no difficulty locating the corresponding parcel of land.

The "For More Info" Column will lead you to more information about the underlying Patents. See the *Legend* at right, and the "How to Use this Book" chapter, for more information.

ID	Individual in Patent	Sec.	Sec. Part	Date Issued	Other Counties	For More Info . . .
2204	BIXLER, John	17	E½SE	1841-05-25		A1
2205	" "	17	SWSE	1841-05-25		A1
2189	BLYTHE, James B	9	NWNE	1835-10-23		A1
2190	" "	9	SWSW	1835-10-23		A1
2173	BOREN, Ezekiel	9	NENW	1835-09-10		A1
2175	" "	9	SENW	1837-03-30		A1
2172	" "	3	E½E½	1839-08-01		A1 F
2174	" "	9	NESW	1840-10-01		A1
2207	BOREN, John	8	E½NW	1825-04-08		A1
2208	" "	8	SWNW	1835-09-05		A1
2206	" "	7	NWNE	1835-10-23		A1
2209	" "	8	W½SW	1835-10-23		A1
2212	BOREN, John D	17	NWSE	1837-08-01		A1
2218	BOREN, John M	18	NWNE	1837-03-20		A1
2219	" "	18	SENE	1837-03-20		A1
2246	BOREN, Samuel H	7	SESE	1837-03-18		A1
2245	" "	17	SWNW	1837-03-30		A1
2191	BRILES, James	13	W½NE	1840-10-01		A1
2154	BRILS, Allen	12	W½SW	1839-08-01		A1
2210	BROTHERS, John	12	SENW	1840-10-01		A1
2240	CALVERT, Patrick	18	NENE	1837-08-05		A1
2225	CARTER, Joseph	18	E½SW	1831-12-08		A1
2243	CARTER, Rane	18	NENW	1837-03-20		A1
2165	CHAFFIN, Edwin	11	NWNW	1839-08-01		A1
2166	" "	11	SWNW	1839-08-01		A1
2167	" "	2	W½W½	1839-08-01		A1
2178	DAVIS, George	13	NWSE	1839-08-01		A1
2179	" "	14	NWSW	1841-12-10		A1
2202	EMMERSON, Jesse	6	E½	1835-10-23		A1 F
2258	FINCH, William	18	SWSW	1839-02-01		A1
2160	FISHER, Daniel	17	NWNW	1835-09-10		A1
2220	FORREST, John M	18	SWNE	1835-10-07		A1
2213	GEISLER, John	14	SESW	1840-10-01		A1
2180	GREP, George	1	E½	1841-12-10		A1 G19 F
2214	HANFT, John	13	E½SE	1839-08-01		A1
2215	" "	13	SWSE	1840-10-01		A1
2216	HARDMAN, John	12	NENE	1848-04-10		A1
2217	" "	12	SWNE	1848-04-10		A1
2251	HARRIS, Stephen	7	NENW	1835-10-01		A1
2252	" "	8	NWNW	1835-10-01		A1
2250	" "	7	NENE	1838-09-01		A1
2249	" "	18	NESE	1840-10-01		A1
2265	JOHNSON, Winchester	18	SENW	1837-08-01		A1
2184	JORDAN, George W	9	SWNE	1835-10-23		A1
2183	" "	3	W½W½	1839-02-01		A1
2148	LAND, Abraham	3	E½W½	1839-02-01		A1

ID	Individual in Patent	Sec.	Sec. Part	Date Issued	Other Counties	For More Info . . .
2149	LAND, Abraham (Cont'd)	3	W½E½	1839-08-01		A1 V2149
2147	LONG, Abner N	18	W½NW	1831-01-04		A1
2181	LOW, George	13	E½NW	1839-08-01		A1
2150	LUTZ, Adam	12	SENE	1845-05-01		A1
2259	MANGRUM, William	10	W½NE	1835-10-23		A1
2157	MARTIN, Berry	15	NWNE	1839-08-01		A1
2158	MARTIN, Charles	15	W½SE	1840-10-01		A1
2237	MARTIN, Nelson	14	N½SE	1839-08-01		A1
2238	" "	14	NESW	1841-05-25		A1
2253	MARTIN, Thomas	15	NWNW	1839-08-01		A1
2182	MARVEL, George	9	W½NE	1829-07-02		A1
2200	MCCONNELL, Jehiel	7	SENE	1837-03-30		A1
2201	" "	7	SWNE	1837-03-30		A1
2161	MCDONALD, Daniel	15	SENW	1840-10-01		A1
2163	MCDOWELL, Daniel	15	S½NE	1838-09-01		A1
2162	" "	11	SESW	1840-10-01		A1
2247	MILLER, Samuel	7	SESW	1835-09-05		A1
2151	MITCHELL, Alexander	1	E½W½	1845-06-01		A1 F
2221	MITCHELL, John	9	SWSE	1850-10-01		A1
2241	MONTGOMERY, Pretuimon	14	NWNW	1839-08-01		A1
2242	" "	15	NENE	1839-08-01		A1
2244	MONTGOMERY, Robert	7	SENW	1837-03-30		A1
2176	MOORE, George A	17	SENW	1837-03-18		A1
2177	" "	17	SWNE	1837-08-01		A1
2145	MURPHEY, Aaron	8	E½SE	1835-09-05		A1
2146	MURPHY, Aaron	17	SENE	1837-03-30		A1
2156	MURPHY, Arron	9	NWSW	1841-05-25		A1
2153	POWELL, Alexander	15	E½SW	1839-08-01		A1
2152	" "	15	E½SE	1841-05-25		A1
2192	POWELL, James	13	E½SW	1839-08-01		A1
2256	REDMAN, Wesley	17	NENW	1835-10-01		A1
2257	" "	17	NWNE	1837-03-15		A1
2230	ROBINSON, Martin L	15	NENW	1835-10-23		A1
2229	" "	10	E½NE	1839-08-01		A1
2231	ROBINSON, Michael D	10	E½SE	1837-08-05		A1
2232	" "	12	E½SW	1840-10-01		A1
2233	" "	14	S½SE	1840-10-01		A1
2234	ROBINSON, Michael Dean	14	SENE	1840-10-01		A1
2239	ROBINSON, Nicholas	9	NWSE	1835-10-01		A1
2226	ROSBOROUGH, Joseph	8	E½NE	1829-07-02		A1
2260	RUTLEDGE, William	11	E½NW	1839-08-01		A1
2155	SHAFER, Anthony	12	NWNE	1844-08-01		A1
2180	SHAFER, Charles V	1	E½	1841-12-10		A1 G19 F
2180	SHAFER, Elizabeth	1	E½	1841-12-10		A1 G19 F
2159	STASER, Conrad	13	W½SW	1840-10-01		A1
2211	STASER, John C	13	SENE	1840-10-01		A1
2222	STEWART, John	12	NENW	1839-08-01		A1
2228	STEWART, Luther W	1	W½W½	1839-08-01		A1
2227	SUMNERS, Joseph	11	E½NE	1838-09-05		A1
2164	SUTTON, David	4	NWSW	1837-08-05		A1
2223	TRIBLE, John	12	SE	1824-08-09		A1
2168	TURNER, Elijah	7	W½SW	1831-01-04		A1
2262	WATKINS, William	15	SWSW	1837-11-07		A1
2261	" "	15	NWSW	1839-08-01		A1
2188	WILKINSON, Isiah	7	N½SE	1837-03-30		A1
2264	WILKINSON, William	7	NESW	1835-10-28		A1
2263	" "	15	SWNW	1841-05-25		A1
2193	WILLIAMS, James	14	NENW	1840-10-01		A1
2194	" "	14	S½NW	1840-10-01		A1
2195	" "	14	W½NE	1840-10-01		A1
2248	WILLIAMS, Simon	18	S½SE	1837-03-30		A1
2254	WILLIAMS, Thornton	13	W½NW	1839-08-01		A1
2255	" "	14	NENE	1840-10-01		A1
2197	WILSON, James	8	E½SW	1832-06-06		A1
2198	" "	8	W½SE	1832-06-06		A1
2196	" "	7	SWSE	1835-10-23		A1
2199	" "	9	SESW	1838-09-01		A1
2224	WRIGHT, John	13	NENE	1839-08-01		A1
2169	YAGER, Elijah	2	E½W½	1839-08-01		A1
2185	YAGER, George	11	NESW	1840-10-01		A1
2186	" "	11	NWSW	1840-10-01		A1
2187	" "	11	SWSW	1840-10-01		A1
2203	YAGER, Joel	11	N½SE	1838-09-01		A1

ID	Individual in Patent	Sec.	Sec. Part	Date Issued	Other Counties	For More Info . . .
2235	YAGER, Moses	11	SESE	1840-10-01		A1
2170	YEAGER, Elijah	11	W½NE	1839-02-01		A1
2171	" "	2	E½	1839-02-01		A1
2236	YEAGER, Moses	11	SWSE	1839-08-01		A1

N

Patent Map

T4-S R11-W
2nd PM Meridian

Map Group 22

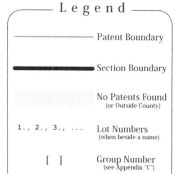

Township Statistics

Parcels Mapped	:	121
Number of Patents	:	116
Number of Individuals	:	82
Patentees Identified	:	80
Number of Surnames	:	56
Multi-Patentee Parcels	:	1
Oldest Patent Date	:	8/9/1824
Most Recent Patent	:	10/1/1850
Block/Lot Parcels	:	0
Parcels Re - Issued	:	0
Parcels that Overlap	:	1
Cities and Towns	:	0
Cemeteries	:	2

Note: the area contained in this map amounts to far less than a full Township. Therefore, its contents are completely on this single page (instead of a "normal" 2-page spread).

Legend

— Patent Boundary

— Section Boundary

No Patents Found
(or Outside County)

1., 2., 3., ...   Lot Numbers
(when beside a name)

[ ]   Group Number
(see Appendix "C")

Scale: Section = 1 mile X 1 mile
(generally, with some exceptions)

Map Grid (Sections)

Section 6
FINCH William 1839
LONG Abner N 1831
HARRIS Stephen 1835
BOREN John 1835
EMMERSON Jesse 1835

Section 19
CARTER Joseph 1831
WILLIAMS Simon 1837

Section 7
TURNER Elijah 1831
MONTGOMERY Robert 1837
MCCONNELL Jehiel 1837
WILKINSON William 1835
HARRIS Stephen 1835
BOREN John 1835

Section 18
JOHNSON Winchester 1837
CARTER Rane 1837
MILLER Samuel 1835
WILSON James 1835
WILKINSON Isiah 1837
MCCONNELL Jehiel 1837
BOREN Samuel H 1837
FORREST John M 1837
BOREN John M 1835
HARRIS Stephen 1840

Section 17
CALVERT Patrick 1835
FISHER Daniel 1835
REDMAN Wesley 1837
MOORE George A 1837
BOREN Samuel H 1837
REDMAN Wesley 1837
MOORE George A 1837
BOREN John D 1837
BIXLER John 1841
MURPHY Aaron 1837

Section 8
BOREN John 1835
WILSON James 1832
WILSON James 1832
ROSBOROUGH Joseph 1829
MURPHEY Aaron 1835

Section 5
HARRIS Stephen 1835
SUTTON David 1837

Section 16
Gibson County

Section 21
Vanderburgh County

Section 9
MURPHY Arron 1841
BLYTHE James B 1835
WILSON James 1838
MARVEL George 1829
BOREN Ezekiel 1835
BOREN Ezekiel 1837
JORDAN George W 1835
ROBINSON Nicholas 1835
MITCHELL John 1850

Section 4
BLYTHE James B 1835
BOREN Ezekiel 1835

Section 20

Section 22
WATKINS William 1837
WILKINSON William 1839
WATKINS William 1841
POWELL Alexander 1839
MCDONALD Daniel 1840
MARTIN Charles 1840

Section 15
MARTIN Thomas 1839
ROBINSON Berry 1839
MONTGOMERY Pretuimon 1839
MONTGOMERY Pretuimon 1839
MCDOWELL Daniel 1838
POWELL Alexander 1841

Section 10
MANGRUM William 1835
ROBINSON Michael D 1837
ROBINSON Martin L 1839

Section 3
JORDAN George W 1839
LAND Abraham 1839
LAND Abraham 1839
BOREN Ezekiel 1839

Section 23
DAVIS George 1841
GEISLER John 1840
MARTIN Neilson 1841

Section 14
WILLIAMS James 1840
WILLIAMS James 1840
MARTIN Neilson 1839
ROBINSON Michael D 1840

Section 11
CHAFFIN Edwin 1839
CHAFFIN Edwin 1839
CHAFFIN William 1839
RUTLEDGE William 1839
YAGER George 1840
YAGER George 1840
MCDOWELL Daniel 1840
YAGER Elijah 1839
YAGER Joel 1838
YAGER Moses 1839
WILLIAMS James 1840
YEAGER Moses 1840

Section 2
CHAFFIN Edwin 1839
YAGER Elijah 1839
YAGER Elijah 1839
SUMNERS Joseph 1838

Section 24
STASER Conrad 1840
POWELL James 1839
STASER John C 1840
HANFT John 1840

Section 13
WILLIAMS Thornton 1839
WILLIAMS George 1839
LOW George 1839
ROBINSON Michael D 1840
BRILES James 1840
DAVIS George 1839
HANFT John 1839

Section 12
BRILS Allen 1839
BROTHERS John 1840
STEWART John 1839
ROBINSON Michael D 1840
TRIBLE John 1848

Section 1
STEWART Luther W 1839
MITCHELL Alexander 1845
STEWART Anthony 1844
HARDMAN John 1845
LUTZ Adam 1845
SHAFER John 1824
HARDMAN John 1841
GREP [19] George 1841
WRIGHT John 1839

Road Map

T4-S R11-W
2nd PM Meridian

Map Group 22

Note: the area contained in this map amounts to far less than a full Township. Therefore, its contents are completely on this single page (instead of a "normal" 2-page spread).

Cities & Towns
None

Cemeteries
Powell Cemetery
Willaims Cemetery

Legend

— Section Lines

═ Interstates

━ Highways

— Other Roads

● Cities/Towns

✝ Cemeteries

Scale: Section = 1 mile X 1 mile
(generally, with some exceptions)

County Line

Vanderburgh County

Gibson County

County Road 1150

County Road 525

County Road 450

County Road 1200

County Road 425

County Road 400

Owensville

County Road 325

✝ *Williams Cem.*

✝ *Powell Cem.*

County Road 200

Sunset

Pine Tree

County Road 150

County Road 1250

State Road 68

19	18	7	6
20	17	8	5
21	16	9	4
22	15	10	3
23	14	11	2
24	13	12	1

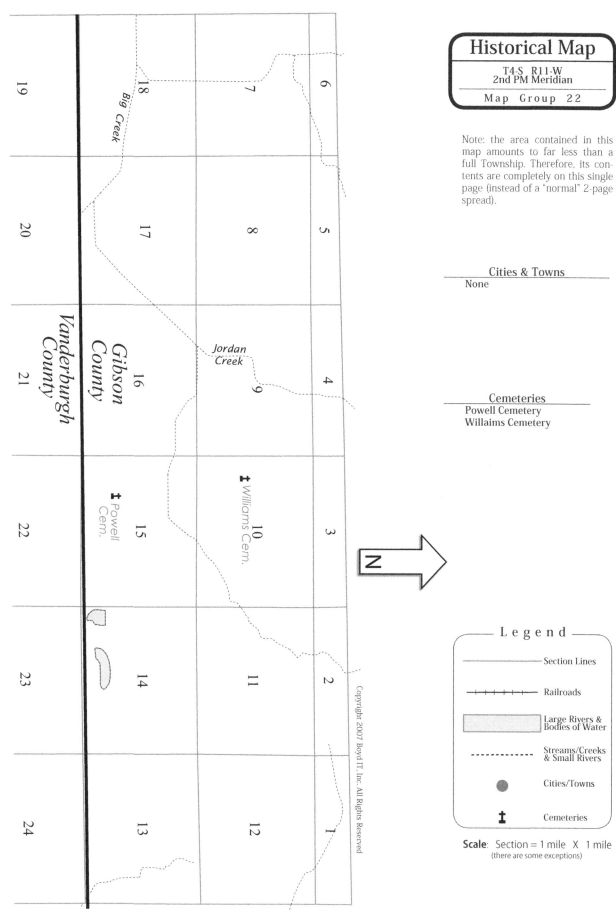

Historical Map

T4-S R11-W
2nd PM Meridian

Map Group 22

Note: the area contained in this map amounts to far less than a full Township. Therefore, its contents are completely on this single page (instead of a "normal" 2-page spread).

Cities & Towns
None

Cemeteries
Powell Cemetery
Willaims Cemetery

Legend

Section Lines

Railroads

Large Rivers & Bodies of Water

Streams/Creeks & Small Rivers

Cities/Towns

Cemeteries

Scale: Section = 1 mile X 1 mile
(there are some exceptions)

Map Group 23: Index to Land Patents

Township 4-South Range 10-West (2nd PM)

After you locate an individual in this Index, take note of the Section and Section Part then proceed to the Land Patent map on the pages immediately following. You should have no difficulty locating the corresponding parcel of land.

The "For More Info" Column will lead you to more information about the underlying Patents. See the *Legend* at right, and the "How to Use this Book" chapter, for more information.

ID	Individual in Patent	Sec.	Sec. Part	Date Issued	Other Counties	For More Info . . .
2316	ANDERSON, Isaac	15	NESE	1839-08-01		A1
2317	" "	15	SESW	1839-08-01		A1
2318	" "	15	SWSE	1839-08-01		A1
2325	ARBURN, John	13	NENW	1849-04-10		A1
2356	BAECHEL, Michael	10	E½SE	1841-05-25		A1
2357	" "	11	SE	1841-05-25		A1
2358	" "	3	W½	1841-05-25		A1
2359	" "	9	SENE	1841-05-25		A1
2367	BALLARD, Thomas	12	NESW	1839-08-01		A1
2368	" "	12	NWSE	1839-08-01		A1
2293	BESING, Frederick	1	E½NE	1848-07-01		A1 F
2294	" "	12	NENE	1850-12-10		A1
2355	BROSE, Mary	17	SW	1839-08-01		A1
2302	BUSING, Henry	11	W½NE	1841-12-10		A1
2303	" "	12	NWNE	1845-05-01		A1
2304	" "	12	SWNE	1850-12-10		A1
2300	BYERS, George	9	SWNW	1839-02-01		A1
2327	CARTER, John	12	SESW	1839-08-01		A1
2370	COVEY, William	13	SESE	1835-10-23		A1
2369	" "	13	NESW	1837-08-01		A1
2371	" "	14	NENE	1838-09-01		A1
2282	CRUSE, Christian	8	SW	1839-08-01		A1
2283	" "	8	W½SE	1839-08-01		A1
2295	CRUSE, Frederick	1	W½E½	1848-04-10		A1 F
2305	CRUSE, Henry	17	E½SE	1839-08-01		A1
2306	" "	17	NW	1839-08-01		A1
2307	" "	17	W½NE	1839-08-01		A1
2308	" "	17	W½SE	1840-10-01		A1
2273	DASH, Andres	7	SWSW	1841-05-25		A1
2309	DICKMEIR, Henry	10	W½SW	1840-10-01		A1
2278	DICKMIRE, Arnold	10	SWNW	1850-12-10		A1
2361	DIKMAR, Oruhlt	10	NESW	1848-04-10		A1
2269	DILLBECK, Abraham	12	SESE	1839-08-01		A1
2272	DOUGLASS, Albert W	18	NWNW	1840-10-01		A1
2292	DUFF, Elijah	15	NWSE	1838-09-01		A1
2291	" "	15	E½NE	1841-05-25		A1
2320	DUFF, Jackson	15	SWNE	1840-10-01		A1
2319	" "	15	NWNE	1841-05-25		A1
2347	DUFF, Joseph	14	E½SW	1835-10-01		A1
2372	EMBREE, William	13	NESE	1838-09-01		A1
2310	FISHER, Henry	11	W½NW	1841-12-10		A1
2311	" "	12	E½NW	1844-08-01		A1
2276	GENTER, Anton	6	W½	1845-05-01		A1
2277	" "	6	W½E½	1845-06-01		A1 V2277
2281	GREATER, Charles	7	NWNW	1845-05-01		A1
2373	HAMPTON, William	1	E½W½	1841-05-25		A1

ID	Individual in Patent	Sec.	Sec. Part	Date Issued	Other Counties	For More Info . . .
2374	HAMPTON, William (Cont'd)	1	W½W½	1841-05-25		A1
2375	" "	2	E½E½	1841-05-25		A1 F
2266	HILL, Aaron W	13	W½SE	1838-09-01		A1
2328	HOLCOMBE, John	13	E½NE	1839-02-01		A1
2329	"	13	SENW	1839-08-01		A1
2330	"	13	W½NE	1839-08-01		A1
2353	IRELAND, Levin	14	SENE	1835-10-23		A1
2352	" "	13	SWNW	1837-08-05		A1
2350	"	11	E½NE	1840-10-01		A1
2351	"	12	W½NW	1840-10-01		A1
2377	IRELAND, William	14	NWNE	1838-09-05		A1
2376	" "	14	NENW	1841-12-10		A1
2385	JONES, William T	14	SWSE	1839-02-01		A1 R2379
2331	KUHL, John	7	SWNE	1841-12-10		A1 V2285
2380	KURTZ, William	10	NWNW	1855-01-03		A1
2381	"	14	SENW	1855-01-03		A1
2301	LOLLMAN, George	6	E½E½	1848-05-01		A1 F
2267	LOYD, Abel	18	NESW	1839-08-01		A1
2268	" "	18	SENW	1839-08-01		A1
2382	LOYD, William L	18	NWSW	1839-08-01		A1
2354	LUKRING, Lewis	2	W½	1841-12-10		A1
2366	MAIL, Solomon	8	NENE	1837-03-18		A1
2288	MCGARRAH, David D	5	E½	1837-03-18		A1 F
2287	" "	4	W½W½	1841-05-25		A1
2289	" "	5	E½W½	1841-05-25		A1
2280	MCGEHEE, Benjamin F	18	SENE	1838-09-07		A1 G27
2279	" "	18	NENE	1840-10-01		A1
2332	MORRIS, John	13	NWNW	1839-08-01		A1
2312	MYER, Henry	8	SWNW	1848-05-10		A1
2365	NEABARGER, Sebastian	18	SWSW	1840-10-01		A1
2275	OBERT, Anthony	18	SWSE	1841-12-10		A1
2274	"	18	SESE	1848-05-01		A1
2363	OWENS, Randolph	18	SWNW	1838-09-07		A1
2348	REITZEL, Joseph	18	NESE	1844-08-01		A1
2349	" "	18	NWSE	1848-05-01		A1
2333	ROCKWELL, John	13	SESW	1838-09-07		A1
2323	ROCKWELL, John A	13	W½SW	1838-09-07		A1
2324	" "	14	W½SW	1838-09-07		A1
2313	ROLFSMEYER, Henry	7	E½NE	1840-10-01		A1
2314	" "	7	E½SE	1840-10-01		A1
2280	ROSE, Jesse	18	SENE	1838-09-07		A1 G27
2284	SANDALL, Christian	7	E½SW	1840-10-01		A1
2285	"	7	W½NE	1840-10-01		A1 V2331
2286	"	7	W½SE	1840-10-01		A1
2290	SHARNST, David	11	E½NW	1841-12-10		A1
2270	SMIDT, Adam	8	E½SE	1840-10-01		A1
2383	STALLINGS, William	10	NWNE	1837-11-07		A1 R2384
2384	"	10	NWNE	1841-05-25		A1 R2383
2296	STASER, Frederick	18	NENW	1840-10-01		A1
2297	" "	18	W½NE	1840-10-01		A1
2326	STASIR, John C	18	SESW	1840-10-01		A1
2298	STRICTMOERDER, Frederick	11	SW	1841-05-25		A1
2299	STUNKEL, Frederick	3	E½E½	1841-12-10		A1 F
2315	STUNKEL, Henry	2	W½E½	1841-12-10		A1 V2315
2360	WEHNER, Michael	17	NENE	1839-08-01		A1
2271	WIDENER, Adam	7	NWSW	1841-12-10		A1
2378	WILHOW, William J	14	NESE	1837-08-05		A1
2322	WILKISON, James T	12	SENE	1849-04-10		A1
2321	WINKELMANN, Jacob	15	E½NW	1849-04-10		A1
2379	WITHRAW, William J	14	SWSE	1835-10-15		A1 R2385
2345	WITHROW, John	9	W½SE	1830-12-02		A1
2342	" "	9	NENE	1838-09-01		A1
2346	" "	9	W½SW	1838-09-01		A1
2335	" "	15	SESE	1839-02-01		A1
2334	" "	15	NESW	1840-10-01		A1
2336	" "	15	W½NW	1840-10-01		A1
2337	" "	15	W½SW	1840-10-01		A1
2338	" "	17	SENE	1840-10-01		A1
2339	" "	8	SENE	1840-10-01		A1
2340	" "	9	E½NW	1840-10-01		A1
2341	" "	9	E½SE	1840-10-01		A1
2343	" "	9	NWNW	1840-10-01		A1
2344	" "	9	W½NE	1840-10-01		A1

ID	Individual in Patent	Sec.	Sec. Part	Date Issued	Other Counties	For More Info . . .
2364	WITHROW, Ritchson	14	NWSE	1840-10-01		A1
2362	WITTMAN, Pierre	7	SWNW	1844-08-01		A1

Patent Map

T4-S R10-W
2nd PM Meridian

Map Group 23

Township Statistics

Parcels Mapped	:	120
Number of Patents	:	109
Number of Individuals	:	69
Patentees Identified	:	69
Number of Surnames	:	60
Multi-Patentee Parcels	:	1
Oldest Patent Date	:	12/2/1830
Most Recent Patent	:	1/3/1855
Block/Lot Parcels	:	0
Parcels Re - Issued	:	2
Parcels that Overlap	:	4
Cities and Towns	:	2
Cemeteries	:	1

Note: the area contained in this map amounts to far less than a full Township. Therefore, its contents are completely on this single page (instead of a "normal" 2-page spread).

Legend

- —— Patent Boundary
- ▬▬ Section Boundary
- No Patents Found (or Outside County)
- 1., 2., 3., ... Lot Numbers (when beside a name)
- [ ] Group Number (see Appendix "C")

Scale: Section = 1 mile X 1 mile (generally, with some exceptions)

Map Grid (Sections)

Section 6: GENTER Anton 1845; GENTER Anton 1845; LOLLMAN George 1848

Section 5: MCGARRAH David D 1841; MCGARRAH David D 1837; MAIL Solomon 1837; WITHROW John 1840; MYER Henry 1848; KUHL John 1841

Section 7: GREATER Charles 1845; WITTMAN Pierre 1844; WIDENER Adam 1841; DASH Andres 1841; SANDALL Christian 1840; SANDALL Christian 1840; ROLFSMEYER Henry 1840; ROLFSMEYER Henry 1840

Section 18: NEABARGER Sebastian 1840; LOYD William L 1839; OWENS Randolph 1838; DOUGLASS Albert W 1840; LOYD Abel 1839; STASIR John C 1840; LOYD Abel 1839; STASER Frederick 1840; STASER Frederick 1840; OBERT Anthony 1841; OBERT Anthony 1848; REITZEL Joseph 1848; REITZEL Joseph 1844; MCGEHEE [27] Benjamin F 1838; MCGEHEE Benjamin F 1840

Section 8: CRUSE Christian 1839; CRUSE Christian 1839; CRUSE Christian 1839; WITHROW John 1840; WEHNER Michael 1839; SMIDT Adam 1840; BYERS George 1839

Section 17: BROSE Mary 1839; CRUSE Henry 1839; CRUSE Henry 1840; CRUSE Henry 1839; CRUSE Henry 1840; WITHROW John 1840

Section 4: MCGARRAH David D 1841; WITHROW John 1840; WITHROW John 1830; WITHROW John 1840; BAECHEL Michael 1841

Section 9: WITHROW John 1840; WITHROW John 1840; WITHROW John 1830; WITHROW John 1840

Section 16: *Gibson County* / *Vanderburgh County*

Section 3: KURTZ William 1855; DICKMIRE Henry 1841; DICKMAN Arnold 1850; STALLINGS William 1837; STALLINGS William 1841; BAECHEL Michael 1841; STUNKEL Frederick 1841

Section 10: DICKMEIR Henry 1840; DIKMAR Orphil 1848; BAECHEL Michael 1841

Section 15: WITHROW John 1840; WITHROW John 1840; ANDERSON Isaac 1839; ANDERSON Isaac 1839; WITHROW John 1839; WINKELMANN Jacob 1849; DUFF Jackson 1841; DUFF Elijah 1838; ANDERSON Isaac 1839; DUFF Jackson 1840; DUFF Elijah 1841

Section 2: LUKRING Lewis 1841; FISHER Henry 1841; SHARNST David 1841; STUNKEL Henry 1841; HAMPTON William 1841; BUSING Henry 1841; IRELAND Levin 1840

Section 11: IRELAND William 1841; STRICTMOERDER Frederick 1841; BAECHEL Michael 1841

Section 14: ROCKWELL John A 1838; DUFF Joseph 1835; KURTZ William 1855; WITHROW Ritchson 1840; WITHRAW William J 1835; JONES William T 1839; IRELAND William 1855; IRELAND Levin 1835; WILHOW William J 1837; IRELAND Levin 1838; COVEY William 1838

Section 13: ROCKWELL John A 1838; ROCKWELL John A 1838; ROCKWELL John 1838; MORRIS John 1839; ARBURN William 1849; IRELAND John 1839; COVEY William 1837; HOLCOMBE John 1839; CARTER John 1839; BALLARD Thomas 1839; BALLARD Thomas 1839; HOLCOMBE John 1839; HOLCOMBE John 1839; HILL Aaron W 1838; EMBREE William 1838; COVEY William 1835; DILLBECK Abraham 1839

Section 1: HAMPTON William 1841; HAMPTON William 1841; FISHER Henry 1844; BUSING Henry 1845; BUSING James T 1849; CRUSE Frederick 1848; BESING Frederick 1848; BUSING Frederick 1850; WILKISON James T 1849; CRUSE Frederick 1848

Section 12: FISHER Henry 1844; BUSING Henry 1845; BALLARD Thomas 1850

217

Road Map

T4-S R10-W
2nd PM Meridian

Map Group 23

Note: the area contained in this map amounts to far less than a full Township. Therefore, its contents are completely on this single page (instead of a "normal" 2-page spread).

Cities & Towns
Saint James
Warrenton

Cemeteries
Nobles Cemetery

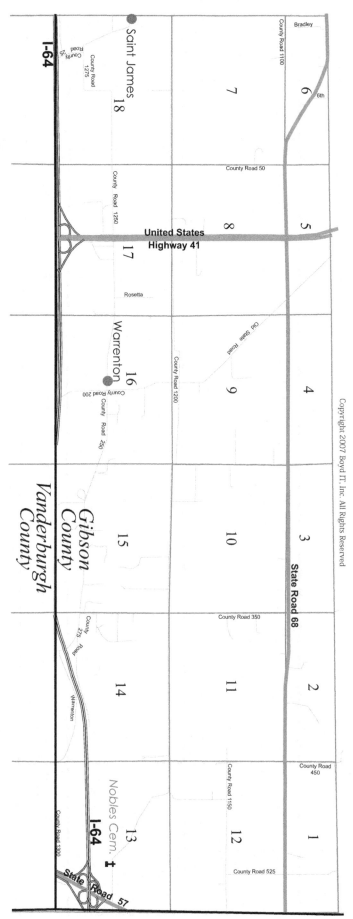

N

Legend

——————— Section Lines

═══════════ Interstates

━━━━━━━━━━ Highways

——————— Other Roads

● Cities/Towns

♱ Cemeteries

Scale: Section = 1 mile X 1 mile
(generally, with some exceptions)

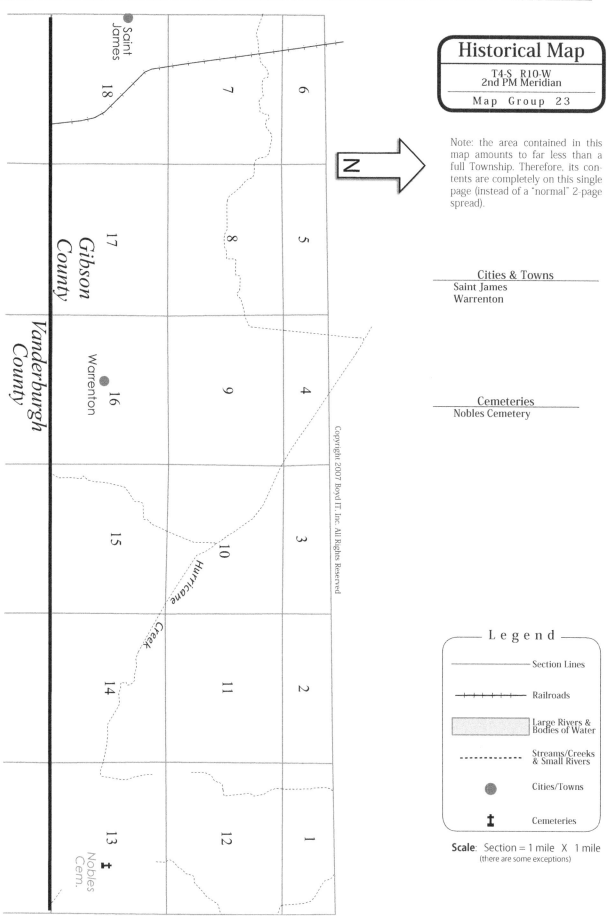

Historical Map

T4-S R10-W
2nd PM Meridian

Map Group 23

Note: the area contained in this map amounts to far less than a full Township. Therefore, its contents are completely on this single page (instead of a "normal" 2-page spread).

Cities & Towns
Saint James
Warrenton

Cemeteries
Nobles Cemetery

Legend
———— Section Lines

+-+-+-+- Railroads

Large Rivers & Bodies of Water

- - - - - Streams/Creeks & Small Rivers

● Cities/Towns

✝ Cemeteries

Scale: Section = 1 mile X 1 mile
(there are some exceptions)

Appendices

Appendix A - Acts of Congress Authorizing the Patents Contained in this Book

The following Acts of Congress are referred to throughout the Indexes in this book. The text of the Federal Statutes referred to below can usually be found on the web. For more information on such laws, check out the publishers's web-site at *www.arphax.com,* go to the "Research" page, and click on the "Land-Law" link.

Ref. No.	Date and Act of Congress	Number of Parcels of Land
1	April 24, 1820: Sale-Cash Entry (3 Stat. 566)	2382
2	February 1801: Canadian Refugee Warrant Act (1 Stat. 100)	3

Appendix B - Section Parts (Aliquot Parts)

The following represent the various abbreviations we have found thus far in describing the parts of a Public Land Section. Some of these are very obscure and rarely used, but we wanted to list them for just that reason. A full section is 1 square mile or 640 acres.

Section Part	Description	Acres
<none>	Full Acre (if no Section Part is listed, presumed a full Section)	640
<1-??>	A number represents a Lot Number and can be of various sizes	?
E½	East Half-Section	320
E½E½	East Half of East Half-Section	160
E½E½SE	East Half of East Half of Southeast Quarter-Section	40
E½N½	East Half of North Half-Section	160
E½NE	East Half of Northeast Quarter-Section	80
E½NENE	East Half of Northeast Quarter of Northeast Quarter-Section	20
E½NENW	East Half of Northeast Quarter of Northwest Quarter-Section	20
E½NESE	East Half of Northeast Quarter of Southeast Quarter-Section	20
E½NESW	East Half of Northeast Quarter of Southwest Quarter-Section	20
E½NW	East Half of Northwest Quarter-Section	80
E½NWNE	East Half of Northwest Quarter of Northeast Quarter-Section	20
E½NWNW	East Half of Northwest Quarter of Northwest Quarter-Section	20
E½NWSE	East Half of Northwest Quarter of Southeast Quarter-Section	20
E½NWSW	East Half of Northwest Quarter of Southwest Quarter-Section	20
E½S½	East Half of South Half-Section	160
E½SE	East Half of Southeast Quarter-Section	80
E½SENE	East Half of Southeast Quarter of Northeast Quarter-Section	20
E½SENW	East Half of Southeast Quarter of Northwest Quarter-Section	20
E½SESE	East Half of Southeast Quarter of Southeast Quarter-Section	20
E½SESW	East Half of Southeast Quarter of Southwest Quarter-Section	20
E½SW	East Half of Southwest Quarter-Section	80
E½SWNE	East Half of Southwest Quarter of Northeast Quarter-Section	20
E½SWNW	East Half of Southwest Quarter of Northwest Quarter-Section	20
E½SWSE	East Half of Southwest Quarter of Southeast Quarter-Section	20
E½SWSW	East Half of Southwest Quarter of Southwest Quarter-Section	20
E½W½	East Half of West Half-Section	160
N½	North Half-Section	320
N½E½NE	North Half of East Half of Northeast Quarter-Section	40
N½E½NW	North Half of East Half of Northwest Quarter-Section	40
N½E½SE	North Half of East Half of Southeast Quarter-Section	40
N½E½SW	North Half of East Half of Southwest Quarter-Section	40
N½N½	North Half of North Half-Section	160
N½NE	North Half of Northeast Quarter-Section	80
N½NENE	North Half of Northeast Quarter of Northeast Quarter-Section	20
N½NENW	North Half of Northeast Quarter of Northwest Quarter-Section	20
N½NESE	North Half of Northeast Quarter of Southeast Quarter-Section	20
N½NESW	North Half of Northeast Quarter of Southwest Quarter-Section	20
N½NW	North Half of Northwest Quarter-Section	80
N½NWNE	North Half of Northwest Quarter of Northeast Quarter-Section	20
N½NWNW	North Half of Northwest Quarter of Northwest Quarter-Section	20
N½NWSE	North Half of Northwest Quarter of Southeast Quarter-Section	20
N½NWSW	North Half of Northwest Quarter of Southwest Quarter-Section	20
N½S½	North Half of South Half-Section	160
N½SE	North Half of Southeast Quarter-Section	80
N½SENE	North Half of Southeast Quarter of Northeast Quarter-Section	20
N½SENW	North Half of Southeast Quarter of Northwest Quarter-Section	20
N½SESE	North Half of Southeast Quarter of Southeast Quarter-Section	20

Section Part	Description	Acres
N½SESW	North Half of Southeast Quarter of Southwest Quarter-Section	20
N½SESW	North Half of Southeast Quarter of Southwest Quarter-Section	20
N½SW	North Half of Southwest Quarter-Section	80
N½SWNE	North Half of Southwest Quarter of Northeast Quarter-Section	20
N½SWNW	North Half of Southwest Quarter of Northwest Quarter-Section	20
N½SWSE	North Half of Southwest Quarter of Southeast Quarter-Section	20
N½SWSE	North Half of Southwest Quarter of Southeast Quarter-Section	20
N½SWSW	North Half of Southwest Quarter of Southwest Quarter-Section	20
N½W½NW	North Half of West Half of Northwest Quarter-Section	40
N½W½SE	North Half of West Half of Southeast Quarter-Section	40
N½W½SW	North Half of West Half of Southwest Quarter-Section	40
NE	Northeast Quarter-Section	160
NEN½	Northeast Quarter of North Half-Section	80
NENE	Northeast Quarter of Northeast Quarter-Section	40
NENENE	Northeast Quarter of Northeast Quarter of Northeast Quarter	10
NENENW	Northeast Quarter of Northeast Quarter of Northwest Quarter	10
NENESE	Northeast Quarter of Northeast Quarter of Southeast Quarter	10
NENESW	Northeast Quarter of Northeast Quarter of Southwest Quarter	10
NENW	Northeast Quarter of Northwest Quarter-Section	40
NENWNE	Northeast Quarter of Northwest Quarter of Northeast Quarter	10
NENWNW	Northeast Quarter of Northwest Quarter of Northwest Quarter	10
NENWSE	Northeast Quarter of Northwest Quarter of Southeast Quarter	10
NENWSW	Northeast Quarter of Northwest Quarter of Southwest Quarter	10
NESE	Northeast Quarter of Southeast Quarter-Section	40
NESENE	Northeast Quarter of Southeast Quarter of Northeast Quarter	10
NESENW	Northeast Quarter of Southeast Quarter of Northwest Quarter	10
NESESE	Northeast Quarter of Southeast Quarter of Southeast Quarter	10
NESESW	Northeast Quarter of Southeast Quarter of Southwest Quarter	10
NESW	Northeast Quarter of Southwest Quarter-Section	40
NESWNE	Northeast Quarter of Southwest Quarter of Northeast Quarter	10
NESWNW	Northeast Quarter of Southwest Quarter of Northwest Quarter	10
NESWSE	Northeast Quarter of Southwest Quarter of Southeast Quarter	10
NESWSW	Northeast Quarter of Southwest Quarter of Southwest Quarter	10
NW	Northwest Quarter-Section	160
NWE½	Northwest Quarter of Eastern Half-Section	80
NWN½	Northwest Quarter of North Half-Section	80
NWNE	Northwest Quarter of Northeast Quarter-Section	40
NWNENE	Northwest Quarter of Northeast Quarter of Northeast Quarter	10
NWNENW	Northwest Quarter of Northeast Quarter of Northwest Quarter	10
NWNESE	Northwest Quarter of Northeast Quarter of Southeast Quarter	10
NWNESW	Northwest Quarter of Northeast Quarter of Southwest Quarter	10
NWNW	Northwest Quarter of Northwest Quarter-Section	40
NWNWNE	Northwest Quarter of Northwest Quarter of Northeast Quarter	10
NWNWNW	Northwest Quarter of Northwest Quarter of Northwest Quarter	10
NWNWSE	Northwest Quarter of Northwest Quarter of Southeast Quarter	10
NWNWSW	Northwest Quarter of Northwest Quarter of Southwest Quarter	10
NWSE	Northwest Quarter of Southeast Quarter-Section	40
NWSENE	Northwest Quarter of Southeast Quarter of Northeast Quarter	10
NWSENW	Northwest Quarter of Southeast Quarter of Northwest Quarter	10
NWSESE	Northwest Quarter of Southeast Quarter of Southeast Quarter	10
NWSESW	Northwest Quarter of Southeast Quarter of Southwest Quarter	10
NWSW	Northwest Quarter of Southwest Quarter-Section	40
NWSWNE	Northwest Quarter of Southwest Quarter of Northeast Quarter	10
NWSWNW	Northwest Quarter of Southwest Quarter of Northwest Quarter	10
NWSWSE	Northwest Quarter of Southwest Quarter of Southeast Quarter	10
NWSWSW	Northwest Quarter of Southwest Quarter of Southwest Quarter	10
S½	South Half-Section	320
S½E½NE	South Half of East Half of Northeast Quarter-Section	40
S½E½NW	South Half of East Half of Northwest Quarter-Section	40
S½E½SE	South Half of East Half of Southeast Quarter-Section	40

Section Part	Description	Acres
S½E½SW	South Half of East Half of Southwest Quarter-Section	40
S½N½	South Half of North Half-Section	160
S½NE	South Half of Northeast Quarter-Section	80
S½NENE	South Half of Northeast Quarter of Northeast Quarter-Section	20
S½NENW	South Half of Northeast Quarter of Northwest Quarter-Section	20
S½NESE	South Half of Northeast Quarter of Southeast Quarter-Section	20
S½NESW	South Half of Northeast Quarter of Southwest Quarter-Section	20
S½NW	South Half of Northwest Quarter-Section	80
S½NWNE	South Half of Northwest Quarter of Northeast Quarter-Section	20
S½NWNW	South Half of Northwest Quarter of Northwest Quarter-Section	20
S½NWSE	South Half of Northwest Quarter of Southeast Quarter-Section	20
S½NWSW	South Half of Northwest Quarter of Southwest Quarter-Section	20
S½S½	South Half of South Half-Section	160
S½SE	South Half of Southeast Quarter-Section	80
S½SENE	South Half of Southeast Quarter of Northeast Quarter-Section	20
S½SENW	South Half of Southeast Quarter of Northwest Quarter-Section	20
S½SESE	South Half of Southeast Quarter of Southeast Quarter-Section	20
S½SESW	South Half of Southeast Quarter of Southwest Quarter-Section	20
S½SESW	South Half of Southeast Quarter of Southwest Quarter-Section	20
S½SW	South Half of Southwest Quarter-Section	80
S½SWNE	South Half of Southwest Quarter of Northeast Quarter-Section	20
S½SWNW	South Half of Southwest Quarter of Northwest Quarter-Section	20
S½SWSE	South Half of Southwest Quarter of Southeast Quarter-Section	20
S½SWSE	South Half of Southwest Quarter of Southeast Quarter-Section	20
S½SWSW	South Half of Southwest Quarter of Southwest Quarter-Section	20
S½W½NE	South Half of West Half of Northeast Quarter-Section	40
S½W½NW	South Half of West Half of Northwest Quarter-Section	40
S½W½SE	South Half of West Half of Southeast Quarter-Section	40
S½W½SW	South Half of West Half of Southwest Quarter-Section	40
SE	Southeast Quarter Section	160
SEN½	Southeast Quarter of North Half-Section	80
SENE	Southeast Quarter of Northeast Quarter-Section	40
SENENE	Southeast Quarter of Northeast Quarter of Northeast Quarter	10
SENENW	Southeast Quarter of Northeast Quarter of Northwest Quarter	10
SENESE	Southeast Quarter of Northeast Quarter of Southeast Quarter	10
SENESW	Southeast Quarter of Northeast Quarter of Southwest Quarter	10
SENW	Southeast Quarter of Northwest Quarter-Section	40
SENWNE	Southeast Quarter of Northwest Quarter of Northeast Quarter	10
SENWNW	Southeast Quarter of Northwest Quarter of Northwest Quarter	10
SENWSE	Souteast Quarter of Northwest Quarter of Southeast Quarter	10
SENWSW	Southeast Quarter of Northwest Quarter of Southwest Quarter	10
SESE	Southeast Quarter of Southeast Quarter-Section	40
SESENE	SoutheastQuarter of Southeast Quarter of Northeast Quarter	10
SESENW	Southeast Quarter of Southeast Quarter of Northwest Quarter	10
SESESE	Southeast Quarter of Southeast Quarter of Southeast Quarter	10
SESESW	Southeast Quarter of Southeast Quarter of Southwest Quarter	10
SESW	Southeast Quarter of Southwest Quarter-Section	40
SESWNE	Southeast Quarter of Southwest Quarter of Northeast Quarter	10
SESWNW	Southeast Quarter of Southwest Quarter of Northwest Quarter	10
SESWSE	Southeast Quarter of Southwest Quarter of Southeast Quarter	10
SESWSW	Southeast Quarter of Southwest Quarter of Southwest Quarter	10
SW	Southwest Quarter-Section	160
SWNE	Southwest Quarter of Northeast Quarter-Section	40
SWNENE	Southwest Quarter of Northeast Quarter of Northeast Quarter	10
SWNENW	Southwest Quarter of Northeast Quarter of Northwest Quarter	10
SWNESE	Southwest Quarter of Northeast Quarter of Southeast Quarter	10
SWNESW	Southwest Quarter of Northeast Quarter of Southwest Quarter	10
SWNW	Southwest Quarter of Northwest Quarter-Section	40
SWNWNE	Southwest Quarter of Northwest Quarter of Northeast Quarter	10
SWNWNW	Southwest Quarter of Northwest Quarter of Northwest Quarter	10

Section Part	Description	Acres
SWNWSE	Southwest Quarter of Northwest Quarter of Southeast Quarter	10
SWNWSW	Southwest Quarter of Northwest Quarter of Southwest Quarter	10
SWSE	Southwest Quarter of Southeast Quarter-Section	40
SWSENE	Southwest Quarter of Southeast Quarter of Northeast Quarter	10
SWSENW	Southwest Quarter of Southeast Quarter of Northwest Quarter	10
SWSESE	Southwest Quarter of Southeast Quarter of Southeast Quarter	10
SWSESW	Southwest Quarter of Southeast Quarter of Southwest Quarter	10
SWSW	Southwest Quarter of Southwest Quarter-Section	40
SWSWNE	Southwest Quarter of Southwest Quarter of Northeast Quarter	10
SWSWNW	Southwest Quarter of Southwest Quarter of Northwest Quarter	10
SWSWSE	Southwest Quarter of Southwest Quarter of Southeast Quarter	10
SWSWSW	Southwest Quarter of Southwest Quarter of Southwest Quarter	10
W½	West Half-Section	320
W½E½	West Half of East Half-Section	160
W½N½	West Half of North Half-Section (same as NW)	160
W½NE	West Half of Northeast Quarter	80
W½NENE	West Half of Northeast Quarter of Northeast Quarter-Section	20
W½NENW	West Half of Northeast Quarter of Northwest Quarter-Section	20
W½NESE	West Half of Northeast Quarter of Southeast Quarter-Section	20
W½NESW	West Half of Northeast Quarter of Southwest Quarter-Section	20
W½NW	West Half of Northwest Quarter-Section	80
W½NWNE	West Half of Northwest Quarter of Northeast Quarter-Section	20
W½NWNW	West Half of Northwest Quarter of Northwest Quarter-Section	20
W½NWSE	West Half of Northwest Quarter of Southeast Quarter-Section	20
W½NWSW	West Half of Northwest Quarter of Southwest Quarter-Section	20
W½S½	West Half of South Half-Section	160
W½SE	West Half of Southeast Quarter-Section	80
W½SENE	West Half of Southeast Quarter of Northeast Quarter-Section	20
W½SENW	West Half of Southeast Quarter of Northwest Quarter-Section	20
W½SESE	West Half of Southeast Quarter of Southeast Quarter-Section	20
W½SESW	West Half of Southeast Quarter of Southwest Quarter-Section	20
W½SW	West Half of Southwest Quarter-Section	80
W½SWNE	West Half of Southwest Quarter of Northeast Quarter-Section	20
W½SWNW	West Half of Southwest Quarter of Northwest Quarter-Section	20
W½SWSE	West Half of Southwest Quarter of Southeast Quarter-Section	20
W½SWSW	West Half of Southwest Quarter of Southwest Quarter-Section	20
W½W½	West Half of West Half-Section	160

Appendix C - Multi-Patentee Groups

The following index presents groups of people who jointly received patents in Gibson County, Indiana. The Group Numbers are used in the Patent Maps and their Indexes so that you may then turn to this Appendix in order to identify all the members of the each buying group.

Group Number 1
AMES, John; BARLOW, John

Group Number 2
AMORY, Francis; AMORY, George W

Group Number 3
BALENTINE, Harvey; KAVANAUGH, B T; HINDE, T S

Group Number 4
CARPENTER, Alvin B; CARPENTER, Willard

Group Number 5
CROCKETT, John; HALL, Samuel; ROBBISON, Henry

Group Number 6
DAVIS, Joel; DAVIS, William R

Group Number 7
DAVIS, Joel; WATTS, Asa

Group Number 8
DAVIS, William R; JOHNSON, George

Group Number 9
DAY, Levi; DAY, Marcrum

Group Number 10
DECKER, John; MILN, William

Group Number 11
DICK, Thomas; PURCELL, Andrew

Group Number 12
EMBEE, Elisha; HALL, Samuel

Group Number 13
EMBREE, Elisha; HALL, Samuel

Group Number 14
EMISON, Samuel; WESTFALL, Thomas

Group Number 15
EVANS, Thomas S; LANSDOWN, Abner

Group Number 16
EWING, John; MILBURN, Robert

Group Number 17
EWING, Thomas; GOORLEY, Robert; HUMMER, William

Group Number 18
GRAY, James; WALDEN, Robert D

Group Number 19
GREP, George; SHAFER, Charles V; SHAFER, Elizabeth

Group Number 20
HAMER, William; MOUNCE, Smith

Group Number 21
HANNAH, William; MYERS, James

Group Number 22
HARRIS, Gillam; MOCK, Abraham; STORMONT, Robert

Group Number 23
HOLCOM, Hosea; HOWE, Willis

Group Number 24
HOWE, Willis; KIRKMAN, Joseph Jackson

Group Number 25
KEY, John L; KEY, Stewart C; KEY, William

Group Number 26
MCGARY, James; MCGARY, Jesse; MCGARY, John

Group Number 27
MCGEHEE, Benjamin F; ROSE, Jesse

Group Number 28
MCMULLIN, Hugh; MCMULLIN, Thomas

Group Number 29
MEISENHELTER, Emanuel; MEISENHELTER, Samuel

Group Number 30
MILLS, Samuel C; SKELTON, Jacob

Group Number 31
PRATT, George W; SULLIVAN, William; THACHER, George M

Group Number 32
REAVIS, William; REYNOLDS, Joseph H

Group Number 33
SKELTON, Jacob; STEPHENS, Joshua W

Group Number 34
STEWART, Scoby; RUSSELL, Abraham

Group Number 35
TERRELL, Walter; TERRELL, James P

Group Number 36
TOWNSEND, Erastus; TOWNSEND, Milo

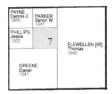

Extra! Extra! (about our Indexes)

We purposefully do not have an all-name index in the back of this volume so that our readers do not miss one of the best uses of this book: finding misspelled names among more specialized indexes.

Without repeating the text of our "How-to" chapter, we have nonetheless tried to assist our more anxious researchers by delivering a short-cut to the two county-wide Surname Indexes, the second of which will lead you to all-name indexes for each Congressional Township mapped in this volume :

For your convenience, the "How To Use this Book" Chart on page 2 is repeated on the reverse of this page.

We should be releasing new titles every week for the foreseeable future. We urge you to write, fax, call, or email us any time for a current list of titles. Of course, our web-page will always have the most current information about current and upcoming books.

Arphax Publishing Co.
2210 Research Park Blvd.
Norman, Oklahoma 73069
(800) 681-5298 toll-free
(405) 366-6181 local
(405) 366-8184 fax
info@arphax.com

www.arphax.com

How to Use This Book - A Graphical Summary

Part I
"The Big Picture"

Map A ▸ *Counties in the State*

Map B ▸ *Surrounding Counties*

Map C ▸ *Congressional Townships (Map Groups) in the County*

Map D ▸ *Cities & Towns in the County*

Map E ▸ *Cemeteries in the County*

Surnames in the County ▸ *Number of Land-Parcels for Each Surname*

Surname/Township Index ▸ *Directs you to Township Map Groups in Part II*

The <u>Surname/Township Index</u> can direct you to any number of **Township Map Groups**

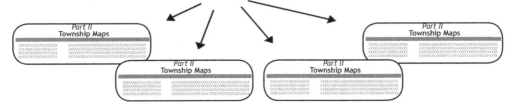

Part II
Township Map Groups
(1 for each Township in the County)

Each Township Map Group contains all four of of the following tools . . .

Land Patent Index ▸ *Every-name Index of Patents Mapped in this Township*

Land Patent Map ▸ *Map of Patents as listed in above Index*

Road Map ▸ *Map of Roads, City-centers, and Cemeteries in the Township*

Historical Map ▸ *Map of Railroads, Lakes, Rivers, Creeks, City-Centers, and Cemeteries*

Appendices

Appendix A ▸ *Congressional Authority enabling Patents within our Maps*

Appendix B ▸ *Section-Parts / Aliquot Parts (a comprehensive list)*

Appendix C ▸ *Multi-patentee Groups (Individuals within Buying Groups)*

Made in the USA
Coppell, TX
13 November 2022